LATER
LIFE

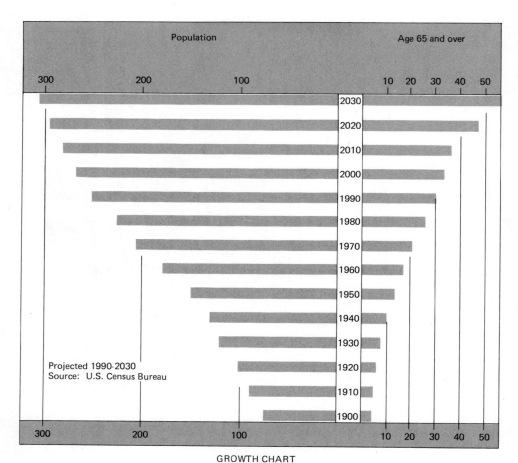

Population			Age 65 and over				
300	200	100	10	20	30	40	50

2030
2020
2010
2000
1990
1980
1970
1960
1950
1940
1930
1920
1910
1900

Projected 1990-2030
Source: U.S. Census Bureau

| 300 | 200 | 100 | 10 | 20 | 30 | 40 | 50 |

GROWTH CHART
Bars show the millions of persons age 65 and older compared with
total population from 1900. The chart extends to the year 2030.

LEWIS R. AIKEN
PEPPERDINE UNIVERSITY

LATER LIFE
SECOND EDITION

HOLT, RINEHART AND WINSTON

New York   Chicago   San Francisco   Philadelphia
Montreal   Toronto   London   Sydney
Tokyo   Mexico City   Rio de Janeiro   Madrid

LIBRARY OF CONGRESS CATALOGING IN PUBLICATION DATA

Aiken, Lewis R., 1931–
   Later life.

   Bibliography: p. 284
   Includes indexes.
   1. Aging.   2. Aged.   3. Gerontology. I. Title
QP86.A38 1982   362.6   81-6744
ISBN 0-03-059751-X   AACR2

Cover Design: Gloria Gentile
Book Design: Marsha Picker

Preface

There are many reasons why a particular subgroup of the population is singled out for special study. The seriousness of the problems posed or the benefits offered by the subgroup to society as a whole and an increase in the power of the subgroup by virtue of its size and leadership are two related reasons why gerontology has become a more popular field during recent years. In terms of problems posed, old age is costly to society. The costs of health care, retirement payments, housing, and social services are all increasing rapidly. Expenditures for the elderly now comprise approximately 33 percent of the federal budget.

People who are 65 years of age or older constitute 11 percent of the American population, but they account for 40 percent of physicians' office visits and occupy 33 percent of the hospital beds in the United States. Because of the growing power of the elderly and their spokespersons, Medicare and Medicaid may eventually give way to some form of national health insurance, which may well cost society even more money. With respect to retirement income, the social security system is fast becoming overburdened, being supported by a ratio of approximately three workers for every benficiary today, compared to a projected ratio of 2 to 1 by the year 2000.

In spite of recent improvements in services to the elderly, many continue to be treated as second-class citizens who are waiting on the shelf for death to overtake them. Furthermore, costs are assessed not only in monetary units. It is costly to the young and middle-aged as human beings, both now and in the years ahead when they will be the aged, to treat older people as anything other than respected, valuable members of society.

The elderly can offer skills, wisdom, and psychological support to younger age groups. The anticipated labor shortages of the 1980s and 1990s in many countries, produced by low population growth during the 1960s and 1970s, will necessitate retaining people in the work force for a longer period of time. This circumstance could also help to relieve the financial stress on the retirement system. The findings of several surveys and many other research investigations have shown that most older people desire to be and are capable of being productive members of society.

If for no other reason, the sheer numbers of elderly people will force society to take greater notice of them in the future. Today, nearly 26 million Americans are 65 or older, a figure that is projected to rise to over 32.4 million by the end of the century. Not only are the elderly increasing in numbers, but the proportion of the over-65 group in the total population is growing even faster. These numbers mean political power for the elderly, power that will undoubtedly result in better medical care, increased housing subsidies, larger retirement incomes, and expanded social services for this age group.

Thus far, research and other efforts directed toward understanding the aged have not been very systematic or ambitious. A few centers have concentrated on topics such as personality development and sexual behavior of the elderly and attitudes of younger people toward the elderly, but few comprehensive longitudinal interdisciplinary investigations have been conducted. Encouraged by federal and private foundation support and stimulated by the growing social, economic, and political significance of the aged, professional interest and hence the body of information on later life has expanded greatly in recent years.

One purpose of this book is to identify and review what is known about later life and the methods by which this information was obtained. The author has attempted to accomplish this purpose in a fairly nontechnical manner, but a certain amount of specialized language has proved necessary. The Glossary, which appears at the back of the book, contains definitions of most of the technical terms used in the book. The Index of Terms and Organizations should also prove helpful.

Another, perhaps even more important, purpose in writing the book was to motivate and point to some directions for further study and research on this most interesting and increasingly influential stage of human existence. Many readers may also be interested in providing services to the elderly or in intervention on their behalf. To assist in this process, suggestions and guidelines for action and interaction with elderly people are given in the text.

The emphasis of this text is on the psychology of later life. But psychology is actually a multidisciplinary field, and later life is merely the final stage in the developmental progression of a biosocial organism. Consequently, the reader will encounter many facts and concepts from biology, sociology, economics, philosophy, and even a few literary quotations in the book. Some information about the earlier stages of life and how they help prepare a person for old age has also been included. All of this material can contribute to our understanding of the total human being—a biological, social, economic, philosophical, and sometimes poetic creature. The many-sided character of human nature becomes especially clear when looking at old age, the final developmental period of life and a time for summing up.

LEWIS R. AIKEN

Contents

The Study of Aging

Human life, like the lives of all animals, begins with a single cell and progresses through a series of developmental stages. The human fetus becomes an infant; the infant, a child; the child, an adolescent; and the adolescent, an adult. The final stage of human development is old age, which can be the best or worst time of life.

PERSPECTIVES ON OLD AGE

Traditionally, old age has been the stage of one's life when the decrements outweigh the increments, when opportunities are reduced rather than expanded (Williamson, Evans, & Munley, 1980). The definition of old age, however, depends on the characteristics of older people and also on the attitudes and needs of society.[1] Society, of course, is a collection of individuals, and the stage of development of these individuals affects their perceptions of what "being old" is. To a young child a person of 30 or 40 years appears old, whereas a middle-aged adult may consider 75 years as the beginning of old age.

Influenced to a great extent by retirement legislation, society as a whole has come to view the beginning of old age as sometime during the seventh decade of life. This somewhat arbitrary benchmark, most often considered to be age 65, represents a chronological definition of old age. But chronological age by itself is rarely an accurate index of a person's biological, psychological, or social age. In defining **biological age**, one takes into account features such as posture, skin texture, hair color and thickness, strength, speed, and sensory acuity. On the other hand, **psychological age** is determined by one's feelings, attitudes, and manner of looking at things. Finally, **social age** is determined by the social roles and activities of a person and whether they are considered appropriate for an individual at a particular age or stage of maturity.

From a strictly medical viewpoint, age is assessed in terms of functional capacity—the ability to engage in purposeful activity. Physicians also distinguish between primary aging, or senescence, and secondary aging, or senility. **Senescence** refers to genetically determined changes in body structure and function resulting in increased vulnerability; **senility** refers to disabilities produced by illness or injury as a person ages. Thus the medical viewpoint is consistent with the notion that a person can be old at 40 or 80 years, depending on his or her overall health, attitude, and other circumstances.

Biological, psychological, and social age all interact in defining **age norms**—the physical and behavioral characteristics displayed by most people at a particular stage of development. These norms, and therefore the stage of an individual's development, change as a function of certain developmental milestones, ceremonies, or rites of passage, such as entering school, graduating, getting married, and retiring from employment. Viewed from this developmental perspective, aging is a continuous, lifelong process, and hence there is no specific point at which one can be said to be "old" for the first time. The developmental perspective also recognizes that the process of aging or becoming old is due to a complex interaction of biological, psychological, and social factors. Consequently, the study of aging must be interdisciplinary, involving a variety of subjects and professions.

LONGEVITY AND LIFE EXPECTANCY

Biological organisms vary greatly in their rate and pattern of development, and the life span of an organism is related to its particular developmental rate and pattern. Length of life, the **longevity** of an animal, varies from a few hours in adult mayflies and a few days in fruit flies and houseflies[2] to over a hundred years in some humans, large birds, and Galapagos turtles. Even greater longevity is found in the plant kingdom, where giant redwoods and bristlecone pines live for thousands of years.

Very Old Humans

On the human level, the unofficial longevity record is held by Methuselah, who is reported to have lived for 969 years. The *Guiness Book of World Records* lists Delina Filkins of New York, who died in 1928 at the

Figure 1-1 Shirin Gasonov, a Russian farmer who was born over a hundred years ago, inspects a vineyard near his home. (Photo reprinted with permission of Sovphoto/eastfoto.)

age of 113, as having the longest officially verified life span in modern times. The oldest person on the U.S. Social Security rolls was a former slave named Charlie Smith, who was listed as being 136 in 1978.

Other famous, probably exaggerated, accounts of very old people are the cases of Thomas Parr, who was presented to Charles I of England as a 152-year-old curiosity, and Javier Pereira, a Colombian Indian who claimed to be 167 years old. Physicians who examined Pereira when he visited the United States in 1956 concluded that he was indeed "very old," but exactly how old they could not determine. Shirali Mislimov, a native of the Caucasus region of the Soviet Union, is said to have been 168 when he died in 1973. Another Soviet citizen, Rustam Mamedov, who in 1977 stated that he clearly recalled the Crimean War of 1854 and the Turkish War of 1878, maintained that he was 142. Further examination has revealed, however, that these men actually did not know their correct ages and undoubtedly exaggerated them. During the nineteenth century, birth records in the Caucasus region were kept by the local church. By arranging with church authorities to add 40 or 50 years to his age or by assuming the identity of an older man, a young man of draft age could deceive Tsarist inspectors into believing that he was much older than his actual chronological age. During Stalin's time the myth of the ancient Russians was kept alive because the great ages of these men presumably demonstrated the superiority of life under communism (Longworth, 1978).

Life Expectancy and Longevity Throughout History

Human **life expectancy**—the average length of time in years that a person born during a certain year can be expected to live—has increased throughout history. From an estimated 20 to 30 years during the days of ancient Greece and Rome, life expectancy rose very slowly to 35 years in the Middle Ages and Renaissance, to 45 years in mid-nineteenth century America, 47 years in 1900, and 73.3 years 1978 (see Fig. 1-2). It is estimated

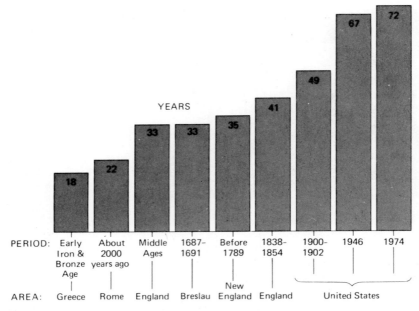

YEARS

PERIOD:	Early Iron & Bronze Age	About 2000 years ago	Middle Ages	1687– 1691	Before 1789	1838– 1854	1900– 1902	1946	1974
	18	22	33	33	35	41	49	67	72
AREA:	Greece	Rome	England	Breslau	New England	England	United States		

Figure 1-2 Average life expectancy throughout history. (From Smith, D. W., Bierman, E. L. & Robinson, N. M., *The biologic age of man*, 2d ed. Philadelphia: W. B. Saunders, 1978, p. 25.)

that life expectancy in the United States will be approximately 82 years by the year 2000.

These figures, however, do not tell the whole story. Because of the shorter life expectancy in former times, a twentieth-century time traveler would be suprised by the small numbers of older people to be found in earlier historical periods. But the traveler might very well encounter a few very old people even in ancient times. These rare individuals would be those of sound constitution and adaptability who had survived the many diseases, wars, and other dangers that were commonplace and took a heavy toll of the child and adult populations. Furthermore, the oldest people in former times were approximately the same ages as those living today. For example, although inscriptions on tombs suggest that life expectancy was 20 to 30 years in ancient Greece, Sophocles wrote *Oedipus Rex* at the age of 75 and won a prize for drama at 85. Marcus Seneca, a renowned Roman orator, lived for 93 years (53 BC to 39 AD). In summary, there are more older people today than in earlier times, but they do not live much longer than their historical counterparts. The average life span has increased, but the maximum life span appears to have remained essentially the same.

Relative to the population as a whole, there were no substantial increases in the number of old people until the nineteenth century. Associated with this increase in the elderly population were the first dramatic breakthroughs in medicine and public health. It was also during the nineteenth century that the large numbers and consequently the increasing needs of this sector of the population prompted certain European governments to institute reforms and social service programs for the elderly.

One of the major causes of shorter life expectancy during previous centuries was the higher rate of infant mortality rather than the greater mortality among older groups. Even in twentieth-century America, **infant mortality,** defined as death before the age of 1 year, has decreased from almost 100 per 1000 births in 1915 to 30 per 1000 births in 1930 and 14 per 1000 births in 1977 ("U.S. Death Rate Falls," 1978). Next to infancy, the greatest decline in death rate has occurred in early childhood, followed by a smaller decrease in the 5- to 55-year age range and an even smaller decline in the 55+ age group. Advances in the treatment of influenza, pneumonia, tuberculosis, diphtheria, typhoid fever, and scarlet fever by the use of sulfa drugs, antibiotics, and other medicines and public health measures (e.g., mass immunization campaigns) have greatly reduced the incidence of death during infancy and early childhood in particular.

The Elderly Population in Twentieth-Century America

Demographic statistics show that the percentage increase in the population of the United States during this century has been two and one-half times as great in the 65-and-over bracket as in the under-65 bracket. The number of people in the United States who are 65 years of age or older has increased from 3.1 million in 1900 to 20 million in 1970 and 25.5 million in 1980 (U.S. Bureau of the Census, 1981). Every day there are approximately 1600 more Americans over 65 than the day before, and on the average those who now reach 65 can look forward to 16 additional years of life. Population projections indicate that the number of Americans who are 65 and over will rise to over 32 million by the year 2000 and reach a possible 56 million by 2030, at which time people born in the post-World War II baby boom will be over 65. From 11.3 percent of the national population in 1980 and a projected 12.2 percent in the year 2000, it is estimated that 18.2 percent of the population will be 65 or over in the year 2030 (U.S. Bureau of the Census, 1977, 1981). Furthermore, the proportion of the very old (75 years and older) among the elderly has increased steadily since 1900 and is projected to continue rising (see Fig. 1-4).

The increasing proportion of older people in the U.S. population since the late 1950s has also been due in part to the declining fertility rate. The effect of a declining **fertility rate**, defined as the number of children per woman of childbearing age, is to reduce the proportion of people in younger age categories while increasing the proportion of older people in the population as a whole. For example, the number of Americans aged 65 and above increased from 20 million in 1970 to 24 million in 1978, but the number of children under five decreased from 20 million in 1960 to 17 million in 1970 and 15 million in 1978 (U.S. Bureau of the Census, 1978). The U.S. fertility rate declined from 3.76 children in 1957 to 1.75 in 1976,

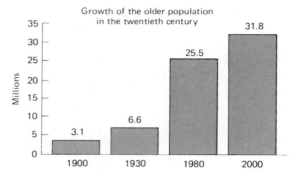

Figure 1-3 Growth of the U.S. older population in the 20th century. (Adapted from U.S. Dept. of Health & Human Services, 1979 and U.S. Bureau of the Census, 1981.)

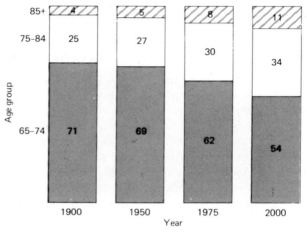

Source: National Center for Health Statistics

Figure 1-4 Increase in pecentages of very old among the elderly in U.S. from 1900, projected to year 2000. (From *Our future selves.* U.S. Dept. of Health, Education, and Welfare. DHEW Pub. No. 77-1096, p. 9. Courtesy of Administration on Aging.)

and by the late 1970s the United States and many other Western countries were well on their way to zero population growth (ZPG). If the drift toward ZPG continues, it is estimated that by the year 2030 the percentage of people below 20 years of age will have decreased to approximately 8 percent, whereas the percentage of people 55 years and older will have increased by the same percentage.

Also indicative of the growing elderly population is the increase in median age. The median age was 16 years in 1790, when the first U.S. Census was taken. It had risen to 28 years by the time of the 1970 census and to 30 years by 1980 (U.S. Bureau of the Census, 1981). If the present trend continues it will approach 35 years by the year 2000 and 40 years by

2030. In addition to declines in infant mortality and the fertility rate, the steady rise in the median age and the proportion of elderly people can be attributed in some measure to the decline in deaths due to heart disorders and other killer diseases among 45 to 75 year olds. This is reflected in the fact that the death rate for people between 45 and 54 dropped six times faster and the death rate in the 65 to 74 age group more than four times faster between 1973 and 1975 than during the preceding 13 years ("The Graying of America," 1977).

The marked increase in the U.S. elderly population documented by the preceding statistics amply attests to what gerontologist Robert Butler has called the "graying of America." This growth is expected to have a pronounced effect on our economic and social institutions during the years to come and has already begun to create problems. For one thing, it has increased the **dependency ratio**—the ratio of the number of dependent (retired) persons to the number of active wage earners in the population. The rising dependency ratio is causing difficulties for the social security system in particular, which could be bankrupt if the dependency ratio becomes too large.

The graying of America also carries with it the challenge that the addition of "years to life" not be wasted and that new opportunities for personal development be provided, which will also add "life to years." As is discussed in more detail in Chapter 8, the growing political power of the aged, which promises to surpass that of the black power and women's movements of the past two decades, is exerting a great deal of influence in realizing this challenge. In particular, compared with their counterparts of today, the "young—old" group of people aged 55 to 75 years, who have retired from a first career but want to remain active and involved, are expected to be healthier, better educated, and more demanding of a greater variety of options in life than their predecessors (Neugarten, 1975).

GROUP DIFFERENCES AND OTHER FACTORS IN LONGEVITY

Human longevity and the proportion of older people in the population vary with factors such as sex, ethnicity, nationality, geography, exercise, diet, personality, and especially heredity. Studies relating these factors to longevity have, of necessity, been primarily correlational rather than experimental, but the findings are interesting and pose some intriguing questions.

Sex Differences

Longevity varies considerably with the sex of the person. Statistics on aging among women during different historical periods are more difficult to obtain than those on men, but it is estimated that the average life span of women in pre-Christian days was approximately 25 years and had reached only 30 years by the fifteenth century. Death during childbirth was a major cause of the difference in longevity between the sexes in earlier times.

In 1900 life expectancy was 51.1 years for white American women and 48.2 years for white American men. By the year 1976 these figures had risen to 77.3 and 69.7 years, respectively (see Table 1-1). As the statistics

Table 1-1 LIFE EXPECTANCY OF AMERICANS AT BIRTH AND AGE 65 IN 1900 AND 1976*

| | Year | | | |
| | 1900 | | 1976 | |
Group	At Birth	At Age 65	At Birth	At Age 65
Blacks				
Men	32.5	10.4	64.1	13.8
Women	35.0	11.4	72.6	17.6
Whites				
Men	48.2	11.5	69.7	13.7
Women	51.1	12.2	77.3	18.1

*Data from U.S. Bureau of the Census, *Current Population Reports,* Series P-23, No. 78.

indicate, the increase in life expectancy has been greater for women than for men. Although the ratio of women to men in the general population is approximately 51 to 49, among Americans in the 65-years-and-older bracket is approximately 148 to 100. Today, women tend to outlive men by 8 years on the average. One out of every eight American women, compared with one out of eleven American men, is 65 years or older. In fact, women begin to outnumber men by age 25 (see Table 1-2). The ratio of older

Table 1-2 NUMBER OF WOMEN PER 100 MEN IN UNITED STATES IN 1980 BY AGE*

Age (Years)	Women per 100 Men
14 and under	95.6
15–24	98.4
25–44	102.6
45–64	110.3
65 and over	147.9
Total U.S. population	105.9

*Data from U.S. Bureau of the Census (1981).

women to older men is projected to become even greater by the year 2000, at which time it is estimated there will be 154 women for every 100 men in the 65-and-over category.

The widening sex differences in longevity and life expectancy is due primarily to the fact that although there are more boy babies than girl babies, at every period of life males are more susceptible than females to disease. This is especially true for heart disease, cancer, and respiratory disorders, which are more common in later life. Among the 1.2 million older people who died in 1978, the cause of death was heart disease in 44 percent of the cases; cancer, in 19 percent; and stroke, in 12 percent. These three disorders accounted for the deaths of 67 percent of the older men but only 54 percent of the deaths of older women in this group (U.S. Dept. of Health & Human Services, 1981).

Marital Status

It is a statistical fact that, on the average, married people live longer than unmarried people, but the reasons are not clear. One plausible explanation is that married people eat better and take better care of their health than unmarrieds. Three other reasons that have been offered for the greater longevity of married people are (Kobrin & Hendershot, 1977): (1) marriage selects rather than protects, in that longer-living people are also more likely to marry or stay married; (2) society views unmarried people as odd or unusual, a circumstance that places them under social stress and consequently wears them down physically; (3) close interpersonal ties, which are more likely to be absent in unmarried people, are important in maintaining a sense of well-being, which, in turn, promotes longevity.

The relationship between marriage and longevity is not a simple one, because the effects of marriage interact with those of sex. Women live longer than men, but the difference is much less for married than for unmarried people. Gove (1973) also interpreted this finding in terms of social ties. He noted that unmarried women tend to have stronger ties than unmarried men to family and friends but that compared with those of married men the roles of married women are more confining and frustrating. As a result, from a psychological viewpoint women are seen as benefiting less from marriage and suffering less from being single than men.

Kobrin and Hendershot (1977) tested Gove's (1973) theory concerning the importance of social ties to longevity in a national sample of people who had died between the ages of 35 and 74. They found a complex interaction in the relationships of sex, marital status, and living arrangement to mortality rates. Among the men, those who were heads of families lived longest, followed by those who were living in families but not as heads. Those men who lived alone had the lowest average longevity. Among the women, those who were heads of families lived longest, but, in contrast with the men, those women who lived alone had the second highest longevity. Lowest of all women in average longevity were those who lived in families but not as heads.

The findings of Kobrin and Hendershot are, in general, consistent with those of Gove: Close social ties and higher social status, which are more likely to be found in marriage than outside it, favor greater longevity. This is truer for men, however, than for women. Unmarried men typically have fewer social ties and less social status than married men, but unmarried women usually retain interpersonal ties and may have even greater social status than they would as dominated members of a family.

Ethnic Differences

Another important variable related to longevity and life expectancy is ethnicity. Asian-Americans, blacks, Latinos, and American Indians, in order of decreasing life expectancy, have shorter life spans than white Americans (U.S. Bureau of the Census, 1981). Approximately 11.3 percent of the total U.S. population is black, but only 8 percent of blacks are elderly. On the average, black men live five years less than white men, and black women live five years less than white women. Similar differences between blacks and whites have been reported for median ages. The 1980 census found the median age of black Americans to be 24.9 years, and for white Americans, 31.3 years.

One reason for the shorter life expectancy of blacks is that hypertension is more than twice as common among black Americans as among white Americans. On the other hand, the life expectancy of black men who reach age 65 is nearly equal to that of their white counterparts. Similarly, the life expectancy of black women who reach age 65 is almost equal to that of 65-year-old white women (see Table 1-1).

The life expectancies of several other ethnic minorities in the United States are even lower than that of blacks. For example, Mexican-Americans have a life expectancy of approximately 57 years, and American Indians, of about 44 years. In the 1980 census the median ages were 23.2 years for Latinos, 23 years for American Indians, Eskimos, and Aleuts, and 28.6 years for Asians and Pacific Islanders (U.S. Bureau of the Census, 1981). But due undoubtedly to improved nutrition and medical care, gains in life expectancy for minority groups in the United States have been even greater than those for American whites during recent years.

Some of the environmental factors associated with ethnic group differences in life expectancy are poverty, lack of education, and the related conditions of poor housing, sanitation, and nutrition, as well as inadequate health care. Better social and economic conditions and the resulting greater availability of life's necessities—good housing and working conditions, clean water and nourishing food, adequate medical care—also help to explain why people tend to live longer in technologically more advanced societies.

Nationality

Statistics compiled by the Population Reference Bureau (1981) indicate that, of the 4.5 billion people in the entire world in mid-1981, approximately 261 million were 65 years of age or over. As Table 1-3 shows, over 32 percent of the world's population but only 16 percent of the persons 65

Table 1-3 SOME DEMOGRAPHIC STATISTICS FOR EIGHT WORLD REGIONS*

Region	Total Population (in millions) 1981	Total Population (in millions) 2000ᵃ	Population 65 and Over (in millions) 1981	Population 65 and Over (in millions) 2000	Life Expectancy at Birth (years)
Africa	486	833	15	27	49
East Asia	1185	1438	71	116	69
Europe	486	511	63	74	72
Latin America	366	562	15	28	64
Northern America	254	286	28	33	74
Oceania	23	30	2	3	69
South Asia	1423	2126	43	84	54
USSR	268	310	24	37	69
Entire World	4492	6095	261	403	62

ᵃProjected population figures.
*Source: *1981 World Population Data Sheet* (prepared by Carl Haub, Demographer), Washington, D.C.: Population Reference Bureau, April 1981.

and over live in South Asia. Another 11 percent of the entire population lives in Africa, but only 6 percent of those 65 and over live on that continent. The relatively small percentage of elderly people living in the less developed countries of South Asia and Africa can be contrasted with the situation in Europe and Northern America, where 16 percent of the total population but 35 percent of the 65-and-over population lived in 1981. Tables 1-3 and 1-4 paint a similar picture in terms of longer life expectancies in more developed than in less developed nations.

Although North America and Europe are similar in possessing large elderly populations, during the twentieth century the annual rate of increase in the 65-and-over population has been greater in the United States and Canada (about 3 percent) than in most European countries. For example, the yearly gain in older people has averaged only 1 percent in France and Sweden. In addition to being proportionally larger, the elderly population has grown faster in highly industrialized Western countries than in the developing countries of Africa, Asia, and Latin America. It is anticipated, however, that the underdeveloped nations of the world will manifest substantial gains in the proportions of elderly people in their populations during the remainder of this century. As the economic and social conditions of these countries improve, changes in living conditions and health care, combined with a previously high fertility rate, are expected to result in a dramatic increase in life expectancy.

Obviously, even today not everyone in less technologically advanced cultures dies at an early age. Individuals having very long life spans are found in sizable numbers among the Hunza people in the Karakoram Range of the Himalayas, the Abkhasians of the Soviet Republic of Georgia, and the Vilcabambans of Ecuador. Nearly fifty out of every 100,000 people

Table 1-4   LIFE EXPECTANCY AT BIRTH IN NATIONS OVER 50 MILLION POPULATION*

Nation	Population (in millions)	Life Expectancy (in years)
Bangladesh	92.8	47
Brazil	121.4	64
China (Mainland)	985.0	68
France	53.9	73
India	688.6	52
Indonesia	148.8	50
Italy	57.2	73
Japan	117.8	76
Mexico	69.3	65
Nigeria	79.7	48
Pakistan	88.9	52
USSR	268.0	69
United Kingdom	55.9	73
United States	229.8	74
Vietnam	54.9	62
West Germany	61.3	72

*Source: *1981 World Population Data Sheet* (prepared by Carl Haub, Demographer). Washington, D.C.: Population Reference Bureau, April 1981.

in the Caucasus region of the Soviet Union, contrasted with about five of 100,000 Americans, reportedly live to be 100 or more. Birth records of the Hunza are more difficult to obtain than those of the Abkhasians and Vilcabambans, but UNESCO data indicate that the Hunza are the only people in the entire world who are completely free of cancer.

State and Climate

The distribution of older people in the United States varies with locality (see Table 1-5). The most populous states—California and New York—also contain the largest numbers of people 65 and older. Florida, Illinois, Ohio, Pennsylvania, and Texas have large elderly populations, too. In fact, nearly half the elderly population in the United States lives in these seven states. The great majority of these people (approximately 70 percent) live in urban areas and towns, with only 5 percent residing in rural areas and the remainder in fringe areas.

The higher percentage of elderly people in certain states, for example, Florida, can be explained by the greater migration of older people to those states. On the other hand, the high percentage of the elderly residing in many other states is the result of a larger number of young people moving out of state to seek adventure and opportunity. Data showing that life expectancy varies with state may be explained in a similar fashion as being due to age-related immigration and emigration. Differences in ethnic

Table 1-5 NUMBER AND PERCENTAGE OF POPULATION AGE 65 AND OVER BY STATE IN 1980 CENSUS*

State	Number	Percent	State	Number	Percent
Alabama	439,938	11.3	Montana	84,559	10.8
Alaska	11,530	2.9	Nebraska	205,576	13.1
Arizona	306,971	11.3	Nevada	65,767	8.2
Arkansas	312,331	13.7	New Hampshire	102,967	11.2
California	2,414,755	10.2	New Jersey	859,682	11.7
Colorado	247,261	8.6	New Mexico	115,690	8.9
Connecticut	364,864	11.7	New York	2,160,558	12.3
Delaware	59,284	10.0	North Carolina	602,273	10.2
District of Columbia	74,202	11.6	North Dakota	80,447	12.3
Florida	1,684,972	17.3	Ohio	1,169,437	10.8
Georgia	516,808	9.5	Oklahoma	376,042	12.4
Hawaii	76,230	7.9	Oregon	303,284	11.5
Idaho	93,680	9.9	Pennsylvania	1,531,107	12.9
Illinois	1,261,160	11.0	Rhode Island	126,922	13.4
Indiana	585,425	10.7	South Carolina	287,287	9.2
Iowa	387,498	13.3	South Dakota	91,014	13.2
Kansas	306,179	13.0	Tennessee	517,524	11.3
Kentucky	409,853	11.2	Texas	1,371,040	9.6
Louisiana	403,939	9.6	Utah	109,220	7.5
Maine	140,918	12.5	Vermont	58,166	11.4
Maryland	395,594	9.4	Virginia	505,204	9.4
Massachusetts	726,531	12.7	Washington	431,417	10.4
Michigan	912,321	9.9	West Virginia	237,868	12.2
Minnesota	479,746	11.8	Wisconsin	564,228	12.0
Mississippi	289,357	11.5	Wyoming	37,218	7.9
Missouri	648,289	13.2	Total U.S.	25,544,133	11.3

*Source: U.S. Bureau of the Census (1981).

composition, nutrition, climate, sanitation, and health resources may also play a role. A combination of several of these factors may explain why data provided by the National Center for Health Statistics show that life expectancy is highest in Hawaii and lowest in Washington, D.C. The state having the next highest life expectancy is Minnesota, and the next lowest is South Carolina ("People in Hawaii Live Longer," 1977).

Specific types of climate have often been prescribed for patients having certain disorders. A warm dry climate that is relatively free of air pollutants is, for example, prescribed in certain cases of emphysema and other respiratory conditions. Tuberculosis sanitaria are frequently located at high altitudes, and altitude has also been associated with heart disease. It is also noteworthy that all three of the long-living peoples of the world referred to earlier reside in mountainous regions.

More systematic data on the relationship between longevity and altitude were obtained by Mortimer, Monson, and MacMahon (1977). Reviewing deaths in New Mexico between 1957 and 1970, these investigators found

403 deaths from coronary heart disease per 100,000 men who were living at the lowest altitude but only 291 deaths from the same cause per 100,000 men living at the highest altitude.

Exercise and Diet

The importance of regular physical exercise at any stage of life cannot be overemphasized. Many people who do not realize that immobility can cause serious physical disorders are stricken by illness at a time in their lives when they are not even thinking about old age. Enforced limitations on one's activities can increase the rate of both physical and mental deterioration, a fact clearly demonstrated in studies conducted by N. D. Mankovsky of the Soviet Institute of Gerontology. Mankovsky found that 50- to 60-year-old people who are put to bed for three weeks and prevented from moving show many of the same symptoms as heart attack patients. From these experiments and interview data collected on very old people, Mankovsky concluded that work is a valuable remedy against premature aging ("Soviets Say . . .," 1977).

Exercise, especially at high altitudes, causes the heart to work harder and thus become conditioned for emergencies. The long-living peoples of the Caucasus, Himalayas, and Andes are all agrarians who get plenty of exercise. The Vilcabambans in particular are quite explicit in attributing their longevity and good health to walking a great deal.[3]

Regular exercise is a contributing factor to health and longevity, but too much exercise may be just as bad as too little. Furthermore, it is difficult in nonexperimental studies to isolate the effects of exercise from those of nutrition. Gots (1977) argued that perhaps even more important than altitude and exercise in contributing to a long, healthful life is what one eats. This is not a surprising conclusion, because it is well known that being overweight is associated with a shorter life span. Less well known is the fact that underweight people also have shorter life spans than people of average weight ("Study Finds . . .," 1980).

Granted that exercise and nutrition are correlated with longevity, what is the best diet? One plan has been offered by the long-living Abkhasians—a diet low in calories, meat, eggs, and salt. Reduced food intake, and especially a diet low in fats and calories, has also been found to be related to a healthier, longer life in technologically more advanced societies. In any event, certain nutritionists recommend the following diet for those who wish to increase their chances of a long life:

1. Lower protein intake and more protein from vegetables (grains, legumes, cereals), and less from animal products (red meat, whole milk, eggs).
2. Less fat, especially animal fat.
3. Fewer calories—enough to satisfy energy requirements but not more.
4. Skim-milk instead of whole-milk products.
5. Chicken and fish more often and red meats only three or four times a week.

6. Greater portions of whole grains, beans, rice, nuts, fresh fruits, and vegetables that provide essential vitamins, minerals, and fiber.

It is generally agreed that moderation in eating, smoking, and drinking (alcoholic beverages), combined with regular moderate exercise, are related to a lower incidence of heart, brain, and liver disorders. Relative freedom from the pressures and worries of civilization, as in the case of the Abkhasians, Hunza, and Vilcambambans, may also contribute to longevity. Psychological factors, such as maintaining an interest in one's surroundings and feeling useful and accepted by others, can be just as important as exercise, diet, and nonsmoking (see Report 1-1). From a study of factors promoting the long lives of the Abkhasians, Benet (1974, 1976) concluded that equal in importance to work and diet is a social structure that permits a meaningful old age and a sense of group belongingness.

Heredity

Many different biological factors can have an influence on longevity. Children born of older mothers, for example, have a higher incidence of congenital disorders that shorten life.[4] Of particular importance, however, is the genetic makeup of the individual. Certain authorities feel that the role of heredity in longevity has been overemphasized, but length of life does tend to run in families. Most gerontologists, although admitting that smoking, environmental pollution, diet, exercise, and health care are related to longevity, would probably agree that the rate of aging depends to a marked degree on genetic endowment.

Evidence of a hereditary basis for longevity comes from casual observation, as well as from scientific studies of the life spans of people having different degrees of genetic relationship. One finding of such investigations is that the correlation between the life spans of different people varies directly with the degree of genetic relationships. Parents who live long tend to have children who also live long. Fraternal twins generally live to much the same age, but, as would be expected with a characteristic affected by heredity, the ages at death of identical twins are even closer (Kallmann & Jarvik, 1959). Based on studies of identical twins reared apart, Kallmann calculated that at least 60 percent of the range of individual differences in longevity is due to genetic factors.

From a study of identical twins who were 60 years and older, Kallmann and Sander (1963) concluded that there is a substantial degree of stability in both physical and mental traits over a lifetime. In spite of pronounced differences in environment in some instances (e.g., New York doctor vs. Western rancher, English-speaking vs. foreign-language-speaking), elderly identical twins were just as difficult to tell apart as when they were younger; they had similar hair patterns and wrinkle patterns, and their energy levels were approximately equal. A particularly dramatic example of biological similarity persisting throughout a lifetime was found in the case of a pair of

Report 1-1 CENTENARIANS TELL SECRET: EXERCISE MIND AND
BODY*

JOHN H. AVERILL, *Times Staff Writer*

WASHINGTON—A congressional committee listened in fascination and admiration
Wednesday as a panel of eight centenarians, two of them in wheelchairs, passed along some
secrets on how to live beyond age 100.

Their advice boiled down to this: remain active and have a hobby.

"Teach people to have a hobby," said Harry Lieberman of Great Neck, N.Y., who took
up painting when he was 80 and now has his work exhibited in 10 museums around the
world.

Lieberman, who will be 103 today, told the House Select Committee on Aging that unless
old people have something to do "they become bitter."

Lieberman, who wears his sparse whitish hair in a ponytail and sports a mustache and
goatee, said he spent six years in idleness after retiring from a confectionary business at age
74—"and those were the worst six years of my life."

"You make the laws," Lieberman said to the congressmen as he urged them to find ways
to help old people remain active. "You have to have something in your hands, and not be
torn up as an old man," he added.

Rep. Claude Pepper (D-Fla.), the committee chairman, said the purpose of the hearing
was to look into the "centenarian explosion."

"Only 3,200 Americans lived past their centennial in 1969," he explained. "Today that
number exceeds 13,000."

Pepper, who at 79 is the oldest member of the House, said that when he was born in 1900
the life expectancy of children born that year was 49. Today it is 72.

He called the eight centenarian witnesses arrayed along a table in front of the committee
"living evidence of whole new horizons for life extension."

Two witnesses punctured any belief that use of alcohol and tobacco are insurmountable
barriers to a person's living a century.

"I enjoy chewing tobacco, and my father taught me how to drink whiskey when I was a
boy," said 111-year-old George Washington White, who used to be a fireman on the
Southern Railway's famous No. 97 Crescent Limited. Since losing his teeth, White said, he
eats raw eggs and oatmeal.

L. Perry West, a 101-year-old retired brick manufacturer, attributed his longevity to a life
of physical fitness. But he also said he enjoyed cigars and pipes until he turned 100 and that
he still indulges in "alcoholic drinks and beverages in moderation."

A Los Angeles centenarian, Maria Majar de Quiroz, who is 100, addressed the committee
in Spanish with her granddaughter interpreting. Mrs. Quiroz and her husband moved to Los
Angeles from Mexico in 1919, and when her husband died in 1924 she cleaned houses and
did sewing to support her eight children. She took her first airplane ride when she flew to
Washington for the hearing. She attributed her long life to "hard work."

Remaining active also was the prescription offered by Dr. W. L. Pannell, 100, who still
practices medicine in East Orange, N.J. "Try to keep up activities," Pannell told the
committee in a firm voice, "exercise your mind and body."

Three elderly black women—Lizzie Dickens, 103, of Whitakers, N.C.; Ida Johnson, 102,
of Anderson, S.C.; and Nanreen Walton, 104, of Hickory, N.C.—credited their long life to
hard work and prayer.

"The Lord has taken care of me," said Mrs. Dickens, who is now confined to a
wheelchair.

twin sisters. Both became blind and deaf in the same month, developed senile psychosis, and died within a few days of each other.

Heredity is important, perhaps the most important of all factors affecting longevity. But neither heredity nor environment by itself determines how rapidly an individual ages. As implied in the following quotation from Hans Selye (1976, p. 82), heredity and environment interact in their effects on longevity:

> It is as though, at birth, each individual inherited a certain amount of adaptation energy, the magnitude of which is determined by his genetic background, his parents. He can draw upon this capital thriftily for a long but monotonously uneventful existence, or he can spend it lavishly in the course of a stressful, intense, but perhaps more colorful and exciting life. In any case, there is just so much of it, and he must budget accordingly.

PROFESSIONAL INTEREST AND RESEARCH IN AGING

As is true today, people in ancient times were aware of the effects of time on their physical and mental abilities. Attempting to reverse or postpone these effects, they consulted magicians, priests, physicians, or anyone purporting to have a remedy or palliative to combat the ravages of time.

The ancient Romans looked upon old age itself as a disease, and stemming from this belief was the search for a way to "cure" the disease and discover the secret of eternal life. Efforts to find this secret, and the related searches for the philosopher's stone and the fountain of youth, occupied the time and energies of many brave and brilliant men.[5] Needless to say, their quest was unsuccessful, although it has not been abandoned even today. Public attention and support have shifted, however, to attempts to make old age more pleasant rather than indefinite in length.

The Social Security Act of 1935 arbitrarily defined "old" as age 65 and above, but "old age" can actually be divided into several substages. Barrett (1972) made a case for three substages in the gerontological (old age) period. He labeled ages 58 to 68 as the "Period of Later Maturity," ages 68 to 78 as the "Early Longevous Period," and age 78+ as the "Later Longevous Period." Neugarten (1975) differentiated between the "young—old" of 55 of 75 years and the "old—old" of 75.+. Dividing old age into substages, similar to the practice of delineating several developmental stages at the other end of the life scale, reflects the growing professional interest in problems of aging and the aged. To some extent, research emphasis has shifted in recent years from early childhood to middle and late life. Developmental researchers who have elected to make the shift have joined others whose professional interests lie in the fields of geriatrics and gerontology.

Geriatrics

Geriatrics is a branch of medicine dealing with the health problems of the aged, both the treatment and the prevention of disease and injury. This medical specialty was founded by an American, Ignaz Nascher, and the first geriatric clinic in the United States was opened in Boston in 1940. Responding to the fact that older people constitute one of the major groups requiring medical care, many hospitals now have special clinics for the aged.

According to Butler (1975), a very small percentage of medical school faculty are experts in problems of the aged. Butler, who has continually stressed the need for greater interest and research in geriatric medicine, believes that medical schools have failed to motivate students toward careers in this specialty because they are not exposed to healthy older people. He recognizes that if a sufficient number of trained geriatricians were available, the diseases of old age could be made less debilitating, less burdensome, and hence less costly.

In any event, medical schools are expanding their research and training programs in this area as professional interest grows. The growth of interest in problems of the aged is witnessed by the increasing membership in professional organizations and the growing number of publications on geriatrics. The major professional organization of physicians who specialize in geriatrics is the American Geriatrics Society. From its beginning in 1950 as a society of only 352 members, it has grown to over 7000 today. Three American medical journals in the field of geriatrics are the *Journal of the American Geriatrics Society; Geriatrics;* and the *Journal of Geriatric Psychiatry.*

Being practical people, medical scientists will probably discover additional ways to slow down aging long before they understand the process itself (Comfort, 1972). To date, they have succeeded in increasing the average life span, but as indicated earlier in the chapter, this has been accomplished mainly by saving the lives of infants and young people rather than by prolonging the lives of the very old. Some years ago Brown (1966) cited a number of research directions that may help prolong life, among them organ transplants, control of cells and tissues so damaged organs and limbs can be regenerated, and the development of virus cells or cells with special inhibitors or stimulator substances. As we shall see in Chapters 2 and 3, this list has been extended in the intervening years.

Gerontology

Many renowned philosophers and scientific pioneers, including Francis Bacon, Benjamin Franklin, and Francis Galton, wrote about aging and its problems. Sir Edmund Halley, an eighteenth-century British astronomer, was the first to conduct a scientific analysis of life expectancy.

Interest in sociological and psychological research on aging was encouraged by various writings and activities in the nineteenth and early twentieth centuries. Noteworthy among these were the writings of the Frenchman Frederic Le Play, the surveys of the Briton Charles Booth, and statistical studies of birthrates, death rates, and the relationships of age to crime rates and suicide initiated by the Belgian Adolphe Quetelet. The psychologist G. Stanley Hall wrote the first important American book on aging, *Senescence: The Second Half of Life,* in 1922, when Hall himself was in his eighth decade of life.

The science of **gerontology**, which grew out of these early efforts, is the study of biological, psychological, medical, sociological, and economic factors having a bearing on old age. The gerontology of today is an interdisciplinary field, based on the premise that solutions to the problems of aging require the cooperative efforts of specialists in many fields. Biologists contribute their knowledge and research concerning the biological processes involved in aging; psychologists study changes in mental abilities, personality, and behavior with age; sociologists study the social roles and status of older people and other aspects of group behavior in old age. Obviously, there is a great deal of overlap among the activities of the various specialists, a fact that is recognized and accepted in the multi- or interdisciplinary approach.

Some authorities consider a Russian, V. Korenchevsky, to be the father of gerontology, whereas others reserve that honor for the American E. V. Cowdry. Cowdry certainly made important contributions to the field, among which were his pioneer volume *Problems of Aging* (1939) and establishment of the International Association of Gerontology (IAG) in 1948.

The International Association of Gerontology, a worldwide organization of gerontologists with branches in many countries, originally focused on medicine and biology but expanded its professional activities in the 1950s to include the social sciences. The primary professional association of gerontologists in the United States is the Gerontological Society, a multidisciplinary organization founded in 1945, which has divisions of Biological Sciences, Clinical Medicine, Psychological and Social Sciences, and Social Research, Planning and Practice. Together with several other professional and governmental organizations, the Gerontological Society promotes interdisciplinary research on aging. Research studies and position papers on topics in gerontology are presented at annual meetings and published in the *Journal of Gerontology* and *The Gerontologist,* the official journals of the Gerontological Society.

Training in gerontology is, like the field itself, multidisciplinary. Larger, well-established training and educational programs, such as those at the University of Southern California and Duke University, have been complemented in recent years by dozens of smaller programs at universities and colleges throughout the United States. Students who enroll in these programs take courses in sociology, psychology, social work, and education. They may also study medicine, biology, physiology, home economics, anthropology, theology, public administration, and hospital administration. It is just as well that gerontology training programs are interdisciplinary, because the professional and paraprofessional occupations related to aging and the aged are also quite varied. Job listings at meetings of national and regional gerontological societies include work in hospitals, nursing homes, community recreation programs, counseling, housing, nutrition, research, and teaching (U.S. Dept. of Health, Education, and Welfare, 1977a). As indicated by the kinds of jobs available, gerontology is primarily an applied field. Be that as it may, research on aging and old age is also an active area.

Research Methods

Because of the high cost of research and the many methodological problems facing researchers in gerontology, advances in our knowledge of aging are often difficult to achieve. The problem of financial support is perhaps easier to solve than methodological problems.

Psychologists and other social scientists who receive substantial training in research methodology have devoted considerable attention to developmental research methods. Among the many methodological questions they must face are those concerned with instrumentation, sampling, and research design. Questions of instrumentation have centered on the reliability, validity, and adequacy of the norms of psychological tests and other measuring instruments designed for and standardized on younger age groups when these instruments are applied to older groups. Unfortunately, tests and inventories that possess satisfactory reliability and validity when administered to children or young adults often lose these characteristics when extended to older groups. Consequently, when these instruments are employed in research on the psychological and social characteristics of the elderly the conclusions are often incorrect. It is becoming more generally recognized that the reliability, validity, and norms for a standardized test or inventory must be determined with samples of older people if the instrument is to be used in gerontological research or diagnosis.

Another serious methodological problem in research on the aged involves the representativeness of the group of older individuals sampled. For example, grossly incorrect conclusions pertaining to older people in general may be drawn from studies conducted with samples of the institutionalized elderly. All too often gerontological researchers have limited themselves to studying readily available groups of old people in nursing homes or retirement communities—neither of which is representative of the elderly in general.

Assuming that problems of instrumentation and sampling have been taken care of, the gerontological researcher must next decide what scientific procedures to use. Although it is the method of choice for investigating cause-effect questions, experimentation is used infrequently in gerontology. Because of their greater social acceptability and ease of implementation, biographical or life-history studies, controlled or uncontrolled observations, surveys, and correlational methods have been more popular. These nonexperimental methods may provide interesting descriptions of people or events and allow researchers to draw conclusions concerning the relationships among things. But unlike experimentation, the results of observational, survey, and correlational investigations cannot be interpreted in cause-effect terminology.

The most popular of all procedures in developmental research employing chronological age as the independent variable and some measure of physical or behavioral change as the dependent variable are longitudinal and cross-sectional research methods. These methods involve the collection of observational, psychometric, and survey-type data on different age groups or on the same age group (cohort) followed over time. Although causal interpretations are seldom warranted by the findings of developmental investigations, the time-related changes in physical and behavioral characteristics observed in longitudinal and cross-sectional studies often help to narrow down the list of possible causes of such changes.

In a **longitudinal investigation,** the same individuals are followed up and reexamined over a period of several months or many years. An example would be retesting the same group of people every 5 years for a period of 25 to 50 years to investigate changes in mental abilities across the life span. Illustrative of longitudinal studies of elderly people are those conducted by the Center for the Study of Aging and Human Development at Duke University.

Longitudinal investigations might appear to be the best way to study age-related changes in human characteristics, but most developmental research on aging is based on cross-sectional studies. A **cross-sectional investigation** involves comparing different age groups of people on some characteristic. Adolphe Quetelet is credited with being the first scientist, in 1838, to apply this method to the study of human development. An example of a cross-sectional investigation is to test separate groups of 40-, 50-, 60-, and 70-year-olds with an intelligence test and compare the average score of each age group with those of other age groups. Conclusions concerning the relationship of intelligence to chronological age can then be drawn.

Cross-sectional studies are less expensive than longitudinal studies and, with effort, can be completed in a relatively short period of time. They do not require long-term commitments by researchers, and subjects are not so easily lost as a result of moving away, dying, or loss of interest in the project. A possible shortcoming of cross-sectional studies is that they necessitate some kind of initial matching of the different age groups. For example, in studying the relationship of intelligence to age, one would certainly want to match the various age groups on education before comparing them on intelligence. The problem is that matching is often difficult to accomplish, and even so, differences in educational opportunity could still affect the results of the investigation. The main difficulty in interpreting the results of a cross-sectional study is that the investigator cannot be certain whether the observed differences among age groups are produced by the aging process itself, by generational or cultural differences **(cohort differences)**, or by time-related changes in the attitudes and values of society.

With regard to the validity of research findings, both cross-sectional and longitudinal studies have limitations. Because a person's age is related to the cultural context in which he or she was brought up, cross-sectional studies confound (i.e., mix up) the effects of age and cohort differences. Longitudinal studies, on the other hand, tend to confound the age of the person with the time at which the behavioral or other measurements are made. Time of measurement is an important variable because the physical, social, and psychological context in which the measurement takes place changes with time. Furthermore, changes in scores on the same tests administered to the same individuals at different times may be attributable to practice effects or increasing familiarity of the material rather than to age per se.

What is needed in order to obtain a clearer picture of the effects of age, apart from cohort and time-of-measurement differences, is a combination of the cross-sectional and longitudinal approaches. Arguing in this vein, Schaie (1967) proposed a three-component model that includes three types of comparisons (Table 1-6). A simple cross-sectional study would involve the three times of birth (cohort) comparisons in any column of Table 1-6 (cells A-D-G, B-E-H, or C-F-I). A simple longitudinal study involves the

Table 1-6 REPRESENTATION OF CROSS-SECTIONAL, LONGITUDINAL, AND TIME-LAG DESIGNS FOR DEVELOPMENTAL RESEARCH*

Time of Birth (Cohort)	Time of Measurement		
	1960	1970	1980
1930	30	40	50
	A	B	C
1920	40	50	60
	D	E	F
1910	50	60	70
	G	H	I

Time Lag

Ages in years are above letters in table

*From Jack Botwinick, *Aging and behavior,* 2d. ed., p. 148. Copyright © 1978 by Springer Publishing Company, Inc., New York. Used by permission. (See text for explanation of table.)

three comparisons in any row of the table (cells A-B-C, D-E-F, or G-H-I). In a third type of age-related comparison, the **time lag design**, several cohorts are examined, each at a different time period. As depicted by the three boxes in the lower left to upper right diagonal of Table 1-6 (cells G-E-C), the subjects in a time lag study are all of the same age at the times of measurement, but they were born at different times (i.e., they belong to different cohorts) and are measured or examined at different times.

In summary, a cross-sectional study confounds age and cohort differences, a longitudinal study confounds age-related differences with differences due to time of measurement, and a time lag study confounds cohort differences with differences related to time of measurement. Only by the combined use of all three types of studies can one hope to unravel the true effects of age on human characteristics, free of the confounding effects of cohort differences and the time at which the measurements are made.

Further efforts to separate differences in behavior due to age, cohort, and time of measurement have been made by Baltes (1968) and by Schaie and Parham (1977). Schaie has proposed three additional research designs—cohort-sequential, time-sequential, and cross-sequential, whereas Baltes advocates a longitudinal sequences design and a cross-sectional sequences design. Because these designs are rather complex and their merits debatable, they will not be discussed further here. The interested reader is encouraged to consult recent writings by Schaie and his coworkers for details (e.g., Baltes & Schaie, 1973; Schaie & Parkham, 1977).

Research Agencies

Private foundations provide some financial support for research on aging, but the greatest amounts of money and other assistance come from governmental organizations and agencies. Federal support for research and research training concerned with the biological, medical, psychological, and sociological aspects of aging was formerly the responsibility of the Adult Development in Aging Branch of the National Institute of Child Health and Human Development. A very small percentage of the budget of the National Institute of Mental Health was also allocated to research on the psychiatric and psychological problems of old age.

Currently, many federal agencies are involved in research and training programs that benefit the elderly. The research and training programs on aging of four agencies—the Administration on Aging, the Office of Nursing Home Affairs, the National Institute on Aging, and the Office of Education—are described in Table 1-7. The newest of these federal agencies, and the one concerned primarily with research, is the National Institute on Aging. In 1975 this agency took over the Gerontology Research Center in Baltimore as its internal program and assumed the aging grants functions of the National Institute of Child Health and Human Development. Dr. Robert Butler (see Fig. 1-5), whose eminent

Table 1-7 DEPARTMENT OF HEALTH, EDUCATION, AND WELFARE TRAINING AND RESEARCH PROGRAMS BENEFITING THE ELDERLY*

Administration on Aging	
Multidisciplinary Centers of Gerontology	Grants to public and private nonprofit agencies and institutions to establish or support centers for such activities as training personnel, research and demonstration projects, and consultation services.
Personnel Training	Project grants for training persons employed or preparing for employment in gerontology and for publicizing available career opportunities in the field of aging.
Research and Demonstration Programs	Project grants for established research and demonstration projects involving the living patterns and living standards of the elderly and delivery of services to them, and to help identify and meet transportation problems of the elderly.
Office of Nursing Home Affairs	
Nursing Home Care, Training and Research Programs	Project grants and contracts to provide short-term training for employees of long-term care facilities and for supporting studies of long-term care. Office of Nursing Home Affairs responsible for training nursing home inspectors and certifying nursing homes participating in Medicare and Medicaid programs.
National Institute on Aging	
Research on Aging Process and Health	Conducts and supports research relating to biological, behavioral, and sociological aspects of the aging process and the special health problems of the elderly.
Office of Education	
Research on Problems of the Elderly	Federal grants to institutions of higher learning to plan, develop, and implement programs specifically designed to apply the resources of higher education to the problems of the elderly.

*Adapted from Select Committee on Aging. *Federal responsibility to the elderly.* Washington, D.C.: U.S. Government Printing Office, 1976, p. 13.

career in gerontology was motivated to some extent by the fact that he was reared by his grandparents, became the first director of the National Institute on Aging in 1976.

Among the activities that the National Institute on Aging has pursued in the area of biology are research on senility, untoward drug reactions in the elderly, osteoporosis (see Chapter 4), and prosthetic devices for the

Figure 1-5 Robert N. Butler, M. D., the first Director of the National Institute on Aging of the National Institutes of Health. (Reprinted by courtesy of Dr. Robert N. Butler.)

elderly. The institute's research support is, of course, not limited to biology, and an effort has been made to strike a balance between support of biological and social science research on aging. The research budget of the National Institute on Aging, which was approximately $70 million in 1980, may seem like a great deal but is small compared to the hundreds of millions of dollars authorized for the National Cancer Institute.

Other nations are following the lead of the United States in supporting research on aging. The British Council for Aging, for example, has enlisted the cooperative efforts of experimental and behavioral gerontologists, geriatricians, and caring agencies in basic research on aging.

SUMMARY

Old age is generally considered to begin in the early to middle 60s, a viewpoint that neglects the fact that people age at different rates and that both biological and psychological factors must be taken into account in defining old age. For a number of reasons, primary among which are the decline in infant mortality and reduction in deaths caused by certain disorders of adulthood, life expectancy has risen steadily during the twentieth century. The increase in average longevity has resulted in a greater proportion of elderly people in the population and an attendant shift in the social status of and concern about this age group. All people do not, of course, age at the same rate. Many different factors—sex, marital status, ethnicity, nationality, geographical area, exercise, diet, smoking, pollution, and especially heredity—have been found to be related to longevity.

The two professions that are most concerned with the processes and problems of aging are geriatrics and gerontology. Geriatrics is a medical specialty that deals with health and disease in old age; gerontology is an interdisciplinary field encompassing all aspects of knowledge about aging.

A variety of methodological approaches—longitudinal, cross-sectional, time lag—have been applied in developmental research on aging. These different research methodologies are necessitated by the fact that many variables other than the process of aging itself, in particular, differences in cohorts and times of measurement of the criterion variable, affect the outcomes of developmental investigations.

Research and training programs to benefit the elderly have received increased support from the public and private sector during the past decade. The National Institute on Aging is the newest of the federal agencies that screen and support research projects concerned with aging and the aged. Interest in the biological, psychological, and sociological problems of aging is international in scope, and research on these problems is being actively pursued throughout the world.

SUGGESTED READINGS

Atchley, R. C. *The social forces in later life* (2d ed.). Belmont, Calif.: Wadsworth, 1977, Chapter 1.

Benet, S. *Abkhasians: The long-living people of the Caucasus.* New York: Holt, Rinehart and Winston, 1974.

————. *How to live to be 100: The life-style of the people of the Caucasus.* New York: Dial Press, 1976.

Birren, J., & Renner, J. Research on the psychology of aging. In J. E. Birren & K. W. Schaie (Eds.), *Handbook of the psychology of aging.* New York: Van Nostrand Reinhold, 1977.

Butler, R. *Why survive? Being old in America.* New York: Harper & Row, 1975, Chapter 1.

Comfort, A. *A good age.* New York: Crown, 1976.

Hendricks, J., & Hendricks, C. D. (Eds.). *Dimensions of aging* (2d. ed.). Cambridge, Mass.: Winthrop, 1981, Part 1.

Kalish, R. A. (ed.). *The later years: Social applications of gerontology.* Monterey, Calif.: Brook/Cole, 1977, Section I.

Palmore, E. (Ed.). *International handbook on aging.* Westport, Conn.:Greenwood Press, 1980.

Woodruff, D. S. *Can you live to be one hundred?* New York: Chatham Square, 1977.

NOTES

[1] Attitudes toward aging and old age are not discussed at length until Chapter 8. However, the reader may wish to check his (her) own attitude and knowledge about aging right now by taking the "Facts on Aging" quiz on page 167.

[2] The immature larvae and pupae of these insects, however, may live for months or even years.

[3] Research has shown that U.S. mail delivery men, who walk a great deal, live two years longer on the average than mail sorters and other postal employees whose jobs do not take them away from the post office (see Simmons, 1977).

[4] Interestingly enough, women who have borne children tend to live longer than those who are childless. The greater longevity of childbearing women has been attributed to increased secretion of the female hormone estrogen (see Woodruff, 1977).

[5] Other discounted beliefs on how to attain long life range from shedding one's skin like a snake to inhaling the breath of young girls. Seemingly fantastic from a modern viewpoint, these procedures have their counterparts in the goat gland surgery, ground sheep embryo treatments, and elixirs of life (e.g., Gerovital) that have been recommended for prolonging life in the twentieth century.

Physical Structure and Function

Although inevitable in living things, aging is not a uniform biological process. As described in the last chapter, there are marked inter- and intraspecies differences in the rate of aging and longevity. Furthermore, biological factors do not act alone in influencing the process of aging; psychological, social, and even economic factors interact with biology in determining the nature and rapidity of aging. Deterioration in the sensory and motor systems of the body, for example, affect a person's attitude and activities, which in turn influence the rates at which these systems deteriorate. It is well substantiated that the progress of a disease and the decline in general health are affected by the joint action of biological and psychosocial variables.

Not only does aging vary among different species and members of a species, but there are also differences within a single individual in the rate at which various bodily structures age. For example, the reproductive system of humans usually ages more rapidly than the nervous system. Even here, however, psychological and other experiential variables affect the rate and degree of decline. "Use it or you'll lose it" is a slogan that applies to sex, mental ability, and many other functions of the human organism.

PHYSICAL APPEARANCE

The thriving mass market for skin creams, scalp preparations, dental adhesives, cleansers, and assorted cosmetics is a testimony to the concern over the changes in physical appearance accompanying aging. The preoccupation of our culture with staving off the ravages of time and retaining a youthful appearance is motivated by the same desire as yesteryear's search for the fountain of youth. Although people gulp vitamins and go on crash diets to maintain a younger appearance, nowhere is more money and effort expended than on the skin. This is due not only to the fact that a person's skin is highly visible to other people, but also because it is possible to do something to improve the appearance of the skin—at least temporarily.

The Skin

As a person ages, the amount of collagen in the human skin decreases. Because collagen, a fibrous protein material, is the primary ingredient of skin, the loss of collagen causes a decline in the total amount of skin. In fact, the structure of the skin is so affected by aging that a dermatologist can usually estimate a person's age within a range of 5 years by examining a 2-millimeter section of his or her skin. Other changes in the skin that are correlated with aging are the various spots and growths frequently seen on older hands and faces. Quite common are "liver spots" (lentigo senilis), darkly pigmented areas that appear on the backs of hands and wrists but actually have nothing to do with the liver. The skin of older people is more easily broken and heals less rapidly than when they were younger. Consequently, purplish spots (senile purpura) caused by cutaneous bleeding are also found on older skin, as well as small red benign tumors (cherry angiomas) and various malignant skin cancers (basal cell carcinoma).

To the casual observer, the skin of an older person is rougher, less resilient, paler, and splotchier than that of younger people. The decrease in fat and muscle tissue under the skin causes it to wrinkle and sag. Older people also perspire less than they did when younger, and therefore their skin is drier. Many continually attempt to retard or disguise these age-related changes by cosmetics, face lifting, and other treatments. Greater concern is usually expressed over the appearance of the face, hands, and other exposed parts because of their visibility and tendency to show age changes more readily than areas of the body that are usually covered. Treatments for aging, wrinkling skin are fairly expensive and only temporarily effective. These include such processes as injection of silicone under the skin or mildly wounding the skin to induce it to lay down more collagen.

Other Changes in Appearance

Another noticeable sign of aging is graying or whitening hair. The hair on the scalp also becomes sparser in most men and women, but a sometimes disturbing growth of hair is observed in the nostrils and ears of men and the upper lips and chins of women. Aging also brings an increase in the incidence of varicose veins and a decrease in subcutaneous fat. The loss of teeth, coupled with a decrease in subcutaneous fat, leads to pronounced wrinkling around the area of the mouth.

Facial appearance in old age is also affected by changes in the eyes. The eyelids thicken with age, the eye sockets develop a hollowlike appearance, and a cloudy ring (arcus senilis) forms around the cornea of the eye. The occurrence of cataracts, which are more common in old age, can also affect a person's appearance.

The effects of aging on overall body shape and stature are found in broadening of the hips and narrowing of the shoulders. Loss of collagen between the spinal vertebrae causes the spine to bow and height to shrink, and the tendency of older people to stoop makes them appear even shorter than they are. Postural changes are especially noticeable in older women who develop a widow's or dowager's "hump" at the back of the neck. This "widow's hump" is the result of osteoporosis, a disorder, common in older women, which results in a gradual loss of bone mass.

The magnitude of age-related changes in appearance varies with each individual and is influenced by diet, health care, and environmental conditions (prolonged exposure to sunlight, air and water pollution, etc.). Inadequate diet and poor health care, combined with air and water pollutants, cause certain groups of people to be more susceptible to the physical signs of old age than other groups. Thus many women of lower socioeconomic status, lacking hormonal treatments during menopause, tend to manifest symptoms of aging sooner than middle-class women. In addition, laborers who work in unhealthful environments age more rapidly than those who spend their days in clean offices (Perry, 1974).

Age changes in health and physical appearance are overwhelming and even disastrous to the self-images and security of some people, whereas others are able to transcend their physical disabilities and be happy in spite of an altered appearance and declining health. Because of the greater cultural expectations of beauty in the female sex, the physical manifestations of aging appear to be of greater concern to women in general than to men (Nowak, 1974). The cultural stereotype that men become more distinguished-looking as they age but women merely look older supports this concern. Furthermore, changes in bodily appearance can affect a person's social and occupational, and hence economic, status. This is especially true when an aging individual continues to pursue an occupation in which physical attractiveness is very important.

INTERNAL ORGANS AND SYSTEMS

The alterations in appearance accompanying aging are the results of both external and internal changes in the human body. The structure of all organs and organ systems gradually deteriorates, and consequently their functioning becomes less efficient in old age. Loss occurs at all levels— cellular, organ, and systemic, and especially in functions involving several different systems.

The effects of age-related physical deterioration and disease are seen in the older person's lessened ability to cope with stress and adapt to environmental changes. Any change, including aging itself, can be stressful, and consequently can pose a problem of adjustment for the elderly. This is particularly true of people in the "old−old" category of 75 to 85 years—the age group in which the deterioration of internal and external organs, which will be discussed in the next two sections, is especially pronounced.

Even in the very old, however, reduction in the efficiency of functioning and adaptability are neither uniform nor inevitable. Furthermore, changes in organismic structure are far from perfectly correlated with decrements in function. A person's previous history of disease and injury and the kind of life he or she has lived play important roles in determining the magnitude and rate of functional deterioration with age. Psychological factors also affect the individual's responses to physical deterioration and the ability to cope with or compensate for declines in the structure and functions of the body's vital systems.

Cardiovascular System

No organ is more vital in the human body than the heart, and the failure of this organ is responsible for the deaths of a large number of people. Contrary to the general rule that most body structures decrease in weight as a person ages, deposits of fat and calcium cause the weight of the heart to increase. It loses some of its resiliency, however, making the number of heartbeats fewer and more irregular and its blood volume output substantially less. As indicated in Table 2-1, the amount of blood pumped by the heart (cardiac output) at rest in a typical 75-year-old man is only about 70 percent of that of a 30 year old, and the blood flow to the brain, only about 80 percent. It also takes longer for the heart of an older person to return to its normal pumping and beating levels after excitement or exercise.

As noted earlier, the total amount of collagen, a protein substance that is the chief constituent of connective tissue fiber, decreases with aging in the skin and between spinal vertebrae. But the number of cross-linkages in collagen molecules increases with age in certain internal organs. The elasticity of blood vessels is so affected by the building up and changing of collagen molecules that the arteries of an octogenarian may be as solid as metal. Unfortunately, medical science has not yet discovered a way to reverse these age-related changes in collagen and the resulting loss of elasticity in body tissues.

In any event, collagen is responsible for the increased sluggishness of an old heart and the hardening of the arteries. These changes in the heart and coronary arteries result in reduced blood flow through the body, and consequently the rate at which oxygen and nutrients are carried to the cells and waste products are carred away is reduced. The reduction in oxygen supply to the body tissues is one reason why older people usually fatigue more rapidly than the young.

Table 2-1 PHYSICAL CHARACTERISTICS OF AN AVERAGE 75-YEAR-OLD MAN
COMPARED TO A 30-YEAR-OLD MAN*

Physical Characteristic	Comparative Percentage
Nerve conduction velocity	90
Body weight for males	88
Basal metabolic rate	84
Body water content	82
Blood flow to brain	80
Maximum work rate	70
Cardiac output (at rest)	70
Glomerular filtration rate	69
Number of nerve trunk fibers	63
Brain weight	56
Number of glomeruli in kidney	56
Vital capacity	56
Hand grip	55
Maximum ventilation volume (during exercise)	53
Kidney plasma flow	50
Maximum breathing capacity (voluntary)	43
Maximum oxygen uptake (during exercise)	40
Number of taste buds	36
Speed of return to equilibrium of blood acidity	17
Also:	
Less adrenal and gonadal activity	
Slower speed of response	
Some memory loss	

*From Shock, N.W.: "The physiology of aging." Copyright 1962 by Scientific American, Inc. All rights reserved.

Respiratory System

As is true of the heart, the functioning of other internal organs is affected by age. But all organs of the body do not age at the same rate. The heart and blood vessels age at one rate, the liver at another, the nervous system at a third rate, and so on. The effectiveness of the lungs diminishes even more rapidly than the heart; both the vital capacity (maximum one-breath capacity) and the oxygen uptake of the lungs decrease markedly. As indicated in Table 2-1, the vital capacity of the lungs of a 75 year old is only 56 percent of that of a 30 year old, whereas the maximum oxygen uptake during exercise is only 40 percent. Maximum ventilation volume during exercise and maximum voluntary breathing capacity are only 53 and 43 percent, respectively, at age 75 of what they were at age 30.

The age-related structural changes that are responsible for the decline in functioning of the lungs include weakening of the muscles lining the rib cage and reduced expansion of the lungs (Leaf, 1973). Combined with the increased sluggishness of the heart, these structural decrements cause older people to experience shortness of breath and take longer to return to normal breathing after exerting themselves to an unusual degree.

Musculoskeletal System

Among the more noticeable changes produced by aging are a loss of several inches in height, a stooped posture, and knobby knees. Deposits of mineral salts in the bones increase, and the dense part of the bones becomes spongier and more fragile. In addition to changes in stature and posture, stiffness and pain in the joints of the lower spine, hips, and knees are common. The quantity of synovial fluid, which serves to lubricate the joints and hence to reduce friction, decreases and may lead to arthritic pain. The flexibility and extent of movement of the joints also decline, effects that are contributed to by changes in muscles. Because the bones are more brittle in later life, fractures of the vertebrae, ribs, and hips—which are slow to heal—often occur.

The loss in overall body weight that usually accompanies aging is in part caused by a decrease in the total amount of muscle tissue, which also leads to a decline in strength. For example, the hand grip strength of an average 75-year-old man is only 56 percent of that of 30 year old (see Table 2-1). Muscular strength actually begins to decline in the late 20s, the rate of decline varying with the particular muscle group and the extent to which a person exercises. But effort, especially when exerted in short, intense bursts, does not depend on the muscles alone. Decrements in the functioning of the heart and lungs, as well as in the mobility of the tissues and joints, also affect a person's maximum strength.

Gastrointestinal System

Although digestive difficulties are not the most serious problems of later life, the digestive and eliminative processes do not usually function as well in the old as in the young. Among the age-related changes in the gastrointestinal system are a decline in digestive enzymes, a decrease in stomach motility, and reduced intestinal peristalsis. The glands in the stomach walls begin to atrophy, and the slower movement of food through the digestive tract resulting from the smaller number of contractions increases the likelihood of constipation. At one end of the alimentary canal, the loss of teeth, ill-fitting dentures, and gum disorders such as gingivitis cause difficulties in chewing. Due in part to a lifetime of poor dental hygiene and malnutrition, over 50 percent of older people lose all their teeth. And at the other end of the alimentary canal, the appearance of hemorrhoids creates problems of elimination.

Efficient functioning of the gastrointestinal system in old age is important, because what a person eats and how well the food is digested can influence his or her sense of well-being and rate of aging. Older people usually exercise less than when they were young, so those who want to keep from gaining weight must reduce their intake of calories as they age. On the other hand, the elderly require more rather than less protein in their diet. Because meat, a major source of protein, is more expensive than other foods, alternative protein-rich foods such as peas must be eaten more frequently to keep costs down.

Selecting and consuming a nutritious, balanced diet in old age is also affected by declines in the acuity of the senses of taste and smell and the resulting flat, unappetizing flavor of many foods. Perhaps less obvious is the fact that declines in the senses of vision, feeling, and even hearing can influence eating habits in old age. Thus the appearance and texture of foods, as well as the sounds that one makes when preparing and chewing them, affect their palatability. Finally, psychosocial factors such as whether one eats alone or with companions play a role in nutrition and the enjoyment of eating.

Genitourinary System

The effectiveness of the kidneys, like that of the lungs, diminishes even more rapidly than that of the heart as a person ages. By age 75 the number of functioning excretory units (glomeruli) has declined by 56 percent and the glomerular filtration rate to 69 percent of their age 30 values (see Table 2-1). Older people excrete less urine and also have less creatine in the urine they excrete. The decline in bladder capacity and enlargement of the prostate gland are responsible for many of the urinary problems of older men. Loss of bladder and bowel control, which is often a source of concern and embarrassment, is more common in old age.

Age-related changes are less distinctive in the male than in the female sex organs. There is a decrease in the volume and force of the ejaculate, and the testes show some shrinkage with age. Severe testicular atrophy, however, is not commonplace. In contrast, reduction in the size of the cervix and uterus is quite pronounced in older women. Atrophy of the vagina mucosa also occurs unless estrogen replacement therapy is used.

The decrease in both male and female sex hormones with aging is a part of changes in the endocrine system as a whole. As noted earlier, digestive enzymes and gastric acids diminish; declines are also observed in steroid and thyroid hormones as well as in ACTH. Impairment of the body's regulatory devices also affects homeostatic functions such as temperature control. Older people adjust less well to extremes of temperature, both hot and cold, than younger adults.

Nervous System

There is some dispute over the matter, but it is a generally accepted fact that human beings are born with essentially all the brain neurons (approximately 10 billion) that they will ever have. The size and complexity of these neurons increase as the individual matures, but neurons in the brain and spinal cord, unlike those outside the central nervous system, do not regenerate when destroyed by injury or disease. It has been reported that by age 75 the brain weight of an average man has declined to 56 percent and the number of nerve trunk fibers to 63 percent of the age 35 values. These losses result from decreases in the number and size of neurons with aging.

Previous estimates that 100,000 brain neurons are lost each day after age 30 are undoubtedly exaggerations, and most authorities now agree that in the absence of disease the brain's ability to function may not be greatly impaired in old age. It is noteworthy that mental abilities improve during childhood and adolescence despite the fact that brain cells are lost regularly from birth onward. Nevertheless, it is generally agreed that the ability of the brain to process information is affected by a decrease in the number of neurons, a measurable loss in the velocity of nerve impulses, and a reduction with aging in the blood supply to the brain. It is estimated, for example, that the cerebral blood supply of a 75-year-old man is only 80 percent of that of a 30 year old.

Age-related changes in the brain have an effect on the sleeping−waking cycle, although environmental and psychological factors also play important roles in sleep. By age 60 to 70 the daily amount of sleep has decreased by an average of 1 to 2 hours. Many older people sleep poorly at night, catching up by means of "cat naps" during the day. Insomnia is very common, especially in older women. The elderly sleep less, and the sleep that they get is neither as deep nor as refreshing as the sleep of the young.

William Dement and his associates have shown that sleep actually consists of four stages, ranging from light to very deep sleep. The cycle from light to deep sleep and back again to light sleep takes about 1½ hours on the average. It is during Stage 1, the stage of lightest sleep, that the rapid eye movements (REMs) indicative of dreaming occur. The intermediate stages, Stages 2 and 3, comprise about 60 percent of sleep time and Stage 4—the stage of deepest sleep—about 20 percent of sleep time. Some dreaming without REMs does occur in Stages 2, 3, and 4, but much less than in Stage 1. It has been found that the REM period of sleep (Stage 1) shortens somewhat and Stage 4 (deepest sleep) shortens appreciably in old age. During the later hours of night sleep, old people typically alternate between Stage 2 and REM (Roffwarg, Muzio, & Dement, 1966).

SENSATION, PERCEPTION, AND MOVEMENT

Aging is accompanied by modifications in the structure and functioning of all the sense organs. Due in part to decrements in the sense receptors themselves and in part to changes in the peripheral nerve pathways and the central nervous system, the thresholds for vision, hearing, taste, smell, and the skin senses all become higher. A general effect of aging is to dull sensations and to slow down responses to sensory stimuli. These sensory changes are usually gradual, beginning in the 30s and 40s but becoming pronounced only after age 60 or so. Furthermore, as with age-related changes in internal organs and systems, the magnitude and quality of the decline vary with the particular person and the sensory modality.

Vision

The two most important senses, vision and hearing, are the ones that show the greatest decline with age. Visual acuity, however, does not suddenly disappear at age 45 or 50. The ability to see details is actually relatively poor in young children, improving gradually to about age 20, then remaining fairly constant until it begins declining in the early 40s. A part of the loss in visual acuity during middle and late life is caused by a decrease in the size of the pupil, resulting in less light reaching the retina. Another change that contributes to poorer detail vision, especially at near distances, is a hardening of the lens of the eye and resulting problems of accommodation. This disorder, known as **presbyopia** and correctable with prescription lenses, is not considered a severe impairment.

More severe losses of vision in old age are produced by cataracts, glaucoma, and retinal degeneration. The most common is the increased cloudiness (and decreased transparency) of the lens known as cataracts, a condition that is almost "normal" in very old people. Even more severe than cataracts is glaucoma—damage to the optic nerve resulting from increased intraocular pressure. People with glaucoma initially experience a reduction in the size of the visual field, and eventually blindness. A number of other diseases (e.g., diabetes) can result in degeneration of the retina and hence a gradual loss of vision.

The process of aging also causes the eyes to lose some of their ability to adjust to darkness, resulting in difficulties in driving at night and necessitating brighter lights for reading and other close work. The ability to distinguish the colors of objects also declines. Because the yellowing lenses of older eyes act as filters for greens, blues, and violets, these colors become particularly difficult to distinguish.

The rapidity of detecting visual stimuli, especially when they are presented in quick succession, also declines in old age. The reduced speed with which the pupils of the eye react to light increases the time needed to detect visual stimuli. Small changes in the environment become quite difficult to perceive and must be repeated or intensified if the individual is to see them.

More complex than elementary sensations are perceptions, consisting of sense impressions plus the meanings or interpretations given to them by the observer. Of particular interest to developmental psychologists who study perception are illusions. Older people tend to be less receptive than young adults to certain perceptual illusions and aftereffects (Necker cube illusion, Ebbinghaus illusion) but are more receptive to other illusions (Müller-Lyer illusion) (Fig. 2-1). The frequency at which a flickering light is

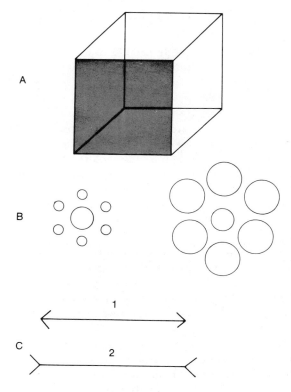

Figure 2-1. (A) Necker cube illusion, devised by L. A. Necker in 1832. The shaded surface can be made to appear on the front or back surface of the cube. (B) Ebbinghaus illusion, devised by H. Ebbinghaus. The circles in the middle of the two patterns are of equal size, but the one in the left pattern appears larger than the one in the right pattern. (C) Müller-Lyer illusion, devised by F. Müller-Lyer in 1889. Line I appears shorter than line 2, although they are the same physical length.

perceived to fuse into a steady beam ("CFF" or "critical fusion frequency") is also lower for older than for younger adults.

Certain age-related differences in the susceptibility to visual illusions (e.g., the CFF) may be attributed to changes in the lenses or pupils of the eyes. Other perceptual changes seem to require interpretation in terms of central nervous system dynamics. One attempt to provide a general principle to account for perceptual changes with age is represented by the stimulus persistence theory, which has been formulated as follows (Axelrod, Thompson & Cohen, 1968, p. 193):

> In the senescent nervous system, there may be an increased persistence of the activity evoked by a stimulus, i.e., . . . the rate of recovery from the short-term effects of stimulation may be slowed. On the assumption that perception of the second stimulus as a discrete event depends on the degree to which the neural effects of the first have subsided, the poorer temporal resolution in senescence would then follow.

This theory has been used to explain why older people react more slowly than younger ones to a series of stimuli presented in rapid succession. According to the principle stated above, it takes longer for an older person to recover from the effects of one stimulus before he or she is ready to respond to a second stimulus.

Although it is true that the elderly are usually unable to evaluate and respond to stimuli as quickly as younger adults, the stimulus persistence theory does not explain all research findings on perception in the aged. Other psychological theorists point to the greater cautiousness of older people as an explanation of their slower responses to visual stimuli. In any event, visual losses in later life can to some extent be compensated for by eyeglasses, intensified lighting, and the use of colors that can be readily seen (more yellow, orange, and red; less green, blue, and violet). Sufficient time to adapt and make decisions based on visual information should also be provided.

Hearing

Because of gradual atrophy of the auditory nerve and end organs within the inner ear, people actually begin to lose their hearing ability quite early in life. Sensitivity to sounds, particularly sounds of high frequency, begins diminishing as early as age 20. Referred to as **presbycusis,** this disorder is even more common in the aged than visual impairment. Thus more than half the individuals with hearing loss are over 65.

Deterioration in hearing is due to the aging process and also to structural damage inflicted by years of noise bombardment and accidents involving the ears. The loss may be so gradual that a person is not even aware that anything is wrong, other than the fact that for some reason people don't speak as clearly as before. Because men tend to lose their hearing sooner than women, the older husband who turns up the radio or television set to hear more clearly can easily blast his wife out of the house. This sex difference in hearing may be the result of greater exposure of men to louder noises on the job.

Presbycusis has a greater effect on the hearing of sibilants such as *s, sh,* and *ch,* which are carried by speech frequencies of over 3520 hertz (Shock, 1952b) (also see Fig. 2-2). Consequently, an older person may hear "ave" instead of "save" and "alk" instead of "chalk." Because the discrimination of speech sounds is particularly affected by presbycusis, it is recommended that one speak in a lower tone of voice and enunciate clearly when addressing an elderly person. Older people also experience difficulty in understanding rapidly spoken words, caused perhaps by a combination of problems in hearing and processing information rapidly. Therefore it is wise to speak more slowly than normal when talking to a very old person. Background noise also has a greater disruptive effect on the auditory comprehension of the elderly, so understanding will be better in a quiet room than in a noisy street or social gathering.

Hearing, like vision, is not simply a matter of sensation. It is a perceptual experience produced by the interaction of auditory sense impressions and past experiences. Barrett (1972) noted, for example, that a

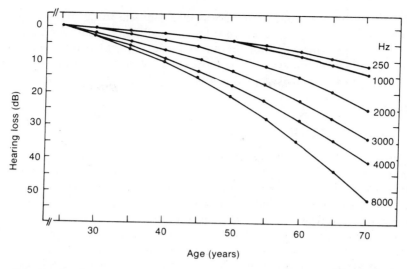

Figure 2-2. Hearing loss as a function of age for tones of various frequencies. (From Jack Botwinick, *Aging and behavior*, 2d ed., p. 371. Copyright © 1978 by Springer Publishing Company, Inc., New York. Used by permission.)

hearing loss need not affect an old person's appreciation of familiar music, because auditory memory can fill in tonal gaps and lead one to "hear" frequencies to which he or she is no longer sensitive.

Semantics, or the meanings that words have for the speaker and the listener, also affect the perception of auditory messages. As people grow older they appear to lose some of their ability to stretch the meanings of words, and this impairs their understanding of the total idea that the speaker is attempting to communicate. Consequently, speech therapists who work with the elderly recommend that special care be taken to make certain that very old people understand what is said to them.

Other sense modalities interact with hearing to facilitate the understanding of auditory messages. Vision and hearing can compensate for each other to some extent, so the speaker should make certain to face the older listener. Getting the older person's attention by touch or gesture is also a good suggestion.

Loss of hearing, even more than loss of sight, can produce a sense of isolation, loneliness, and emotional distress. The results in some hard-of-hearing cases may be paranoid symptoms.[1] The fact that hard-of-hearing elderly people are especially prone to paranoid behavior was documented in a study by Cooper et al. (1974). The study was conducted on 132 mental patients with an average age of 68 years. None of the patients had been mentally ill before the age of 50, but at the time of the study 65 were paranoid and 67 (the "control group") had other psychiatric problems. Over 46 percent of the paranoid patients had a hearing loss, compared to 38 percent of the controls—a statistically significant difference. Because the deafness of the paranoid patients was of a long-standing, bilateral nature, usually produced by chronic middle-ear problems, deafness had begun long before the onset of the mental disorder. It was concluded that the existence of a long interval between the onset of deafness and the paranoid psychotic condition provides an opportunity for prevention of the mental disorder.

Taste and Smell

Both taste and smell decline with age. A decrease in the number and functioning of taste buds begins at about age 50, and by age 70 a typical man has less than half the taste buds than he had in his 20s. There is some loss in olfactory cells as well, which, combined with the greater hairiness of the nostrils in old age, affects the sense of smell.

Taste sensitivity begins to decline appreciably at age 60, particularly in men. All four tastes—sweet, salt, sour, and bitter—show declines, but the decline is greater for sweet than for the other three taste modalities. Foods that seem sickeningly sweet to younger people are often quite palatable to the elderly. Older people also tend to use greater amounts of salt, pepper, and other seasonings in their food. The preference for sweet, spicy foods shown by many elderly people must be monitored carefully if nutritional requirements are to be met and digestive upsets avoided.

The taste of food is affected by the sense of smell, which also becomes less keen in old age. The aged tend to prefer stronger essences and may not be bothered by odors that are unbearable to younger adults (e.g., the odor of strong urine). A number of other factors play a role in taste and smell. As is generally known, serious respiratory illness affects the sense of smell, and consequently affects the sense of taste. In addition, experience can at least partially compensate for a loss of taste and smell receptors. It is noteworthy, for example, that wine tasters and gourmets are often elderly.

Cutaneous (Skin) Senses

The traditional four cutaneous senses are touch (or pressure), pain, warmth, and cold. A variety of receptors are involved in the sense of touch, but their functioning is not well understood. Touch sensitivity appears to increase from birth to middle age, becoming less acute in old age.

The ability to experience pain also declines with age, being only about one-third as great in an average 70 year old as in an average 20 year old (Arehart-Treichel, 1972). Older adults do not seem to be so sensitive to pain as younger ones, which can be a serious deficit when an elderly person is unaware of an injury that needs attention. Loss of pain sensitivity is not, however, uniform across the body. For example, the decline is greater in the arms and face than in the legs. Cultural and personality factors also influence the perception of pain and probably the rate at which it declines in old age.

Temperature sensitivity is also affected by aging, but whether it increases or decreases is debatable. Older people usually adapt less well to extremes of heat and cold and cannot tolerate them as well as the young. The elderly frequently have feelings of discomfort—sensations of being either too hot or too cold—even when the external temperature remains constant. Because of their vulnerability to accidental hypothermia—a loss of body heat that is potentially fatal, it is recommended that temperatures in homes and facilities for the elderly be kept higher than 65° F, even as high as 83° F if it is not uncomfortable. This is especially true when the residents are over 75 years, have arteriosclerosis or some other vascular disorder, or are taking certain medications.

Vestibular Senses

Receptors for the vestibular senses, or senses of posture and balance, are located in the semicircular canals and otolith organs of the inner ear. Of particular significance in maintaining one's balance are the small calcite crystals known as otoliths. Deterioration of these microscopic structures appears to be one reason why many old people fall so easily and have more difficulty reorienting themselves than the young. The growth in number and size of the otoliths from the fetal stage until the late teens is correlated with improvement in the sense of balance. Beginning at about age 50, the otoliths show signs of deterioration, a structural change that signals a decline in the sense of balance. By age 70, the number of otoliths in the inner ear has greatly decreased and balance sensitivity has followed suit (Ross, 1979).

Motor Abilities

Owing to decreased strength and energy and increased stiffness in the joints, movement becomes more difficult with age. Older people are less able to do hard work, especially if it must be done rapidly, and it takes them longer to recuperate from strenuous effort. On visits to the doctor, the elderly frequently complain of weakness and fatigue, but four-fifths of those over 65 manage to get around from place to place fairly satisfactorily. They may have to walk slowly, "shuffling" along, and use a cane, but they usually get where they want to go. When the individual suffers from arthritis or another chronic disorder, however, physical activity can be quite troublesome.

Speed of responding on tasks requiring fast reflexes or reactions, especially reaction time situations in which the person must choose among several alternatives, shows an age decrement (Fig. 2-3). The ability to coordinate various movements, fine muscle movements in particular, also declines (Botwinick, 1970; Shock, 1952a). Although some slowing of movement always occurs in old age, practice, motivation, and physical exercise affect the speed and skill of performing psychomotor tasks.

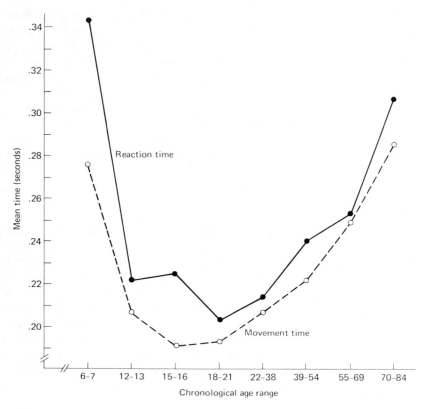

Figure 2-3. Age changes in reaction time and movement time. (Data from Hodgkins, 1962.)

Furthermore, the range of individual differences in the motor abilities of older people is quite large. For example, it has been found that superbly healthy men in their 70s and 80s perform as well as normal men of 20 (Birren, et al., 1963; Botwinick & Thompson, 1968). The study by Birren et al. (1963) compared the physical and mental abilities of healthy men in the 65 to 91-year-old age range with those of a group of young men whose average age was 21. It was found that the older men were as good as the younger ones on several physiological measures. There were no differences between the two groups of men, for example, in blood flow to the brain and the consumption of oxygen during exercise.

In spite of declining sensorimotor abilities, nearly 60 percent of older Americans have valid driver's licenses. Unfortunately, drivers over 65 tend to have more accidents per distance driven and to be at fault in the accidents more often (see Fig. 2-4). Recognizing that many older people must travel by car but that those with disease or disability pose a danger for themselves and others, a special screening examination for the aged has been advocated (Butler, 1975). The examination, which would have to be passed every year after age 50, would consist of visual, auditory, and

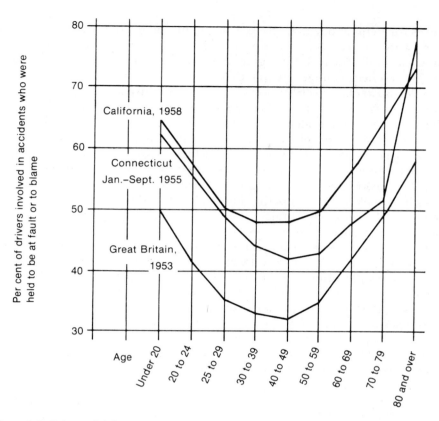

Figure 2-4. Drivers of different ages involved in accidents and held to be at fault. According to these statistics, the safest drivers are in the age range 30–60. (After McFarland, Tune, & Welford, 1964. Reprinted with permission.)

reaction time tests, as well as measures of judgment in driving situations. Combined with certification that the person is in good physical condition, such an examination could appreciably lower the high accident rate of elderly drivers. Because losing a driver's license is discouraging to anyone who values the speed and convenience of automobile transportation, a person who failed any part of the test battery would be given an opportunity to make up the deficiency. Refresher courses, such as the one developed at the University of Michigan's Institute of Gerontology, have been designed to assist older people in overcoming such driving deficiencies.

Getting Inside of an Old Skin

Except in the rare case of a completely age-segregated society, people of different chronological ages must interact and cope with one another. Because social interactions are usually enhanced by understanding, procedures for helping one age group develop an understanding and appreciation of the problems and motivations of another age group could be of practical value. Such is the argument of Kastenbaum (1971) and Pastalan (1974). To help younger people experience the relative slowness of older people, Kastenbaum (1971) contrived a procedure by which a younger person is placed in an accelerated environment and forced to deal with it in the same way an old person must deal with the real world.

Even more comprehensive is the research of Pastalan (1974) and his co-researchers at the University of Michigan's Institute of Gerontology. These investigators devised a special method for studying the sensorimotor problems associated with old age and creating understanding in younger people. Labeled the "Empathic Model," the method involves the use of mechanical devices to simulate the loss of sensation and movement that people experience as they grow older. Some of these devices are coated lenses, noseplugs and earplugs, and fixatives or gloves to desensitize touch. Among the lessons learned by a young person who dons these gadgets are that old people often experience difficulties in seeing traffic signs and distinguishing words from background noise (see Report 2-1).

Using the Empathic Model, researchers have identified several sources and types of perceptual problems accompanying old age: difficulty seeing in natural and unbalanced artificial light because of glare; fading of colors, greens and blues most and reds least; poorer depth perception and slower visual recovery in moving between brighter and darker places; the blurring of sounds, especially those containing high frequencies, by background noise. Other sensory and motor problems revealed by the Empathic Model are the facts that food does not taste as good as it formerly did (and therefore many old people do not eat well), degrees of temperature are more difficult to distinguish (posing potential hazards in bathing and washing dishes), and fine muscular control declines (making the turning of pages and dials difficult).

As a result of findings employing the Empathic Model, changes in lighting, color combinations, and other features of the environment that take into account the sensory abilities and motor skills of older people have been recommended. The purposes of these recommendations, which are made to designers and administrators of housing and other facilities for the elderly and to workers in agencies or institutions serving the aged, are to increase both the safety and pleasurability of the environments for the elderly. Illustrative of the kinds of recommendations that have been made are those pertaining to driving: Make road signs larger and more distinctive; remove unnecessary lights, signs, and other roadside distractions.

THEORIES AND RESEARCH ON THE AGING PROCESS

As is true of different body organs and systems, the rate of aging varies from person to person. At one end of the continuum are the centenarians of the Caucasus, Himalayas, and Andes. At the other end are the victims of

Report 2-1*

SAGINAW, Mich. (AP)—Four junior high students became old people for a day to see how they felt and how others acted toward them.

"I found myself getting very irritable because I couldn't get around as well as I normally do," said 13-year-old Mike Russell of Zilwaukee.

He and others are students at Saginaw's North Intermediate School. Their health education teacher, Albert Garcia, helped apply the bandages, earplugs and splints to simulate physical handicaps.

The experiment was similar to those conducted at the University by Dr. Tamerra Moeller's students in her class on the psychology of aging.

"We tend to forget all of the adjustments a person must make as a result of the physical processes of aging," Dr. Moeller said. "Declining vision or hearing, chronic illness, memory loss—these processes are painful and unnerving."

Armed with this information, the students and their teacher devised ways to experience for a few hours some of those same physical ailments.

They used earplugs to reduce hearing, noseplugs to stifle smell, gloves to make hands slow and awkward, as they might be with arthritis, and bandages or splints to make arm and leg movements difficult.

A couple of them also put patches on one eye. They had first tried to use crinkled plastic wrap to get the impression of eyesight blurred by cataracts, but the paper kept slipping.

"The eyepatch was the biggest problem," said Mike. "I kept misjudging distance. The first surprise was that I couldn't catch a table tennis ball. Then I tried to pick up a pencil and missed. I even misjudged steps."

Terry Colby, 13, said: "When I went home at noon my mother said, 'You're not coming to the table with those gloves on.'

"I told her I had to, it was part of an experiment for health class. The gloves really cut down on movement, and even though I was slow and careful, I still spilled my glass of Kool-Aid."

Thirteen-year-old Holly Neuman had a plastic bag over her right hand and a bandage on the left eye.

"I couldn't turn the pages of my books," she said. "I also found the eye that wasn't covered got tired."

Ray Lucas, 13, spent the day with tape across his nose, and that helped him discover how closely the sense of taste is linked to the sense of smell.

"At noon, I had a deviled egg sandwich that tasted blah," he said. "Even the water tasted funny. My candy bar wasn't too good, either."

*Used by permission of the Associated Press.

---

a disease known as **progeria.** One extremely rare form of this disease that has its onset in childhood is Cockayne's syndrome (see Report 2-2). A victim of this disorder shows signs of premature senescence and appears to "die of old age" while still a child or young teenager. Another type of progeria, Werner's syndrome, has its onset in the late teens. People with Werner's syndrome develop many of the signs of aging—graying and falling hair, deteriorating skin, cataracts, tumors, and arteriosclerosis—between the ages of 20 and 40. Cockayne's and Werner's syndromes, however, are considered to be caricatures of aging rather than true aging. Thus the victims of these disorders show many external signs of aging but not the changes in age pigment and collagen of true aging.

Report 2-2   SHE'S AN 'OLD WOMAN' AT ONLY 5*

SAN DIEGO (AP)—Penny Vantine appears to have sipped from the fountain of old age. She's going deaf, has arthritis, high blood pressure, cataracts in both eyes, blue mottled skin on her arms—and she's only 5 years old.

Penny doesn't just look old, she is old. Doctors say she is aging at the rate of 15 to 20 years every year. She has the looks and many of the ailments of a woman in her 80s, doctors say.

She has been losing weight and now weighs only 9 pounds and stands 29 inches tall.

Before long, she will probably die—essentially of old age, says her doctor, Harold M. Sterling.

"She is probably going to have a cardiac or respiratory illness she can't handle," says Sterling. "She will either have a heart attack or pneumonia."

Sterling fears it will happen this year. He says nothing can be done for her.

Penny suffers from a rare disorder called Cockayne's Syndrome. Many doctors have never heard of it and there are only a handful of cases in all medical literature.

It is believed to be caused by some metabolic or endocrine defect that places the victim irretrievably into a kind of time machine capable of suddenly bringing on old age and senility.

"She reminds me of a cranky, little old lady," said Susy Kaplan, recreation director at Children's Convalescent Hospital, where Penny lives. But she said the aged child is loved by everyone.

Penny's mother, Jeanne Mitchell, lives in Olympia, Wash., where there are no facilities for her daughter.

Penny has been cared for here at skilled nursing homes and came to Children's Hospital when nursing homes could no longer give her proper medical care.

Some Cockayne patients are mentally retarded, but because Penny no longer talks, Sterling said he can't tell. She had a speaking vocabulary of about 15 words when she came to Children's, but Sterling thinks Penny has become so depressed she refuses to talk.

She has been a medical curiosity among physicians, nurses, therapists, and other professionals. Hundreds of them have been to Children's to view her.

They talked in front of her, often commenting on her frightful condition and Sterling believes the comments have had their effect on her.

"After they left, you would find her all curled up in a ball like this," he said, covering his head with his arms. "When a child doesn't answer back when she is spoken to, everybody thinks she doesn't know what is going on."

*From *Stockton* (Calif.) *Record*, February 15, 1979. Used with permission of the Associated Press.

Theories of Aging

In an effort to discover clues to the biology of aging, scientists who study the aging process have taken a special interest in both long- and short-lived people. Perhaps the first medical researcher to study the problem was Hippocrates, who viewed the cause of aging as a decline in body heat. Other theories of aging advanced in pre-twentieth century times were Erasmus Darwin's notion that it is due to a loss of irritability in neural and muscular tissue and Eli Metchnikoff's concept of "autointoxication" (Wallace, 1977).

One set of modern theories of aging may be termed "breakdown" theories, according to which aging is the result of wear and tear, stress, or exhaustion of organs and cells. Illustrative of theories in this category is the homeostatic imbalance theory, which attributes aging to the breakdown in homeostatic, or self-regulatory, mechanisms that control the internal environment of the body. Other examples of breakdown theories are immunological theory and autoimmunity theory. The former views aging as due to the gradual deterioration of the immune system, so that the body can no longer protect itself adequately against injury, disease, and malfunctioning cells. According to the latter, on the other hand, age changes are caused by the response of the body to mutations produced in itself. The body becomes unable to differentiate between substances produced within itself and those produced outside, and consequently it creates antibodies to attack both.

Autoimmunity theory is a type of breakdown theory, but it is also a "substance" theory, because it sees the production of a substance unrecognizable to the body as a cause of aging. Other examples of "substance theories" are cross-linkage theory, free-radical theory, and hormonal theory. Cross-linkage is the inadvertent coupling of large intracellular and extracellular molecules that cause connective tissue to stiffen. It has been suggested that cross-linkages of DNA molecules prevent the cell from reading genetic information properly (see Shock, 1977). As a consequence, enzymes that are sufficiently active to maintain the body and its functions are not produced. Some authorities maintain, however, that although cross-linkage is associated with aging, it is an effect or correlate of the process rather than a cause of aging itself.

Another substance theory of aging at the cellular level points to the accumulation of chemical "garbage" such as free radicals as the primary agent. **Free radicals**, which are highly reactive molecules or parts of molecules, may connect to and damage other molecules. Finally, illustrative of hormonal theories is Denckla's (1974) conception of aging as being caused by the release of antithyroid hormones by the hypothalamus. These "blocking hormones" presumably inhibit the absorption of thyroxin, which is necessary for metabolism, by the cells of the body.

Noting the great similarity in length of life among genetically related persons, many researchers have become convinced that there is an "aging clock"—a genetically determined aging program—somewhere in the body. The aging clock presumably dictates the rate and time at which, barring physical mishap, one can expect to age and die. Some authorities believe that the aging clock is in the brain, perhaps in the hypothalamus. Others interpret the evidence as pointing to the existence of aging clocks in the individual body cells. A proponent of the individual cell theory is Leonard Hayflick, whose experiments demonstrated that there is a built-in limit to the number of times that individual cells can subdivide before they die. Tortoise cells divide 90 to 125 times, human cells 40 to 60 times, and chicken cells 15 to 35 times (Hayflick, 1970). Hayflick estimates that because of genetically based limits on cell division, 110 years would be the maximum life expectancy obtainable if cancer, cardiovascular disorders, and all other diseases were eradicated.

All the preceding theories of aging have their supporters, but the various positions are obviously not mutually exclusive. This is not necessarily a shortcoming, because there is evidence of multiple sites or causes of aging. Aging can occur at the tissue level, the cellular level, or in the cell nucleus. At the tissue level aging is related to an increase in collagen; at the cellular level, to a deterioration of mitochondria—the little energy machines in the cytoplasm of the cell; and at the nuclear level, to mutations of DNA and the cross-linkage of molecules within the cell nucleus (Anderson, 1974).

In addition to multiple sites, the evidence points to at least two kinds of aging processes: (1) the accidental damage to the molecules, membranes, or parts of the body and (2) the "wired-in," genetically programmed "aging clock," previously mentioned. Such a clock presumably consists of a series of special on-off gene "switches," which, when the organism has reached maturity, turn off certain cell activities while turning on new cells that cause the destruction of the body's protein building blocks. Belief in the existence of such a genetic program has resulted in increased research directed at the DNA and RNA molecules responsible for cell replication. In addition, research on the role of the hypothalamus and endocrine glands—the pituitary and thymus glands in particular—continues.

Prolonging Life

Whether the socioeconomic problems that would be created by a greatly extended average life span could be solved is of concern to many gerontologists, but scientists and laypersons alike remain quite receptive to efforts to prolong life. C. S. Lewis once asked: "Why this preoccupation with squeezing out more spatiotemporal existence? Could it be a lack of confidence in what comes hereafter?" Whatever the answer to Lewis's question may be, the number of diets, drugs, surgical procedures, and other methods that have been tried to obtain greater longevity is legion. One approach that works to a degree in lengthening the lives of small animals is calorie restriction which begins around the time of birth. However, it appears that while lengthening life, underfeeding results in animals that are less resistant to stress than normally fed ones (Anderson, 1974). Another experimental method for lengthening life is hypothermia—lowering the body temperature by 2 to 3 degrees Celsius, a procedure that can extend the lives of small animals by 20 to 25 percent.

It is a sensible idea to eat lightly but nutritiously at any age, but caloric restriction and body cooling will not dramatically increase the longevity of humans when initiated after puberty. Consequently, most people who are preoccupied with living longer, and looking and feeling better as well, have turned to dieting, drugs, and other methods. Unfortunately, these procedures are not always effective, or they can have double-edged effects. For example, many people who were concerned about the role of cholesterol in arteriosclerosis and heart attacks switched from saturated to polyunsaturated fats. But as Rosenfeld (1976) points out, polyunsaturated fats increase the oxidation reactions of cells, thereby creating more free radicals and hence more cellular damage of the sort associated with aging.

The situation with drugs and vitamins is not much clearer. One drug—Gerovital—is purported by its advocates to be able to treat a host of old age afflictions, including angina pectoris, arteriosclerosis, arthritis, gray hair, high blood pressure, and wrinkled skin, as well as depression and other psychological disorders. The difficulty is that Gerovital is prepared from procaine hydrochloride, commonly known as Novocain, which has been shown to have no significant effect on the physical or psychological problems of old age.

Reasoning that aging is associated with too much tissue or cellular oxygen, researchers have reported some success in prolonging the life spans of animals by the use of dietary supplements of antioxidants such as vitamins C and E: For example, there is some evidence that doses of vitamin E in the diets of rats can increase the life span of these animals by 39 percent or more (Harman, 1972). In an experiment by Packer and Smith (1974), human cells that were treated by vitamin E were found to be significantly more resistant to the physical stress produced by exposure to oxygen and visible light. The experimenters attributed their results to the fact that as a natural antioxidant, vitamin E countered the oxygen and light before they could oxidize (damage) the molecules of the body cells. Unfortunately, Packer and Smith themselves, in addition to other investigators, were unable to replicate their own initial findings (Packer & Smith, 1977).

Summarizing the results of his experiments with vitamin E and those of others, Harman (Harman, Heidrick, & Eddy, 1976) concluded that the decline in the immune system with age is the result of the degrading action of free radicals on the body cells. Therefore, he maintained, the antioxidant abilities of vitamin E can help retard the decline of the immune system by protecting the cells from free radicals. But as Packer and Smith discovered, vitamin E, in its role as an antioxidant, does not always increase the life span of cells. Rather, they speculate, when vitamin E does extend cellular life span, the results are produced by the interaction of vitamin E with some unidentified chemical or chemicals.

SUMMARY

Age-related changes in the skin, muscles, and bones of the human body, and the consequent altered appearance of the individual, represent a source of stress that may be weathered well or poorly. Changes in the internal and external organs and systems of the body are also associated with old age. There is a general decrement in the cells and tissues of all internal organs, resulting in declines in efficiency of the functioning of the cardiovascular, respiratory, musculoskeletal, gastrointestinal, and genitourinary systems. The infiltration of collagen into body tissues is associated with the reduced functioning of the heart in particular. Decreases in the quantity of brain neurons, the blood flow to the brain, and the speed of nerve impulses affect the capacity of the brain to process information in old age. The pattern of sleeping is also affected, with elderly people sleeping less and also not as deeply as younger people.

Presbyopia is the most common visual disorder of aging, but cataracts and glaucoma are more serious. Other age-related changes in the eye necessitate stronger light and larger print. A gradual loss of sensitivity to high and middle pitches (presbycusis) is also observed in old age. Declining sensitivity to sound can usually be helped by a hearing aid, although psychological factors play a role in the understanding of speech and the appreciation of music. Taste, smell, touch, pain, temperature sensitivity, and the sense of balance also decline with age.

Movement becomes more difficult and reaction time slower with aging, but there is a wide range of individual differences in motoric functioning. The use of mechanical devices worn by younger observers (the Empathic Model) can assist them in understanding the sensorimotor deficits associated with aging. Such experiments have also proved useful in the design of facilities and devices for older people.

Among the various explanations that have been offered to account for biological aging are "breakdown" theories such as homeostatic imbalance theory and the autoimmunity theory and "substance" theories such as the cross-linkage theory and the accumulation of free radicals in cells. A comprehensive theory of aging must take into account at least two processes: accidental damage to molecules, membranes, or organs and the functioning of a wired-in, genetically programmed "aging clock."

Experiments in lengthening the lives of animals have involved caloric restriction, hypothermia, and various drugs. Antioxidants such as vitamins C and E have received particular attention, and some success has been reported. The overall results of such experiments, however, permit no definitive conclusions regarding the effects of these vitamins or other chemicals on the aging process.

SUGGESTED READINGS

Bergman, M. Changes in hearing with age. *The Gerontologist,* 1971, *11* (2), Part I, 148−151.

Corso, J. Sensory processes and age effects in normal adults. *Journal of Gerontology,* 1971, *26,* 90−105.

———. Auditory perception and communication. In J. E. Birren & K. W. Schaie (Eds.), *Handbook of the psychology of aging.* New York: Van Nostrand Reinhold, 1977.

Engen, T. Taste and smell. In J. E.

Birren & K. W. Schaie (Eds.), *Handbook of the psychology of aging.* New York: Van Nostrand Reinhold, 1977.

Fozard, J. L., Wolf, E., Bell, B., McFarland, R. A., & Podolsky, S. Visual perception and communication. In J. E. Birren & K. W. Schaie (Eds.), *Handbook of the psychology of aging.* New York: Van Nostrand Reinhold, 1977.

Kurtzman, J., & Gordon, P. *No more dying: The conquest of aging and the extension of human life.* Los Angeles, Calif.: Tarcher, 1976.

Rockstein, M., & Sussman, M. *Biology of aging.* Belmont, Calif.: Wadsworth, 1979.

Rosenfeld, A. *Prolongevity.* New York: Knopf, 1976.

Rosenfeld, A. Are we afraid of living longer? The strange resistance to aging research. *Saturday Review,* 1977, *5* (May 27), 10–13.

Shock, N. W. Biological theories of aging. In J. E. Birren & K. W. Schaie (Eds.), *Handbook of the psychology of aging.* New York: Van Nostrand Reinhold, 1977.

Shore, H. Designing a training program for understanding sensory losses in aging. *The Gerontologist,* 1976, *16*, 157–165.

NOTE

[1]Paranoid conditions are mental disorders characterized by systematic delusions of grandeur or persecution, or by ideas of reference. Delusions are firmly held beliefs that the patient will not relinquish even in the face of contrary evidence.

Health
and
Disease

It is true that most people do not die of the "natural" causes of old age; they die from the diseases accompanying it. The purpose of this chapter is to examine the various diseases affecting older people and how they are treated so that the reader can better understand the problems of the aged and how they cope. Coping with disease involves both physical and psychological factors, because a person's sense of well-being and attitude toward life are obviously affected by his or her physical health. For a healthy individual, old age can be another interesting and challenging time of life; for someone seriously ill, it can be terrifying and depressing.

DISEASE AND DISABILITY

The type and incidence of health problems in old age are affected by a number of variables. Older men, for example, are more vulnerable to disease than older women, especially to heart disorders, lung cancer, respiratory conditions, and accidents. They are also more often the victims of homicide and suicide (Riley & Foner, 1968). Other demographic variables related to illness and death are socioeconomic status and ethnicity. Poorer people have a higher incidence of disease and a shorter life span than the more affluent, and a similar, probably related, difference exists between blacks and whites. Many of the sex, socioeconomic, and ethnic group differences in disease and longevity are undoubtedly the results of environmental conditions such as pollution, diet, and sanitation rather than of heredity. Thus men more than women are likely to encounter pollution on the job, and poor people usually eat less nutritious food and have less adequate medical care than the more affluent.

Historical Perspective

Because of advances in medicine and improved living conditions, it seems that older people today would be healthier than those of yesteryear. It is certainly true that due to more sanitary living conditions, better nutrition, mass immunization, and antibiotics, the types of diseases that have the most debilitating effects on the elderly have changed. Measles, diphtheria, influenza, and pneumonia are no longer such threats to the aged. Nevertheless, despite the conquest of these diseases and the fact that most older people are fairly healthy, as a group they continue to have a significantly higher rate of illness than other age groups. Eleven percent of the American population is over 65, but they occupy more than 25 percent of the hospital beds in this country.

Although the gains in average longevity during this century have been remarkable, the incidences of heart disease, cancer, and stroke remain high. Three-fourths of all older Americans die of one of these three disorders. A large percentage also suffer from arthritis, rheumatism, orthopedic handicaps, and mental disorders. Consequently, it is debatable whether older people of today are healthier than those during times past. It has even been suggested that by interfering with the Darwinian principle of survival of the fittest, medical science has succeeded only in creating a larger but weaker human population.

As indicated in Chapter 1, the expected life span of a 65-year-old American today is close to what it was in 1900. At that time, a 65 year old could expect to live 13 more years, compared to 16 more years now—an increase of only 3 years. If cancer, one of the current major causes of death in the aged, were completely eradicated, the average life span would rise by only 1.2 to 2.3 years. But if all cardiovascular and kidney diseases were conquered, the average life span would increase by approximately 10 years (Butler, 1975; Myers & Pitts, 1972). This is a significant, if not dramatic, increase in longevity (see Table 3-1).[1]

CHRONIC CONDITIONS

In contrast to acute disorders, which are of relatively short duration, chronic disorders are long-standing conditions such as cardiovascular disorders, hypertension, various respiratory ailments, arthritis, diabetes, rheumatism, and gastrointestinal disorders. Although young people have more acute illnesses, older people are more susceptible to chronic disorders. Only about 25 percent of men and 10 percent of women over 65 are

Table 3-1 GAIN IN EXPECTATION OF LIFE AT BIRTH AND AT THE AGE OF 65 DUE TO ELIMINATION OF VARIOUS CAUSES OF DEATH*

Cause of Death	Gain (Yr.) in Expectation of Life If Cause Was Eliminated	
	At Birth	At Age of 65
Major cardiovascular-renal diseases	10.9	10.0
Heart diseases	5.9	4.9
Vascular diseases affecting central nervous system	1.3	1.2
Malignant neoplasms	2.3	1.2
Accidents, excluding those caused by motor vehicles	0.6	0.1
Motor vehicle accidents	0.6	0.1
Influenza & pneumonia	0.5	0.2
Infectious diseases (excluding tuberculosis)	0.2	0.1
Diabetes mellitus	0.2	0.2
Tuberculosis	0.1	0.0

*Source: Life tables published by National Center of Health Statistics, U.S. Public Health Service & U.S. Bureau of Census, "Some Demographic Aspects of Aging in the United States," February 1973.

seriously handicapped by illness, but approximately 75 percent have one or more chronic conditions that restrict their activities. Even though these diseases do not kill, they can make life extremely unpleasant for oneself and others.

Arthritis, an inflammation of the joints accompanied by pain and stiffness that result in movement difficulties, is especially common in old age. The arthritic individual experiences problems in getting around and engaging in formerly routine movements and activities. Although there is no known cure for rheumatoid or spinal arthritis, the symptoms can be relieved by drugs and other treatments. Most other chronic conditions can also be treated, if not cured, and some can probably be prevented.

Among the other less serious chronic disorders that respond well to treatment are cataracts, hernias, hemorrhoids, and varicose veins. More serious chronic conditions include prostate disorders, chronic respiratory illness, and diabetes mellitus. The symptoms of diabetes, which is common among the elderly, are weight loss, abnormal thirst, and frequent urination. Caused by a breakdown in the body's ability to use glucose, diabetes in the aged is often fatal without strict adherence to treatment and diet.

Chronic respiratory disorders such as bronchitis, emphysema, and fibrosis are especially common in older men, again, undoubtedly because of their greater exposure to cigarette smoke and air pollutants. Other respiratory disorders that are potentially fatal to elderly patients are tuberculosis, influenza, and pneumonia. The last two are usually acute illnesses that may accompany other physical disorders. Pneumonia was once so common that it was known as the "old man's friend" because of its frequent association with death in that age-sex group.

Osteoporosis

As a person ages, the dense part of bone structure becomes spongier and more fragile, causing vertebral, rib, and hip fractures, pain in the joints of the lower spine and hips, and a loss of several inches in height. A common cause of these changes is **osteoporosis,** a gradual long-term loss in the mass of the bones. In this disorder, which is four times as common in women as in men, the bones become less dense and more porous. Women who have gone through the menopause are often given estrogens to control osteoporosis, in addition to large doses of calcium, vitamin D, fluoride, and perhaps growth hormones.

Jowsey and Holley (1973) maintained that the degenerative changes of osteoporosis are triggered by a decrease in the calcium/phosphorus ratio rather than by the total amount of calcium in the body. Consequently, they advocated treating osteoporosis by increasing the amount of phosphorus in the patient's diet. Other physicians have prescribed exercise to help relieve the pain and muscle spasms and possibly even reduce the rate of bone loss of postmenopausal osteoporosis. In a study at the Mayo Clinic, however, little relationship was found between loss of muscle strength and loss of bone mineral (Sinaki, Opitz, & Wahner, 1974). This finding casts doubt on the value of muscular exercise in combating the bone mineral loss of osteoporosis.

Accidents

Chronic degenerative musculoskeletal diseases of later life such as osteoporosis and arthritis, and the resulting orthopedic impairments, are worsened by accidents. Injuries incurred during a traffic accident in which an older pedestrian is hit by a vehicle, or by a fall around the house, are especially common. As a result of these incidents, which are more likely to occur when the victim has poor vision, poor hearing, an impaired sense of balance, or a neurological disorder, long-term hospital or home care may be required. Because healing and recuperation are slower in older people, an accident representing only a temporary setback to a younger person may result in a permanent disability in an elderly individual.

Realizing that good safety habits, combined with good mental and physical health, can help prevent accidents, the National Institute on Aging (1980) has made the following recommendations:

To help prevent falls:

1. Illuminate all stairways and provide light switches at both the bottom and the top.
2. Provide night lights or bedside remote-control light switches.
3. Be sure both sides of stairways have sturdy handrails.
4. Tack down carpeting on stairs and use nonskid treads.

5. Remove throw rugs that tend to slide.
6. Arrange furniture and other objects so that they are not obstacles.
7. Use grab bars on bathroom walls and nonskid mats or strips in the bathtub.
8. Keep outdoor steps and walkways in good repair.

To help prevent burns:

1. Never smoke in bed or when drowsy.
2. When cooking, don't wear loosely fitting flammable clothing; bathrobes, nightgowns, and pajamas catch fire.
3. Set water heater thermostats or faucets so that water does not scald the skin.
4. Plan which emergency exits to use in case of fire.

To help prevent injuries when riding public transportation:

1. Remain alert and brace yourself when a bus is slowing down or turning.
2. Watch for slippery pavement and other hazards when entering or leaving a vehicle.
3. Have fare ready to prevent losing your balance while fumbling for change.
4. Do not carry too many packages, and leave one hand free to grasp railings.
5. Allow extra time to cross streets, especially in bad weather.
6. At night wear light-colored or fluorescent clothing and carry a flashlight.

Attention to these simple suggestions can help prevent many of the more than 800,000 injuries and 24,000 deaths in elderly Americans caused by accidents each year (National Institute on Aging, 1980).

Cardiovascular Disorders

Diseases of the heart (44 percent), cancer (18 percent), and cerebrovascular diseases (13 percent) lead the list of the various causes of death in older Americans (see Table 3-2). Among the different types of cancer, those involving the gastrointestinal tract, the kidneys, the prostate gland, and the skin are more common in the elderly, whereas cancers of the lungs, breast, and cervix are more frequent prior to old age. The overall fatality rate of cancerous disorders is approximately 50 percent, but it is higher in middle and late life.

Cardiovascular disorders, although a common chronic condition and the ranking cause of death in the elderly, are, of course, not limited to this age group. But the probability of death from cardiovascular disease is 150 times greater in a 75 year old than in a 35 year old. Mortality due to heart disease and stroke is also higher in men than women and higher in blacks than in whites. Hypertension (high blood pressure), a frequent accompanier of heart failure and cerebral hemorrhage, is also more prevalent in men and blacks than in women and whites.

The incidence of cardiovascular disorders has been linked to a number of factors—obesity, lack of exercise, heavy smoking, psychological stress,

Table 3-2 DEATH RATES FOR THE TEN LEADING CAUSES OF DEATH, FOR PERSONS 65 YEARS AND OVER, BY AGE: 1976*

Cause of death (by rank)	Deaths per 100,000 Population			
	Total, 65 Years and Over	65 to 74 Years	75 to 84 Years	85 Years and Over
All causes	5,428.9	3,127.6	7,331.6	15,486.9
Diseases of the heart	2,393.5	1,286.9	3,263.7	7,384.3
Malignant neoplasms	979.0	786.3	1,248.6	1,441.5
Cerebrovascular diseases	694.6	280.1	1,014.0	2,586.8
Influenza or pneumonia	211.1	70.1	289.3	959.2
Arteriosclerosis	122.2	25.8	152.5	714.3
Diabetes mellitus	108.1	70.0	155.8	219.2
Accidents	104.5	62.2	134.5	306.7
Motor vehicles	25.2	21.7	32.3	26.0
All other	79.3	40.4	102.2	280.7
Bronchitis, emphysema, and asthma	76.8	60.7	101.4	108.5
Cirrhosis of liver	36.5	42.6	29.3	18.0
Nephritis and nephrosis	25.0	15.2	34.1	64.6
All other causes	677.5	427.8	908.6	1,683.8

*Source: U.S. Department of Health, Education and Welfare, National Center for Health Statistics, *Monthly Vital Statistics Report*, Vol. 26, No. 12, Supplement 2, March 1978.

and high blood cholesterol level. The relationship between cardiovascular disorder and blood cholesterol is seen in the lower frequency of heart conditions in cultures of Asia and Africa, whose diets include higher intakes of vegetables and lower intakes of animal fats than those of people in most North American and Western European countries.

A heart attack, which is an anxiety-arousing experience at any age, can have a profound psychological effect on the victim. Consequently, heart attack patients frequently require medical treatment and a curtailment of their activities, as well as psychotherapeutic assistance. Some heart patients develop a condition known as *angor anima*, a fear of impending death, which can precipitate another attack. In any event, there are important physical and psychological reasons for keeping heart patients relaxed and untroubled.

Great strides have been made in the treatment of heart disease and other cardiovascular disorders during the past few years, and break-throughs in the treatment of cancer, arthritis, and other crippling diseases are expected at any time. The fact that pacemaker, artificial valve, open-heart surgery, and heart transplant are household terms attests to the progress in treating cardiac disorders and in educating the public about these matters.

ORGANIC BRAIN DISORDERS

Organic brain disorders are one of the most common causes of death in old age, but many people who are diagnosed as having an organic disorder live for years, manifesting gradual, insidious changes in personality. These are the **chronic brain syndrome** cases, which can be treated symptomatically but not "cured." On the other hand, the symptoms of **acute brain syndrome,** although frequently severe, are transient and reversible.

Elderly patients comprise more than half of the first admissions to mental hospitals, and most of these are suffering from chronic brain syndrome. One chronic condition found more often in the "young—old" than in the "old—old" is alcoholism. When untreated, chronic alcoholism can result in a brain disorder known as Korsakoff's syndrome, a relatively rare condition occurring most often in 50 to 60 year olds. The symptoms of Korsakoff's syndrome include disorientation, impulsiveness, loss of memory, confabulation,[2] and inflammation of the peripheral nerves of the body. More common in later life, however, are cerebral arteriosclerosis and senile brain disease. These irreversible conditions account for approximately 50 percent of all cases of major mental disorders in old age.

Cerebral Arteriosclerosis

Cerebral arteriosclerosis (hardening of the arteries of the brain) usually has its onset in the mid-60s, and the victim dies of a heart attack or stroke within three to four years. In old age the walls of the arteries of the brain become thickened, and the diameter of the vessels is reduced owing to fatty deposits. These accumulations of fatty tissue and calcified material, known as **plaque**, clog the channels of the arteries and interfere with blood circulation. As a result the vessels are unable to carry enough nutrients, vitamins, and oxygen in the blood to the brain, and the probability of a blockage or rupture increases.

The blockage (thrombosis) or rupture (hemorrhage) of a cerebral blood vessel, referred to as a cerebrovascular accident (CVA), or stroke, can result in heart failure. Blockage of a small blood vessel is technically known as a "small stroke," and blockage of a large vessel as a "major stroke," or CVA. Cerebral arteriosclerosis affects over 3 million people in the United States, with CVAs killing more than 200,000 annually (Terry & Wisniewski, 1974). A typical patient is in his early 70s and manifests the organic brain syndrome symptoms of confusion, disorientation, incoherence, restlessness, and occasionally hallucinations. Complaints of headaches, dizziness, and fatigue also occur, with some patients becoming paralyzed on one side (hemiplegia) and having seizures. Superimposed on these symptoms are the anxiety and depression resulting from the severe stress of a CVA. As with any stress situation, maladaptive personality traits that existed before the trauma are accentuated by a CVA.

Elizabeth R. was admitted to a hospital at age 73. The present attack began about 5 years before her admission, when the patient developed the idea that she was being hypnotized by her relatives. She heard voices, with members of her family cursing her and telling her that she was no good. Other voices hinted that someone wanted to kill her. The patient's husband is blind, and just before her admission to the hospital she tried to pour scalding water over him. She thought he hypnotized her and wanted to kill her. For five months, the patient refused to sit at the same table with her husband. She argued constantly with her family and with neighbors, cursing constantly anyone who came near her. She was afraid that she would be killed and thought that she must kill other people for protection. She boiled water all day long to break the "spell" and kept the lights on at all times in different places in the house to scare away the evil spirits. She believed that when the train whistled near her home, it ordered her to do different things. She grew increasingly destructive and dangerous toward her blind husband, who attempted to quiet her by hitting her with his cane. At the hospital, the patient said, "The electric light catches me every time I walk from room to room. My husband makes money behind my back. He hypnotizes me. My grandfather sent you doctors to see me."

*From Kisker, 1972, p. 391.

Senile Brain Disease

Senile brain disease is caused by neuronal degeneration, which leads to atrophy (shrinking) and related degenerative changes in the brain during old age. The shrinkage, which can reduce the brain to 15 to 30 percent of its normal weight, occurs primarily in the frontal cortex, the temporal cortex, and the associated white matter. The disorder becomes apparent after age 65, peaks in frequency at about age 70, and then begins to decline. During the past 30 years the incidence of this disorder in the general population has doubled. Over one-third of the people who live past 80 have senile brain disease, which is ranked number five among all killer diseases. It is estimated that 50 percent of the people who enter nursing homes for the aged are suffering from senile brain disease, and one-fourth of all people admitted to mental hospitals have this disorder. Slightly more women than men develop the condition.

Among the psychological symptoms of senile brain disease—a syndrome referred to as **senile dementia**—are self-centeredness, difficulty assimilating new experiences, and childish emotionality. The changes in personality are gradual, beginning with simple memory failure (e.g., difficulty remembering names). As the disorder progresses, memory, confusion, and disorientation in time and place become progressively worse. For example, the patient may be unable to remember when he ate last, whether or not he took his medicine, and whether the stove was turned off. He may lose the ability to perform certain routine tasks, showing little interest in external events, untidiness, and a preoccupation with eating, eliminating, and other bodily functions. Memory, speech, and personal habits deteriorate even further as time progresses.

Most older people never become so severely disturbed as to be labeled "senile," and the extent of pathological behavior in those who do is influenced by the patient's environment and premorbid personality. The importance of psychological factors is seen in the fact that postmortem examinations of the brains of senile patients reveal little or no relationship between the degree of brain damage and the magnitude of deterioration in behavior (Gal, 1959). Recognizing the variety of behavioral symptoms in senile brain disease, Coleman (1976) categorized the symptom picture into several reaction tendencies or types: simple deterioration, paranoid reaction, presbyophrenic type, depressed and agitated types, delirious and confused types.

Although true senile brain disease is considered irreversible, many patients who manifest symptoms of senility can be treated. A special X-ray technique known as computerized tomography can help determine the degree of brain atrophy, and if little or no atrophy is present it may be that the patient is suffering from a disorder other than senile brain disease, such as thyroid deficiency, anemia, diabetic coma, or even a heart attack. Butler (1975) reported that physicians often fail to distinguish between reversible and irreversible brain disorders. He pointed out that malnutrition, anemia, heart failure, drugs (overdoses of tranquilizers and barbiturates in particular), alcohol, CVAs, and reactions to dehydration have all been misdiagnosed as irreversible brain disease. Severe depression, the clinical picture of which includes forgetfulness, difficulty concentrating, and helplessness, has also been mislabeled as senile brain disease.

Among the symptoms of reversible brain disorder listed by Butler (1975), of which medical diagnosticians should be aware, are: a fluctuating level of awareness (from mild confusion to stupor to delirium), disorientation, misidentification of people, and impairment of intellectual functions. Hallucinations, unusual aggressiveness, and a dazed expression may also be present. Many of these same symptoms, of course, occur in irreversible senile brain disease, but they may go untreated if the physician does not recognize the presence of a treatable, reversible disorder.

Other than custodial care and medication for the control of emotions, little is done to treat patients who are accurately diagnosed as having senile brain disease. Severely senile patients simply while away the time in institutions, remaining there and receiving minimal care for the rest of their lives. Because senile patients tend to accumulate in mental hospitals, which are supposed to be treatment centers, relatives are advised to move them to less expensive facilities that are expressly custodial in nature.

Presenile Dementia

The clinical picture in presenile dementia is similar to that of senile brain disease, except that it occurs in a younger age group. Alzheimer's and Pick's diseases are the major disorders in this category, but Jakob–Creutzfeldt disease and even parkinsonism and Huntington's chorea are sometimes classified as presenile dementia. All of these disorders are named after men who discovered or conducted research on the respective condition.

The degree of brain atrophy in Alzheimer's disease, a type of atrophy known as neurofibrillary degeneration, is greater than that usually found in senile dementia. The average age of onset of the disorder is 56, with deterioration progressing rapidly and death occurring in an average of four years after onset. Alzheimer's patients are usually overactive, agitated, and under emotional stress and frequently show disturbances in language and movement. Pick's disease, which is one and one-half times more common in women than in men but less common than Alzheimer's disease, has an average age of onset in the late 40s. The progress of Pick's disease is slow and insidious, involving first the frontal and temporal lobes and causing difficulty with thinking, fatigability, and lowered inhibitions. As the disorder progresses the patient becomes disoriented and apathetic, and intellectual functions are affected. Both Alzheimer's and Pick's diseases are considered to have a genetic basis, with no specific treatment for either condition other than routine hospital or custodial care.

HEALTH CARE AND TREATMENT

It is undeniable that good health is important to a feeling of satisfaction with life. To a limited extent, discomfort and disease in old age can be combated with medical treatment, but attention to preventive health measures before and during old age is a better defense.

Preventive Health Measures

The truth of the proverb that "an ounce of prevention is worth a pound of cure" is particularly evident with respect to health in old age. As the body's ability to ward off the effects of disease, accidents, and other stressors declines with aging, it becomes essential to take precautions against accidents, to exercise and eat sensibly, and to receive periodic medical checkups.

Exercise. Regular exercise of an appropriate nature has a general salutary effect on the individual, both physically and psychologically, in old age as at other stages of life. In particular, it reduces the incidence of factors contributing to heart disease and hence promotes longevity. Walking, calisthenics, swimming, and jogging in moderation increase oxygen consumption, ventilation capacity, cardiac output, blood flow, and muscle tonus. Furthermore, exercise helps prevent obesity, rids the body of poisons, and decreases the response time of body cells and organs. Physical exercise also increases a person's ability to cope with psychologically stressful situations.

A noteworthy study of the effects of exercise on physiological state and sense of well-being was conducted by Herbert de Vries (1975). One-hundred-twenty-five older men residing at Leisure World, a retirement community in Laguna Hills, California, participated in a program involving calisthenics, jogging, walking, and swimming. Improvements occurred on a number of measures, particularly maximum oxygen usage and oxygen pulse. The overall endurance and physical fitness of the participants, as indicated by oxygen intake, were definitely enhanced by the program.

Nutrition. Eating alone or from loneliness and skipping meals because food is too expensive or because of loss of interest in cooking or eating can cause serious nutritional problems for the elderly. Dietary restrictions, dental and digestive problems, reductions in the sensitivity of taste and smell, as well as depression can interfere with the enjoyment of food. Good nutrition is also hampered by the high cost of food and the unavailability of transportation for many of the elderly. Lacking the social stimuli traditionally associated with meals, isolated older people frequently end up eating unplanned snacks or "picking" at their food. Actually, it is generally recommended that the aged eat four or five light meals instead of a smaller number of heavier meals each day. In most cases these meals should include fewer carbohydrates and more proteins than was typical for the individual prior to old age.

Realizing that a large percentage of the elderly either fail to select a nutritionally balanced diet or cannot afford one, the federal government provides funds for several tax-supported nutrition programs. The Nutrition Program for Older Americans makes available, through state agencies, low-cost group meals and home-delivered meals for persons 60 years of age and older. A part of this program known as "Meals on Wheels" provides for the delivery of hot food to the homes of the aged, and another section of the program arranges for transportation to nutrition sites in the community.

Another nutrition program, even more extensive than the nutrition program for the elderly because it involves all age groups, is the Food

Stamp Program. Under this program, individuals or families with low incomes are eligible for stamps, which can be exchanged for foodstuffs. Also, homebound or handicapped people over 60 years can exchange food stamps for meals delivered to their homes. Finally, emergency foodstuffs and related supplies and services are available to low-income elderly under several programs administered by the Community Services Administration.

Drugs. Elderly people consume 25 to 35 percent of the drugs sold in the United States. Many of these drugs are for chronic conditions such as cardiovascular disorders and arthritis; others are sedatives and tranquilizers that the aged take in quantity to control the anxiety, depression, and insomnia common in old age. These drugs are often misused, due in no small part to the overreadiness of physicians to write prescriptions for them. Physicians frequently prescribe both too much medication and combinations of medications that produce bad reactions in older patients. The elderly may also be unable to read labels or to open drug containers and may lack the funds or transportation to obtain needed drugs.

Addiction to drugs is common to both older and younger people, but the problem of alcohol addiction is more serious in later life. Chronic alcoholism increases the likelihood of accidents, and, combined with poor nutrition, can lead to a number of serious, quite possibly fatal, disorders. Another addiction that increases the probability of poor health and shorter longevity is cigarette smoking.

Psychological Factors. One of the cornerstones of modern medicine is the fact that patient attitudes and psychological stress play important roles in health and disease. For example, the psychological examination of patients who manifest symptoms of coronary heart disease has revealed a pattern of behavior known as "Type A," which is characterized as "driven, aggressive, ambitious, competitive, preoccupied with achievement, impatient, and having restless movements and staccatolike speech" (Jenkins, Rosenman & Friedman, 1967). Type A behavior is considered to be a significant risk factor in the causation and recuperation from a heart disorder.

Type A's, unlike the more relaxed, easygoing, and patient individuals labeled as Type B's, appear to thrive on change. Unfortunately change, whether unpleasant or pleasant, produces a disruption in daily living that places a stress on the individual. Holmes and Rahe (1967) maintained that the stress of change, requiring a readjustment on the part of the individual, increases one's susceptibility to disease. The degree of increased susceptibility varies with the extent of readjustment necessitated by the change. These investigators constructed a "Social Readjustment Rating Scale" on which events requiring changes in the pattern of daily living are scaled from 0 to 100, depending on the degree of readjustment required (see Table 3-3).

Physician Attitudes. The attitude of the patient, as well as the attitude of the physician can play a crucial role in the health of the elderly patient.

Table 3-3   SOCIAL READJUSTMENT RATING SCALE*

Rank	Life Event	Mean Value
1	Death of spouse	100
2	Divorce	73
3	Marital separation	65
4	Jail term	63
5	Death of close family member	63
6	Personal injury or illness	53
7	Marriage	50
8	Fired at work	47
9	Marital reconciliation	45
10	Retirement	45
11	Change in health of family member	44
12	Pregnancy	40
13	Sex difficulties	39
14	Gain of new family member	39
15	Business readjustment	39
16	Change in financial state	38
17	Death of close friend	37
18	Change to different line of work	36
19	Change in number of arguments with spouse	35
20	Mortgage over $10,000	31
21	Foreclosure of mortgage or loan	30
22	Change in responsibilities at work	29
23	Son or daughter leaving home	29
24	Trouble with in-laws	29
25	Outstanding personal achievement	28
26	Wife begin or stop work	26
27	Begin or end school	26
28	Change in living conditions	25
29	Revision of personal habits	24
30	Trouble with boss	23
31	Change in work hours or conditions	20
32	Change in residence	20
33	Change in schools	20
34	Change in recreation	19
35	Change in church activities	19
36	Change in social activities	18
37	Mortgage or loan less than $10,000	17
38	Change in sleeping habits	16
39	Change in number of family get-togethers	15
40	Change in eating habits	15
41	Vacation	13
42	Christmas	12
43	Minor violations of the law	11

*Reprinted with permission from the *Journal of Psychosomatic Research,* 11, T. H. Holmes and R. H. Rahe, "The Social Readjustment Rating Scale," Copyright 1967, Pergamon Press, Ltd.

Unfortunately, many physicians hold negative attitudes and stereotypes concerning older people. All in all, health professionals are significantly more negative in their attitudes toward treating the elderly than they are toward treating younger people (Spence, Feigenbaum, Fitzgerald & Roth, 1968). For example, Butler (1975) noted that future physicians, whose first encounter with an older person in medical school is in the form of a cadaver, may engage in gallows humor and refer to older patients as "crocks," "turkeys," and "dirt-balls," Comfort (1976) reports knowing licensed physicians who ridiculed and humiliated older patients whom they viewed as insulting to their medical skills.

It is hoped that these attitudes are not general, because the elderly average significantly more physician visits than persons under 65. However, even well-meaning physicians are sometimes inadvertently condescending to older patients, calling them by their first names and in other ways treating them as inferiors. To some extent one may sympathize with doctors who feel that treating the elderly is less satisfying because treatment results are less positive than those obtained with younger patients. Doctors have also reported more difficulty in communicating with older patients and of insufficient time to treat them ("Docs Find . . . ," 1978). Certainly, more adequate medical education to help physicians deal with elderly patients is part of the solution to the problem of physician attitudes—a prescription with which Robert Butler and other geriatric physicians would undoubtedly concur.

Nursing Homes

Although a "typical" elderly individual is not likely to be found in a nursing home, hundreds of thousands of people who are 65 or over reside in approximately 25,000 nursing homes in the United States. The great majority of these patients are white, with blacks and other minorities contributing a much smaller proportion of residents than their numbers in the general population might suggest. Approximately 70 percent of nursing-home residents are women, the majority of whom suffer from chronic brain disorders, heart disease, or cancer. They have been placed in these homes because they became disoriented and confused, wandered away from home, were incontinent, and/or showed the need for extensive nursing care (Butler, 1975).

Only about 5 percent of Americans over 65 are in nursing homes or other long-term health-care facilities at any given time, but 25 percent can expect to spend a portion of their later lives in such institutions. Some experts argue that 10 to 15 percent of the elderly population should be in nursing institutions, whereas others feel that only about 2 percent actually require this kind of care.

The reputation that nursing homes have of being "houses of death" comes from the high mortality rate in these institutions. Up to 20 percent of all deaths in the elderly population occur in nursing homes (Kastenbaum

& Candy, 1973), frequently during the first weeks or months of residency. In fact, research evidence shows that both doctors and nurses often let terminally ill nursing-home patients just die, making little or no effort or taking no "heroic measures" to prolong the lives of these patients (Brown & Thompson, 1979).

One factor related to survival in a nursing institution is the attitude of the patient. A depressed attitude suggests a poor prognosis, and an angry or hostile attitude a good prognosis for living more than a few months after being admitted to a nursing home (Ferrare, 1962). A related variable is the degree of control that the patient feels over the situation: Patients who feel that they have some control over their environments tend to have more positive attitudes and hence survive longer.

Illustrative of the relationship between degree of control and the attitudes of patients are the results of an experiment by Langer and Rodin (1976). The subjects, nursing-home patients between the ages of 65 and 90, were divided into three groups. One group was told by the home adminis- trator that they still had a great deal of control over their own lives and should therefore decide how to spend their time. For example, they were encouraged to decide whether or not they wanted to see a movie that was being shown and were made responsible for taking care of a plant. A second (comparison) group of patients was assured that the nursing home staff was concerned with their well-being, but they were not encouraged to assume greater control over their own lives. They were told that the staff would inform them when they were to see the movie, and although they were also given a plant, they were told that the nurses would take care of it. A third (control) group of patients was given no special treatment. Subsequent ratings of the happiness, alertness, and activity of the residents were obtained from the nurses and the residents themselves. The results showed significant increases in the happiness, alertness, and activity of the group urged to assume greater control over their lives, whereas the ratings of the comparison group on these variables declined. Follow-up data obtained 18 months later (Rodin & Langer, 1977) revealed even more impressive results. Not only did the patients in the first (experimental) group continue to be more vigorous, sociable, and self-initiating than those in the comparison and control groups, but the death rate in the first group was only half that of the other two groups.

The federal government began paying for nursing-home care through Medicaid in 1966, and the result has been very profitable for many business people. Money invested in a private nursing home may yield 40 percent or more interest on one's investment in a single year. Unfortunately, the quality of the home typically fails to keep pace with the investors' profits. Ideally, a nursing home should provide excellent medical and convalescent care in a homelike atmosphere. It should be run by a trained hospital administrator who recognizes the need for both liveliness and quietness, depending on the patient and the situation, and makes provisions for them. This picture is reportedly truer of homes in England, Holland, and

Scandinavia than in the United States and many other Western countries, where institutions for the aged too often merit the title of "deathbed dormitories" (de Beauvoir, 1972) (see Reports 3-3 and 3-4).

The quality of nursing homes varies widely, depending to some degree on whether the home is a skilled nursing facility, an intermediate care facility, or a nonskilled institutional or private home facility. Los Angeles'

Report 3-3   A PROFILE OF AMERICA'S ONE MILLION NURSING HOME PATIENTS*

They are old:	Average age 82; 70 percent are over 70.
Most are female:	Women outnumber men three to one.
Most are widowed:	Only 10 percent have a living spouse. Widowed, 63 percent; never married, 22 percent; divorced, 5 percent.
They are alone:	More than 50 percent have no close relatives.
They are white:	Whites, 96 percent; blacks, 2 percent; others, 2 percent.
They come from home:	Some 31 percent come from hospitals, 13 percent from other nursing homes, the remainder from their own homes.
Length of stay:	An average of 2.4 years.
Few can walk:	Less than 50 percent are ambulatory.
They are disabled:	At least 55 percent are mentally impaired; 33 percent are incontinent.
They take many drugs:	Average 4.2 drugs a day.
Few have visitors:	More than 60 percent have no visitors at all.
Few will leave:	Only 20 percent will return home. Some will be transferred to hospitals, but the vast majority will die in the nursing home.

*From *Parade*, July 17, 1977, p. 10.

Report 3-4   A GRANDDAUGHTER'S FIRST VISIT TO A NURSING HOME*

The smell of the place was so strong that I stepped back, trying to fight it off. . . . We stood for a moment looking at the recreation room. . . . A few of the residents chatted together. Several of them looked up hungrily at us, and one old lady in a wheelchair beckoned to me with a clawlike hand. Two bored attendants exchanged laconic comments, and a nurse in a starched white cap wiped the face of a sweating, palsied old man. A few old people had visitors and, jealously guarding them in inescapable clusters of chairs, they leaned forward to grab onto every word. The visitors looked guilty and uncomfortable and miserably self-conscious.

After the visit in the car, my mother turned to me. The brittle smile was gone from her face and she looked exhausted. "Well, Deb, what did you think?" I looked out at the street. "It's awful," I said flatly. "It's horrible and ugly and smelly and I can't understand," my voice rose, "how you can let Gram be so miserable!" My mother turned her head slightly so I couldn't look directly into her eyes. My father glanced away from the icy street long enough to give Mom a look of compassion.

"We know, Deb," he said mildly. "We know. But there's really nothing else to do."

*After Saul, 1974, pp. 63, 68. Reproduced with permisssion.

Keiro ("Home for Respected Elders"), for example, is a nursing home in which members of the Japanese-American community have no misgivings about placing their parents. On the other hand, nursing care in many private homes is so poor that a number of experts have advocated replacing all existing nursing homes with government-owned and professional-staffed facilities. People who entrust their parents to a nursing home should be much more concerned about such matters as nurse/patient ratio, the availability of creative facilities and physical therapy equipment, and the frequency of physicians' visits (Jacoby, 1974). Furthermore, federal standards for these institutions, which were actually lowered in 1974, should be raised and enforced.

Because of the scandals involving nursing homes and the increasing cost of institutional treatment, health care of the elderly is beginning to move away from hospital-based and nursing-home treatment to home health care, day-care centers, and preventive medicine clinics for the elderly. These alternatives are potentially less costly than hospitals and nursing homes and are also less likely to foster the feelings of depersonalization and dependency seen so often in institutional residents.

Among the various alternatives to institutionalization that have been proposed is the multigenerational household. One investigator (Sussman, 1977) reported that members of 60 percent of the 365 households that he interviewed indicated they would be willing to care for elderly relatives in their homes, particularly if the family were financially reimbursed by a monthly check of $200 to $400. Only about 20 percent of the respondents stated that they would not accept an older person in their home under any circumstances, primarily because of a bad experience with an aged relative.

Health-Care Costs and Insurance

Compared to people under 65, the elderly spend many more days in bed, visit doctors a greater number of times, have longer and more frequent stays in the hospital, and consume more medications. In the face of high inflation, the costs of health care represented by these facts would be impossible for the elderly and their families to meet without turning to federal and state governmental agencies for assistance. Expenditures for health care have become the second largest item in the federal budget, even outranking appropriations for defense. Approximately two-thirds of the health expenditures of individuals over age 65 and three-tenths of those for people under 65 are paid by the federal government (U.S. Dept. of Health & Human Services, 1979).

The major federal health-care programs benefiting the elderly are described in Table 3-4. Medicare and Medicaid, which are administered by the Social Security Administration, are the best known and most widely applicable of these programs. Medicare, which since 1965 has covered all people who are eligible for social security benefits, is divided into two parts. Part A (Health Insurance for the Aged—Hospital Insurance) pays for a large portion of hospital care up to 90 days, plus a lifetime reserve of 60 days if more than 90 days are needed. Part A also includes certain items for health care after leaving the hospital, including up to 100 days in an extended care facility.

Coverage under Part A of Medicare is automatic, being financed by a portion of the social security tax, but individuals must apply for Part B (Supplemental Medical Insurance) and pay for it by a deduction from their social security checks. The premiums, however, take care of less than 30 percent of the cost of Part B; the federal government pays the remainder. After a $60 deductible amount, Part B pays for 80 percent of the costs of outpatient physician services, certain types of therapy, home health services, and other services and supplies.

Despite its seemingly high cost, the Medicare program pays less than half the hospital and doctor bills of the elderly. The remainder must come from personal savings, private medical insurance, or other sources. Well over half the aged make up the deficit from private health insurance, but those who cannot even afford the monthly premium of Part B of Medicare

Table 3-4 MAJOR FEDERAL HEALTH CARE PROGRAMS BENEFITING THE ELDERLY*

Program	Executive Agency	Description
Health Resources Development Construction and Modernization of Facilities (Hill-Burton Program)	Health Service Administration of HEW	Federal formula grants and loans to public and private agencies, and to state governments for construction, expansion, or modernization of long-term care institutions and other outpatient and inpatient facilities. Federal share of project cost determined by designated state agency.
Construction of Nursing Homes and Intermediate Care Facilities	Federal Housing Administration (Housing and Urban Development)	Federal government insures loans to nonprofit agencies or individual sponsors to finance the construction, rehabilitation, or equipment supply of certified nursing homes or intermediate care facilities.
Grants to States for Medical Assistance Programs (Medicaid)	Social and Rehabilitation Service of HEW	Federal grants to states to cover 50 to 80 percent of costs of medical care for eligible low-income families and individuals. Within federal guidelines, states establish eligibility and scope of benefits.

Table 3-4   (cont.)

Program	Executive Agency	Description
Program of Health Insurance for the Aged and Disabled (Medicare)	Social Security Administration of HEW	Coverage of specified health care services for persons aged 65 or older and eligible disabled persons covered by social security. Part A (Hospital Insurance) covers hospital and post-hospital skilled nursing home care and home health services. Part B (Supplemental Medical Insurance), subject to premiums, covers physicians and other specified outpatient services.
Veterans Domiciliary Care Program	Veterans Administration	Federal funds for federal facilities, and project grants to states to construct and rehabilitate domiciliary care facilities for veterans, provides medical and personal care in residential-type setting to aged and disabled veterans not requiring hospitalization; provides payments to facilities for provision of such services.
Veterans Nursing Home Care Program	Veterans Administration	Federal funds for federal facilities, and grants to states for construction of homes providing nursing home care to veterans, and for covering medical care services for veterans receiving such care.

*Adapted from Select Committee on Aging. *Federal responsibility to the elderly.* Washington, D.C.: U.S. Government Printing Office (1976), pp. 6-7.

must look elsewhere for health-care funds. Medicaid (Medical Assistance Program), the benefits of which come from federal grants to the states, was designed for just such people. Medicaid covers 50 to 80 percent of medical care, the type and extent of coverage varying from state to state. Anyone who is eligible for old age assistance or welfare is usually eligible for Medicaid, but the applicant for Medicaid must demonstrate a financial need ("means test").

There have been many criticisms of federal health-care programs, from both the elderly themselves and health-care professionals. For example, older people often object to the requirement that they must pay the first

$60 and 20 percent of the remaining portion of their medical expenses in each calendar year. Furthermore, poor people who cannot pay for Part B of Medicare may also be humiliated by the Medicaid means test. Health-care professionals may object to the paperwork involved in filing health insurance claims, governmental "control" of medical services, and the Medicare definition of "reasonable charge." Both doctors and patients may object to the apparent unfairness of other Medicare provisions. As an illustration, when an elderly patient who has been hospitalized with an acute medical condition (e.g., a broken leg) is transferred to a nursing home for convalescence, Medicare will pay most of the bill. But when he or she is sent directly home or judged unlikely to recover, Medicare will pay none of the posthospital bill. Furthermore, Medicare does not cover the cost of spectacles, dental work, hearing aids, foot care, or drugs prescribed outside the hospital. Elderly patients are learning, however, that even when only part of a claim is initially paid by Medicare, filing an appeal will often result in at least a portion of the unpaid balance being reimbursed (Porter, 1980b).

Added to the ever-increasing cost of medical bills, the criticisms and shortcomings just noted indicate the need for changes in the approach of the federal government to health care for the elderly. Robert Butler (1975) has maintained that current federal medical programs will eventually be extended to some form of national health insurance. Beyond national health insurance, he envisages that it may even be necessary for medicine in the United States to become a public utility.

Whatever revisions may occur in the Medicare law, it is hoped that they will represent simplifications rather than an ever-increasing complexity of its provisions. In the coming decades, more emphasis will also be placed on preventive medicine and perhaps less on spectacular medical achievements such as organ transplants that make headlines but cost a great deal of money and benefit relatively few people.

SUMMARY

Disease and disability are related to age, sex, socioeconomic status, and ethnicity. Although the maximum life span has not increased significantly during this century, the disorders most commonly causing death have changed. Also, with extended life expectancy, more people are reaching old age and suffering from various chronic disorders associated with that period of life. The chronic conditions, related mostly to old age, are arthritis, respiratory disorders, digestive and eliminative problems, and osteoporosis. Osteoporosis, a gradual loss of bone mass, which is four times as frequent in older women as in older men, can lead to painful fractures of the spine, hips, and rib cage. Traffic accidents and falls around the house are also frequent causes of injuries in older people.

Heart disease, cancer, and stroke are the three biggest killers in old age. Obesity, lack of exercise, heavy smoking, psychological stress, and high blood cholesterol level are all related to the incidence of cardiovascular disorders. Great strides have been made in treating heart disease, and there is evidence that its incidence is declining.

Organic brain disorders that are fairly common in old age are cerebral arteriosclerosis and senile brain disease. Confusion, disorientation, incoherence, restlessness, and occasionally hallucinations occur in cerebral arteriosclerosis. Self-centeredness, difficulty in assimilating new experiences, and childish emotionality are symptoms of senile brain disease. The symptoms of irreversible senile brain disease are similar to those of many other reversible conditions (e.g., overdoses of certain drugs, malnutrition, and dehydration). Consequently, the physician must be wary of misdiagnosing one of these reversible conditions as senile brain disease. Alzheimer's disease, Pick's disease, and Jakob–Creutzfeldt disease are irreversible presenile disorders involving the destruction of brain tissue and a psychological symptom picture similar to that of senile brain disease.

Preventive health measures recommended for the elderly include regular exercise, good nutrition, judicious usage of both prescribed and nonprescribed drugs, periodic medical checkups by a physician who has a positive attitude toward older people, and freedom from severe psychological stress. Unfortunately, lack of exercise, poor nutrition, misuse of drugs, and treatment by physicians having negative attitudes toward elderly patients are all too common in later life. Nutrition programs for the elderly such as "Meals on Wheels" have been prompted by the recognition that many elderly people are unable to select or afford a nutritionally balanced diet.

Varying greatly, the quality of nursing and rest homes for the elderly is a source of continuing national concern. A number of alternatives to institutional care of the elderly have been proposed, including home health care, day-care centers, and preventive medicine clinics. At the very least, closer supervision of the facilities, staff, and practices of nursing homes needs to be maintained by official agencies.

In spite of the billions of dollars appropriated each year by the federal government for Medicare and Medicaid, medical and dental bills continue to deplete the savings and income sources of many elderly people. Combined with the ever-increasing costs of health care, the complexity and apparent inequity of many Medicare provisions will necessitate changes during the next few years, eventuating perhaps in some form of national health insurance.

SUGGESTED READINGS

Barrows, C. H., & Roeder, L. M. Nutrition. In C. E. Finch & L. Hayflick (Eds.), *Handbook of the biology of aging.* New York: Van Nostrand Reinhold, 1977.

Brody, S. J. Comprehensive health care for the elderly: An analysis. The continuum of medical, health, and social services for the aged. *The Gerontologist,* 1973, *13*, 412–418.

Butler, R. N. *Why survive: Being old in America.* New York: Harper & Row, 1975. Chapters 8 and 9.

Butler, R. N., & Lewis, M. I. *Aging and mental health* (2d ed.). St. Louis, Mo.: Mosby, 1977.

Conditions tragic in adult care homes. *Aging,* 1980, *303/304* (Jan/Feb), 24–29.

De Vries, H. The physiology of exercise and aging. In D. Woodruff & J. E. Birren (Eds.), *Aging: Scientific perspectives and social issues.* New York: Van Nostrand, 1975.

Harris, R. Graduate training in geriatrics: New dimensions and trends. *Aging,* 1979, *295*(May), 28–34.

Hazzard, W. R., & Bierman, E. L. Old age. In D. W. Smith, E. L. Bierman, & N. M. Robinson, (Eds.), *The biologic ages of man.* Philadelphia: Saunders, 1978.

Kart, C. S., & Manard, B. (Eds.). *Aging in America. Readings in social gerontology.* Part VI. Institutionalization. Port Washington, N.Y.: Alfred Publishing, 1976.

Posner, B. M. *Nutrition and the elderly: Policy development, program planning, and evaluation.* Lexington, Mass.: Lexington Books (Heath), 1979.

NOTES

[1] The elimination of these disorders is already underway. The results of a study by the Mayo Clinic indicate that the number of cerebrovascular accidents ("strokes"), especially among the elderly, has declined appreciably during the past 30 years. Possible causes of the decline are better treatment of high blood pressure, a decrease in smoking since the surgeon general's report of 1964, and dietary changes ("Reports Show . . . ," 1979).

[2] A person who confabulates tries to fill in gaps in his or her memory by guessing or lying.

Mental Abilities

A popular view of old age is that it is a time when abilities decline, activities are more restricted, and dependence on others becomes more of a necessity. A common belief is that old people have poor memories, cannot think clearly, and undergo a general decline in mentality. As discussed in Chapter 2, sensorimotor abilities usually show a marked decline in old age. But as we shall see in the present chapter, mental abilities do not deteriorate quite so rapidly, and judgment and wisdom can compensate for the losses in physical and mental abilities that do occur. Certainly, many very old people remain independent and active almost until the time of death, adapting successfully and maintaining their level of mental ability.

CREATIVITY

Evidence that creative production does not necessarily decline in old age can be found by analyzing the biographies of famous artists, scholars, and scientists. Pianist Artur Rubinstein was still playing brilliantly at age 89, some say with greater sensitivity and skill than ever. Many famous men—Goethe, Picasso, Edison, and Burbank—continued their highly creative endeavors into the ninth decade of life. Giuseppe Verdi produced the joyous, exuberant opera "Falstaff" at age 80, and Justice Oliver Wendell Holmes, Jr. formulated many of his most impressive legal opinions while in his 90s.

> Cato learned Greek at eighty; Sophocles
> Wrote his grand Oedipus, and Simonides

Bore off the prize of verse from his compeers,
When each had numbered more than four score years.
And Theophrastus, at four score and ten,
Had just begun his *Characters of Men*.
Chaucer, at Woodstock with the nightingales,
At sixty wrote the Canterbury Tales;
Goethe at Weimar, toiling to the last,
Completed Faust when eighty years were past.

Longfellow, Morituri Salutamus

Old people learn new things, develop new skills, and may become truly creative for the first time during later life. Grandma Moses was 73 when she started painting, and held her first exhibition at age 80. By the time of her death at 101 she had achieved international fame as an artist. One may argue, however, that these are exceptions and that creative performance typically peaks much sooner than old age. An early study found that the period of peak productivity in the arts was 30 to 39 years and that productivity declined thereafter (Lehman, 1953). Lehman (1962, 1966) subsequently reported a similar pattern of an early peak and a decline with age in scientists. Likewise, chess masters tend to reach a performance peak in their 30s, although they typically show little decline until their 50s. A dramatic illustration of a continuing high level of mental functioning in chess is that of the chess master Blackburne, who gave nine exhibitions between the ages of 76 and 79, averaging 21 games at each exhibition and winning 86 percent of them (Buttenwieser, 1935).

A problem with Lehman's (1953) conclusion that creativity usually peaks in the 20s and 30s is that many of the people who were studied died when they were still fairly young. This circumstance produced a bias favoring early peak creativity, a methodological shortcoming that Dennis (1966) attempted to correct. Dennis's investigation of 738 people who lived to age 79 or beyond reported comparative longitudinal data on the productivity of three major groups—scholars, scientists, and artists (art, music, and literature). Although people in the fine arts and literature tended to produce more in their 20s than scholars and scientists, the period of greatest output for all three groups was in the 40s or shortly thereafter. The performance of scholars declined little after age 40, but the output of artists and scientists decreased appreciably after age 60. Other studies have found that inventors and historians tend to reach maximum productivity around age 60.

Differences in the period of peak productivity of various groups depend on individual creativity, as well as on the length of the training period. This period is longer for scientists and scholars than for artists (Dennis, 1966). Productivity in the arts seems to depend more on individual creativity than experience and therefore peaks early. Creative production in scholarly or scientific endeavors, on the other hand, demands a longer training period, and consequently, creativity in these fields shows a later peak.

The results of these studies and the examples of numerous creative people indicate that creative performance is not limited to a particular chronological age range. Given adequate ability, sound health, sufficient encouragement, and opportunity, a person can be creative at any age. However, potentially creative people who are not properly stimulated or rewarded, or who are not given a chance to demonstrate their abilities will, all too often, settle into a routine existence in which their potential remains unfulfilled. Only a society that recognizes the wide variations in individuals, regardless of age, and provides opportunities for these differences to be manifested can hope to make optimal use of its older citizens.

GENERAL INTELLIGENCE

In addition to curiosity, motivation, and flexibility, an extremely important factor in creativity at any age is ability. Of the many efforts that psychologists have made to measure general and specific mental abilities, research and application in the area of intelligence testing have been in the forefront. Unlike creative performance, which is actually a criterion variable, measures of general intelligence and specific mental abilities have been used primarily as predictors of future performance. The instruments employed to measure these variables attempt to assess maximum mental performance—what a person is capable of achieving with adequate motivation and opportunity.

Wechsler Adult Intelligence Scale

Traditional intelligence tests, which are loaded with school-type tasks, were not designed originally to assess the abilities of older people. Early tests such as the Stanford-Binet Intelligence Scale were directed primarily at school-age children, the major purpose of the tests being to determine the abilities of children to profit from scholastic work. The first individual tests of intelligence constructed specifically for adults were the Wechsler-Bellevue Intelligence Tests, published originally in 1939 and revised as the Wechsler Adult Intelligence Scale (WAIS) in 1955.

The WAIS, which consists of eleven subtests and is scored for Verbal, Performance, and Full Scale intelligence quotients (IQs), was standardized on a wide age range of adults. The old age standardization sample consisted of over fifty men and fifty women in each of four age groups (60 to 64, 65 to 69, 70 to 74, 75 and over), but the number of cases in each age/sex group on which the IQ tables were based was considerably smaller. Furthermore, the examinees in the old age groups were selected by quota-sampling procedures from metropolitan Kansas City, which was described as a "typical American city." For these and other technical reasons, the sample used in computing the IQ tables on the WAIS for age 60 and above turned out not to be truly representative of older U.S. citizens. Recognition of this fact is seen in the provision for more representative sampling of older adults in the 1981 revision of the WAIS.

A graphic plot of the average WAIS subtest scaled scores for the four old-age groups is presented in Figure 4-1 (p. 78). It will be noted that the average scaled scores for these groups are higher on the first six subtests (the Verbal Scale) than on the last five subtests (the Performance Scale). Because the mean subtest scaled score for people in general is 10, the old-age sample scored below the general population mean on all subtests, but particularly on Digit Symbol (DS)—a speeded test. It will also be observed that there is a general decline in the average scaled scores on all subtests after ages 60 to 64.

Testing Older Adults

In addition to difficulties of score interpretation caused by inadequate norms, there are special problems in administering intelligence tests to older people. To begin with, older people, whose behavior is less susceptible to control by psychologists and educators, are frequently reluctant to be tested. Among the reasons for the uncooperativeness of elderly examinees are: lack of time, perception of the test tasks as trivial or meaningless, and fear of doing badly or appearing foolish (Welford, 1958). Older adults, to an even greater extent than more test-conscious younger adults, do not

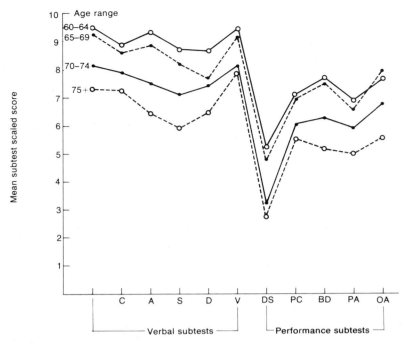

Figure 4-1 Mean WAIS subtest scaled scores for the four subgroups of the old-age standardization group. (From Doppelt & Wallace, 1955.Copyright 1955 by the American Psychological Association. Adapted by permission of the publishers and author.)

relish performing tasks that make them look stupid or that they perceive as having no bearing on their lives.

Because of lower motivation to be tested in the first place, it obviously requires sensitivity and tact on the part of the psychological examiner to obtain valid responses in testing elderly people. Unfortunately, it is often questionable whether a technically proficient but young examiner can establish sufficient rapport with elderly examinees to communicate test directions adequately and stimulate examinees to do their best (Fletcher, 1972). Relatively few mental testers appear to have sufficient training and experience in the psychological examination of the elderly to do a credible job. Most examiners find, however, that once elderly examinees have agreed to be tested, they are just as highly motivated to do their best as are younger examinees (Welford, 1958).

Even when examinees are cooperative and motivated to do well, the time limitations on tests, the presence of sensory defects, and the distractibility and easy fatigability of many elderly people make it difficult for them to perform satisfactorily. For example, one of the most characteristic things about being older is that one's reflexes and physical movements tend to slow down. For this reason, explanations of the declining test scores of the elderly in such areas as learning and memory must take into account the fact that older people do not usually react as rapidly as younger people. Although older people are usually at a disadvantage on timed tests, their performance improves significantly when they are provided sufficient time in which to respond. Consequently, the aged show little or no inferiority in comparison to younger people on untimed tests.

Sensory defects, especially in the visual and auditory modalities, can also interfere with performance in old age. Special test materials such as large-face type and trained examiners who are alert to the presence of sensory defects can be of help. Occasionally, however, an alleged sensory defect may actually be a mask for a problem in reading and auditory comprehension. For example, the author has had the experience of preparing to test an elderly man who, embarrassed by his poor reading ability, conveniently forgot his glasses and hence was unable to read the test materials.

Assuming that all goes well with the testing procedure, the examiner must still avoid confusing scholastic intelligence with everyday mental functioning. Many older (and younger) people who do poorly on intelligence tests manage to cope satisfactorily with the demands of daily living. From a practical standpoint, how well a person functions in everyday life is the best measure of his or her abilities. This has led some authorities to suggest that tests for older people would have greater validity if they consisted of problem situations specific to their lives.

Because the test materials and the method of administration affect test performance, more extensive research needs to be conducted to determine the effects of adjusting test administration procedure to the characteristics of the elderly. Whether such adjustments are advisable depends on what is being measured and the context in which the test results are interpreted. For example, timed tests measure different functions and serve different purposes from untimed tests. It seems reasonable, however, that special procedures of test administration, coupled with sensitivity and patience on the part of the examiner, can afford a better opportunity for elderly examinees to demonstrate their capabilities. Among these suggested procedures, which have been adapted from well-known instructional techniques, are:

1. Provide ample time for the examinee to respond to the test material.
2. Allow sufficient practice on sample items.
3. Use shorter testing periods than with younger adults.
4. Watch out for fatigue and take it into consideration.
5. Be aware of and make provisions for visual, auditory, and other sensory defects.
6. Arrange for the examination room to be as free as possible of distractions.
7. Employ a generous amount of encouragement and positive reinforcement.
8. Do not overstress or force examinees to respond to test items when they repeatedly decline to do so. (Aiken, 1980, p. 123)

Cross-Sectional and Longitudinal Studies

The results of earlier studies of changes in general intelligence with age were almost always based on cross-sectional data (Yerkes, 1921; Jones & Conrad, 1933; Doppelt & Wallace, 1955). From his analysis of scores on the Army Alpha Test administered to American Army officers during World War I, Yerkes (1921) found that average scores on this early group-administered test of intelligence decreased steadily from the late teens through the sixth decade of life. A similar trend was observed by Jones and Conrad (1933) in a study conducted in nineteen New England villages. Wechsler's (1958) analysis of the relationship of mean Full Scale scores on the Wechsler-Bellevue Form I also showed that mean standard scores peaked in late adolescence, remained fairly constant from that point until the late 20s or early 30s, and subsequently showed a steady decline through old age (Fig. 4-2). A composite picture of the findings of cross-sectional investigations through 1960 indicates that scores on general intelligence tests reach a maximum during the late teens or early 20s, show little appreciable further change until ages 30 to 35, and then decrease steadily through old age.

The problems encountered in interpreting the results of cross-sectional studies were described briefly in Chapter 1. Cross-sectional investigations compare people of different cohorts; that is, a group of people brought up in one kind of sociocultural climate is compared with a group brought up in another sociocultural climate. Differences among cohorts in factors such as educational opportunity, which is closely related to intelligence test scores, and the selective migration of brighter people away from home make it difficult to match people of different ages.

The steady rise in both the average educational and socioeconomic levels of Americans during the current century must be taken into account when interpreting the apparent age decline in mental abilities. Intelligence test scores are positively related to both educational level and socioeconomic status. Consequently, it is understandable that older cohorts, those who grew up during less affluent times and had less formal education, would score significantly lower than younger cohorts. Rather than interpreting this result as demonstrating that intelligence declines with age, a more reasonable view may be to show that the increase in test scores in later generations was due to improvements in education and socioeconomic status.

In contrast with cross-sectional studies, the findings of several longitudinal investigations indicate that intelligence test scores may actually increase after early adulthood. It can be argued that because these longitudinal studies have most often been conducted on college graduates or other intellectually favored groups, the increases with age do not necessarily apply to the general population (Bayley & Oden, 1955; Nisbet, 1957; Campbell, 1965; Owens, 1953, 1966). However, longitudinal investigations with people of average intelligence (Charles & James, 1964;

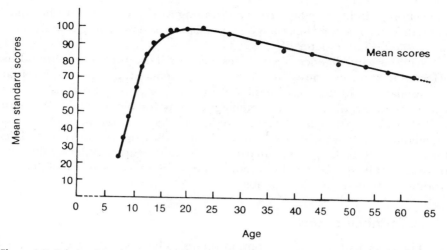

Figure 4-2 Relationship of mean Full Scale scores on the Wechsler-Bellevue Form I to age (7−65 years). (After D. Wechsler, *The measurement and appraisal of adult intelligence,* 4th ed., 1958. New York: Oxford University Press. Used with permission.)

Eisdorfer, 1963; Tuddenham, Blumenkrantz, & Wilkin, 1968) and with noninstitutionalized mentally retarded adults (Baller, Charles, & Miller, 1967; Bell & Zubek, 1960) have yielded similar findings. Botwinick (1976) interpreted these results as suggesting that intelligence continues to increase by small amounts during early adulthood, reaching a plateau between the ages of 25 and 30. Subsequently, people who are below average in intelligence decline somewhat, but above-average people manifest no decline or even improve until age 50. Furthermore, a later study by Baltes and Schaie (1974) found that intelligence may continue to increase even after age 70. As the results of such longitudinal investigations make clear, intellectual decline with aging is by no means inevitable, varying with the task and the individual.

Intellectual Decline with Age: Further Considerations

Deciding whether the research evidence permits any firm conclusions regarding the alleged decline in intelligence during old age is not a simple matter. Different authorities, depending perhaps on their particular theoretical persuasions, disagree. Horn and Donaldson (1976), for example, maintain that decrements in at least some of the important abilities constituting intelligence are likely to occur if one lives long enough. Baltes and Schaie (1976) do not reject this conclusion in toto but maintain that the existence of wide individual differences in intelligence, together with its multidimensionality, modifiability, and the interaction between age and cohort, lead to the conclusion that intelligence is a very plastic variable. Consequently, they feel that psychologists should give more attention to the subject of changing intelligence in a changing world. Efforts must be made to modify behavior, rather than being resigned to its seeming fixedness or inevitable decline in later life.

Whether intelligence test scores rise or fall during adulthood is affected to some extent by the kinds of experiences that a person has that are similar to the tasks on intelligence tests. One must also consider the appropriateness of traditional intelligence tests for older adults. Wesman (1968) argued, for example, that older adults are not necessarily less intelligent than younger ones simply because they do not score as well as the latter on tests designed primarily for younger people. Older adults may possess highly specialized knowledge and skills in areas not included in traditional tests of intellectual abilities.

A Terminal Drop?

The consensus of expert opinion seems to be that intellectual abilities do not invariably decline in old age and that wisdom and experience can compensate for whatever decline may occur. There is, however, an apparent exception to this principle, a psychological phenomenon referred to as the **terminal drop.** The terminal drop is an observed decline in intellectual functions (IQ, memory, cognitive organization), sensorimotor abilities (e.g., reaction time), and personality (assertiveness, etc.) during the last few months or so of life. The research that first demonstrated the terminal drop phenomenon was prompted by a nurse in a home for the aged who claimed that she could predict which patients were going to die soon just by observing that they "seem to act differently" (Lieberman, 1965). Subsequent research (Lieberman & Coplan, 1969; Reimanis & Green, 1971) found declines in several areas of cognitive and sensory-motor functioning and in the general ability to cope with environmental demands in those patients who died within a year of the testing. Similar declines were not found in patients who died a year or more after being tested.

Not all authorities agree that the terminal drop is an authentic phenomenon. The findings of Palmore and his associates (Palmore, 1974; Palmore & Cleveland, 1976) suggest, for example, that the supposed drop is due to conceptual and methodological problems in research on the topic rather than to any sudden loss of ability at the end of a person's life. Consequently, this matter, like so many others in gerontological psychology, remains an open question and a topic for further investigation.

Biological Variables in Intellectual Decline

A number of biological variables—heredity, sex, nutrition, health, and the like—are related to mental functioning in old age. For example, one 20-year investigation of sex differences in the mental ability of octogenarians found that the women were superior to the men (Blum, Fosshage, &

Jarvik, 1972). Furthermore, studies of people in their 70s, 80s, and 90s have found a higher correlation between health and intelligence than between age and intelligence (Birren, 1968; Palmore, 1970). Generally speaking, brighter people are healthier and live longer than the less bright in old age. It has also been suggested that the relationship between mental ability and health in old age may be reflective of personality adjustment, with better adjusted people being both brighter and healthier (Neugarten, 1976).

One health-related factor that affects only a small percentage of older people but interferes with efficiency of intellectual functioning is chronic brain syndrome (Ben-Yishay et al., 1971; Overall & Gorham, 1972). A more common condition is high blood pressure (hypertension), which may be accompanied by cardiovascular disease and stroke. And a serious stroke, which is related to an insufficient flow of oxygen to the brain, can affect both intellectual functioning and the motor skills required for speaking and walking.

The results of an investigation by Wilkie and Eisdorfer (1971) suggest that when intelligence does decline during old age, it may be caused not by aging itself but rather by high blood pressure. Over a 10-year period, these researchers observed 202 men and women who were in their 60s and 70s. The participants were divided into three groups according to their blood pressure—normal, borderline, and high—and were given a complete battery of psychological tests. The relationship between blood pressure and intellectual changes was seen by the end of the tenth year to be a complex function. Participants whose blood pressure was normal showed no significant change in intelligence, whereas those with high blood pressure showed a drop of almost ten points on the intelligence test. The third group (those with borderline blood pressure) actually increased their scores on the test by an average of several points. This last finding was interpreted as support for the theory that slightly elevated blood pressures is needed to maintain good circulation in the brains of old people.

SPECIFIC MENTAL ABILITIES

General intelligence tests measure a combination of several mental abilities, and the pattern of change in performance with age depends on the specific ability being measured. For example, cross-sectional data on the WAIS subtests reveal that scaled scores on the subtests of the Verbal Scale remain fairly constant but scaled scores on the Performance Scale subtests decrease more significantly with age (Wechsler, 1958; see Fig. 4-1). The findings of other cross-sectional studies are similar in that vocabulary and information scores typically manifest no appreciable change, but perceptual-integrative abilities and comprehension of numerical symbols decline more rapidly.[1]

A classical longitudinal study of age changes in mental abilities was conducted by Owens (1953), who compared the army Alpha scores of a group of middle-aged men with their performance on the same test 30 years earlier. It was found that the men scored higher in middle age than as youths on every subtest except arithmetic. Related investigations point to the conclusion that an older person's verbal ability stays fairly constant and may even improve as long as he or she remains in good health. Experience undoubtedly plays a role in determining which abilities decline and which do not, in that well-rehearsèd verbal abilities involving vocabulary usage and verbal comprehension show little or no decrease with age (Arenberg, 1973).

As one ages it may become increasingly difficult to understand new ideas, make complex decisions, master new concepts, or solve laboratory-type problems. But whether these changes are due to a decline in mental aptitude, the interfering effects of prior learning, physical and mental inactivity, loss of motivation to perform various tasks, or some other factor is not clear. Gergen and Back (1966) maintained that as a result of a limited time perspective, old people prefer short-range rather than long-range solutions to problems. Furthermore, the limited time perspective of the elderly may be accompanied by a limited space perspective, in which individuals consider only those factors that are physically close to them. Also related to problem solving is the shift in sex differences in some abilities with aging. The superiority of young men to young women on laboratory-type problems undergoes a change with aging, in that there is no sex difference in this skill during the 50s and women are superior to men in the 60s (Young, 1971). In fact, the data point to a greater overall age-related decline in the mental abilities of men than in those of women (Neugarten, 1976). However, just how much of this difference is due to the highly verbal nature of the tests employed is not clear. Certainly, through-out the life span males tend to score lower than females on verbal-type tasks.

The most comprehensive studies of the differential effects of aging on mental abilities have been conducted by Warner Schaie and his associates (Baltes & Schaie, 1974; Schaie & Labouvie-Vief, 1974; Schaie & Strother, 1968). The results of the investigation by Schaie & Strother (1968), which employed both cross-sectional and longitudinal methods, are illustrated in Figure 4-3. Fifty people in each 5-year age interval from 20 to 70 years were tested with the SRA Mental Abilities Test, and as many as could be located were retested seven years later. The results varied with specific abilities, but some decline was noted using both cross-sectional and longi-tudinal approaches. Figure 4-3 indicates that the cross-sectional approach revealed the greatest decline in abilities with age, and the decline began at an earlier age than with the longitudinal approach.

A later longitudinal study (Baltes & Schaie, 1974) found a decline in the mental factor of "visuo-motor flexibility" but no significant change in "cognitive flexibility" with age. However, increases in the factors of "crystallized intelligence" and "visualization" were observed in the later years. The former term is Raymond Cattell's label for intelligence that is

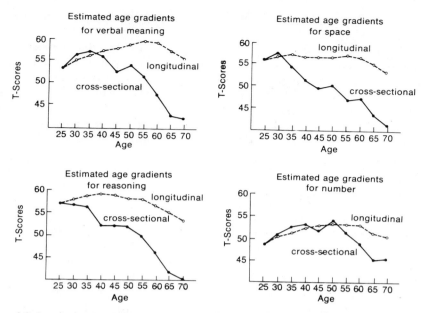

Figure 4-3 Standard scores on four subtests of the SRA Mental Abilities Test as a function of age in cross-sectional and longitudinal studies. (From Schaie & Strother, 1968, pp. 675–676. Copyright 1968 by the American Psychological Association. Reprinted by permission of the publisher and author.)

specific to certain fields, such as school learning or tasks in which habits have become relatively fixed. In contrast to fluid intelligence (g_f), which is general to many different fields and depends primarily on heredity, crystallized intelligence (g_c) depends more on environment.

MEMORY AND LEARNING

A well-known saying is that "old age is the mother of forgetfulness," and a common complaint of the aged is loss of memory (Savitz, 1974). It might appear that memory is a single specific ability, but research findings point to several kinds of memory. **Short-term memory** (STM), or primary memory, is defined as the ability to retain information from a second to a few minutes at most. **Long-term memory** (LTM), or secondary memory, is defined as retention for at least 10 to 20 minutes. Very long-term memory was involved in Kastenbaum's (1966) study of the earliest memories of 276 centenarians. Many of these people were quite engrossed in their memories of the distant past, to a much greater degree than their memories of more recent events. Another illustrative study was conducted by Smith (1963), with a sample size of one, in an attempt to recall verbal materials learned 30, 40, and 50 years before. It was found that forgetting was most rapid after 63 years of age, and more difficult material that had not been overlearned originally or practiced subsequently was most difficult to recall.

Beginning with the classic work of Hermann Ebbinghaus, most laboratory experiments on learning and memory have employed special materials such as nonsense syllables, simple perceptual configurations, or meaningful verbal materials. The majority of these investigations have been concerned with remembering over several days or at least a few hours, but recent research has focused on short-term memory. People use short-term memory in recalling unfamiliar telephone numbers or other information needed for only a short time.

Short-Term Memory

Psychologists have been aware of short-term memory for over a half-century, because many intelligence tests contain items (digit span, for example) that measure the examinee's immediate memory span for numbers or words. But systematic investigations of the characteristics of short-term memory and the factors that affect it began only about 20 years ago (e.g., Peterson & Peterson, 1959; Welford, 1958). A typical experiment consists of showing the subject a very short list of letters, words, or numbers, and immediately thereafter requiring the performance of some unrelated activity to prevent rehearsal of the material. Then after a few minutes the subject is asked to recall the original list. The results of experiments of this sort have revealed how quickly people can forget information when enough time is not provided for the information to be integrated or consolidated into the existing mental framework. It has also been found that short-term memory behaves very similarly to long-term memory. For example, the amount of material recalled decreases progressively with time since original learning.

Numerous investigations have been concerned with the relationhip of short-term memory to age. In one of these (Inglis, Ankus, & Sykes, 1968), 240 people between the ages of 5 and 70 were tested on a rote learning task and a short-term auditory memory task. On both tasks, performance rose until adulthood and then fell in old age. The investigators interpreted the findings as indicating that short-term memory storage is involved in many learning tasks and may be the cause of wide variations in performance across individuals. A similar conclusion was arrived at by Welford (1958), who maintained that short-term memory is involved in several types of learning processes affected by aging.

Certain psychologists have concluded that the similarity between the behavior of short-term and long-term memories indicates no meaningful distinction between the two phenomena. Other psychologists believe, however, that there are two qualitatively distinct processes having different physiological storage mechanisms. Bower (1966), for example, postulated a two-stage theory of memory, the first stage (short-term memory) involving a temporary memory-storage mechanism and the second stage (long-term memory), a more permanent storage mechanism. According to Bower's theory, perceived information first goes into temporary storage and must then be coded in some way by means of a mnemonic (memory-facilitating) operation in order to be placed in permanent storage.

The results of other research have led to a questioning of the notion that older people have good long-term memories but poor short-term memories. According to the findings of Craik (1977), age differences in short-term memory are slight, but older adults have more difficulty than younger adults in retrieving information from long-term memory. The seemingly remarkable ability of elderly people to remember events that occurred decades ago was interpreted by Craik as being due to mental rehearsal of those events over time.

Recognition versus Recall Memory

Another distinction between types of memory is recognition versus recall. Recognition memory is used when one is required to select the correct response from a list or group, whereas recall memory is used when material must be learned "by heart" and the correct response given without using prompts. Schonfield (1965) was interested in determining whether the difficulty that old people appear to have in learning new material is due to a problem of absorbing (storing) the material or of recalling it once it has been stored. His experiment consisted of presenting two lists of twenty-four words each on a screen at intervals of 4 seconds between words. Immediately after the last word was presented, memory was tested by the recall method for one list and by the recognition method for the other list. The participants were 134 people between the ages of 20 and 75, half of whom performed the recognition test first and half the recall test first. The results, which are illustrated in Figure 4-4 (p. 88), revealed no age deterioration in average recognition scores but a consistent drop in recall scores. The investigator concluded that older people do show a defect of memory, but this appears to be a loss of ability to retrieve memories rather than a deficiency in the storage system itself.

Schonfield's (1965) research findings have led many authorities to conclude that the difference between memory in older and younger adults is primarily a matter of retrieval rather than a lack of initial storage of the information in the brain. Subsequent research has, for the most part, confirmed the notion that older people have more difficulty retrieving long-term memories. However, for whatever reasons—sensory deficits, inattentiveness, distractibility, insufficient time, or neurological deficit—the aged also seem to have greater difficulty storing memories initially. This is especially true with more complex material (Adamowicz, 1976). Thus one can reinterpret Schonfield's (1965) research as demonstrating that the elderly do not acquire and store information as well as younger people, and

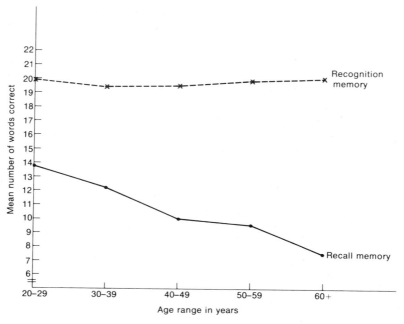

Figure 4-4 Mean scores on recognition and recall tests as a function of age. (Data from Schonfield, 1965.)

as a consequence, have an incomplete knowledge of it. This incomplete knowledge is sufficient for them to recognize the learned material but not to recall it.

Interference and Arousal

Loss of memory in old age has traditionally been attributed to a decline in the number of brain neurons and to large accumulations of **plaque**—collections of altered dendrites and axons in the brain. Decrements in performance with age cannot, however, be explained entirely in terms of structural changes in the nervous system. Motivation and other psychological factors play important roles in both learning and memory. For example, an older person is less likely than a younger one to attempt to learn something that is meaningless or seemingly useless to him—the kinds of tasks that psychologists frequently devise for their research. As the following two investigations demonstrate, interference, which causes attention to shift, and arousal are also significant variables in learning and memory.

Data obtained by Kirchner (1958) indicate that the older person's problem with remembering is due more to the difficulty of retaining information in the presence of interference or shifting attention rather than to simple recall failure. Older people seem to take longer to consolidate new information, and are more susceptible to the interfering effects of other stimuli. Kirchner's experimental task consisted of a row of twelve lights that went on and off at random; each light had a switch just below it. The older subjects did as well as the younger ones when the task was to press the switch below the light that had just gone off, but they did progressively worse than the younger ones when required to press the switch below the next-to-the-last light to go off, the switch below the next-to-the-next-to-the-last light to go off, and so on. The poorer performance of the older subjects was interpreted as a difficulty in retaining information in the face of interference or shifts in attention rather than a failure of recall.

Explanations of an age-related decrement in learning and memory must also take into account the fact that older people often fail to respond when a rapid response is called for. However, as noted previously, they tend to be generally slower than younger age groups, both in learning and in performing. When elderly subjects are given more time in which to respond, their performance improves significantly. Another finding is that older people show heightened, prolonged arousal of the autonomic nervous system during learning. Presumably, the heightened arousal causes them to commit more errors of omission when the learning situation is rapidly paced. Consequently, if autonomic arousal during learning could be controlled by an autonomic-blocking drug such as propranolol, perhaps elderly people would learn more quickly.

Arguing in this manner, Eisdorfer, Nowlin, and Wilkie (1970) paid twenty-eight men volunteers in the age range of 60 to 78 years to have a drug (or placebo) administered to them and subsequently to learn a list of eight high-association words by the method of serial anticipation. Thirteen of the men (the experimental group) were chosen at random to receive the drug propranolol hydrochloride; the remaining fifteen men (the control group) received a saline solution. Heart rate, plasma free fatty acid, and the galvanic skin response were monitored to measure autonomic activity during the learning task. As indicated by these physiological measures, propranolol was at least partially effective in reducing arousal. Furthermore, the men who received the drug performed significantly better on the learning task than the controls.

Effects of Drugs and Other Substances

It is possible that certain drugs or other substances can improve the efficiency of learning and memory, and many drugs have seemed at first to have this effect. The change, unfortunately, is usually short-lived or attributable to improvements in motivation and general health or to a placebo effect. A few years ago interest was shown in Ribaminol, a compound based on the RNA (ribonucleic acid) molecule. This drug, which appeared to speed up protein synthesis in the brain, was tested on hospitalized senile patients and college students. Initial results indicated that the drug had some effect on short-term memory, but the results were not confirmed by further tests (Botwinick, 1967).

Other drugs or substances for which improvements in learning and memory have been reported are Gerovital, sex hormones, and a high choline diet. Evidence to back up such claims is, unfortunately, at best inconclusive.

One physiological theory of age decrement in memory holds that hardening of the arteries starves brain cells of oxygen-bearing blood, causing the cells to stop receiving and processing information. For example, Jacobs, Winter, Alvis, and Small (1969) found that daily breathing of 100 percent oxygen at high atmospheric pressures ("hyperoxygenation") prevented a loss of memory in the old people whom they studied. The benefits of hyperoxygenation reportedly lasted at least two weeks. The results were interpreted as being caused by improvement in the functioning of brain tissues that were deficient in oxygen rather than a reversal of the degeneration process in neurons.

In a further investigation of hyperoxygenation and memory, Boyle ("Can Oxygen Fight . . . ," 1972) oxygenated patients at three atmospheres for 30 minutes—a higher pressure than Jacobs et al. (1969) employed, but for a shorter period of time. As a result of these investigations and several others, many researchers became quite enthusiastic about the procedure, and especially its apparent ability to improve memory of recent events. Attempts to replicate these findings, however, have not been uniformly successful, and the earlier investigations have been severely criticized. It has been suggested, for example, that the care and attention that older people receive while being treated by hyperoxygenation may be suffficient to stimulate their brains and motivate them to remember better (the Hawthorne effect). In any event, hyperoxygenation is not a procedure that will cure memory disorders or empty all institutions for the elderly.

EDUCATION FOR THE ELDERLY

As we have seen, the intellects of older people are not generally impaired and are quite capable of new learning. However, elderly people as a group have less formal education than younger adults. The average elderly person in 1980 had completed 10.2 years of school, compared to an average of more than 12 years for all American adults. Forty-one percent of all elderly people in the United States were high school graduates, and 9 percent were college graduates (U.S. Dept. of Health & Human Services, 1981). These figures can be expected to rise during the remaining years of this century, as the difference between the educational levels of the young and old decrease. The advantage that younger people now have of being exposed to radio, television, and other media and improved transportation facilities during their formative years will be shared by all age groups.

Older Learners

As indicated throughout this book, there are wide individual differences among older people in motivation, experience, and test performance. Although the discussion of many topics deals with the hypothetical "average" older person, a specific elderly individual may be quite different from the average. For example, people who maintain an interest in their surroundings and those who are required to keep using their problem-solving skills decline less rapidly with age. Education is especially important, because highly educated people tend to show greater resistance to intellectual decline. The limited time perspective to which Gergen and Back (1966) referred also seems less evident in the elderly who have more education. Nevertheless, as these investigators have noted, even those older people who have more education than average tend to prefer short-range solutions to problems over long-range ones.

It is frequently alleged that elderly people are rigid or "set in their ways" and have difficulty learning new things, not because of reduced learning capacity but because of old knowledge and habits get in the way of new learning. Although there is some evidence in support of such "interference effects" in laboratory-type tasks (Kirchner, 1958), educational psychologists now emphasize the modifiability of behavior at any stage of life. It is recognized that continued learning and problem solving in later life can sustain and even improve intellectual abilities, attitudes, and interests—all of which interact to influence performance.[2] Even with people of limited abilities, special techniques, coupled with enthusiastic, patient instruction, can sometimes work wonders.

Among the instructional techniques that are recommended when teaching the elderly are to[3]:

1. Provide ample time for students to master the lesson or task.
2. Repeat the material to be learned several times if necessary.
3. Employ a generous amount of positive reinforcement, providing for success experiences as needed.
4. Set short-term goals that students are capable of attaining within a reasonable period of time.
5. Use shorter practice periods than with younger students, because older people are more easily fatigued.
6. Verbalize what you are doing and have the learners do so also, when demonstrating a physical skill.
7. Be aware of and make provisions for those students with visual or auditory defects (e.g., sufficient illumination, books with large print, tape recordings, louder than normal speech).

Formal Education Programs

Directed specifically toward helping those elderly retirees who must live on a subsistence income to become more self-sufficient is the job training provided by such organizations as the Senior Skills Center at Santa Rosa,

California. Enrollees at the center can choose training in office skills, home maintenance, small appliance and electronics repair, or offset printing. There are also classes in home health care, horticulture and gardening, arts and crafts, and English as a second language (Brown, 1977).

The stimulation provided by an educational atmosphere is an enriching experience for many elderly people, and thereby important to their physical and mental health. Recognition of this fact has been demonstrated by programs such as Fordham University's College at Sixty and the Third Age College in Toulouse, France. For several years now, New York City residents who are 65 or older have been enrolled "tuition free" in any undergraduate course at CUNY in which space is available. As one Columbia University dean stated, "Older people are good people to teach. We find them very highly motivated, very thoughtful people and usually highly intelligent. Their life experience is rich."

Community colleges, such as Los Angeles City College and New York City Community College, both with several hundred students over 60, have been especially forward-looking in addressing themselves to the needs of senior citizens. The Institute for Retired Professionals of The New School for Social Research has also developed a program of course work for retired persons. Every term, these institutions and many others throughout the nation register people of 70, 80, 90, and even 100 years old for courses dealing with such complex topics as "Illusions of Peace in the Middle East." It is anticipated that in the future more and more elderly people will be signing up for college courses and that a semester of art history or English literature will become an educational and recreational experience for increasing numbers of them. Older students are taking courses in traditional as well as academic subjects, in practical topics such as living on a fixed income, coping with illness, and adjusting emotionally to old age. Among the other course offerings aimed specifically at older people are "Sex Over 65," "The Psychology of Dying," and "Film Time: Oldies But Goodies."

Student comments about specific courses and their college experiences are enlightening. One older student at Mercyhurst College in Erie, Pennsylvania, stated that she hoped a course on fixed income would teach her to live within her budget ("I know it's late, but I'm still going to try"). A second student gave a more political reason for attending the class: "We have to find out if our social security payments are too low for a decent life and whether we should fight for more" ("Learning for the Aged," 1972). Concerning the interrelationships of older and younger students, an elderly man felt that he had finally been accepted by his youthful fellow students when they asked him if he was interested in marijuana. Another was delighted at being asked out by three young coeds, but disappointed that "nothing came of it."

The most extensive effort to provide higher-educational experiences for older Americans is Elderhostel. Consisting of a network of several hundred colleges and universities in all 50 states and Canada, Elderhostel offers low-cost, one-week summer residential academic programs for people 60 and over and their spouses. A wide range of liberal arts courses is offered every summer, but there are no formal prerequisite courses, no required homework, no examinations, and no grades. In addition to attending classes, students sleep in college dormitories, eat in college dining halls, and participate in a variety of extracurricular activities.[4]

Educational Statistics and Organizations

It would be misleading to present an overly optimistic picture of education for the aged. Whereas 8 percent of people over 65 have graduated from college, 15 percent are functionally illiterate (Butler, 1975; also see Fig. 4-5). The fact remains that the vast majority of adult students

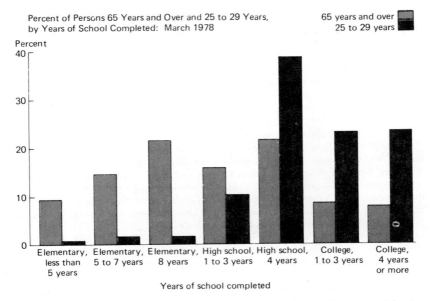

Percent of Persons 65 Years and Over and 25 to 29 Years, by Years of School Completed: March 1978

65 years and over
25 to 29 years

Figure 4-5 Educational characteristics of old and young adults. (From U.S. Bureau of the Census, *Current Population Reports,* Series P-23, No. 85, p. 15.)

in American educational institutions are young, and only about 400,000 older Americans are enrolled in courses. More specifically, the results of one survey (Quirk, 1976) gave the following percentages of adults in various age brackets who stated that they were enrolled in an educational institution or taking courses: 34 percent of those 18 to 24 years old, 15 percent of those 25 to 39, 5 percent of those 40 to 54, 5 percent of those 55 to 64, and only 2 percent of those over 65. Thus education for the elderly is still a relatively modest enterprise. Furthermore, although the majority of elderly people are alert and intellectually capable, they often discover on returning to school after a long absence that they must spend time relearning how to learn or redeveloping the needed study skills and routines. It is difficult to pick up the books again and break through the nonscholarly habits of a lifetime.

Several professional organizations provide educational information and services to retired persons. The Institute for Retired Professionals of The New School for Social Research paved the way in the area of educational opportunities and activities for the elderly. The largest organization in this category is The Institutes of Lifetime Learning, a combined effort of the National Retired Teachers Association and the American Association of Retired Persons. As the members of these organizations recognize, not only should opportunities be provided for retired persons to take course work and training but also their services as teachers of the young should be utilized to a greater extent. Much of our culture, which is not communicated very well by most courses in history and the social sciences, could probably be taught more effectively by knowledgeable elderly people. More generally, many qualified older persons could serve as professional aides, tutors, and advisors to the young (Odell, 1976).

SUMMARY

The popular view of old age as a time of declining mental abilities is certainly not true of all elderly people, and in any case it requires considerable qualification. Although the period of peak productivity among scholars, scientists, and artists is typically reached before later life, many people have continued their creative endeavors into the seventh, eighth, and even ninth decades of life.

Testing older adults poses particular problems of test administration and interpretation that can affect the validity of the test results. The old age norms on standardized intelligence tests are usually not truly representative of that age group in the American population as a whole. Also, older adults are typically not as motivated as younger people to take psychological tests, which they often perceive as having no importance to their lives.

The findings of developmental studies of general intelligence depend significantly on the research methodology employed. In general, the results of cross-sectional studies reveal a decline in overall mental ability after the late 20s or early 30s. Cross-sectional studies do not, however, adequately control for cohort differences. In any case the findings of longitudinal studies indicate little or no decline in general mental ability after early adulthood.

The entire question of age-related changes in mental abilities is still very much open and will require the application of a combination of methodological approaches to answer satisfactorily.

Among the specific mental abilities that have been found to decline with age are the ability to understand new ideas and both short-term and long-term memory. The initial storage and subsequent retrieval of memories from storage appear to be affected by age-related changes in the brain. Evidence also indicates that older people take longer to respond and to consolidate new information, are more susceptible to interference or distraction, and manifest heightened and prolonged autonomic arousal during learning. Deficits in learning and memorizing new information are affected by sensory changes and practice and are more noticeable when the material is complex.

Some of the biological variables that are known to affect mental ability in old age are heredity, sex, nutrition, and health. Various substances and treatments (Ribaminol, Gerovital, choline, hyperoxygenation, etc.) have been alleged to improve memory in the aged, but the findings of research with these substances and others have been criticized because of inadequate controls and other methodological shortcomings.

Education and training programs for the elderly are receiving increased attention, and many educational institutions have designed specific courses of study and training for this age group. Certainly, the elderly constitute a relatively small percentage of the American student population, but the success of educational programs for them indicates that many old people can and want to continue learning. This is especially true when the particular assets and limitations of older learners are taken into account in the instructional process. A number of organizations provide educational information and services to the elderly, who can perform in the role of students and also as teachers.

SUGGESTED READINGS

Alpaugh, P. K., Renner, V. J., & Birren, J. E. Age and creativity: Implications for education and teachers. *Educational Gerontology*, 1976, *1*(1), 17–40.

Arenberg, D., & Robertson-Tchabo, E. Learning and aging. In J. E. Birren & K. W. Schaie (Eds.), *Handbook of the psychology of aging*. New York: Van Nostrand Reinhold, 1977.

Botwinick, J. Intellect and abilities in J. E. Birren & K. W. Schaie (Eds.), *Handbook of the psychology of aging*. New York: Van Nostrand Reinhold, 1977.

Craik, F. I. M. Age differences in human memory. In J. E. Birren & K. W. Schaie (Eds.), *Handbook of the psychology of aging*. New York: Van Nostrand Reinhold, 1977.

Edel, L. Portrait of the artist as an old man. *American Scholar*, Winter 1977–78, 52–68.

Hebb, D. O. On watching myself get old. *Psychology Today*, 1978, *12* (Nov.), 15–23.

McLeish, J. *The Ulyssean adult: Creativity in the middle and late years*. New York: McGraw-Hill, 1976.

Mead, M. Grandparents as educators. *The Saturday Evening Post*, 1977, *249*(2), 54–59.

Poon, L. (Ed.), *Aging in the 1980's: Psychological issues*. Washington, D.C.: American Psychological Association, 1980, Section 5.

Siegler, I. C. The terminal drop hypothesis: Fact or artifact? *Experimental Aging Research*, 1971, *1*, 169–185.

NOTES

[1]An exception is the task of detecting a simple figure in a complex one, a skill that appears to improve with age.

[2]Bischof (1969, p. 224) concluded that "Old dogs can learn new tricks, but they may be reluctant to do so, particularly when they are not convinced that the new trick is any better than the old tricks which served them so well in the past. They may not learn new tricks as rapidly as they did in the past. But if they started out as clever young pups, they are very likely to end up as wise old hounds."

[3]Adapted from "Implications for Teaching," the third in the filmstrip series *Perspectives on Aging* (Concept Media, 1500 Adams Ave., Costa Mesa, CA 92626).

[4]The national headquarters of Elderhostel is at 100 Boylston Street, Suite 200, Boston, MA 02116; telephone 617-426-7788.

Adjustment and Personality

Personality is the unique organization of traits and behavioral patterns that typify an individual, making of him or her psychologically different from others. As with all human characteristics, personality is the product of a continuous interaction between heredity and environment. Consequently, personality does not necessarily stop changing when physical growth ceases; it usually continues developing as long as there are new experiences and challenges. Just as infancy, childhood, adolescence, and early and middle adulthood pose developmental tasks that must be mastered, so, too, does the period of later maturity present its own challenges and crises.

DEVELOPMENTAL TASKS AND CRISES

Problems of adjustment during later life are caused more by the changes accompanying the process of aging, rather than by the fact that one has aged. Among the more stressful experiences affecting one's outlook and expectations at this time of life are altered physical appearance, chronic illness, retirement, and the death of a loved one. Physical changes in old age are especially difficult to cope with, because the appearance and feelings of one's body influence the self-concept.

There is a tendency for older and younger people alike to minimize their physical and mental limitations and disabilities, but this is a normal self-protective response. Most people do not like to think of themselves as aging or disabled, and such thoughts produce feelings of discomfort and anxiety. But everyone ages and aging can affect personality adjustment. Furthermore, the level of personality adjustment and mental health may affect the rate at which a person ages.

Some people are overwhelmed by the changes produced in their bodies by aging and literally grieve for the physical and psychological losses they have suffered. Others are able to transcend or overcome these physical changes and find satisfaction in spite of declining strength, appearance, and health. In any event, a person's perception of his or her health—which is rarely identical to the actual state of health—is closely related to expressed satisfaction with life (Palmore, 1974).

Coping with Old Age

In order to compensate for a changing body and new social and occupational roles, older people adopt new diets, develop new skills, and find new ways of using their increased leisure time. Considerable readjustment to changing social values and mores is required, and experiencing a loss of status and self-satisfaction is common.

To the extent that it can be measured, reported overall satisfaction and happiness with life appear to decline gradually after the late 20s. For example, in 1977 a Gallup poll was conducted to determine how expressed happiness varied with chronological age and several other demographic variables. The poll question asked of 1516 adults was "Generally speaking, how happy would you say you are—very happy, fairly happy, or not too happy?" From an analysis of replies to this question, the pollsters concluded that to be happy is to be young, married, and to have a college background (Gallup, 1977).

Young adulthood is also recalled by a large percentage of older people as having been the happiest time of their lives. In two separate surveys conducted some years ago, Morgan (1937) and Landis (1942) found that approximately 50 percent of the elderly respondents viewed the years of young adulthood as happiest in retrospect (Table 5-1). Subsequent research has shown, however, that the stage of life perceived as having been the "happiest" varies considerably with the individual and with socioeconomic status and ethnicity.

Crises and Goals of Development

Sigmund Freud considered sexual factors to be of primary significance in personality development, but modern psychoanalysts and psychologists place greater emphasis on learning and culture. Illustrative of the importance given to social factors in personality development in more recent psychoanalytic writings is Erik Erikson's descriptive taxonomy of the crises (conflicts) and goals in eight stages of life. According to Erikson (1963), the psychosocial development of a person can be described in terms of these

Table 5-1 PERIOD OF LIFE THAT SEEMED HAPPIEST IN RETROSPECT TO TWO SAMPLES OF ELDERLY PEOPLE

	Percentage of Respondents	
Happiest Period	**Sample 1***	**Sample 2****
Childhood (5 to 15 years)	15	11
Youth (15 to 25 years)	19	19
Young adulthood (25 to 45 years)	49	51
Middle age (45 to 60 years)	12	6
Later life (60 years and over)	5	5
Undecided	0	8

*After Morgan (1937). Respondents were 370 New York residents between the ages of 70 and 90.
**After Landis (1942). Respondents were 450 Iowa residents between the ages of 65 and 98.

progressive stages. During each stage a particular crisis or conflict comes into prominence and must be resolved if psychological development is to proceed normally. As indicated in Table 5-2 (p. 100), the crisis of trust versus mistrust in infancy must be resolved by acquiring a basic sense of trust. And the major crisis of early childhood—autonomy versus doubt—is resolved by attaining a sense of autonomy.

Erikson refers to the major crisis of middle age as one of generativity versus self-absorption. Middle age is the time of life when most people take an inventory of their lives and accomplishments. Realizing that one's personal future is limited, the middle-aged individual's time perspective begins to shorten. Perhaps spurred on by the awareness that death is imminent, he or she comes to the conclusion that if a radical change in life-style or direction is to be made it had better be now.

The major crisis of old age is, according to Erikson, integrity versus despair, and the primary goal is to become an integrated and self-accepting person. How the individual handles this crisis depends on personality characteristics that have been developing for years and also on his or her physical health, economic situation, and the meaningfulness of the social roles that can be played successfully. Thus rather than resulting from aging per se, a sense of despair in old age is more often the consequence of the poor health, financial insecurity, social isolation, and inactivity that so often accompany that stage of life.

People in despair view life with a feeling of profound regret that they have not made greater use of their assets, that potentialities have not been realized nor opportunities seized, and that the chances of achieving their goals lessen with every passing day. Such people are keenly aware of old age as the "no-solution problem" referred to by gerontologists. Feeling that time is now too short to begin anew or to try to achieve success and contentment by a different approach, hopeless individuals find it difficult to accept the inevitabilty of death. In such cases, life is ended with a whimper of despair, rather than with a bang, demonstrating through this attitude the errors in one's philosophy of life.

Table 5-2 ERIKSON'S STAGES OF PSYCHOSOCIAL DEVELOPMENT*

Stage	Crisis (Conflict)	Goal (Resolution)	Description
Infancy	Trust vs. mistrust	Acquire a basic sense of trust	Consistency, continuity, and sameness of experience lead to trust. Inadequate, inconsistent, or negative care may arouse mistrust.
Early childhood	Autonomy vs. doubt	Attain a sense of autonomy	Opportunities to try out skills at own pace and in own way lead to autonomy. Overprotection or lack of support may lead to doubt about ability to control self or environment.
Play age	Initiative vs. guilt	Develop a sense of initiative	Freedom to engage in activities and parents' patient answering of questions lead to initiative. Restrictions of activities and treating questions as a nuisance lead to guilt.
School age	Industry vs. inferiority	Become industrious and competent	Being permitted to make and do things and being praised for accomplishments lead to industry. Limitations on activities and criticism of what is done lead to inferiority.
Adolescence	Identity vs. role confusion	Achieve a personal identity	Recognition of continuity and sameness in one's personality, even when in different situations and when reacted to by different individuals, leads to identity. Inability to establish stability (particularly regarding sex roles and occupational choice) leads to role confusion.
Young adulthood	Intimacy vs. isolation	Become intimate with someone	Fusing of identity with another leads to intimacy. Competitive and combative relations with others may lead to isolation.
Middle age	Generativity vs. self-absorption	Develop an interest in future generations	Establishing and guiding next generation produces sense of generativity. Concern primarily with self leads to self-absorption.
Old age	Integrity vs. despair	Become an integrated and self-accepting person	Acceptance of one's life leads to a sense of integrity. Feeling that it is too late to make up for missed opportunities leads to despair.

*After Erikson (1963), as adapted by Robert F. Biehler, *Child Development: An Introduction,* 2d. edition. (Boston: Houghton Mifflin Company, 1981), pp. 122–123.

Although Erikson does maintain that each of the eight crises described in Table 5-2 assumes a central importance at a given time of life, all eight are actually important throughout an individual's life span. Furthermore, personality is not an "all or none" affair; one pole of a given crisis does not usually overwhelm the other pole. Thus most people develop some degree of mistrust, but they are able to maintain a proper balance of trust and mistrust. Likewise, the great majority of older people cannot be characterized as integrated on the one hand versus despairing on the other. Certainly, the "despairing person" described in the last paragraph is an accurate picture of only a small minority of the aged. But no matter how realistic they have been in their attitudes toward life, despair is no stranger to the elderly; almost everyone experiences it at some time. Indeed, a certain amount of despair is realistic, and the usual achievement of old age is not the total victory of integrity over despair but rather a favorable balance between the two.

Good Adjustment and Identity

In contrast to the totally despairing person, the individual who has developed an effective set of solutions to the major tasks and crises of life during the preceding stages of development can look forward to old age as the capstone of a life well lived. Such a person has no overwhelming regrets and would be willing to go through it all again, but thinks less about the past and more about using the remaining time wisely. Having come to terms with personal goals and achievements, a well-adjusted older person is self-accepting and lives hopefully rather than helplessly. Old age is welcomed as an opportunity to take stock of and clarify a lifetime of experience. Finding responses to these experiences satisfactory, this individual is in a much better position to cope with the inevitable stresses and changes of later life.

It is often said that the well-adjusted elderly person has a clear sense of identity. However, one must be cautious about viewing old age as merely a "summing up" period of no further development. Self-development and the search for identity—Erikson's major goals of adolescence—continue throughout life. As Butler (1971, p. 51) phrased it: "When identity is established or maintained, I find it an ominous sign rather than a favorable one. A continuing life-long identity crisis seems to be a sign of good health." An individual's new identity in old age comes from finding new uses for what has been learned during the previous years and developing new ways of coming to terms with reality. That reality consists of weaknesses as well as strengths and a changing world that is not always to one's liking.

PERSONALITY CHARACTERISTICS OF THE ELDERLY

Observations concerning personality characteristics of the elderly go back to ancient times. Aristotle, for example, viewed older men as conservative and greedy, a viewpoint that is probably shared by sizable numbers of people today. In contrast, Cicero spoke of the greater wisdom and tolerance found in the elderly than in their younger contemporaries.

The scientific study of personality, which began in the early 1900s, has employed a variety of procedures and instruments—observations, ratings, inventories, and projectives. Unlike the WAIS and a few other cognitive tests, little interest has been shown in standardizing these personality assessment devices on groups of older people. A few instruments, such as the Test of Behavioral Rigidity (Schaie & Parham, 1975), the Senior Apperception Test (Bellak & Bellak, 1974), and the Gerontological Apperception Test (Wolk & Wolk, 1971), have been designed specifically for older adults, but these are exceptions and the norm groups are usually small and selective. Consequently, psychological researchers frequently generalize about personallity in old age from small samples of people who may or may not be representative of larger groups of the elderly.

Continuity of Personality

The unique pattern of traits and behaviors characterizing a person as a special human being shows considerable continuity across the life span. Although Kastenbaum (1971) maintained that the behavior of the young and old is similar if their environments are the same, Dibner (1975) concluded that older people are more like what they have always been than like their peers. One manifestation of this consistency of behavior is seen in the fact that people who have been most active and interested during their earlier years tend to remain so in later life.

Evidence from casual observation and research indicates that both positive and negative traits tend to persist throughout an individual's lifetime. From her talks with older people, Curtin (1972) concluded that those who were maladjusted had usually been uninvolved, passive, or unhappy when they were younger. They did not become radically different personalities on the day they turned 65; rather, they had much the same temperament as when they were 30, 40, or 50. Curtin also observed that aging does not solve but instead compounds one's personal problems. People who have difficulty coping with life at age 30 will most like have similar problems at 65.

More systematic evidence for the continuity of personality comes from several research studies. From the results of an extensive investigation described more fully later in the chapter, Reichard, Livson, and Petersen (1962, p. 171) concluded that:

> With the exception of the mature group, many of whom had reported difficulties in personal adjustment when younger, these personality types were relatively stable throughout life. Poor adjustment to aging among the angry men and the self-haters seemed to stem from lifelong personality problems. Similarly, the histories of the armored and rocking chair groups suggest that their personalities changed little throughout their lives.

The findings of Woodruff and Birren's (1972) 25-year longitudinal study involving retesting with the California Test of Personality also support the proposition that personality remains fairly stable across time.

Neugarten (1971, 1973) found, in a series of investigations, that if we know about an individual's personality in middle age and how events in his or her earlier life have been dealt with, then we can make broad predictions about how the person will react to old age. Neugarten recognizes that personality does change, but the changes are quantitative rather than qualitative. That is, the pattern of one's personality traits, established early in life, becomes more pronounced in response to the stresses of later life.

In conclusion, whether or not an individual adapts successfully to later life is determined in large measure by how well he or she is already adjusted on reaching old age. Nevertheless, human personality is not completely static; it is modified to some extent by the very process of aging and the success of one's efforts to cope with the challenges and problems that aging presents (e.g., see Report 5-1).

Self-Acceptance and the Self-Concept

As people develop and become aware of the differences between their own aims and those of others, they usually come to behave in more realistic and socially appropriate ways. The reactions of other people to an individual's presence and behavior cause the person to modify that behavior and also affect his or her view of himself or herself. These reflected evaluations from people who are significant to the individual, in addition to the successes and failures in dealing with other aspects of the environment, result in the acquisition of a self-concept. The self-concept includes the overall value that one places on oneself as a personality, as well as evaluations of one's own body and behavior. Biological factors such as physical appearance, health, innate abilities, and certain aspects of temperament are important in determining the frequency and kinds of social experiences that a person has and the degree of social acceptance that is attained. But these biological factors interact in complex ways, and they always operate in a social context. Therefore the social evaluations placed on the physical and behavioral characteristics of an individual who possesses a particular biological makeup—and consequently his or her self-evaluation—depend on the specific sociocultural group to which the person belongs.

The results of a number of investigations have provided insight into self-concept and self-acceptance in old age. Referring to Kuhlen's (1956) finding that the degree of personal happiness in most people reaches a maximum in the middle adult years, Bloom (1961) speculated that self-acceptance would follow a similar trend. The hypothesis was confirmed in an investigation of male surgery patients, ranging in age from 20 to 70 years, at a New York Veterans Administration hospital. Degree of self-acceptance increased steadily from age 20 until the middle to late 50s and then declined. Caution must be exercised in generalizing from Bloom's study, because different results are obtained with different samples. Kaplan and Pokorny (1969), for example, suggested that the events occurring in later life and not age per se affect the self-concept. Thus these investigators found that a more negative self-concept was associated with having a lower standard of living than one had hoped for, and living alone or with relatives rather than as a couple.

Destiny Control and Self-Confidence

People who feel weak and powerless—characteristics considered by many to be earmarks of old age—tend to resign themselves to a poor socioeconomic and physical condition. In fact, it has been shown that both the physical and mental health of older people are influenced by the feeling of having some control over the important events in their lives. Those who feel they have outlived their options and must submit blindly to whatever fate holds in store become easily depressed or angry. That this sense of "destiny control" changes with age was documented in a longitudinal study by Gutmann (1964). It was found that a typical 40-year-old man, who sees himself as having the energy and capacity to control his external environment, is willing to take risks and accept challenges. In contrast, a typical 60 year old tends to see the world as more dangerous and complicated and no longer as likely to be within his control.

Obviously, both the active, assertive orientation of the average middle-aged man and the more passive-conforming orientation of the older man represent reasonable attempts to adjust to the environment. As the investigations of Gutmann (1964) and others make clear, during the period between 40 and 60 years an individual's self-perception in relation to the environment gradually shifts from that of being generally strong and capable of overcoming obstacles to viewing the world as a complicated, dangerous place in which compliance and accommodation are the best policy. Thus by age 60 or 70, a formerly bold, outer-directed orientation may have changed from involvement with people and things to an increasing preoccupation with the inner life (Ullmann, 1976).

Interiority and Loneliness

During the sixth and seventh decades of life an individual's interactions with people and other externals show a trend toward simplification or less active involvement. On the whole, the elderly become more preoccupied with their inner experiences and the satisfaction of their own personal needs. This movement from active to passive mastery, or **interiority,** as it has been labeled by Neugarten (1968), is an inner orientation beginning in middle age and continuing until death. Increased interiority in old age is a

Figure 5-1 Bernice L. Neugarten, a prominent researcher in the field of personality development in middle and late life. (Courtesy of Dr. Bernice L. Neugarten.)

tendency that occurs among elderly people in most geographical regions, nations, ethnic groups, and cultures (Gutmann, 1977). One of its common manifestations across cultures is increased interest in the supernatural and religious devotion in later life.

A turning inward of the personality can have either a positive or a negative effect, possibly leading to feelings of greater self-reliance or to a sense of inadequacy and depression. The positive side of interiority and associated egocentrism is illustrated by May Sarton's (1978) statement that "It is the privilege of the old to feel less guilt about the undone, and what a joy that is!" What is positive for the elderly person, however, may not be viewed in the same light by younger people. Thus a preoccupation with oneself and the resulting lack of attention to external matters may be viewed by others as a self-centered disregard of socially appropriate behavior.

Rigidity and Flexibility

Older people sometimes appear to be easily annoyed with the ways of the younger generation. One study of men 70 years and older found that they were frequently annoyed by the behavior of teenagers, as well as by heavy drinking and intolerance in others. Their own inability to accomplish things, and feelings of helplessness and aloneness were other common sources of annoyance to these older men (Barrett, 1972).

Younger adults might attribute such annoyances to inflexibility or contrariness, seeing older people as irritable, quarrelsome, and crotchety individuals who "live in the past." The presumption that the elderly are rigid is not limited to teenagers. People of all ages view the aged as less adaptable, less willing or unable to change their ways of doing things and more reluctant to try new approaches to personal and social problems.

Robert Butler (1974) refers to the so-called inflexibility of older people as a myth. To Butler, the structure of a person's character seems to be fairly well established by the time of old age. But unless one is severely hampered by brain damage, low mentality, or lack of education, people can and do change right up to the time of death. Perhaps the word "cautious" is a better description of the elderly than "inflexible" or "rigid." A lifetime of experience has taught them not to expect miracles and to be suspicious about what can be accomplished by physicians, politicians, social planners, and others in positions of authority.

Older people are probably less likely to risk being wrong for the sake of being right or fast (Botwinick, 1967), but if the directions and structure of a task are clear, the elderly person will usually do his or her best. It is also true that old people are sometimes reluctant to make complex decisions in ambiguous situations, but the flexibility with which they respond depends on lifelong habits and behaviors. Some people, young and old, can absorb new information more readily than others, and consequently are less resistant to change. Those with higher intelligence and greater self-confidence are more willing to accept reasonable risks rather than adhering rigidly to what has worked in the past. In contrast, the senile patient is more likely to be rigid and unadaptable in the face of environmental change.

Personality Types

The uniqueness of human personality is especially pronounced in old age, with the aged manifesting an even wider range of personality characteristics than their younger contemporaries. Neugarten, Havighurst, and Tobin (1968) were more impressed by the differences than with the similarities among the personalities represented in a group of 70 year olds whom they studied. These personality differences are quite apparent in the various patterns of coping and defensive behavior observed in older adults.

In a classic study of aging and personality Reichard, Livson, and Petersen (1962) obtained 115 ratings of the personality characteristics of forty well-adjusted and thirty poorly adjusted older men. The findings pointed to the presence of five personality types or clusters: mature (constructive), rocking chair (dependent), armored (defensive), angry (hostile), and self-hating. These five types represent fairly specific methods of coping with the problems of old age. The **mature** men, who were relatively free of neurotic conflicts, could accept themselves and grow old with few regrets. Also fairly well adjusted were the **rocking chair** types, who viewed old age in terms of freedom from responsibility and as an opportunity to indulge their passive needs. The **armored** types, who were somewhere in the middle in terms of adjustment, defended themselves against anxiety by keeping busy. The first of the poorly adjusted types, the *angry* men, expressed bitterness and blamed other people for their failures. Also maladjusted were the **self-haters**, who, depressed rather than angry, blamed themselves for their disappointments and misfortunes. These people, hating themselves and old people in general, viewed later life as a useless, uninteresting period.

Further evidence for the variety of individual differences in personality and adjustment in old age was obtained in a study by Neugarten, Havighurst, and Tobin (1968). The study was concerned with the relationships of long-standing personality characteristics and social activity to happiness in a sample of people aged 70 to 79. The four major personality traits, derived from an assessment of each person on forty-five dimensions, were: integrated, armored-defended, passive-dependent, and unintegrated. The life satisfaction of each person was rated according to the extent to which the person appeared to take pleasure in daily activities, regarded life as meaningful, accepted responsibility for his or her past life, felt successful in having achieved major goals, had a positive self-image, and was generally optimistic about life. A measure of role activity consisted of observers' ratings of the extent and intensity of the social roles of parent, spouse, grandparent, kin-group member, and church member. A wide range of activity patterns and life-styles, depending on the type of personality possessed by the individual, was noted.

Among the **integrated** personalities, who functioned well and had complex inner lives as well as intact intellective abilities and egos, were three patterns of role activity. The **reorganizers** engaged in a wide variety of activities, the **focused** types devoted most of their energies to a few important roles, and the **disengaged** people possessed high satisfaction with their lives but had voluntarily moved away from role commitments.

The men and women who were labeled as **armored-defended** personalities were striving, achievement-oriented people who pushed themselves. The two patterns of aging that were observed in this group were the **holding-on** people who believed that they would be all right as long as they kept busy, and the **constricted** individuals, who reduced their involvement with other people and experiences and defended themselves against aging by concentrating on losses and deficits.

Two patterns of aging were also found in the **passive-dependent group—succor-seeking** people with strong dependency needs who expressed medium satisfaction with life as long as they had at least one or two people to lean on, and **apathetic** people, who were passive individuals with few activities or social interactions and little interest in their surroundings.

The fourth main type of personality observed in this investigation was the disorganized or **unintegrated**, who had serious psychological problems.

The overall results of this investigation support the common observation that whether a person remains active or gradually disengages during later life depends on personality characteristics as much as anything else. Well-integrated personalities tend to adjust well to old age, whereas people who are dissatisfied or unhappy with themselves and their previous experiences have adjustment difficulties. Level of activity is also important to life satisfaction: Those who keep a young, active, problem-solving attitude are better adjusted. Furthermore, activity and motivation are interacting variables, motivation for living and orientation toward others being affected by whether or not a person is engaged in useful activities.

Happiness and Survival

As the findings of Reichard et al. (1962) and Neugarten et al. (1968) indicate, different personalities have different ways of adjusting to the changes and stresses of old age. Elderly people do not have to be continually "on the go" in order to be happy. But neither do they have to be perfectly happy in order to survive. For example, in his study of the residents of an old people's home in Chicago, Lieberman (1973) discovered that the best survivors were the "grouches." Furthermore, the modal personality of successful adjusters varies with external circumstances. Thus Stephens (1976) found that older occupants of slum hotels who adjusted successfully to their circumstances did so by adopting a life-style characterized by suspiciousness, hustling, and rugged individualism.

Granting that there is a difference between happiness and survival and that people who are perfectly well adjusted in one situation can be maladjusted in another, several authorities (Butler, 1975; Hochschild, 1973; Medley, 1976; Neugarten, 1973) have proposed a number of factors that seem to be important for effective adjustment in a wide variety of circumstances encountered by the elderly. Among these are: (1) some degree of independence, (2) a sense of accomplishment, (3) satisfaction in interpersonal relationships, (4) interest or involvement in some activity, and perhaps most important, (5) flexibility or willingness to change. In general, older people who are able to plan ahead without being overly rigid in those plans and who feel wanted and useful are more apt to be happy and to survive longer.

DISORDERS OF ADJUSTMENT AND PERSONALITY

Despite the fact that the majority of elderly people do adjust to the stresses and changes accompanying old age, disorders of adjustment and personality are more common in older than in younger adults. As indicated earlier in the chapter, maladjusted young adults tend to become maladjusted older adults. However, the same individual who at 30 or 40 years was able to withstand pressure and frustration can, under the stress of retirement or loss of a loved one, experience a severe adjustment problem.

Documenting the pronounced decline in mental health after young adulthood are the results of Meltzer and Ludwig's (1971) cross-sectional study of 143 industrial workers in five age groups: 20 to 29, 30 to 39, 40 to 49, 50 to 59, and 60 to 69. As illustrated in Figure 5-2, the "mental health index" is highest in the 30 to 39 age group, shows a marked decline in the 40 to 49 age group, and then levels off until the 60 to 69 age range. The more negative mental health index in the older groups is a reflection of the lower self-confidence, greater sense of failure, weaker resistance to stress, and lesser orientation toward reality than in younger adults.

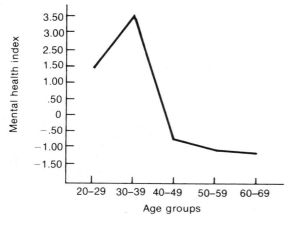

Figure 5-2 Changes in mental health with age. (Adapted from Meltzer & Ludwig, 1971.)

The Meaning of Mental Disorders

To a great extent, normality and abnormality of behavior are statistical concepts that vary in meaning with culture and time. Sociocultural factors, such as the attitudes and tolerance of others, are important in determining what is normal or acceptable behavior. These factors are emphasized when we define as **abnormal** a person who has poor interpersonal relations, displays socially inappropriate behavior, and has no acceptable goals. According to this definition, if one repeatedly violates social norms, he or she is considered to be abnormal. But whether abnormal behavior is punished, ignored, treated, or even praised depends on society's interpretation of the value of the behavior and the extent to which other people are willing to accept it.

Most psychologists are not content with a purely cultural or statistical definition of abnormality. They look further into the personal experiences of the individual, studying the satisfactions attained, the tension, anxiety, depression, and sense of isolation that are felt and the amount of effort expended, in determining whether one is mentally disordered. Thought processes, perceptions, and attitudes are also important. Society may be willing to tolerate strange behavior or even be unaware of a person's problems, and he or she may continue to function fairly effectively over a lifetime while experiencing invisible anxieties and insecurities.

Normal personality changes occurring with age are exaggerated in people who become mentally disordered, with disturbances running the gamut from transient situational problems to severe psychotic reactions. The trend today is to avoid assigning nonuseful diagnostic labels to mental disorders whenever possible and to attempt to identify causes of disordered behavior. Consequently, the labels employed in this chapter should in no way be viewed as either completely descriptive or explanatory of the behavior of the disordered person in question.

Only about 10 percent of the people in the United States and other industrialized Western nations are considered to be sufficiently disturbed in thought processes, emotion, or behavior to be classified as mentally disordered. This includes both the milder mental disorders (psychophysiological disorders, psychoneuroses, character disturbances), the incidence of which remains fairly constant into old age; and the more serious psychotic conditions, which are more common after age 50. People with severe mental disorders, both the young and the old, occupy about 50 percent of the hospital beds in the United States.

It is frequently maintained that the "stress of modern living" is responsible for the high incidence of mental illness in the twentieth century. Because diagnostic criteria and other factors affecting mental hospital admissions statistics vary with time and place, the question of whether people are more likely to become mentally ill in contemporary society than in the past is difficult to answer. Available data indicate, however, that the twentieth century has not produced a greater proportion of most mental disorders (Goldhamer & Marshall, 1953). It is true that the number of first admissions to mental hospitals increased during the first six decades of the present century, but the rate did not change, and the average length of residence in the hospital decreased. In recent years there has been a drop in first admissions to mental hospitals for all patients—young and old. Unfortunately, this drop is not due to a decrease in the number of mentally disturbed people, but rather than to the fact that other facilities and institutions—nursing homes in particular—are handling larger numbers of mental patients.

Although the rate of serious psychotic disorders in men under 40 and women under 50 has not changed appreciably since 1885 (Goldhamer & Marshall, 1953), there has been an increase in mental disorders associated with old age. The increase is interpreted as being due largely to the fact that people are living longer and consequently are more likely to develop symptoms of mental disorder produced by changes in the brain accompanying old age (see Chapter 3). The particular physical and interpersonal stresses to which the elderly are subjected should also not be overlooked as causative factors. Whatever the reasons, approximately 3 million, or 15 percent of all elderly Americans are considered to be mildly to severely mentally disordered. A sizable number of these individuals, about 1 million in all, are deemed sufficiently disturbed to have been placed in mental hospitals or nursing homes (Pfeiffer, 1977).

Age differences interact with sex, location of residence, and socioeconomic status in affecting the incidence, severity, and type of mental disorder. The majority of elderly people admitted to mental hospitals are women, due to a combination of factors, including the fact that elderly women outnumber elderly men in the general population. Other contributing factors are the stresses of widowhood and the lower likelihood that older women have someone to take care of them at home. A larger percentage of mentally disturbed elderly people also live in urban rather than in rural areas, probably because more older people—both normal and abnormal—reside in cities and not necessarily because cities are more stressful places in which to live. Having someone at home to care for them may also help explain why smaller numbers of rural-dwelling older people who are mentally disturbed come to the attention of authorities. Finally, severe mental disorders are more common in the elderly who have lower than average incomes for their age group (see Butler & Lewis, 1977; Busse & Blazer, 1980).

Defense Mechanisms

Many types of psychological reactions to stress, some adaptive and others maladaptive, occur in old age. Among the maladaptive responses are denial, anger, withdrawal, and dependency. In denial, the person simply denies the seriousness of a problem or that it even exists. Another reaction to stress is becoming angry at someone or something, perhaps someone other than the direct cause of frustration. This is the case in displaced aggression, in which the victim has nothing to do with the frustrating circumstance but is merely a convenient scapegoat.

Elderly people may also withdraw in potentially threatening situations, feeling that being close to others is too risky and that self-isolation or retreat into fantasy is the best way to cope. Another type of reaction to frustration and conflict is to become helpless or overly dependent on other people. Old people with strong dependency needs may also exaggerate and exploit a physical illness and associated depression. Dependency is often fostered by well-meaning people who respond to older people as if they were unable to do anything for themselves and were in constant need of assistance.

All these **defense mechanisms** are maladaptive because they are not permanent solutions to problems and usually create further difficulties for the person. Used to excess, many defense mechanisms can lead to more serious mental disturbances, for example, paranoia as a result of excessive anger or senile regression as a result of withdrawal (see Verwoerdt, 1969b).

Psychophysiological Disorders

Prolonged stress and anxiety can result in a variety of psychophysiological symptoms: anxiety, depression, irritability, fatigue, loss of appetite, headache, backache, and so on. Almost any organ or system of the body may show structural and functional changes under prolonged stress. Peptic ulcers and other gastrointestinal reactions are the most publicized psychophysiological disorders, but the course and severity of migraine headaches, skin conditions, chronic backache, and bronchial asthma are also affected by persisting emotional stress. In fact, it is generally acknowledged by medical scientists that all physical illnesses and their courses are influenced by the emotional state of the patient.

A longitudinal study (Vaillant, 1979), which for 30 years followed up 204 men who were students at Harvard University in the 1940s, has provided evidence linking personality adjustment to physical disorders. Those men who had been diagnosed as "poorly adjusted" proved much more likely to become seriously ill and die in their middle years than those diagnosed as "well adjusted." In contrast to the well adjusted, the group of poorly adjusted individuals had a greater incidence of cancer, coronary disorders, high blood pressure, emphysema, back disorders, and suicide. From these results, Vaillant concluded that the status of one's personality adjustment or mental health has a definite influence on his or her physical health in midlife. Good adjustment and positive mental health appear to retard the physical decline that begins in the middle years of life, whereas poor adjustment hastens it.

Psychoneuroses

The psychodynamic explanation of neurotic behavior is that it serves to control the anxiety caused by the threatened breakthrough of unacceptable unconscious impulses. Although recognizing the fact that neurotic symptoms serve to control anxiety, behavior-oriented psychologists emphasize the learned nature and anxiety-reducing function of such symptoms rather than their unconscious origin. Among the neurotic symptoms are: conversion hysteria (sensory or motor disturbances of psychogenic origin), dissociative conditions (psychological amnesia, fugue, multiple personality), obsessions, compulsions, phobias, hypochondriasis, and depression. Especially common are anxiety reactions, in which anxiety is not reduced or controlled by another neurotic symptom.

For the most part, neurotic behavior in old age is merely a continuation and intensification of personality characteristics that have been present since youth. The particular neurotic symptoms depend, however, on the existing personality structure as well as on the social reinforcement the individual receives for the symptoms. The greater frequency of hypochondriasis in elderly women, for example, is probably a function of the fact that the dependent, sick role is a more socially acceptable behavior pattern in women than in men.

Depression and Suicide

Although depression is just as frequent in young adulthood as in later life, it is one of the most common of all reactions to stress and change in old age (Butler & Lewis, 1977). Ten to 20 percent of all elderly people are depressed, as indicated by chronic feelings of worthlessness, guilt, loss of interest in things, eating and sleeping problems, physical aches and pains, fatigue, and difficulty remembering ("Scientists Hope. . . ," 1980). It is understandable from this list of symptoms how psychological depression, like chronic alcoholism, has often been misdiagnosed as senile brain disease (see Chapter 3).

The intensity of depressive states varies from relatively mild reactions to specific situational factors (loss of a loved one, social isolation, physical problems, financial insecurity, and institutionalization) to more serious depression that has no clear connection with external events. Depression does tend to run in families, especially the nonreactive type of depression that is apparently not precipitated by environmental circumstances.

Suicide attempts are an ever-present danger in cases of depression, with over 25 percent of all suicide victims being over age 65. The high incidence of suicide among the elderly is reflected in statistics from both the nineteenth and twentieth centuries. The overall suicide rate is lower among the middle aged, but this is due primarily to sex differences. Thus as illustrated in Figure 5-3, the increase in the number of suicides during

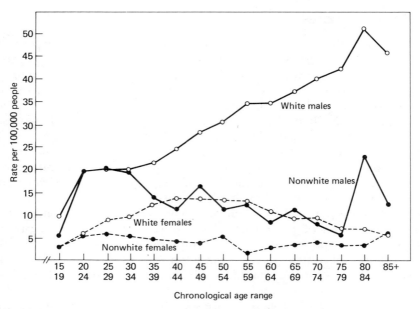

Figure 5-3 Suicide rate as a function of chronological age, sex, and ethnicity. (Adapted from *Vital statistics of the United States, 1970, Vol. II. Mortality, Pt. A.* Rockville, Md.: U.S. Public Health Service, 1974.)

later life is caused primarily by the high rate in white men. The suicide rate for women actually declines slightly after age 40, but it increases steadily for men in general. Consequently, the ratio of men to women who commit suicide had risen to 7 to 1 by the mid-70s.

The cause of the sex difference in suicide rate among the elderly is not clear, but it is certainly affected by the different roles that men and women are expected to play in our culture and the resulting changes in those roles with aging. The assertive, achievement-oriented role of a typical middle-aged man is not so adaptable to the retirement situation as the more passive, nurturant role assumed by a typical middle-aged woman. Consequently, the greater change in behavior and self-esteem necessitated in the older man creates more stress and resulting depression when he is unable to find satisfaction in his new situation. The result is a greater potential for suicidal behavior. As documented by Marshall (1978), however, this is less likely to happen in an older man whose income from social security, pensions, and other sources is sufficiently high.

One tends to think of "suicide pacts" as a phenomenon of romantic youth, but double suicide also occurs among elderly couples. Newspapers occasionally carry stories of old couples, who, because they have been the victims of crime, neglect, or chronic illness, become despondent and decide to end their lives together.

Character Disorders

Maladaptive personality patterns, or character disorders, may also persist into old age. Although these conditions are more common in younger age groups, there are elderly alcoholics, drug addicts, and sex deviates. Many elderly alcoholics are simply continuing a lifelong habit, whereas others, in response to boredom, loneliness, or grief, take up drinking for the first time in old age. Unfortunately, chronic alcoholism is sometimes misdiagnosed as senility, and consequently is not treated properly.

Elderly antisocial ("psychopathic") personalities, individuals with little conscience or regard for the feelings or rights of others, are less numerous than alcoholics. Most psychopaths appear to "burn out" by their 40s, their antisocial behavior decreasing markedly by the fifth decade of life.

Psychotic Disorders

Patients diagnosed as having a psychophysiologic disorder, neurosis, or character disorder can benefit from treatment and sometimes require hospitalization. Such patients, however, rarely manifest the severe distortion of reality, bizarre behavior, or extensive personality disorganization seen in institutionalized psychotics.

A large percentage of older Americans admitted to mental hospitals and nursing homes each year are diagnosed as psychotic. Their symptoms vary, but a diagnosis of psychosis implies the presence of a disorder in which the ability to recognize reality is severely distorted. The distortion of reality is manifested in deficits of perception, language, and memory, as well as in changes in mood. Approximately 50 percent of those patients who are diagnosed as psychotic have a detectable brain disorder of the sort discussed in Chapter 3. In the remaining 50 percent of the patients, who are referred to as **functional** psychotics, no brain damage or other organic cause for the disorder has been discovered.

Schizophrenia. The two major types of functional psychoses— schizophrenia and affective psychoses—both increase in frequency with aging and are more common in elderly women. Schizophrenics, who comprise the largest category of functional psychotics, have severe disturbances in thinking and sometimes perception. They withdraw from contact with reality and lose empathy with other people. Disturbances in concept formation and regressive, bizarre behavior are characteristic of schizophrenics, and hallucinations (false perceptions) and delusions (false beliefs) may also occur. Delusions of grandeur and persecution are most common in paranoid conditions, which may or may not be accompanied by a schizophrenic process.[1] On rare occasions, two or more people share the same delusional system, as in folie à deux ("insanity of two") or, even less frequently, folie à trois ("insanity of three") (see Report 5-2).

Report 5-2   FOLIE A TROIS*

Three elderly spinster sisters, aged 72, 68, and 65, were admitted to a psychiatric hospital after a neighbor called the police to report that one of them threatened to "slit the throat" of a 10 year old neighbor boy. These sisters had worked, eaten, and lived together for more than 40 years.

When interviewed in the hospital, each of the sisters told an almost identical story about how this 10 year old boy had been "sent by them" to remove the NO TRESPASSING sign from their front lawn. Close questioning revealed that many years earlier these women had posted such a sign on their lawn because both of their neighbors "were spying" on them by coming on their lawn and looking through the front window. It was also learned that these sisters had sued one of their neighbors with regard to a boundary dispute about their property lines. They lost the suit and attempted to find another lawyer to take up their case again, but no lawyer would do so. The boy they had threatened was the grandson of their neighbor, and they described him as "rotten to the core from the day he was born."

The two younger sisters also related that they and their sister had a good deal of trouble at vacation spots, usually rooming houses near resort areas, because other people were after their money and belongings. The oldest sister vehemently denied having had such difficulties and explained that her younger sisters occasionally "told such lies," but that she would "set them right" as soon as she saw them on the ward.

When the younger sisters were again interviewed several days later, they both volunteered the information that their story about their rooming house troubles was untrue and that their neighbor had a way of influencing them to tell such stories. They then disclosed that they thought the doctor was conspiring with their neighbor against them and that he had better not ask them any more questions because he was being paid to keep the three in the hospital.

About three weeks after admission, the oldest sister had a massive cerebrovascular accident and died within hours of the attack. The two younger sisters at first became severely depressed, but then, as often happens with separation from the dominant person in such *folies,* several weeks after the death, they began talking about going back to their home and spoke of "letting bygones be bygones."

*From *Essentials of Abnormal Psychology,* 2d Edition, p. 288, by Benjamin Kleinmuntz. Copyright © 1980 by Benjamin Kleinmuntz. Reprinted by permission of Harper & Row, Publishers, Inc.

Some schizophrenics are in or in-and-out of mental hospitals for a large portion of their lives, growing old in institutions (see Report 5-3). Generally speaking, these long-term patients are meek and mild individuals who have adapted to institutional life and would probably be unable to cope with the decisions and stresses outside an institution. If they are not being actively treated for the disorder, a nursing home or some other less expensive facility is preferable to life in a mental hospital.

Manic-Depressive Psychoses.   Second in frequency to schizophrenia are affective psychoses, which involve disturbances in mood—either extreme elation (mania), profound depression, or periodic fluctuation between the two; in addition to extremes of mood, there is a loss of contact with reality. The major types of affective psychoses are manic-depressive psychosis and involutional melancholia. The symptom picture in the circular type of manic-depressive psychosis, which is seen in about 25 percent of patients diagnosed as manic or depressive psychotics, consists of severe mood swings from depression to elation, remission, and then recurrence. With aging, the times of occurence of the manic and depressive phases of the cycle become more regular and hence predictable. During the manic state the patient is overtalkative, elated or irritable, and shows increased motor activity and bizarre ideation. During the depressive phase of the cycle the patient is deeply depressed in mood and activity, becoming agitated in some instances and stuporous in others.

Psychiatrists also differentiate between the manic and depressed types of manic-depressive psychosis. The symptoms of the manic type, which is less common than the depressed type, include overtalkativeness, elation or irritability, increased motor activity, and the rapid production of bizarre ideas. Hostile, paranoid behavior of an accusatory nature may also occur. The depressed type is characterized by feelings of deep depression, together with motor inhibition and either mental slowness or agitation (see Report 5-4).

Involutional Melancholia. Textbook descriptions of the so-called "change of life" disorder, involutional melancholia, list the following symptoms: extreme depression, agitation, self-deprecation, feelings of guilt and failure. This disorder, which is termed "involutional" because of its onset after age 40, is more common in women than in men. It is relatively rare, and occurs during middle to later life in the absence of any prior history of depression. Many authorities, however, seriously question the need for such a diagnostic category, because psychotic depression can occur at any stage of life and does not show a sudden rise in frequency after age 40 (Winokur, 1973).

TREATMENT OF MENTAL DISORDERS

The elderly can avail themselves of a wide range of community, state, and federal treatment facilities. Unfortunately, these facilities, and community mental health clinics in particular, are not used sufficiently by old people. Among the reasons cited by Butler (1975) for this state of affairs are pessimism and lack of interest by the general practitioners and clergymen who serve as referral sources and by mental health practitioners them- selves. Lack of enthusiasm for treatment of the elderly and for gerontologi- cal research is also revealed by the fact that less than 5 percent of the budget of the National Institute of Mental Health is typically allocated to studies of mental disorders in old people. Other reasons why elderly people fail to make adequate use of treatment facilities are inexperienced or poorly educated mental health workers, lack of knowledge of resources on the part of the elderly, and a scarcity of transportation to the clinic or other mental health facility.

Voluntary and Involuntary Admission

In spite of this bleak picture, older patients, realizing the need for help or encouraged by others to obtain it, may seek assistance at a community mental health facility or ask to be admitted to a mental hospital for examination and treatment. A patient who is voluntarily admitted to a mental hospital can sign out at any time unless, in cases where the patient is considered dangerous to himself or others, the head of the hospital is granted a legal postponement of release. Involuntary admission or com- mitment,[2] the laws and procedures for which vary from state to state, may be obtained after a petition is made by a family member or another person who is responsible for the patient. Following the petition is a legal hearing at which it is determined whether the patient is harmful to him- or herself or others, and if so, a decision is then made as to where he or she should be admitted for treatment. The length of the commitment varies according to the judgment of institutional officials and other authorities, but it is usually 30 to 60 days. The commitment period may be extended indefinitely by subsequent legal action.

Physical Treatment Methods

The prognosis with older patients who are seriously mentally ill is not always good, and the goals of treatment may be more limited than with younger patients. Decreasing the patient's suffering so that his or her complaints and the complaints of others about him or her are minimized is important. A combination of physical and psychological procedures is almost always needed in order for treatment to be effective. Among the physical treatment measures are drugs, special diets, electroshock, and neurosurgery.

For many years electroshock therapy (EST) was the recommended treatment for both schizophrenia and psychotic depression, but tranquilizing and antidepressant drugs gradually replaced EST in the great majority of cases.[3] The most commonly prescribed drugs for mental disorders are tranquilizers such as chlordiazepoxide (Librium) and diazepam (Valium) for anxiety, chlorpromazine for psychotic behavior, tricyclic antidepressants such as imipramine and amitriptyline for depression, and lithium for manic excitement.

Psychological Treatment Methods

It might seem that older people, by virtue of the fact that they have lived until old age, have a proven track record of coping with the stresses of life. Old age, however, brings its own special crises—physical deterioration, retirement, widowhood—and a continuing need for helpful understanding and emotional assistance. These psychological methods of treatment are also of great importance, especially with nonpsychotic conditions. Psychological treatment methods, which are discussed in detail in the next chapter, include counseling for milder problems of adjustment and psychotherapy for more serious personality disorders. The effectiveness of both physical and psychological treatments, and especially the latter, depends on the cooperation and efforts of people with problems to help themselves.

Whether the adjustment problem is large or small, mental health in old age is enhanced by maintaining a sense of interest, curiosity, and wonder. Problems and crises do occur, but the conquest of disillusionment and cynicism stemming from unresolved conflicts and frustrations begins with the recognition of one's feelings. People must learn to cope with old age and its special problems in the same way that they learn any skill. Only by maintaining a continued focus on learning and growth in the face of seeming hopelessness can the elderly person use the final days of life valuably and serve as an example to others and have an influence on their lives.

SUMMARY

People vary extensively in their ability to cope with the tasks and problems of later life. Declining health and physical appearance, the loss of employment and loved ones, and erosion of the sense of significance and meaningfulness of one's life can lead to depression and despair. On the other hand, more integrated persons who possess effective mechanisms for coping with the stresses of aging and who are willing to search for a new identity in old age can find new challenges and sources of gratification in this stage of life.

Personality, the unique organization of abilities, traits, and behavior patterns that characterize an individual, manifests a substantial degree of consistency across the life span. People who are well adjusted in youth and middle adulthood tend to remain so in later life; people who are maladjusted in earlier life continue to have adjustment difficulties in old age. Although the self-concept may decline in later life, rather than being a function of age per se the decline is related to decreased socioeconomic security and other events that occur in old age.

An age-related trend toward interiority or introspection, which is perhaps a normal coping response to the stresses of aging, has been observed. Increased rigidity or inflexibility is also said to characterize the aged, but a more accurate description of the elderly is "realistically cautious" rather than "rigid."

Reichard and his colleagues found evidence for five types of adjustment patterns in older men: mature, rocking chair, armored, angry, and self-hating. Similarly, in a study of the relationships of personality and social activity to happiness in older people, Neugarten and her colleagues noted four major personality types—integrated, armored-defended, passive-dependent, and unintegrated—with two or three subcategories under each of the first three types. A well-integrated personality and an active, problem-solving attitude were found by Neugarten to be associated with better adjustment in old age. Having socially meaningful roles to play is also important.

Owing to a combination of organic changes and psychological stress, the mental health of the aged tends to be poorer than that of younger adults. Young adulthood is most often characterized by the elderly as the "happiest time of life." Mental disorders are more common in old age than at other times of life, but the incidence varies with sex, socioeconomic status, urban versus rural residence, and other demographic variables.

Psychophysiological disorders, psychoneuroses, depression, and character disorders occur at all stages of life. Depression, in particular, is equally common in the young and old and often poses the problem of suicide. Suicide is more frequent in older white men than in any other group, showing a steady increase with age.

Psychotic disorders, which are characterized by pronounced distortions of reality and may also involve disturbances in perception, language, memory, and mood, are less common and more serious than other functional disorders. The two main types of functional psychoses are schizophrenia and affective psychoses. Among the latter are manic-depressive psychosis and involutional melancholia.

The treatment of milder mental disorders does not require institutionalization, but admission (commitment)—either voluntary or involuntary—is often necessary with more severe disorders. Treatment may involve a combination of physical (drugs, electroshock, surgery) and psychological (psychotherapy, milieu therapy) methods. Mental health in old age is also affected by a person's attitude toward living and the perceived meaningfulness and value of his or her existence.

SUGGESTED READINGS

Britton, J. H., & Britton, J. A. *Personality changes in aging.* New York: Springer, 1972.

Busse, E. W., & Pfeiffer, E. (Eds.). *Mental illness in later life.* Washington, D.C.: American Psychiatric Association, 1973.

Eisdorfer, C., & Wilkie, F. Stress, disease, aging, and behavior. In J. E. Birren & K. W. Schaie (Eds.), *Handbook of the psychology of aging.* New York: Van Nostrand Reinhold, 1977.

Kaplan, O. J. *Psychopathology of aging.* New York: Academic Press, 1979.

Monge, R. H. Structure of the self-concept from adolescence through old age. *Experimental Aging Research,* 1975, *1,* 281–291.

Neugarten, B. L. Personality changes in late life. A developmental perspective. In C. Eisdorfer & M. P. Lawton (Eds.), *The psychology of adulthood and development.* Washington, D.C.: American Psychological Association, 1973.

Neugarten, B. L. Personality and aging. In J. E. Birren & K. W. Schaie (Eds.), *Handbook of the psychology of aging.* New York: Van Nostrand Reinhold, 1977.

Pfeiffer, E. Psychopathology and social pathology. In J. E. Birren & K. W. Schaie (Eds.), *Handbook of the psychology of aging.* New York: Van Nostrand Reinhold, 1977.

Sheehy, G. *Passages: The predictable crises of adult life.* New York: Dutton, 1976.

Vaillant, G. E. How does the best and brightest come of age. *Psychology Today,* 1977, *11*(4), 34–41.

Weinberg, J. Psychopathology. In J. Hendricks & C. D. Hendricks (Eds.), *Dimensions of aging.* Cambridge, Mass.: Winthrop Publishers, 1979.

NOTES

[1]As noted in Chapter 2, the isolation and frustration produced by severe hearing loss in old age may contribute to paranoid symptoms.

[2]Mental health professionals and legal experts object to the term "commitment" with its implications of imprisonment, and have recommended that it be replaced with "hospitalization," "admission," or some other less offensive term.

[3]Because of the negative side effects that many of these drugs have on older patients, electroshock therapy is now coming back into popularity.

Counseling and Psychotherapy

Old age, perhaps more than any other stage of life, is a time of problems. Many of the problems encountered by older people are similar to those of younger adults: family and peer relationships, physical illness, financial and living conditions. Others, such as the stress of retirement or the death of a spouse, are more characteristic of later life. In any event, the depression, anxiety, grief, loneliness, dissatisfaction, and lack of self-respect felt by many young and middle-aged individuals are also experienced by the elderly.

How older people handle or cope with their problems is as much a matter of subjective perception as it is objective reality. Thus almost all the elderly experience anxiety, but by virtue of a better self-concept and more optimistic outlook, some are able to manage their anxieties while others are devastated by them. All older people who have problems do not require the assistance of professional counselors. Most, by themselves or with the help of family members and friends, are quite successful in coping with the losses and changes of old age. However, others need counseling or psychotherapy to assist them in dealing with life's vicissitudes and in finding satisfaction or contentment.

BACKGROUND AND RESOURCES

The distinction between **counseling** and **psychotherapy** is not sharp. Both involve the discussion of one's problem(s) with another, usually professionally trained, individual. In counseling, these discussions are usually of shorter duration; the techniques employed, somewhat more superficial; and the goals, more limited than those of psychotherapy. The object of these discussions, which are encouraged by the development of a positive interpersonal relationship between the counselor (therapist) and counselee (client, patient), is to provide a psychological climate in which the counselee can examine his or her problems and to find solutions to them.

Counseling is not restricted to any one profession; psychiatrists, psychologists, social workers, nurses, ministers, teachers, and many non- or paraprofessional persons do counseling. However, the practice of psychotherapy for the treatment of more serious personality disorders is usually limited to psychiatrists and clinical psychologists.

Lombana (1976) described a variety of situations in which remedial counseling or psychotherapy is needed by the elderly. Serious mental health concerns, especially depression, may require in-depth personal counseling. People with debilitating physical problems, which are aggravated by emotional reactions, require supportive counseling. Included in supportive counseling are techniques such as sensitive listening and reassurance, as well as efforts to motivate the person, elevate his or her spirits, and reinforce the will to recover and survive. These approaches are especially necessary when the older person receives little or no emotional support from family and friends.

Counseling is also needed by elderly people residing in nursing homes or similar institutions. Personal counseling and other therapeutic intervention techniques can help them redevelop feelings of worth and independence to sustain them in the institution and to help them cope with life outside. Another type of counseling, avocational counseling, can be combined with retraining to assist retirees in handling feelings of resentment and apathy accompanying forced retirement.

Background and Training of Counselors

The first old age counseling center in the United States was established some years ago in San Francisco by Lillian Martin. The field of later life counseling is, however, still not very popular, and only recently have concerted efforts been made to train counselors in problems of the aged. Many counselors and psychotherapists, because of the purported inflexibility or poorer learning and problem-solving abilities of the elderly, have concluded that psychological treatment is not as effective with older as with younger people. In fact, Sigmund Freud, the father of psychoanalysis, did not advocate the use of psychotherapy with people over 40 years of age. Consequently, those counselors and therapists who subscribe to the stereotype of the aged as rigid, uncooperative, and mentally deteriorated have shown a reluctance to work with them (Kastenbaum, 1963). These perceptions are unrealistic, because there is little evidence that older people are any more difficult to treat or that they gain less from psychological methods than other adults. On the contrary, many elderly individuals are quite receptive to the efforts of counselors and psychotherapists.

Trained psychotherapists or counselors may be psychiatrists, psychologists, clergymen (pastoral counselors), or social workers. Unfortunately, in many states almost anyone can call him- or herself a psychotherapist or counselor and "treat" people for a fee. Because of the danger of psychological quackery, elderly people who need psychological treatment should be aware of the credentials of the persons to whom they are referred. A list of competent professional psychotherapists can usually be obtained from a family physician, clergyman, or public mental health agency. In addition, most mental health organizations publish directories of professionals who are qualified to offer psychological assistance to the elderly. But unless the therapist, no matter how well intentioned, has also been trained in geriatric problems, he or she may make a mistake in diagnosis or treatment.

Considering the growth of counseling programs of various kinds, the need to establish criteria for counselors of the elderly and counseling training programs is apparent (O'Brien & Streib, 1977). The trainees enrolled in counseling programs include professional persons as well as para- and nonprofessionals. It is important that such training be offered to nonprofessionals as well as professionals, because much of the counseling in family service agencies, Red Cross chapters, Senior Citizens and Golden Age clubs, departments of public welfare, recreation centers, nursing homes, and other organizations catering to the elderly is done by nonprofessionals.

Especially noteworthy among the many counselor training programs are the peer counseling (widow-to-widow, patient-to-patient, etc.) pro-

---

Report 6-1   A SUCCESS FOR PSYCHOTHERAPY*

Anna was nearly 80 and living with a married daughter. For the past 5 years Anna had experienced a progressive loss of memory. At first, she just forgot a few insignificant things, such as where she had placed her reading glasses. Gradually, the problem got more serious until she sometimes could not maintain a conversation: she forgot what she had just been told and asked the same question again. At times she would get lost or would even lose her way inside her daughter's house. Anna became more and more of a burden. The advice of Anna's doctor was to have her placed in a home for the aged.

Anna's experience is all too common. Many older persons suffer from some sort of short-term memory impairment: they forget what just happened but can tell you the details of an incident that occurred half a century ago. All sorts of medical theories have been proposed to explain this phenomenon of senility. The one taught in most medical schools is that such mental deterioration is caused by physical changes in the brain . . . and is irreversible. Therefore, most physicians and medically trained psychiatrists tend to give up too easily on an older person with a failing memory.

Fortunately for Anna, her daughter did not take the advice of the first doctor. They saw another physician, who referred Anna to a psychotherapist specializing in geriatric practice. In less than two months, Anna's deteriorating mental condition was reversed. This psychotherapy was not cheap. However, it was less expensive than psychoanalysis and certainly a bargain compared to the cost of keeping Anna in a home for the aged.

*After Brink (1976), p. 24. Used with permission of the National Mental Health Association, Inc.

grams of the University of Southern California and Oakland University in Michigan. The emphasis in these programs is on training counselors to assist the elderly without "taking over" or creating excessive dependency. As noted by Schwartz and Peterson (1979), efforts to help older people should not be made in a "take charge" or patronizing manner. Elderly people need to develop self-confidence in coping with their own problems without relying completely on someone else to solve all their difficulties or to meet all their emotional needs.

THEORIES AND MODELS

Although counseling is possible without adhering to any elaborate theory of personality development and functioning, all counselors have some explicit or implicit framework for understanding other human beings. In fact, every layperson probably has some "theory" as to why people behave as they do. Such theories frequently consist of overgeneralizations or stereotypes but serve as rough guides to expectation and action. Realizing that every individual is different and that human behavior is very complex, professional counselors and psychotherapists have learned to be suspicious of the explanatory power of commonsense theories. It is generally maintained, however, that therapeutic interventions are more likely to be effective when guided by some explicit, professionally developed theory or set of principles concerning personality. Theories that have had the greatest impact on counseling and psychotherapy are psychoanalysis, phenomenology, and behaviorism.

Psychoanalysis

Sigmund Freud and other psychoanalysts have viewed human personality as a kind of battleground where three combatants—the id, ego, and superego—vie for supremacy. The **id**, a reservoir of instinctive drives of sex and aggression housed in the unconscious part of the mind, acts according to the pleasure principle. It runs into conflict with the **superego** (the "conscience"), which acts according to the moral principle. Although the id is inborn, the superego develops as the child internalizes the prohibitions and sanctions that the parents place on the behavior of their offspring. Meanwhile the **ego** acts according to the reality principle, attempting to serve as a mediator between the relentless pressures of the id and superego for control. The id says "Now!" the superego says "Never!" and the ego says "Later" to the individual's basic desires. Although id impulses and the conflict of the id with the superego and ego usually take place in the unconscious mind, they are expressed in thoughts and behavior in various disguised forms.

Freud also believed that human personality develops through a series of psychosexual stages. During each stage a different region of the body is the center of sexual stimulation and gratification, and at that stage conflicts pertaining to the particular body region predominate.

Freud was one of the first personality theorists to recognize that "the child is father to the man," that deprivation and conflict in childhood frequently have permanent effects on personality. His theory of psychosexual stages maintains that frustration and conflict at a particular stage affect the individual's adult character structure by causing **fixation** (a failure to progress psychosexually beyond a particular stage) or **regression** (a partial or complete return to behavior patterns typical of an earlier stage of development).

From the psychoanalytic viewpoint, the basic goal of psychotherapy is to bring into conscious awareness those repressed impulses that are causing anxiety. The primary techniques used to accomplish this goal of achieving insight into the bases of a psychological problem are free association (saying whatever comes into one's mind), analysis of transference (meaning of the relationship that develops between patient and analyst), analysis of resistance (reluctance of patient to discuss sensitive material), analysis of the patient's dreams, and interpretation of statements made by the patient during the course of therapy. Unfortunately, classical psychoanalysis is considered inappropriate for dealing with most of the problems of the elderly. However, it has been helpful with certain intelligent, talkative older patients who suffered from milder mental disorders.

Transactional Analysis

An offspring of classical psychoanalysis that has been somewhat more effective in treating problems of the elderly is **transactional analysis.** As described by Berne (1964), transactional analysis conceives of human personality as composed of three ego states—adult, parent, and child. These three states are similar to the ego, superego, and id of classical psychoanalysis, but unlike psychoanalysis with its emphasis on the unconscious, transactional analysis focuses on conscious, observable behavior. Similar to the Freudian notion of conflict, it is the interaction, or transactions, among these three ego states that leads to maladaptive personality development or emotional problems.

The goals of transactional analysis are to (Berne, 1966):

1. Help the client decontaminate any damaged ego state.
2. Develop in the client the capacity to use all ego states where appropriate.
3. Assist the client in developing the full use of his or her adult state.
4. Help the client rid him or herself of his or her inappropriately chosen life position and life script, replacing them with an "I'm OK" position and a new, productive life script.

To accomplish these goals, the counselor tries to help the client understand the structures of his or her ego states ("structural analysis"), the transactions in which the client usually engages ("transactional analysis"), the payoffs that a client receives for playing certain games ("game analysis"), and the fact that the client's whole life script has been a mistake ("script analysis").

Phenomenological (Self) Theory

Phenomenological, or "self," theorists maintain that attempts to analyze personality into a set of components such as id, ego, and superego or adult, parent, and child do an injustice to its integrated, dynamic nature. In contrast to psychoanalysts, who emphasize sexual and aggressive drives, the unconscious, and the importance of psychosexual stages, phenomenologists stress perceptions, meanings, attitudes, feelings, and the centrality of the self. To phenomenological theorists, people are seen as responding to the world in terms of their unique perceptions of it. The **phenomenal field** is that part of a person's physical environment that is perceived by and has meaning for the person, whereas the **self** is that portion of the phenomenal field that is related to the individual in a personal way. In the language of Abraham Maslow, Carl Rogers, and other phenomenologically oriented psychologists, the individual strives to attain a state of **self-actualization**—a congruence or harmony between his or her real and ideal selves.

Carl Rogers and other psychologists who have been greatly influenced by phenomenological and existential philosophers have emphasized an ahistorical, "here-and-now," approach to counseling. Counselors subscribing to the phenomenological point of view do a minimum of questioning, advising, and interpretation. In Rogers' client-centered counseling, for example, clients assume the responsibility for solving their own problems. The counselor simply accepts what the client says, reflects the feeling tone in the client's statements, or restates the content of a statement made by the client. By providing an accepting, nonjudgmental atmosphere ("unconditional positive regard") in which clients can examine their own experiences freely and be themselves, the counselor encourages clients to use their own positive resources to solve their problems and change their attitudes and behavior.

Rogers emphasized that everyone has the ability to grow and fulfill his or her potentialities, that is, to "become" himself or herself. In successful counseling, clients initially express a rather low evaluation of themselves, but their evaluations become more positive as counseling proceeds. Success, however, is not guaranteed with client-centered counseling, especially with people who are highly dependent or have severe mental disorders. This approach to counseling tends to be more effective with fairly self-sufficient people suffering from minor maladjustments.

There have been a number of extensions of phenomenological (self) theory, some of which have implications for counseling the elderly in particular. A noteworthy model is the one proposed by Carkhuff (1969). Carkhuff described three goals of counseling: self-exploration, self-understanding, and action. To assist the client in attaining these goals, the counselor uses six conditions: empathy, respect, concreteness, genuineness, confrontation, and immediacy. The first four are most important during the initial or facilitation stage of counseling. This stage in the counseling process has as its primary objective the establishment of a working relationship such that the client will feel free to begin self-exploration, which will hopefully lead to self-understanding. During the second, or action, stage of the counseling process the last two conditions—confrontation of the client with discrepancies and getting the client to focus on the immediate situation in counseling—are most important.

Based on the approaches of Rogers and Carkhuff is the nine-step model advocated by Alpaugh and Haney (1978) for counseling older adults (see Fig. 6-1). The objectives of the nine-step model are (1) to provide emotional support to the client and (2) to clarify the client's problems and the issues contained in those problems. The first step in the model, understanding the client, consists of attending to the feelings expressed by the client and the verbal and nonverbal content of the client's communications. The second step, establishing rapport, requires that the counselor be empathic, respectful, and concerned. The third step, defining the problem, is similar to the reflection of the content of the client's communications. The counselor must listen carefully to what the client says and try to determine the central issue. When the problem has been defined, the fourth step—setting a goal—is easy. The goal of the counseling sessions becomes one of finding a solution to the problem. Step five is clarifying issues. The next two steps in the model, listing and exploring alternatives, are concerned with looking at possible solutions to the problem and their

Figure 6-1 The nine-step counseling model. (After Alpaugh & Haney, 1978, p. 68.)

positive and negative features. Step eight, making a decision, does not usually come without considerable soul searching, because most decisions have some negative consequences. The final step, providing closure, comes only after the client and counselor agree that the relationship should be terminated. Closure is achieved by tying up loose ends but leaving the door open for further counseling sessions if the need should arise.

Behavior Theory and Therapy

For many years almost all psychotherapists subscribed to the beliefs of psychoanalytic depth therapists that (1) simply removing symptoms rather than treating root causes does not produce permanent cures, (2) causes, and hence "cures," can only be found by studying the patient's life history in detail, (3) a transference relationship between patient and therapist must develop if therapy is to be successful, and (4) the patient can be cured only by gaining insight into his or her personality. Although these beliefs are not held so tenaciously by phenomenological counselors, the latter still subscribe to the notion that clients must achieve some degree of self-understanding, or "insight," in order to solve their emotional problems. In the past quarter century, however, an increasing number of psychotherapists and counselors, particularly clinical psychologists who have been trained in learning theory, have questioned whether these beliefs are correct. Even some psychoanalysts have expressed doubt concerning the necessity of treating root causes, studying the life history, developing a strong transference relationship, and attaining insight (see Ellis, 1962).

Behavioral approaches to psychological treatment, referred to as **behavior therapy** or **behavior modification**, are based on principles of motivation and learning formulated from the results of laboratory studies of animals and humans (Wolpe & Lazarus, 1966). These principles involve applications of concepts such as positive and negative reinforcement, shaping, discrimination, generalization, extinction, and mediating responses. Behavior theorists have argued that because many adjustment problems are the results of faulty learning, it should be possible to arrange conditions so that the maladjusted behavior is unlearned. For example, a behavior modification approach that has had some success with the elderly, particularly those in institutions, is **contingency management.** This approach makes positive reinforcement (pleasures or privileges of various kinds) contingent on socially approved behavior (e.g., keeping neat and clean, eating properly, interacting with other patients).

Other behavioral techniques have been devised for extinguishing anxiety, which is considered to be at the heart of many emotional disorders. In the technique of **desensitization** the patient is exposed to the anxiety-arousing situation under contrived "safe" conditions. Other, more normal responses can be conditioned to the situation by controlling anxiety responses. In the method of **reciprocal inhibition** the conditioned stimuli for anxiety responses are presented only when the individual makes responses that are incompatible with anxiety. For example, the therapist may encourage the patient to become more relaxed, during which time stimuli that are increasingly more fearful to the patient are presented. The therapist starts with stimuli that normally produce a weak fear response and then presents more frightening stimuli as the patient becomes more and more relaxed. Besides relaxation, assertive behavior, sexual behavior, and eating responses—because they are also incompatible with anxiety—can be used to inhibit anxiety.

Critics of behavior therapy and behavior modification have argued that the techniques treat only the symptoms of a disorder and that other symptoms will be substituted for them if the root causes of the problem are not understood and dealt with by the patient. Reviews of cases treated by behavioral methods (e.g., Grossberg, 1964), however, have found relatively few instances of such symptom substitution.

Reality Therapy

Like behavior therapy, reality therapy did not stem from a complex theory of personality development and adjustment. Rather, this approach is based on a set of practical techniques devised by William Glasser (1965) on the basis of his personal experiences with emotionally disturbed patients. Glasser conceptualizes human personality in terms of how well people meet their needs, especially those to be loved and to feel worthwhile. The goal of reality therapy is to teach the client to meet his or her own needs by using the three R's of "Right, Responsibility, and Reality" as a guide. "Right" is an accepted standard or norm of behavior; "Responsibility" means satisfying one's own needs without interfering with those of others; "Reality" means understanding that there is a real world in which needs must be satisfied.

In reality therapy the counselor uses the following techniques to teach the client to govern his or her life according to the three R's (Hansen, Stevic, & Warner, 1977):

1. Communicating to the client that he or she cares.
2. Getting the client to focus on present behavior rather than feelings.
3. Helping the client to evaluate his or her own irresponsible behavior.
4. Getting the client to make a commitment to a specific plan to change his or her irresponsible behavior.
5. Refusing to accept excuses for failure to stick to a plan but not punishing the client for failing.

TECHNIQUES OF COUNSELING THE ELDERLY

Literally dozens of theories and models have served as frameworks for counseling and psychotherapy, but the ones described in the last section have found the greatest use in the psychological treatment of the elderly.

The focus of all these approaches in working with older people is to attempt to motivate the person to take an interest in things and to use his or her abilities in personally and socially acceptable ways. It is also important that the counselee be helped to feel wanted and valued by his or her family and community.

Whether the counselor is a professional, a peer, or a relative, there is a variety of techniques for achieving the above goals. A list of practical suggestions, incorporating many of the specific techniques that have been used to provide psychological help for the elderly, is given in Table 6-1. These suggestions may be followed by anyone—trained or untrained—who has an interest in assisting older people.

Group Counseling and Psychotherapy

Butler and Lewis (1977) have described several individual and group-oriented techniques for use with the elderly, including telephone outreach therapy, group psychotherapy, life review therapy, and life cycle group therapy. All counseling and psychotherapy is concerned with interpersonal relationships, but the interpersonal aspect is emphasized in group methods. Group counseling is counseling conducted simultaneously with a group of people coordinated by a counselor or therapist. This approach saves time over that required for individual counseling, and the group also provides an opportunity for the counselee to communicate with someone

Table 6-1 SUGGESTIONS FOR GIVING PSYCHOLOGICAL HELP TO OLDER PEOPLE*

---

1. Allow older people opportunities to talk about and resolve their problems and conflicts; pay attention to their reminiscences and try to understand them.
2. Do not be afraid to touch older people; a handshake, a friendly pat, or an arm about the shoulder can satisfy the desire for human contact and open up the discussion.
3. Assist older people to accept the fact that they are growing older, but emphasize the positive aspects of aging (e.g., reduced pressure to perform at high levels).
4. Help older people maintain human contacts and develop new relationships; encourage them to gain new friends to replace those that are lost.
5. Help older people cultivate pleasures of the mind and to find creative outlets in community activities, arts, and hobbies.
6. In counseling the elderly, it is as critical to identify and encourage areas of health as it is to clarify problems.
7. Persons caring for or counseling the ill or handicapped must assist them in finding ways to help themselves in a positive manner that brings at least a measure of the self-esteem necessary for human dignity.
8. Do not try to destroy the defenses of illusion and denial employed by older people. Rather than attacking these defenses directly, work toward understanding and encouraging a realistic lowering of them.
9. Always discuss the facts of death and loss and the problems of grief in the context of possibilities, restitution, and resolution.

---

*Adapted from *Human Relations* (University of California Cooperative Extension, Berkeley, Calif.), Vol. III, No. 3, March 1978 and Butler & Lewis (1977).

other than the counselor. In this way the person is exposed to the kind of interpersonal stress that may have contributed to his or her problem and with which he or she must learn to cope. Group members also gain social support, the realization that their problems are not unique, and the advice and counsel of other people who have had similar problems.

Group counseling, which is less expensive than individual counseling, has proven to be especially valuable in helping older people overcome feelings of loneliness, alienation, and despair. For these reasons, Butler and Lewis (1977) have recommended that group therapeutic procedures be employed in all institutions (nursing homes, hospitals, etc.) and on an outpatient basis for treating the elderly with psychological problems. Nurses are probably most often used as group counselors or therapists in such institutional groups, the usual goals of which are socialization, emotional catharsis, and the management of behavior.

A number of specialized techniques have been employed in counseling and therapy groups, including "Here and Now" approaches, such as group discussion and role-playing, and "There and Then" approaches, such as reminiscence and life review. Reminiscing about personal experiences and other memories can serve as an effective form of therapy for older people who have a sensitive listener. These reminiscences form a part of **life review therapy** and **life cycle group therapy,** which Butler (1974) has advocated as being particularly helpful to older patients.

Life review therapy begins by obtaining an extensive biography of the patient from the patient and family members. Tape recordings, diaries, family albums, and other memorabilia can assist in the life review process. Some of the goals of this type of therapy are atonement for feelings of guilt, getting rid of childhood identifications that continue to cause trouble, and resolution of intra- and interpersonal conflicts.

Life review therapy can be either individual or group. Extended to a group setting consisting of eight to ten members of different ages, life review becomes life cycle group therapy. The groups are oriented toward individuals who are experiencing life crises, ranging from adjustment difficulties in adolescence to fear of impending death. By interacting with people of different generations in a group setting ("age-integrated life cycle group therapy"), the elderly individual comes to see his or her problems in the perspective of the life cycle and continuing development.

Other techniques that have been employed in a group setting are **psychodrama** and **scribotherapy.** Psychodrama is therapeutic role-playing in which clients act out situations related to their conflicts and problems. Members of the group may play the roles of supporting characters to help a particular client reexperience a situation pertaining to his or her problem. In scribotherapy, the group members write down their feelings about certain topics and then, after group discussion and individual interviews, develop them into a news format.

Family counseling, a special type of age-integrated group counseling, involves the elderly counselee and one or more other members of the family interacting with a counselor and each other. Because family relationships are a common source of difficulty for elderly people, it is often important to include the family in the psychological counseling of older people. Herr and Weakland (1979) have provided some useful guidelines for counseling elders and their families.

The limited economic resources of the aged and the stigma of being referred to a psychological counselor frequently make it necessary to conduct family counseling under less than optimal conditions and to settle for limited goals. In any event, family counseling is as much a matter of not doing certain things as it is of doing others. Herr and Weakland (1979) point out that counselors should avoid arguments or overinvolvement with clients and their families and should not put words into their mouths. At the same time, family counselors should be genuine and empathic, express unconditional positive regard, and work toward improving their skills in communicating with older people and their families.

Other Psychotherapeutic Techniques

Many additional techniques that have been employed in counseling and psychotherapy with the elderly are described by Barns, Sack, and Shore (1973). These include reality orientation, resocialization, remotivation, attitude therapy, reinforcement therapy, sensory retraining, biofeedback, and self-image therapy. Each of these techniques, which may be used in combination with other procedures, is more effective with certain kinds of problems or patients. Reality orientation, the backbone of which is the repetition and learning of basic information (e.g., patient's name, place, day, date, time, etc.), is employed with confused patients. Sensory retraining, on the other hand, is most effective with regressed older patients who have difficulty interacting with the environment. In sensory retraining, differentiated stimuli are used to improve the patient's perception of a response to the physical and social environment.

Galton (1978, 1979) described several interesting therapeutic techniques that have been found helpful in treating depressed elderly patients. One is cognitive therapy, in which the patient keeps a diary of pleasant and unpleasant daily experiences and automatic negative thoughts. Patient and therapist meet for an hour each week to discuss and analyze the material recorded in the diary. In this way patients gradually become aware of how they are making themselves miserable.

Another approach described by Galton (1979) is pet-facilitated therapy, in which birds, dogs, or other pets are used to bring out depressed, withdrawn, love-hungry elderly patients. Well-trained wirehair fox terriers, which are particularly resilient, playful, good humored, and aggressively friendly, have been found by Dr. Samuel Corson and his co-workers at Ohio State University to be particularly effective. These "feeling heart" dogs are able to bring out patients emotionally so that they can interact more comfortably with other people and begin the process of psychotherapy.

Prevention and Milieu Therapy

The techniques of counseling and psychotherapy discussed thus far are remedial. But even more valuable to positive adjustment and mental health, at least in the long run, is preventive counseling. Preventive approaches include preretirement counseling and continued health education, as well as information and opportunities for avocational, educational, and recreational activities (Lombana, 1976). For example, nursing homes usually provide a variety of avocational and recreational activities (arts, crafts, music therapy, exercise classes, field trips, etc.) to stimulate and interest older people and emphasize the fact that they are still among the living.

Environmental arrangements or changes of the sort that play a role in prevention can also be used in remediation. All mental health professionals realize that the physical and social surroundings are important in the course and treatment of psychological problems and disorders. It has been found, for example, that the introduction of some simple changes—a record player, a decorated bulletin board, games, dressing patients in white shirts and ties, serving beer and crackers every day at two o'clock—can markedly alter the behavior of patients on a senile ward (Volpe & Kastenbaum, 1967). These changes have resulted in decreased incontinence and a lessened need for restraint and medication, and the mental and social functioning of the patients has improved markedly. Such improvements may be interpreted as stemming from better patient attitudes, accompanied by an increase in the expectations of the institutional staff and the patients of what they themselves are able to do. At least to an extent, mental patients—like people in general—become what they are viewed or labeled as being, doing what others expect them to do.

A similar explanation can be applied to the findings of an experiment by Kahana and Kahana (1970b). Aged male psychiatric patients were assigned at random to one of two types of hospital wards,—age-segregated and age-integrated. The patients on each of the age-segregated wards were all within a fairly narrow age range, whereas those on the age-integrated wards covered the entire adult age range. When reexamined after three weeks, those patients who had been placed on the age-integrated wards showed greater improvements in responsiveness and performance on mental status examinations than those on the age-segregated wards. Apparently, simply being around younger people, who act as more youthful behavior models, can alter the negative attitudes of older patients toward their situation and consequently improve their behavior.

Psychological Training of Workers with the Elderly

Counseling, psychotherapy, milieu therapy, and other methods of helping the elderly with psychological problems should be accompanied by education of the general public about the stereotypes and myths pertaining to old age. Adequate psychological training of professional, paraprofessional, and nonprofessional workers with the elderly is also essential. Most experts agree, for example, that the training of workers in residential centers for the elderly should deal not only with the routines of physical care, but also with techniques for protecting the dignity and rights of patients and trying to get them to accept life and live it to the fullest extent possible.

One method, used to increase the sensitivity of those who work with the elderly, is the "Empathic Model." This model, which was discussed in Chapter 2, has been applied to the training of nurses and technicians in nursing homes. In some instances health personnel who participate in the training sessions have been provided with an "Instant Aging Kit" containing a white wig, wire-rimmed spectacles, and theatrical makeup. Many who don these getups begin to see the world from an old-age viewpoint, thus acquiring greater empathy with the elderly residents.

SPECIFIC COUNSELING AND THERAPEUTIC PROBLEMS

The range and severity of psychological problems confronting the elderly are at least as great as in other age groups, but certain problem areas are more common. These include problems with family relationships,[1] health, finances, living conditions, retirement, death, and bereavement. Counseling and psychotherapy for such problems are offered by a variety of public and private agencies, but in most instances elderly people must take the initiative themselves to come in for counseling (Lowy, 1975). Although in-depth counseling or psychotherapy usually takes many sessions, in certain cases one visit may be sufficient:

> A farmer's wife came and told a tragic story where nothing could be done, but her compassion and strength made it possible to continue. As usual with these cases, I asked if she would care to come again; she looked a little surprised, and said, "There is no need, I've told you everything." She had only wanted to confide in someone she respected, in case there was more she could do, and not to be so alone in her hard life .... One visit was enough for her (Scott-Maxwell, 1968).

Drugs, Death, and Bereavement

Certain types of counseling for the elderly, for example, drug counseling and bereavement counseling, have increased during recent years. The growing need for drug counseling of the elderly is not the result of older people taking illegal drugs, but rather the consequence of errors in prescribing or taking legal prescription and over-the-counter medicines. Drug-induced illness in the elderly is often overlooked because it produces many of the symptoms associated with old age—forgetfulness, weakness, confusion, tremor, and anorexia ("Senior Citizens...," 1978).

With respect to counseling the bereaved and dying, there is no set prescription for dealing with the emotional needs of terminally ill patients and those who are close to them. What the physician, clergyman, or social worker tells the patient and the family must be adapted to the particular needs of the individuals being counseled. Many counseling methods have been employed with the dying, but the emphasis should be placed on helping the patient live each day for itself—as joyfully and peacefully as possible. This may best be achieved in an emotional and social environment with which the patient is familiar, usually at home (Carey, 1976). Carey (1976) also recommends that counselors of terminally ill patients and their families be careful not to force their own moral or religious values on the counselees. In general, the counselor should try to understand and share the feelings of those involved and help them to find their own ways of handling death, whether these be religious or secular.

Bereavement counseling is not greatly different from counseling for any other separation or loss. Counselors of the bereaved need to be supportive and empathic, but at the same time, to encourage the counselee to take a realistic view of things. Often this can be done most effectively by individuals who themselves have experienced the death of a loved one (Silverman, 1969). Much bereavement counseling is one-to-one, but group-oriented approaches are also fairly common. In these "Grief Groups" patients talk about mourning, their feelings concerning death, and how to survive the loss of a loved one. A professional counselor provides information and direction to the group, as well as individual counseling for those members who need it.

Situational and Supportive Counseling

Situational or supportive counseling is frequently needed by elderly people, and for certain situations specific counseling techniques and goals have been delineated. For example, in training law enforcement officers to deal with elderly victims of crime, instructors recommended that officers (Symonds, 1978):

1. Tell the victim they're sorry it happened, they're glad he or she is all right, and that he or she did nothing wrong.
2. Describe to the victim the kinds of feelings that crime victims experience, so that the victim understands that his or her own emotions are actually very normal.
3. Confirm his or her belief that something terrible has happened to him or her, rather than arguing with a victim who does not want to be consoled.

Another common situation calling for counseling is impending retirement. Manion (1976), for example, described a preretirement counseling program fashioned after the T-group model of the National Training Laboratory and a facilitator-learning model. In this small-group approach, preretirees review factual materials on retirement and also are encouraged to examine the needs, attitudes, values, and fears concerned with how they expect to cope with life after retirement. The objectives of this group-centered approach are to develop: skills in self-diagnosis, communication, interpersonal relations, and life planning; attitudes of independence, problem solving, decision-making, and action-taking; an awareness of their retirement options. A group facilitator, who is assigned to each group of ten to twelve persons, helps create an atmosphere of trust, openness, understanding, genuineness, and empathy in which retirement problems and potential solutions can be explored (Manion, 1976).

SUMMARY

Counseling and psychotherapy are similar terms for psychological methods of treatment, or "talking cures." Counseling, however, is usually of shorter duration and does not deal with such deep-rooted problems as psychotherapy. Various professional, paraprofessional, and nonprofessional persons provide counseling services for the elderly, but the practice of psychotherapy is restricted to psychiatrists and clinical psychologists.

Elderly people can benefit from psychological treatment for different problems, but professional counselors and psychotherapists are often reluctant to work with them. It is frequently assumed that older people are too slow or inflexible to benefit from psychological treatment.

Theories or models of personality development and functioning can serve as guides in counseling and psychotherapy. Psychoanalysis, with its emphasis on unconscious processes, psychosexual development, and the three-component structure of personality, has been the most influential theory. However, psychoanalysis has been less helpful in working with the elderly than transactional analysis, phenomenological (self) theory, behavior theory, and reality theory. Derivatives of Carl Rogers's self-theory of personality, when applied to counseling, have been especially popular among those who work with older people. An example is the nine-step model of Alpaugh and Haney (1978), which has as its objectives the provision of emotional support and the clarification of the problems of the elderly and the issues inherent in those problems. The progressive nine steps in this model are understanding the client, establishing rapport, defining the problem, setting a goal, clarifying issues, listing alternatives, exploring alternatives, making a decision, and providing closure. Behavior therapy and behavior modification techniques, in particular, contingency management, have found some use in treating institutionalized older people. Glasser's reality therapy has also been employed with the institutionalized elderly.

Dozens of special techniques have been applied in counseling and therapy with older people. Butler & Lewis (1977) have reported good success with life review therapy and life cycle group therapy in treating guilt feelings, childhood identifications, and interpersonal conflicts in the aged. Other group-oriented approaches are psychodrama, scribotherapy, and family counseling. Barns, Sack, and Shore (1973) list a variety of additional procedures: reality orientation, remotivation, attitude therapy, sensory retraining, biofeedback, and self-image therapy. Cognitive therapy, which involves discussing the contents of a daily diary with a therapist, and pet-facilitated therapy, in which pets are used to bring out withdrawn patients, have enjoyed some success in treating depression in the elderly.

Preventive counseling is considered to be even more essential than remedial counseling, and milieu (environmental) therapy just as important as direct counseling. The effects of the living environment on the attitudes and functioning of older patients have been demonstrated in a number of investigations, including those of Volpe and Kastenbaum (1967) and Kahana and Kahana (1970b). An especially significant part of the environment of an institutionalized elderly person is the institutional staff. It is considered essential to train such workers in caring for both the physical and psychological needs of elderly residents.

There has been a recent upsurge in the number of older people receiving counseling for drug and bereavement problems. Counseling of terminally ill patients—by physicians, nurses, clergymen, and others—has also become more acceptable in recent years. Although approaches to counseling differ to some extent with the specific problem, there are similarities across problem areas in the techniques employed. For example, bereavement counseling is not greatly different from counseling for any other kind of separation or loss.

Much of the counseling conducted with elderly people is situational or supportive in nature. Illustrative of situational counseling are the counseling of elderly crime victims and preretirees. Preretirement counseling, however, has become an extensive, systematic process in many business and industrial organizations. Such preretirement counseling programs are concerned both with presenting factual information pertaining to retirement and exploring the psychological needs and attitudes of participants.

SUGGESTED READINGS

Alpaugh, P., & Haney, M. Counseling the older adult. Los Angeles: University of Southern California Press, 1978.

Barry, J. R., & Wingrove, C. R. (Eds.). Let's learn about aging. New York: Schenkman, 1977, Section IV-B.

Burnside, I. M. (Ed.). Working with the elderly: Group process and techniques. N. Scituate, Mass.: Duxbury, 1978.

Butler, R. N., & Lewis, M. I. Aging and mental health (2d ed.). St. Louis, Mo.: Mosby, 1977.

Gottesman, L. E., Quarterman, C. E., & Cohn, G. M. Psychological treatment of the aged. In C. Eisdorfer & M. P. Lawton (Eds.), Psychology of adult development and aging. Washington, D.C.: American Psychological Association, 1973.

Gurian, B. S. Psychogeriatrics and family medicine. *The Gerontologist,* 1975, *15,* 308–310.

Herr, J. J., & Weakland, J. H. *Counseling elders and their families.* New York: Springer, 1979.

Keller, J., & Hughston, G. *Counseling the elderly: A systems approach.* New York: Harper & Row, 1981.

Landreth, G. L., & Berg, R. C. *Counsel-ing the elderly.* Springfield, Ill.: Charles C Thomas, 1980.

Oberleder, M. Psychotherapy with the aging. In R. A. Kalish (Ed.), *The later years: Social applications of gerontology.* Monterey, Calif.: Brooks/Cole, 1977. 327–332.

Storandt, M., Siegler, I.C., & Elias, M. F. (Eds.). *The clinical psychology of aging.* New York: Plenum, 1978.

NOTE

[1]Counseling for sex problems is discussed in Chapter 7.

Sex and Family Relations

Human beings are gregarious, mutually dependent creatures who need to be close and companionable. The expression of the social need to be with other people promotes security, species propagation, and other ends that protect and maintain humanity. This sociability of the human species is manifested most clearly in the desire to be touched, caressed, or held or by the verbal equivalents of these actions in a lullaby, a love song, or simply a comforting word. Nowhere is the need to be close to another person seen more clearly than in romantic love and sexual behavior.

SEXUAL BEHAVIOR

Although the sexual urge is not lost with a diminishing of reproductive capacity in later life, the ability to reproduce does decline with age in both sexes. There are, however, authenticated instances of men in their tenth decade of life who have sired children and women as old as 57 who have given birth. Even more startling is the feat purportedly accomplished by Rustam Mamedor (142 years old) and his wife (116 years old), who lived in the Caucasus region of the USSR: Their youngest son is said to have been born when Rustam was 107 and his wife 81 (Gots, 1977)! This was, of course, a very rare and questionable blessed event. Women normally lose the capacity to reproduce sometime between the ages of 45 and 50, the stage of life when ova are no longer regularly released from the ovaries and the *corpus luteum* fails to form.

It was formerly believed that aging of the reproductive system was caused directly by a decrease in the sex hormones, testosterone and estrogens, produced by the male and female gonads. Subsequent research, however, implicated insufficient pituitary or hypothalamic sex hormones in reproductive aging. Now it is believed that reproductive aging is caused by defects in the production of chemicals (neurotransmitters) that assist in the release of sex hormones by the hypothalamus. Because the blueprint for production of these neurotransmitters presumably exists at the cellular level, we are back once more to an individual-cell explanation of aging—this time aging in the reproductive system (Arehart-Treichel, 1976).

Incidence of Sexual Activity

Reference to the "sexless older years" is a social stereotype that is contradicted by research findings. The results of investigations from Kinsey (Kinsey, Pomeroy, & Martin, 1948) to Masters and Johnson (1970) point to only a slight decline in sexual interest with age. The Kinsey Report devoted little attention to sexual behavior in old age, but it was noted that 95 percent of the sample of 60-year-old men and nearly 70 percent of the sample of 70-year-old men reported being sexually active.

The findings of a 20-year longitudinal study conducted by Duke University researchers on 254 men and women aged 60 to 94 are very instructive (Pfeiffer, Verwoerdt, & Wang, 1968, 1969) (see Figure 7-1). Two-thirds of the elderly men in this sample stated that they were sexually active, and four-fifths of them admitted to a continuing interest in sex. The percentage of those interested in sex was the same 10 years later, but the number who were sexually active had fallen to 25 percent of the total. However, more than 20 percent of the men reported an *increase* in sexual activity as they grew older. This phenomenon, which was more common among unmarried men and due in large measure to meeting new partners, is dramatic evidence that sexual desire does not necessarily drop in old age.

The findings of surveys of sexual activity in elderly women are somewhat different from those of men. At the beginning of the Duke University study, for example, one-third of the sample of women confessed to a continuing sexual interest and one-fifth reported that they still had sexual intercourse on a regular basis. Both these fractions were approximately the same 10 years later. In addition, whereas the median age for cessation of intercourse in the elderly men was 68 years, it was only 60 years in the women.

As indicated by the elderly men who were interviewed in the Duke University study, being a widower or otherwise unmarried did not decrease their sexual activity. On the other hand, 90 percent of the older women interviewed in the study stated that they stopped having sexual intercourse when their husbands died or became impotent or ill. Even when both partners were healthy, the decision to stop having intercourse was almost always the husband's. Because most sexual activity in old age, especially for

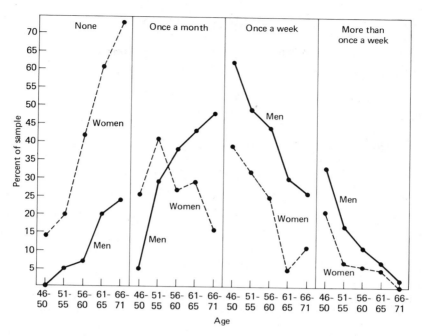

Figure 7-1 Frequency of sexual intercourse in middle and late life. (Data from Pfeiffer, Verwoerdt, & Davis, 1972. *The American Journal of Psychiatry*, vol. 128:10, p. 1264, 1972. Copyright 1972, the American Psychiatric Association. Reprinted by permission.)

women, takes place within a marital relationship, the difference in the sexual behavior of elderly men and women is probably due more to reduced opportunity than to an absence of desire. The reduction in opportunity among older women comes about because of the many more unattached women than men in old age. Among those women who are widowed or unmarried, a lack of available men, a reluctance to engage in sex out of wedlock, concern over personal appearance, and a belief that sex should cease after menopause all contribute to abstinence.

The investigations of Pfeiffer et al. (1969) and others (e.g., Newman & Nichols, 1960) also indicate that older people in lower socioeconomic groups are more sexually active than those in upper socioeconomic groups. Perhaps this is why certain studies have found that elderly blacks, who are more likely than whites to be of low socioeconomic status, are more sexually active than elderly whites. The overall results of studies of ethnic group differences in sexual behavior are, however, conflicting. But whatever the gender, social class, or ethnicity of a person, research underscores the truism "Use it or you'll lose it." Continued sexual activity is most important for the ability to function sexually in old age. As documented by the fact that people who are more sexually active in their youth are also more active in old age, human sexual behavior is a lifelong habit pattern (Masters & Johnson, 1966; Newman & Nichols, 1960). Thus, given good general health and sufficient practice, men can remain sexually active into their 70s and 80s and women as long as they live.

Physiology of Sex

Whereas the Kinsey reports and Duke University studies have helped to dispel the myth that sexual activity in old age is abnormal, precise information regarding the physiology of sex in the elderly was lacking prior to the investigations of Masters and Johnson (1970). In these studies elderly people were interviewed and their physiological responses during the sex act were monitored. One of the findings concerning sexuality in older women, of which laypersons and health professionals alike should be aware, is that menopause does not eliminate sexual need or functioning, especially when hormones are used, and sometimes even increases it. Because the clitoris remains intact and responsive to stimulation through-out old age, elderly women are physically capable of having just as many orgasms as younger women. Much of the older woman's sexual activity, however, does not result in orgasm.

The decrease in estrogen production after menopause is accompanied by both structural and functional changes in women. The cervix and uterus become smaller, and the vaginal walls thinner. The degree of vasoconges-tion of the breasts, clitoris, and vagina is also affected, and vaginal lubrication is reduced. These changes in the vagina can result in discomfort and pain during intercourse and an aching, burning sensation afterward. The extent to which these symptoms are experienced, however, varies from person to person, and sex hormone replacement therapy can help to control them.

The effects of aging on male sexuality can be classified as primary and secondary. Among the secondary (superficial) changes signaling the so-called "male menopause" and produced by a decline in secretion of the male hormone testosterone are loss of hair, increased flabbiness, and elevated voice pitch. The primary changes include a slight shrinkage of the testes, production of fewer sperm, and a decrease in the volume of the ejaculate. In regard to sexual functioning, older men usually take longer to achieve an erection, which may be incomplete but sufficient for vaginal penetration. There are fewer genital spasms, and the force of the ejaculate is reduced—often seeping rather than spurting. The erection is lost more quickly after ejaculation, and it takes longer to have another erection. Finally, orgasm may occur only once every second or third time rather than every time that an elderly man has intercourse.

For both men and women, all four phases of sexual arousal and decline (excitement, plateau, orgasmic, resolution) are prolonged in old age. But none of the age-related physiological changes need detract from sexual appreciation, and the enjoyment of intercourse is usually retained by both sexes. Despite the physiological changes previously noted, the extent to which sexual intercourse is enjoyed by an elderly couple depends to a great extent on the psychological relationship between them.

Attitudes toward Sex

A definition of old age as "the time when a man flirts with girls but can't remember why," the description of sexual life in the elderly as "triweekly, try weekly, try weakly," and one-liners such as "What do you do with a dirty old man? Introduce him to a dirty old woman." suggest the mixture of humor and disapproval with which society views sexual activity in the aged (Puner, 1974). Unfortunately, a disapproving attitude toward sexual activity in the elderly is held by many older people themselves. This is particularly true of older women, who, accepting the traditional stereotype, too often view sexual behavior on the part of old people as lecherous, dirty, and sick. As a consequence, older women patients may find it difficult to admit—even to an older woman physician—that they have sexual desires (Knopf, 1975). Because of negative attitudes and misconceptions regarding sex in later life, older people are cut off more than they need to be from one of the joys of life.

Many social organizations and institutions reinforce the notion that sex is only for the young and that elderly men and women who express an interest in the subject are "dirty old men" or "frustrated old women." The cultural emphasis on youthful beauty all too often causes older women to view themselves as physically unattractive and hence sex as no longer possible for them. And the overreactions of friends, relatives, and caretakers when an elderly person dares to become involved in a sexual affair leads to courtship in an atmosphere of secrecy and shame:

> An elderly woman in a nursing home pads quietly down the dimly lit corridor shortly after lights out for a rendezvous with her lover, a widower and fellow resident of the facility. Suddenly a staff member emerges from a doorway, scolds the woman and sends her back to her room, admonishing that sex is not permitted here. (Ingram, 1980)

A sexual relationship between two elderly people provides more than a means of releasing sexual tensions. The pleasures of companionship and sharing are an essential part of any enduring relationship. Furthermore, there is more to the physical aspect of sex than intercourse. As one 73-year-old man expressed it:

> I don't know if I'm oversexed, but I'm a lover. I like to pet, kiss, hug. I have more fun out of loving somebody I love than the ultimate end. You know, some people—and this is the failure of sex, too—some people want sex and forget the rest of it—the hugging and the petting and I think that's wrong. People say, "What will happen to me when I get older?" Well, I'm still alive! There's no thrill like that today. People try dope, they try smoking, they try drinking. This is the one thing that's good for the body. (Vinick, 1977, p. 12)

To counter the tendency of society—young, middle aged, and old—to label any older person who is interested in sex as a D.O.M. ("dirty old man") or an F.O.W. ("frustrated old women"), one elderly Californian

Report 7-1   MEDIA GUIDELINES FOR SEXUALITY AND AGING*

While the range of age-related stereotypes used in the media is wide, elders are particularly denigrated about their sexuality. Sexuality—used here in its broadest meaning to include sensuality, physical desirability, vitality, physical enjoyment and relationships—is a fundamental human right/capacity. Therefore the portrayal of elders as nonsexual, the ridicule of their sexuality, or the omission of elders from sensual/sexual contexts, is a dehumanizing use of media. The inclusion of sex-positive and elder-centered images should be a vital part of all coverage.

We offer the following guidelines for non-agist portrayal of sexuality in the media:

- DO use words like elder, old, old age; and, in context, words such as experienced, wise, mature, and weathered.
- DON'T use words or expressions like balding, granny, hag, old bag, peppery, spry, old goat, old fogey, little old lady, dirty old man, sagging breasts or face, cranky, cantankerous, grouchy, or housewife (if not applicable).
- DO try to emphasize the positive aesthetic aspects of growing old: a face wrinkled with beauty; gray hair blowing in the wind.
- Be careful, in general, of age-related adjectives. DON'T use the word senile as a general adjective. Instead of saying "She's acting senile," be more specific: "She's acting confused and disoriented"; instead of saying, "Their love affair was almost adolescent in spite of their advanced age," say, "Their love affair was wild and fresh."
- DON'T assume that all elders are heterosexual; as with all ages, a significant proportion of elders are Lesbians, gay men, and bisexuals.
- AVOID portraying old men as needing young women for potent and vital sex. Include the portrayal of sexually active elders with contact with each other. Be careful in portraying old women in relationships with young men as "news"—you may be helping to generate yet another myth.
- All of the above apply to humorous depictions of elders. Avoid implying that sex for elders is absurd by snickering or being oblique about their sex lives or sensuality.

*From Davis (1980), pp. 83–84.

responded with a bumper sticker on his sports car that declared: "I'm not a dirty old man; I'm a sexy senior citizen" (Lobsenz, 1974). There are, of course, more effective measures than bumper stickers for helping elderly men and women satisfy their needs for sex and love without censure, embarrassment, or undue physical difficulties. Stereotypes concerning sex and the elderly on television programs, for example, can be reduced by advocacy of the guidelines recommended by the Gray Panthers. Several of the items in these guidelines are listed in Report 7-1.

Indications of the growing public acceptance of sexuality among the aged are also found in the mixed reactions to the recommendations of several gerontologists and laypersons that private rooms be provided in nursing homes so patients can have sex with each other and/or visitors. It has been suggested that the chronic anxieties of nursing-home patients could be alleviated by sexual intercourse. Although most nursing homes do not publicly sanction conjugal visits and other sexual arrangements among patients, they have begun to show a greater tolerance toward sexual contacts.

Sexual Problems and Deviations

It should be emphasized that sex in old age is not a perversion and that declines in sexual activity are due as much to social and emotional factors as to physiology. It is true that certain physical disorders and drugs (e.g., tranquilizers) can reduce sexual functioning, but equally important are the lack of privacy; insufficient practice; preoccupation with work; and emotions such as anger, anxiety, guilt, and depression (Masters & Johnson, 1970).

A case in point is impotence, a serious concern of many elderly men. Because sexual prowess is a symbol of manliness, the loss of ability to perform the sex act can lower the elderly man's feeling of competence and self-esteem. Although diabetes and removal of the prostate gland may cause impotence, when an elderly man is impotent it is usually a temporary condition produced by overeating, excessive drinking, medications, fatigue, boredom with the sexual partner, or emotional stress. Rather than taking constructive action, the impotent elderly man often perpetuates the condition by avoiding sex altogether and/or turning to alcohol.

As documented by Kinsey et al. (1948) and other researchers, masturbation is fairly common in both young and old, declining only slightly with age. There is, on the other hand, no evidence that voyeurism (peeping), exhibitionism (displaying one's sex organs), pedophilia (sexual relations with children, "child molesting"), or other sexual deviations are anything but rare exceptions in the elderly. There are no adequate statistics concerning the incidence of homosexuality in old age, but its occurrence in older people usually produces the same intense social reaction as in any age group. Indicative of our politically active times are recent efforts both in the United States and the United Kingdom to obtain public acceptance and support of older, especially "widowed," homosexuals.

Sex Therapy

The frequency of sex problems in old age is indicated by the fact that in one community of 10,000 elderly people, therapists were consulted about sex problems twice as often as about any other difficulty (Peterson, 1971). Many of these sex problems would not occur or would be less serious if elderly people received good health care, adequate nutrition, and hormone replacement therapy. In any event, sound physical health and an adequate supply of hormones are seldom sufficient for coping with a problem having strong emotional components. Some form of psychotherapy or reeducation is also required in the majority of cases.

Masters and Johnson (1970) have pioneered in the rapid but effective treatment of cases of sexual inadequacy. Many of their patients, and those of their associates, have been elderly people who had stopped having sexual relations because of misunderstandings concerning the natural physiological changes with age. Report 7-2 describes one such case. It

Mr. and Mrs. A were 66 and 62 years of age when referred to the Foundation for sexual inadequacy. They had been married 39 years. . . .

They had maintained reasonably effective sexual interchange during their marriage. Mr. A had no difficulty with erection, reasonable ejaculatory control, and . . . had been fully committed to the marriage. Mrs. A, occasionally orgasmic during intercourse and regularly orgasmic during her occasional masturbatory experiences, had continued regularity of coital exposure with her husband until five years prior to referral for therapy. . . .

At age 61, . . . Mr. A noted for the first time slowed erective attainment. Regardless of his level of sexual interest or the depth of his wife's commitment to the specific sexual experience, it took him progressively longer to attain full erection. With each sexual exposure his concern for the delay in erective security increased until finally . . . he failed for the first time to achieve an erection quality sufficient for vaginal penetration.

When coital opportunity [next] developed . . . erection was attained, but again it was quite slow in development. The next two opportunities were only partially successful from an erective point of view, and thereafter he was secondarily impotent.

After several months they consulted their physician and were assured that this loss of erective power comes to all men as they age and that there was nothing to be done. Loath to accept the verdict, they tried on several occasions to force an erection with no success. Mr. A was seriously depressed for several months but recovered without apparent incident. . .

The marital unit . . . accepted their "fate." The impotence was acknowledged to be a natural result of the aging process. This resigned attitude lasted approximately four years.

Although initially the marital unit and their physician had fallen into the sociocultural trap of accepting the concept of sexual inadequacy as an aging phenomenon, the more Mr. and Mrs. A considered their dysfunction the less willing they were to accept the blanket concept that lack of erective security was purely the result of the aging process. They reasoned that they were in good health, had no basic concerns as a marital unit, and took good care of themselves physically. . . . Each partner underwent a thorough medical checkup and sought several authoritative opinions (none of them encouraging), refusing to accept the concept of the irreversibility of their sexual distress. Finally, approximately five years after the onset of a full degree of secondary impotence, they were referred for treatment.

*From Masters, W. J., and Johnson, V. E. *Human sexual inadequacy.* (Boston: Little Brown, 1970), pp. 326–328. Used with permission.

required approximately one week of therapy to restore the sexual functioning of this couple. They regained their confidence, and the sexual dysfunction disappeared when they came to realize that the symptoms they were experiencing—increased time to attain an erection and reduced seminal fluid in the man, decreased vaginal lubrication in the woman— were not abnormal in any way and that they could continue to enjoy sexual relations in spite of these age-related changes.

The therapeutic procedures employed by Masters and Johnson produced improvement in 75 percent of the elderly men and 60 percent of the elderly women treated in one investigation. These 56 couples were, however, a select group of individuals whose sexual problems were of fairly short duration. Other therapists have not always reported such dramatic results.

A number of other therapeutic techniques, ranging from the viewing of pornographic movies and live strippers to self-stimulation and sex education programs, have been advocated by sex therapists. Butler and Lewis (1976) are among those who recommend masturbation by elderly people who do not have partners and wish to reduce their sexual tensions. When performed without guilt or other negative feelings, masturbation can help prevent the discomfort and impotence that often results from long abstinence from sexual intercourse. Butler and Lewis (1976) have also joined Masters and Johnson (1970) and other gerontologists in proposing a program of sex education for the aged. Such a program should include information on techniques of intercourse specific to the needs of the elderly, in addition to ways of coping with fears of sexual inadequacy, the reputed dangers of sex to health, and the disapproving attitudes of relatives and the larger society.

MARRIAGE AND UNMARRIAGE

The majority of elderly men are married (78 percent), but the majority of elderly women are unmarried (61 percent). This fact by itself would seem to be a contradiction except when one recalls that a larger percentage of people over 65 are women (60 percent) than men (40 percent). (U.S. Bureau of the Census, 1981). Furthermore, over one-third of elderly married men are married to women who are under 65 years old (U.S. Dept. of Health & Human Services, 1979), due in part to the fact that, on the average, men marry women who are four years younger. These and other statistics on the marital status of older Americans are given in Figure 7-2 and Table 7-1. Note especially that although the percentages of divorced men and women are almost identical, the percentage of women who are

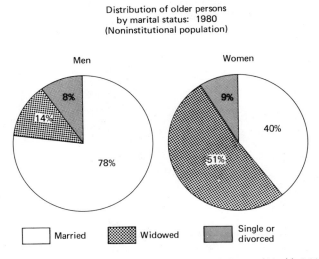

Distribution of older persons
by marital status: 1980
(Noninstitutional population)

Men   Women

Married   Widowed   Single or divorced

Figure 7-2 Distribution of older persons by marital status. (U.S. Dept. of Health & Human Services, 1981.)

Sexual Behavior   **149**

TABLE 7-1 PERCENTAGES OF AMERICANS AGE 65 AND OVER IN FOUR MARITAL STATUS GROUPS*

Marital Status	Year			
	1965	1970	1975	1980
Men				
Single (never married)	7	8	5	5
Married	71	72	79	78
Widowed	20	18	14	14
Divorced	3	2	2	4
Women				
Single (never married)	8	8	6	6
Married	36	36	39	40
Widowed	54	55	52	51
Divorced	2	2	3	3

*Adapted from *The Economics of Aging* by James H. Schultz. © 1976 by Wadsworth Publishing Company, Inc. Reprinted by permission of Wadsworth Publishing Company, Belmont, CA 94002. 1980 figures from U.S. Dept. of Health and Human Services, 1981.

widows (51 percent) is substantially greater than that of men who are widowers (14 percent).

The pattern of sex differences in the percentages of elderly married and widowed men and women is similar for all ethnic groups in the United States. Twice as many elderly men as women are married, and nearly three times as many women as men are widows. Also, as shown in Table 7-1, the percentages of single, married, widowed, and divorced elderly women remained fairly constant from 1965 to 1980. In contrast, the percentages of

TABLE 7-2 PERCENTAGES OF TWO AGE GROUPS OF OLDER AMERICANS IN FOUR MARITAL STATUS CATEGORIES*

Marital Status	Age	
	65 to 74	75 and Over
Men		
Single (never married)	4.3	5.5
Married	81.8	68.3
Widowed	8.8	23.3
Divorced	3.1	1.2
Women		
Single (never married)	5.8	5.8
Married	47.3	22.3
Widowed	41.9	69.4
Divorced	3.3	1.5

*From U.S. Bureau of the Census, *Current Population Reports*, Series P-20, No. 287. Washington, D.C.: U.S. Government Printing Office, 1975, p. 8.

single and widowed elderly men decreased significantly and the percentage of elderly men who were married increased significantly from 1965 to 1975. In addition, as shown in Table 7-2, in 1975 the percentages of married men and women in the 65 to 74 age bracket were higher than the corresponding percentages in the 75+ age bracket. These statistics, plus the fact that the percentages of widows and widowers are higher in the 75+ age bracket than the corresponding percentages in the 65 to 74 age bracket, are as would be expected.

The Marital Relationship

The percentage of elderly Americans who are married has risen during the past ten years, and is predicted to continue increasing during the rest of this century. Chief among the many reasons why marriage appears to be becoming more popular among the elderly are the improved health and economic status of older people. But whatever their reasons for staying married or remarrying, marriage is the most important of all interpersonal relationships for the majority of elderly people.

It was noted in Chapter 1 that married men tend to live longer than unmarried men. This finding has been attributed, at least in part, to the closer social ties and high social status of married men (Kobrin & Hendershot, 1977). Other explanations for the greater average life span of married men have also been offered, but most authorities agree that psychological stress plays a role in longevity. One connection among marital status, longevity, and psychological stress is seen in the fact that the suicide rate is significantly higher for elderly men who are divorced or widowed than for those who are married.

Because of the physiological and psychological changes accompanying aging, the relationship between a married couple undergoes modification in later life. In happy marriages, these changes produce greater equality among marital partners. Equality is more likely because in some ways the sexes become more alike with aging: Both men and women become more eccentric and preoccupied with their own lives and personal needs. But after retirement the role relationships between the sexes may reverse, with women becoming more aggressive or assertive and men more submissive and nurturant. Aging tends to make men more mellow, less ambitious, and less aggressive, whereas women become more assertive and controlling. According to Neugarten (1977, p. 637), "older men seemed more receptive than younger men to their affiliative, nurturant, and sensual promptings; older women to their aggressive and egocentric impulses." This pattern is the opposite of typical sex-role behavior during the early adult years.

Rather than developing suddenly in old age, Gutmann (1964, 1967) maintained that the relatively greater aggressiveness manifested by elderly women results from the release of aggressive urges that have been there all the time. During the years when she is rearing her children, the typical married woman suppresses her aggression, as is required by the nurturant,

Figure 7-3 Changing sex roles in old age. (H. Armstrong Roberts.)

mothering role. But when her children have grown up and moved away, she then feels free to express her aggressiveness with impunity.

Marital Problems and Divorce

Elderly married couples often experience great pleasure in just being alone with each other. This idyllic picture is, however, far from universal. As with all married people, elderly couples experience problems of adjustment. Retirement, chronic illness, lack of money, and reduced sexual interaction are all potential sources of stress and marital friction in later life. Consequently, problems of marital adjustment in old age are particularly severe for elderly couples with insufficient income, physical disabilities, and low education (Duvall, 1977).

Being able to stay happily married into old age is attributable to a combination of affection, shared interests, habit, and a respect for the individuality of one's spouse. Rollins and Feldman (1970) have characterized the happily married older couple as similar to the young, newly married couple in their overall feeling of peacefulness and lack of stress.

Marriage, in old age as at other times, does not guarantee happiness, but older people who are married tend to be happier than those who remain unattached.

As is true of social adjustment in general, marital happiness during old age is positively related to marital happiness in the earlier years. Happy marriages tend to remain happy, whereas unhappy marriages do not improve with age unless there are marked changes in the attitudes and actions of the marital partners. A marriage is, of course, not necessarily a happy one simply because the couple stay together. They may remain incompatible but unseparated for decades, living under an "armed truce" and finally "making the break" when their children have grown up and moved out.

Between one-half and one million elderly Americans (2 to 3 percent of those 65 years and over) are divorced, and another 10,000+ get divorced every year. Despite the magnitude of these figures, the divorce rate among late middle-aged and older adults is significantly lower than the national average. Many people who might be better off divorced remain together because of the cultural stigma attached to divorce. Even in couples who have been married as long as 30 to 50 years, however, divorce is not as rare as it once was. In any event, most people who get divorced remarry sooner or later.

Widowhood

According to U.S. census figures, 51 percent of women but only 14 percent of men in the 65-and-over age bracket are widowed. Because of the shorter life expectancy of black men, the proportion of widows to widowers is greater among blacks than among whites.

As noted previously, the larger percentage of widows compared to widowers can be attributed to the fact that women live longer than men and tend to marry men who are older than they. It is also easier for widowers to remarry, which they usually do and to younger women. This endorses the cultural stereotypes, shared by elderly women themselves, that physical attractiveness is more important in women than men and that aging women are less attractive than aging men.

So where does the elderly widow seek companionship, and how does she live if she is unwilling to search for a new husband or unable to find one? The picture is not as bleak as this question may seem to imply. Widows, both young and old, are much more likely to find companionship with other widows than widowers are with other widowers. It is true that, as a group, elderly widows experience frequent loneliness, especially at first (Lopata, 1973). But the great majority are able to cope with the loss of a husband, a process in which having a close friend or confidant can be of help. In any event, perhaps because it is expected, widowhood is usually less traumatic for older women than for younger ones.

The loss of a husband obviously creates problems for a woman; her income, social life, and living accommodations may all decline. The effects of widowhood, however, are not all bad. Even those who were happily married, and who are admittedly lonely at times, usually become more competent and independent than they were when the husband was alive. This is less likely to occur, however, if the widow was extremely dependent on her husband or identified too closely with him. And strange as it may seem, those widows who experienced the greatest amount of difficulty getting along with their husbands often find themselves least able to get along without them. Whatever the cause—a feeling of guilt, abandonment, or anger produced by frustration, adjustment is often quite difficult for widows whose marriages were unhappy.

Approximately one-half of all widows live alone, and only about 10 percent live with their married children (Lopata, 1971). Some live with relatives, others in a group situation or home, and still others remarry. Many widows prefer to live alone, even when it means being lonely, because they value their freedom and independence. Most elderly widows miss their husband's companionship, but they now have the time to devote to interests and to develop abilities that were suppressed or lay dormant during the years of service to their husband.

Although the problems of adjusting to the loss of a spouse are often worse for a woman than for a man, any man who has lost his wife by death or divorce is faced with loneliness and a need for companionship. An elderly widow usually has more friends available to her than an elderly widower, who may discover that he was more dependent on his wife for physical and emotional support than he realized when she was living. Because men are usually not as close to other people as women, widowers are apparently more lonely and consequently need marriage more than widows do. This is one reason why the great majority of widowers remarry within a year or so after their wife's death.

Remarriage

A few years ago there was a road sign at Sun City, near Tampa, Florida, that said: "DRIVE SLOWLY. GRANDPARENTS PLAYING." For a number of reasons, one being the reduction in social security benefits that formerly occurred when retired people married, the elderly have sometimes engaged in what geriatric counselors refer to as "unmarriages of convenience." These are companionable, sexual relationships not formalized by a license or ceremony. The social security law was changed in 1977 so that newlyweds who are 60 or over now lose none of their benefits. Certain older people, especially men, still confess to enjoying the secretive, "swinging singles" experience of living together without benefit of clergy. But most elderly couples are not swingers, and elect to marry rather than face the censure of conventional society and their own consciences.

Marriage, in old age as at other times of life, does not guarantee happiness, but older people who remarry after the death of a spouse tend to be happier than those who remain unattached. This is perhaps truer for men than for women, because many single women make better adjustments in late life than married women. In any case, twice as many elderly men as elderly women remarry after the death or divorce of a spouse (Butler & Lewis, 1977). Among the factors responsible for the higher remarriage rate in elderly men are the greater number of available elderly women and the cultural bias against elderly women remarrying. Nevertheless, the frequency of remarriages in both older men and older women more than doubled from 1960 to 1973. Interestingly enough, the remarriage rate among the elderly was greater in the West and South than in other sections of the country.

Among the reasons older women give for getting married are companionship, a desire to take care of someone, and intimacy (Jacobs & Vinick, 1979). Thus warmth and aloneness, rather than the physical act of sex, were stressed as reasons for remarrying by the elderly women interviewed by Vinick. Similarly, McKain (1969) found that few newly married elderly people believe in romantic love, but they remarry because of the need for companionship, affection, and regard.

According to Vinick (Jacobs & Vinick, 1979), it is easier for older men and women to remarry than one may think. A typical couple meet through friends at a dinner party or other social occasion, begin seeing each other, and eventually marry. Elderly men are usually more eager to get involved and remarry than elderly women, but sometimes the traditional sex roles are reversed:

Figure 7-4 Social functions sponsored by Golden Age and Senior Citizens organizations provide opportunities for unmarried elderly people to become acquainted. (© Rollie McKenna/Photo Researchers, Inc.)

He was sitting near me at the Golden Agers, and I didn't even know him. He was looking so depressed. You could see that the man needs something. The trouble is, when I see someone lonely, I want to know what's the matter. He was sitting just like a chicken without a head (sic). After that, he went his way, I went my way. So (the next meeting), he was sitting there again. So, my friend said, "Let's sit down with him. It will warm him up a little." It was awfully windy. We sat down, and then we started to talk. You know the way it is . . . (Vinick, 1977, p. 6)

Older people who decide to remarry should consider such factors as how well acquainted they are, whether the proposed marriage meets with the approval of their children and friends, whether they will have sufficient income, how their estate(s) will be divided among their relatives, where they will live (preferably not in a home previously shared with the first spouse), and how they plan to spend the rest of their lives. Such considerations may seem to be unromantic, but a marriage's chances of survival are greater when they are taken into account.

Singlehood

In 1980, 5 percent of the elderly men and 6 percent of the elderly women in the United States had never been married. Considering the fact that elderly singles do not live as long as elderly marrieds, one might expect to find the former group a lonely, dispirited lot. But this does not seem to be the case. For example, the results of interviews conducted by Gubrium (1975) of twenty-two never married people aged 60 to 94 revealed that these singles were less lonely than the average elderly person. On the whole, they were more independent and competent than average. As a result of having lived alone for so many years, they were able to develop feelings of self-reliance and "copability" that the stresses and changes of later life so often demand. Despite having fewer social relationships, they felt happy and satisfied with their lives, expressing no need for an intimate relationship and remaining single by choice rather than by necessity.

Closeness can, of course, be attained in other ways than by sexual and marital intimacy. Well-adjusted singles are frequently close to their pets and nonrelatives. Being free of the demands of a spouse and children, they are also able to devote more time to social interactions outside a family setting. Furthermore, elderly singles usually have closer ties to their relatives than elderly marrieds do, which is particularly true in the case of sisters.

FAMILY RELATIONSHIPS

It is estimated that 94 percent of elderly people have living family members around whom their social life is usually centered (Troll, 1971). Approximately 80 percent have living sisters and/or brothers, but an even greater percentage have children and grandchildren.

Elderly couples live together for an average of 16 years after the last adult child has left home. During this period, which has been called the postparental phase of the family cycle, the children have moved out but are not forgotten. As a result, some elderly women become depressed (the "empty nest" syndrome). Others, by way of contrast, discovering that they now have more time to devote to and achieve satisfaction from their marriage, gain a new enthusiasm for life.

Elderly Parents and Adult Children

Exactly when the last child leaves home varies with ethnic group and social class. Middle-class and white Americans usually have fewer children than lower-class Americans. Consequently, there are more children present and for a longer time in a typical lower-class family. A similar pattern of more children in lower socioeconomic and minority group families prevails in other countries. White elderly Americans also live farther away from their children, although in most instances it is less than an hour's drive (Sussman, 1976).

The nostalgic multigenerational household of yesteryear (see Figure 7-5) was certainly more a matter of economic necessity than desire on the part of older and younger family members. Today, fewer than 30 percent of elderly Americans live with their children, and an even smaller percentage wish to do so. For example, almost 100 percent of the elderly people interviewed by Streib and Thompson (1965) stated that under no circumstances would they consent to move in with their children. Realizing that they would have trouble keeping quiet about mistakes and that their advice would seldom be welcome in their children's homes, the vast majority of elderly people prefer the independence and freedom of living alone.

> Never try to live with your children. It's no good. I stayed there (at her daughter's house) a couple of months and I couldn't stand it. The kids, you know, have to do what they want to do. When I was listenin' to my TV, they were playin' games on the other side. . . . My daughter has a husband you can't take to, you know what I mean? The minute he come home, I went upstairs and I stayed there. (Vinick, 1977, p. 3)

Although not desiring to live with them, most elderly parents continue to receive much satisfaction from their adult children. They expect them to visit often, an expectation with which the children generally concur, and to write frequently when they are too far away for frequent visits. The results of surveys (see Shanas et al., 1968) indicate that contact between elderly parents and their adult children is not merely a matter of expectation; a majority see each other every day.

Most elderly parents and children also continue to assist each other in various ways. Older people provide their children with money, household products (e.g., needlework and woodwork), and services (e.g., baby-sitting,

Figure 7-5 A 19th-century American farm family. Wearing their best clothes, a Mormon family proudly poses before their home. Multigenerational households such as the one depicted here were more a matter of economic necessity than choice. (A.J. Russell Photo, 1868–1869. Union Pacific Railroad Museum Collection.)

legal advice). Because mother–daughter relationships are usually closer than father–son relationships, the most frequent direction of help is from mother to daughter. It is a more common practice for elderly parents to assist their adult children than to receive help from them (Kivett, 1976). In some instances, however, old age may be a time of role-reversal with respect to one's children—the aged parent now playing the role of the nurtured one and the son or daughter the role of caregiver. This is more likely to occur when the adult child feels that the parent is no longer competent to handle his or her own affairs.

Grandparents and Grandchildren

Less closely related to them than their children, but still quite important members of an elderly person's family, are his or her grandchildren. Seventy percent of all elderly Americans have grandchildren, and 40 percent have great-grandchildren. These grandchildren and great-grandchildren have multiple meanings for the elderly, including a source of biological renewal or continuity, the opportunity to succeed in new socioemotional and resource roles, and a potential source of pride and vicarious achievement (Neugarten & Weinstein, 1968). The new social role of grandparent brings with it the pleasure and excitement of a new personality that the grandparent has helped create, or, alternatively, a sense of growing old and a remoteness from the present and future.

The feeling of remoteness and insignificance that many elderly people feel in modern Western society[1] is in great contrast to the esteem in which they were held in preindustrial cultures or are held in oriental countries such as Japan. The wisdom and practical knowledge of the elderly is valued less in the technologically based industrialized societies of the United States and Western Europe than in societies with a traditional reverence for old age. Furthermore, the tendency of our society to segregate the generations has reduced the degree of social interaction and emotional interchange among different age groups, an important function of the extended family of yesteryear. This is unfortunate, because children need their grandparents as much as the latter need their grandchildren. Maintaining too much psychological distance between the young and old because of some irrational fear of old age is a disservice to both groups. Curtin (1972, p. 36) expresses the fear of many adults that:

> mine will be the last generation to know old people as friends, to have a sense of what growing old means, to respect and understand man's mortality and his courage in the face of death. Mine may be the last generation to have a sense of living history, of stories passed from generation to generation, of identity established by family history. It is such an unholy waste.

Grandparents, who can add a sense of identity and stability to the family and society as a whole, vary extensively in their perceptions of the grandparenting role. On the one hand, there are those who see themselves as mere babysitters for someone else's children, and on the other hand, there are those who relate to their grandchildren with joy and love. The latter group often find that the role of grandparent is even more emotionally gratifying than that of parent. To these people the grandparent role involves its traditional elements of teacher and advisor to the young.

The age of the grandparents has some relationship to the way in which they respond to their grandchildren. Younger grandparents are more likely to be somewhat fun-seeking in their role, as if they were the child's playmate. Older grandparents tend to be more distant and formal in their behavior toward their grandchildren, becoming close only on special occasions (Christmas, birthdays, etc.) (Neugarten & Weinstein, 1968).

Most grandparents seem to enjoy the role of grandparent, but this varies with the age of the grandparent as well as with the grandparent's sex and the age and sex of the grandchild. Teenage grandchildren are appreciated least, and grandmothers usually enjoy interacting with their grandchildren more than grandfathers do. The relationship between grandmother and granddaughter is usually the strongest, probably because grandmothers have more pertinent knowledge and skills to communicate to their granddaughters than grandfathers do to grandchildren.

And how do grandchildren perceive their grandparents? To provide answers to this question, Kahana and Kahana (1970a) asked three groups of children (ages 4 to 5, ages 8 to 9, and ages 11 to 12) a number of questions about their grandparents and other elderly people. One finding was that all age groups of children felt closer to their mother's parents than to their father's parents and liked their mother's mother best of all. When asked what kind of grandparents they liked best, the 4 to 5 year olds indicated that they preferred grandparents who gave them food, love, and presents; the 8 to 9 year olds liked grandparents who did fun things with them; the 11 to 12 year olds preferred grandparents who indulged them, letting them do whatever they wished. Kahana and Kahana (1970a) concluded that the particular "style" of grandparenting that fits the child's needs varies with the age of the child. Thus, in grandparenting, as in response to all of later life's challenges, flexibility is required.

SUMMARY

The incidence of intercourse and other sexual outlets in old age varies extensively from person to person. As indicated by the findings of the Kinsey report and Duke University studies, elderly men are more sexually active and interested than elderly women, and the young–old are more active than the old–old. Interest in sex is greater than actual intercourse, and the frequency of intercourse is higher for healthy people and those of lower socioeconomic status. In elderly couples the decision whether to stop having sexual intercourse is usually influenced more by the husband's condition than the wife's and is typically made by him.

The studies of Masters and Johnson revealed that although marked physiological changes in the structure and functioning of the sex organs take place in later life, with proper medical and psychological treatment, most couples can continue having intercourse into their 70s and 80s. The treatment of sexual problems in old age involves physical measures such as hormone replacement, sexual reeducation, and psychotherapy.

The degree of sexual activity in old age is as much a matter of attitudes as it is of physiological changes. Although public attitudes, and the degree to which they are internalized by the elderly, are changing, too many people—both young and old—still regard elderly people who are interested in sex as dirty old men and frustrated old women.

Masters and Johnson have pioneered in rapid, effective treatment of sexual inadequacies at all stages of life. In one investigation, their therapeutic procedures resulted in improvements in 75 percent of the elderly men and 60 percent of the elderly women who were treated. Other techniques, including the viewing of pornographic films and live strippers, self-stimulation, and sex education, have also been used in the treatment of sexual disorders in the aged.

A majority of elderly men but a minority of elderly women are married, a difference due primarily to the substantially larger number of older women than older men. The percentages of married men and women decline with age, as more members of both sexes become widowed. The relationships between married men and women tend to change in later life, with wives becoming more assertive and controlling and husbands more submissive and nurturant.

The percentage of elderly people who get divorced is relatively small, but each year more than 10,000 older Americans obtain divorces. Divorce in both middle-aged and older Americans is becoming more common but not nearly as common as between younger married people.

Because there are many more widows than widowers and widowhood usually causes more difficulties for women than for men, the problems encountered by the widowed elderly are primarily those of widows. Among these problems are reduced income, loneliness and less social life, and poorer living arrangements. Although painful, widows usually learn to cope with these problems and in the process become more competent, independent, and self-confident.

The greater availability of unattached women, added to the fact that men seem to need marriage more than women do, leads to a greater percentage of remarriages in elderly men. Both women and men who remarry or marry for the first time in later life do so more for companionship and closeness than for the physical act of sex.

Research findings indicate that married men are happier and live longer than unmarried men. As a group, elderly women who remain single are neither chronically frustrated nor deeply unhappy. An adult lifetime of living alone and taking care of themselves appears to make them more self-confident and capable, and consequently they do not seem to require intimate relationships with men.

The large majority of elderly parents desire to live in a separate residence from their adult children but to maintain frequent contact with them. These elderly parents continue to attain satisfaction from their children, assisting them in numerous ways. The role of grandparent also provides satisfaction to most older people, but the style in which that role is played varies with the age and sex of both grandparents and grandchildren. Grandmothers, and the mother's mother in particular, interact more with their grandchildren and are usually preferred by the latter to their grandfathers.

SUGGESTED READINGS

Butler, R. N., & Lewis, M. I. *Love and sex after sixty: A guide for men and women in their later years.* New York: Harper & Row, 1976.

Jacobs, R. H., & Vinick, B. H. *Re-engagement in later life: Re-employment and remarriage.* Stamford, Conn.: Greylock Publishers, 1979.

Masters, W. H., & Johnson, V. E. Sex after sixty-five. *The Saturday Evening Post*, 1977, *249*(2), 48–52.

Morgan, L. A. A re-examination of widowhood and morale. *Journal of Gerontology,* 1976, *31,* 687–695.

Robertson, J. F. Significance of grandparents: Perceptions of young adult grandchildren. *The Gerontologist,* 1976, *16,* 137–140.

Rubin, L. *Sexual life after sixty.* New York: Basic Books, 1976.

Solnick, R. (Ed.). *Sexuality and aging* (Rev. ed.). Los Angeles: University of Southern California, 1976.

Sussman, M. B. The family life of old people. In R. H. Binstock & E. Shanas (Eds.), *Handbook of aging and the social sciences.* New York: Van Nostrand, 1976, pp. 218–243.

Treas, J., & Vanhilst, A. Marriage and remarriage among older Americans. *The Gerontologist,* 1976, *16,* 132–136.

Troll, L. E., Miller, S. J., & Atchley, R. C. *Families in later life.* Belmont, Calif.: Wadsworth, 1979.

NOTE

[1]An exception is Ireland, which, because of its primarily agriculturally based economy controlled by older people, continues to hold the elderly in high regard. Another semi-European country in which very old people are admired is the Soviet Union (Hendricks & Hendricks, 1977).

Social Status and Roles

It has been said that, next to dying, the realization that one is aging is the most shocking event of one's life. This is probably truer in a youth-oriented culture such as ours, where people spend considerable time and money trying to slow down or at least camouflage the effects of aging. Many elderly people attempt to conceal their ages from others as well as from themselves. Some never come to use the word "old" as self-descriptive, even when they are in their 70s (Taves & Hansen, 1963). Aside from its connotation that the termination of one's earthly existence is approaching, "old" in our society too often means uselessness, rolelessness, and a consequent loss of status.

STATUS AND ATTITUDES

The relatively low social status, or prestige, accorded the elderly in our society is not universal in time and place. Some primitive societies, in particular, show great respect and even reverence for the aged. For example, the Jivaro Indians of the Andes believe that old people have supernatural powers that increase with age. But in poorer tribal groups the elderly are viewed merely as a burden and are sometimes killed. Other primitive peoples, such as the Eskimos and certain Native American and African tribes, have respected the experience and wisdom of the elderly

163

but left them to die when they could no longer take care of themselves. Older people in these societies have usually accepted the necessity of their demise and even assisted in it. Thus an old man in a South Sea island native group, seeing himself as no longer useful or wanted, might voluntarily paddle out to sea and perish. Similarily, after deciding that he was ready to die, an older Native American warrior would tie himself to a stake in hostile territory and then fight off braves and warriors of the hostile tribe until he was eventually killed.

The status, or position of value, honor, or prestige, of elderly people throughout history has varied with the nature of the society. In nomadic, food-gathering and hunting societies, where strength, speed, and physical skill were critical for survival, the status of the aged—consistent with their contributions to the survival of the group—was typically quite low. In contrast, agricultural societies, depending more on the knowledge and advice of the elderly, have traditonally accorded them high status. In such societies elderly people have been able to amass wealth and hence to demand respect and consideration. Subsistence systems based almost entirely on agriculture characterized Western societies until the nineteenth century, when the machine age and mass education intervened to diminish the high status of the elderly.

It is still true today that the elderly enjoy high status in those countries in which the economy is based almost entirely on agricultural production. Besides economics, however, there are other important variables that affect the prestige of the elderly, such as the type of political system, religion, and cultural traditions. Older Japanese, for example, are accorded great respect, but Japan is a highly industrialized nation.

Despite the fact that their special knowledge and skills may be seen as less valuable in a technologically more advanced society than in a predominantly agricultural one, it might be expected that the Western world's emphasis on humanism and mutual respect would produce more considerate treatment of the elderly. But according to many observers, old people in modern European and American society are not always treated as human beings. Attitudes toward old age, of course, vary considerably from person to person in the same Western nation. Even the intellectual elite of a nation have expressed different viewpoints toward old age. For example, the English poet Robert Browning, in his 1864 poem "Rabbi Ben Ezra," extended an invitation to

> Grow old along with me!
> The best is yet to be,
> The last of life, for which the first was made.
> Our times are in His hand
> Who saith "A whole I planned,
> —Youth shows but half;
> trust God;
> see all nor be afraid.

The response of another English poet, Matthew Arnold, in his 1867 poem "Growing Old," was

> What is it to grow old?
> Is it to lose the glory of form?
> The lustre of the eye?
> Is it for beauty to forgo her wreath?
> —Yes, but not this alone.

Despite the concern and respect of many Western Europeans and Americans for the status of the elderly, to Simone de Beauvoir (1972) it is Western society that truly degrades the old. She noted that sometimes an old man is a respected, venerated sage, but more often he is viewed as a ridiculous, doddering old fool and mocked by the young. Bernice Neugarten (1971) takes a somewhat more optimistic point of view but still recognizes the tendency of American society to stereotype the old as poor, isolated, sick, and unhappy, on the one hand, or as powerful, rigid, and reactionary, on the other. Neugarten points out that these stereotypes influence our behavior and make the prospect of old age very unattractive.

Stereotypes and Misconceptions

Stereotypes, or oversimplified, often caricatural descriptions of the aged, are found not only in popular entertainment media but even in classical literature:

> The sixth age shifts
> Into the lean and slipid pantelone
> With spectacles on nose and pouch on side;
> His youthful hose, well-sewed, a world too wide
> For his shrunk shank, and his big manly voice
> Turning again to childish treble, pipes
> And whistles in his sound. Last seen of all,
> That ends this strange eventual history,
> Is second childishness, and mere oblivion,
> Sans teeth, sans eyes, sans taste, sans everything.
>
> –William Shakespeare, *As You Like It*

Such overgeneralizations and caricatures have often been reinforced by scientific researchers who limit their study of the effects of old age to institutionalized samples of elderly people. Because no more than 5 percent of the elderly are in institutions, and are certainly not representative of the entire old-age population, the resulting unflattering descriptions lead to general misconceptions of what old people are like.

Robert Butler (1974, 1975), who coined the term *ageism* to refer to the social stereotyping of older people as well as to the social discrimination against them, cites many examples of negative attitudes toward the elderly. Future physicians, whose first encounter with an older person in medical school is in the form of a cadaver, may engage in gallows humor and refer to older patients as "crocks," "turkey," and "dirt-balls." Furthermore, Alex Comfort (1976) reported knowing licensed physicians who ridiculed and belittled older people whom they viewed as insulting to their medical skills.

All in all, health professionals are significantly more negative in their attitudes toward treating older people than they are toward treating younger ones (Spence, Feigenbaum, Fitzgerald & Roth, 1968). It has been suggested that the stereotyping of the elderly by professional people may serve as a kind of justification for not attending to their needs. Personnel directors, for example, may use stereotypes as a rationalization for ignoring older workers (Pines, 1976).

To quote Butler (1974, p. 11): "Ageism can be seen as a process of systematic stereotyping of and discrimination against people because they are old—just as racism and sexism can accomplish this with skin color and gender. Old people are categorized as senile, rigid in thought and manner, old fashioned in morality and skills. Ageism allows the younger generations to see older people as different from themselves. Thus they subtly cease to identify with their elders as human beings." This quotation refers to several stereotypes pertaining to the aged. Among the other stereotypes, myths, or misconceptions cited by Butler and other (Comfort, 1976; Perry, 1974; Verwoerdt, 1969a) are the following:

1. Most old people are ill or in poor health.
2. Most old people are senile or in their second childhood.
3. Most old people are rigid or inflexible.
4. Most old people can't do a good job and should retire.
5. Most old people have no sex life.
6. Most old people want to disengage or gradually withdraw from active participation.
7. Most old people live alone, abandoned by their families and other relatives.
8. Most old people do live or should live in institutions (homes, hospitals, etc.).

There are other myths or misconceptions, for example, the myth that conceives of old age as a magic land where everyone is a happy retiree from the worries of the world and the myth that people automatically start going downhill at chronological age 65.

Research on Attitudes Toward Aging and the Aged

Research on attitudes toward old age has employed a variety of techniques, ranging from the simple "Yes—No" poll questions of Gallup, Harris, and Roper to the more carefully constructed attitude questionnaires of Kogan (1961) and Palmore (1980) (see Table 8-1). The results of several older research studies with subjects from age 8 to college level reinforce the notion of a generally negative attitude toward the elderly.

Table 8-1 FACTS ON AGING QUIZ*

The reader is encouraged to test his/her knowledge and attitudes about aging by taking the following quiz. Specific items on the quiz are considered in the appropriate chapters of the text.

Directions: Mark "True" or "False"

1. The majority of old people are senile (i.e., defective memory, disoriented, or demented).
2. All five senses tend to decline in old age.
3. Most old people have no interest in, or capacity for, sexual relations.
4. Lung vital capacity tends to decline in old age.
5. The majority of old people feel miserable most of the time.
6. Physical strength tends to decline in old age.
7. At least one-tenth of the aged are living in long-stay institutions (i.e., nursing homes, mental hospitals, homes for the aged, etc.).
8. Aged drivers have fewer accidents per driver than drivers under age 65.
9. Most older workers cannot work as effectively as younger workers.
10. About 80% of the aged are healthy enough to carry out their normal activities.
11. Most old people are set in their ways and unable to change.
12. Old people usually take longer to learn something new.
13. It is almost impossible for most old people to learn something new.
14. The reaction time of most old people tends to be slower than reaction time of younger people.
15. In general, most old people are pretty much alike.
16. The majority of old people report that they are seldom bored.
17. The majority of old people are socially isolated and lonely.
18. Older workers have fewer accidents than younger workers.
19. Over 15% of the U.S. population are now age 65 or over.
20. Most medical practitioners tend to give low priority to the aged.
21. The majority of older people have incomes below the poverty level (as defined by the federal government).
22. The majority of old people are working or would like to have some kind of work to do (including housework and volunteer work).
23. Older people tend to become more religious as they age.
24. The majority of old people report that they are seldom irritated or angry.
25. The health and socioeconomic status of older people (compared to younger people) in the year 2000 will probably be worse or about the same as that of today's older people.

*After Palmore, 1980. Reprinted by permission of *The Gerontologist,* Vol. 20, No. 6 (1980).
The odd-numbered items are false, the even-numbered ones true.

Kogan and Shelton's (1962) sample of college students tended to downgrade the appearance of old people, felt that the old resent the young, and stated that they preferred to avoid direct personal contact with the aged. Kastenbaum and Durkee (1964) also found that adolescents usually have little regard for the elderly.

The results of later investigations of the attitudes of children (Hickey & Kalish, 1968; Serock, Seefeldt, Jantz & Galper, 1977) substantiate earlier findings that children have a generally unpleasant image of growing old and old people. In a study conducted at the University of Maryland's Center on Aging, Serock et al. (1977) found that most of the 180 children (ages 3 to 11) whom they questioned described the elderly in negative ways. The elderly were seen as "wrinkled, short, and gray-haired," people who "chew funny," "don't go out much," "sit all day and watch TV in their rocking chairs," and "have heart attacks and die." When asked how they felt about growing old themselves, all but a few of the children stated that they simply didn't want to do it.[1] Such stereotypes and attitudes, which are communicated by parents, teachers, and peers, appear in many famous books and plays and are shared by lay and professional people alike. In fact, as Butler (1975) points out, old people frequently look at themselves in a negative light, thereby perpetuating and reinforcing the social stereotypes of old age.

Indirect evidence of the negative image of old age in the elderly themselves was obtained by Kastenbaum and Durkee (1964), who found that people over 70 consistently classified themselves as middle aged. These findings confirm those of Phillips (1962) in a study of 346 people who were 60 years old and above. Sixty-one percent of Phillips's group classified themselves as middle aged, 67 percent thought that other people viewed them as middle aged, and 62 percent stated that they felt younger than most people their age.

To obtain more representative information on the attitudes and images of old age and the aged, the National Council on the Aging (1975) commissioned the Lou Harris public opinion agency to conduct an interview survey of a cross section of American adults. The results of 4,250 interviews make abundantly clear that adult Americans harbor many misconceptions about what old age is really like. Some of the results of the survey, those comparing the general adult sample's expectations of the "serious" problems of old age with the personal experiences reported by the elderly themselves, are summarized in Figure 8-1. Half or more of the general adult group expected poor health, insufficient money to live on, and loneliness to be very serious problems, but one-fourth or less of the elderly sample actually reported these as problems. It is interesting that many of the old people who were questioned gave different answers when asked about other people than they did when asked about themselves. They tended to see themselves as having fewer problems than other old people, such as the "old fogey" or "old biddy" down the street. Somewhat encouraging to aging Americans is the fact that three-fourths of the elderly who were polled confessed that they were pleasantly surprised to find that old age was better than they expected it to be.

Harris concluded that the elderly do have problems—inadequate money, poor health, loneliness, poor medical care, fear of crime, and difficulties in getting from place to place. These problems, however, are not as pervasive as the general public believes them to be, and perhaps the greatest problem of the elderly is the attitude of the general public toward them.

Elderly Images on Television

The fact that television has an impact on the attitudes and values of the entire population of viewers, which includes a large majority of the American population, is undeniable. Unfortunately, the images of the

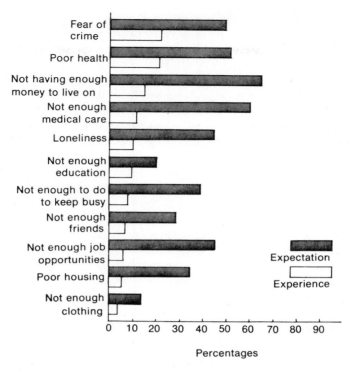

Figure 8-1 Selected results of a Harris survey comparing the general American public's expectations of the serious problems of older people with the personal experiences reported by a sample of older people themselves. (Copyright © 1975 Ziff-Davis Publishing Company.)

elderly depicted on American television have emphasized the traditional stereotype of older people as "ugly, toothless, sexless, incontinent, senile, confused, and helpless." ("New Image. . . ," 1977). Too often they are depicted as narrow-minded, in poor health, floundering financially, and sexually dissatisfied (see Kubey, 1980).

Although a number of well-known actors and actresses in their 60s, 70s, and 80s are still quite active in their profession, until fairly recently elderly people have either been ignored or served primarily as objects of humor and ridicule for comedians. Such comical roles as that of Fred Sanford in the sitcom "Sanford and Son" may be amusing, but they reinforce the negative stereotype of the elderly as lazy, hypochondriacal, and oafish. Furthermore, it has been a rarity to see old people playing themselves; rather, a typical situation has been for a young or middle-aged actor to play an elderly role. When an elderly actor is seen on television, the role is more likely to be that of a pitchman for an arthritis remedy, a denture adhesive, or a laxative rather than a dramatic performance.

Studies conducted by the Annenberg School of Communications (University of Pennsylvania) during the decade 1969 to 1979 revealed some of the disparities between television portrayals of the elderly and their real-life counterparts (see Signorielli & Gerbner, 1977). For example, although over 10 percent of the American population during the years of the study consisted of the over-65 group, less than 3 percent of fictional television characters in the 1365 nighttime programs analyzed were elderly. Elderly people who did appear in television programs tended to be characterized as "stubborn, eccentric, ineffectual, sexually inactive, and downright silly." Furthermore, older women were given fewer romantic roles than older men of the same age, and elderly men were more likely to be cast as madmen or evildoers who ended up dead ("Warped View. . . ," 1979).

Because elderly people watch more television than any other age group, it would appear that the treatment they receive in this medium is inconsistent with their influence. Television advertisers and executives realize, however, that it is young people rather than the aged who consume most of the products advertised on television. With the possible exceptions of instant coffee, upset stomach remedies, soap flakes, and laxatives, older people consume less than the average and are also less likely to try new products or brands ("Elderly Demanding. . . ," 1977). On the other hand, older people have more money to spend than ever before, and advertisers are becoming more conscious of them and making greater efforts to avoid offending them.

Changing Attitudes and Images

The **self-concept**, or personally perceived value, of an individual is determined in large measure by the appraisals and attitudes communicated by other people. In old age a person's self-concept affects the very process of aging. Thus people who are socially devalued and hence have negative self-concepts show the symptoms of biological aging sooner than those who are given more social status and acceptance. Consequently, one might expect that with the gradual erosion of the public's negative attitudes and stereotypes about aging, the elderly will begin to live more energetically and happily.

But how can attitudes and stereotypes pertaining to aging and the aged be changed? For example, does direct personal contact with older people help change attitudes toward them? Yes, to some extent, particularly when the contacts are spontaneous and the elderly people are not ill (Tuckman & Lorge, 1953; Spence. Feigenbaum, Fitzgerald & Roth, 1968; Steinbaum, 1973). Although exposure to the aged and knowledge of the aging process do not necessarily have positive effects, courses in gerontology can help to change attitudes when classroom work and textbook readings are supplemented by positive contacts with the elderly.

Certainly, improvements in the ways of depicting older people in the mass media and books can assist in changing attitudes. Television programs such as "Over Easy" and films such as *Peege* and *Portrait of Grandpa Doc* paint a better picture of old age that seen on most prime time television fare. Blue (1978) also reports that children's fiction now portrays the elderly in a less negative way than it did previously.

The Empathic Model, which discussed in Chapter 2, can also be applied to help younger people understand the elderly and hopefully improve their attitudes toward this age group. The frustrations, social roles, mourning, joblessness, sexual behavior, and political attitudes of the elderly have all been simulated by placing young people in a variety of contrived situations typical of those encountered by the elderly. This procedure serves to give participants greater insight into the situations faced by older people and why they respond as they do (Kastenbaum, 1971; Kastenbaum & Durkee, 1964).

Many other interesting and often ingenious approaches to attitude change have been devised, but needless to say, they are not always successful. After summarizing the findings of a number of studies on the topic, Bennett (1976) concluded that negative attitudes toward the elderly are very difficult to change. Consequently, she anticipates a continuation of the fear and even denial of one's own aging and a reluctance to work with old people. Denial of aging and the aged is, however, a two-edged sword, because in so doing we ultimately deny ourselves. As Butler (1975) put it, "We don't all grow black or Chinese, but we do grow old."

Butler also recognizes that overturning a deeply rooted prejudice is a slow process, requiring continuous effort. According to Anderson (1979) and Cottin (1979), much of this effort will have to be made by the elderly themselves. If society will not change its attitudes toward them, then the elderly will have to change society. This, in essence, is the argument of the Gray Panthers and other political lobbyists for the rights of the aged. And it is a topic to which we shall return later in the chapter.

SOCIAL ROLES

Social roles are patterns of behavior individuals are expected to display under certain conditions or in certain situations involving other people. A person usually has many different roles that he or she is expected to play under different circumstances, for example, the roles of spouse, parent, grandparent, friend, employee, and churchgoer. Each role consists of an acquired set of behaviors that must be learned if the individual is to be socially accepted in the position or status to which the role applies.

Because roles are based on interactions with other people, it is not surprising that the most socially active people play the greatest number of roles. In addition, as is the case with personality traits in general, there is a continuity from youth to old age in the extensiveness of a person's social activities and hence in the number of roles played. Considering old age as a whole, however, a process of role reduction or gradual disengagement from social activities is quite common. Because the psychological needs and self-identity of a person are closely related to his or her social, occupational, and familial memberships, a loss of several of the roles prescribed by these memberships can produce feelings of alienation and marginality.

Some gerontologists have stressed the fact that role loss is a natural, perhaps even desirable, part of later life. On the other hand, Blau (1973) argued that, given the option, older people usually prefer to live their lives with the meaning and purpose that comes from having personally and socially significant roles to play. Eleanor Maxwell ("Aging . . . ," 1976) noted that in certain primitive societies, old people keep young in spirit by "starring" in specific social rituals. For example, an elderly Eskimo woman in the Canadian Arctic may give her all in a tug-of-war contest, whereas elderly Apaches bless babies, and senior members of the Bakongo tribe of Africa train youngsters for adult life. Although the setting up of rituals in which older people can play leading roles would not be easy in our society, Maxwell suggests that if the elderly are encouraged to participate in a variety of social groups they will find leading roles to play.

Some roles last from young adulthood through old age, but even these long-term roles undergo changes with aging. Furthermore, old age brings with it the opportunity to establish new relationships, memberships, and roles. Among the types of social roles that give meaning to one's life in old age are those involving relationships with family and friends as well as the usually less intimate roles stemming from memberships in various organizations. Sex and family roles were described in Chapter 7, and the roles of employee and retiree will be considered in Chapter 9. Other social roles—friendship, social organizational, religious, and political—will be discussed in the remainder of this section.

Friendships

Although friends are usually considered to be less important than close relatives, because of their voluntary nature friendships may be valued even more than relationships with kinfolk (Adams, 1967). Older people tend to have friends who are similar to themselves in status, values, and interests. These friends usually live close by, but easily available transportation can extend the friendship circle beyond the immediate neighborhood. Elderly friends meet in their homes, at church, in community centers, and at many other places within traveling distance.

Friends can be a source of emotional support as well as of information and entertainment and hence contribute to an older person's sense of belongingness, meaningfulness, and social status. Therefore, it is understandable why close personal relationships with friends, which help to cushion the shock of physical deterioration, loss of loved ones, and other sources of stress in old age, are characteristic of physically healthier and personally happier elderly people. One friend is better than none, but because old friends die sooner than young ones, it is better to have several. This is particularly true in the case of older men.

The number and intensity of friendships in old age varies with a variety of factors. Women, who throughout the lives of a family tend to initiate the social interactions of the family with outsiders, usually have more friends and longer-lasting friendships than men (Schonberg & Potter, 1976). Friendships also vary with social standing, people of higher socioeconomic status usually having more friends than those of lower socioeconomic status. Many of these friendships, however, are superficial, and older people in the lower social classes often have single friendships that last for a lifetime (Williamson et al., 1980). Ethnic group differences in number of friendships in old age have also been studied, with whites reporting higher levels of contact with friends and neighbors than blacks or Mexican Americans (Dowd & Bengtson, 1978). In this same study, however, whites reported the lowest frequency of contact and Mexican-Americans the most frequent contacts with their children and grandchildren.

Also related to the number of friendships in old age are length of residence in a particular neighborhood and the density of older people in the neighborhood. Thus being a long-term resident of a locality that has a high density of elderly people is associated with a greater number of friendships. The size of the municipality is also related to friendships: older residents of small towns tend to have more friends than those in larger cities (Riley & Foner, 1968).

Many of the demographic factors associated with a greater number of friendships in old age are brought together in retirement communities. It can be argued that the social identities and self-concepts of most elderly people are maintained most effectively by relationships within their own age group rather than by trying to emulate the behavior of young and middle-aged adults (Rose, 1965). Consequently, retirement communities, by providing a better opportunity to develop friendships with one's own age group, may be the best solution to loneliness and loss of status in old age. It is much easier to become socially isolated and the victim of negative attitudes toward the aged in an age-integrated situation than in an age-segregated setting such as a retirement community.

Organizational Memberships

Many adults obtain a great deal of personal satisfaction and a sense of identity and status from belonging to formal social organizations. The business clubs, trade unions, and other occupation-related organizations are of particular importance to young and middle-aged adults who are active in the work force. The influence of these organizations does not automatically cease when a member retires from formal employment, but it may become less important during the last years of life. Involvement in other social organizations, as with all social activities, declines in old age (see Fig. 8-2). The decline is, however, not universal, and many healthy, outgoing people remain actively involved into their 70s, 80s, and even 90s. This is especially true of older people in the middle and upper social classes, who take a more active part in social organizations and have more

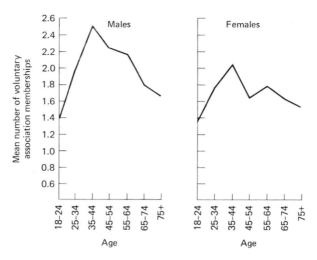

Figure 8-2 Mean number of voluntary memberships of men and women of different ages. Reprinted from *Social Forces*, 55 (September 1976), 43–58. "Age Differences in Voluntary Association Memberships" by Stephen Cutler. Copyright © The University of North Carolina Press.

friends outside the family than older people of lower-class status (Cutler, 1977).[2]

Religion in Old Age

Just as in younger age groups, there are religious fanatics, atheists, and moderates among the aged. Older people as a whole are not doctrinaire, but they do attach more importance to religion than younger people. For example, a national Harris poll (National Council on Aging, 1975) found that 49 percent of adults under 65 and 71 percent of those over 65 felt that religion was very important in their lives. A larger percentage of older than younger adults also believe in immortality, and more of them pray, read scriptures, and are involved in religious organizations (Blazer & Palmore, 1976; Moberg, 1968, 1971). Older women show a greater religious interest than older men, and the middle and upper social classes are more active than the lower class.

Actual church attendance declines from ages 10 to 30–35 and then rises steadily until old age (Bahr, 1970; National Council on Aging, 1975). Church attendance begins to decline again in the last years of life, due undoubtedly to problems with health, transportation, and income.

It is not clear whether the observed increase in religious interest in old age is the result of aging per se or generational differences. The findings are based on cross-sectional studies, and therefore it is impossible to separate age and cohort variables (see Chapter 1). One can argue that the greater religious interest of the elderly is due to the fact that they grew up during a time when families stressed religion more strongly than later

American families and that the effects of this early training persisted throughout life. In any case, there is certainly no good evidence that the greater religious interest of the elderly is caused by the realization that they have little time left on this earth and should therefore begin thinking more seriously about the hereafter.

Politics and the Elderly

Responding to the challenge to fight back against their public image and exploitation as well as to the need for companionship with a purpose, the elderly have become more organized during the past few years than at any time since the Townsend movement of the 1930s. Older people are showing a greater interest in demanding self-respect and protesting such discriminatory practices as fixed retirement ages and segregation by age.

Over six million older Americans, compared to approximately 250,000 a dozen or so years ago, belong to local, state, and national organizations. Chief among these organizations, which are not mere social clubs but political action groups, are the American Association of Retired Persons (AARP), National Council of Senior Citizens (NCSC), Gray Panthers, International Senior Citizens Association (ISCA), National Alliance of Senior Citizens (NASC), and National Caucus on the Black Aged (NCBA) (see the Appendix for a more detailed list and addresses). The two largest of these organizations, AARP and NCSC, boast memberships of several million adults of all ages. The declaration of rights of the twelve-million-member AARP is a general inventory of the concerns of elderly Americans:

> To live with sufficient means for decency and self-respect; to move about freely, reasonably, and conveniently; to pursue a career or interest without penalty founded on age; to be heard on all matters of public interest; to maintain health and well-being through preventive care and education; to receive assistance in times of illness or need or other emergency; to peace and privacy as well as participation; to protection and safety amid the hazards of daily life; to act together to seek redress of grievances; to live life fully and with honor—not for their age but for their humanity. (Offir, 1974, p. 40)

The elderly as a group are admittedly more conservative in their political attitudes than younger people. Kastenbaum (1971) believes that this conservative streak is a reaction to what society has taken away from older people in terms of status and opportunity. He suggests that the elderly might feel less threatened and not so obsessed with clinging to what they possess if they were given more positive social roles to play and equality with younger adults in employment. In any event, the elderly may abandon their political conservatism when the issue pertains to the living conditions and rights of older people. That they can wield a great deal of political power when they are organized behind a common cause is shown by the fact that 90 percent are registered to vote, representing some 15 percent of the electorate, and that they vote quite regularly.

Older people as a group are concerned with self-maintenance, but this does not necessarily imply retaining the status quo. Members of the Gray Panthers, a grass-roots political movement of social activists founded by Margaret ("Maggie") E. Kuhn in the early 1970s, are quite "liberal" or "progressive" in their efforts to improve tax laws, health laws, bus service, and other rights and benefits for the elderly ("Gray Panther Power," 1975). In addition, considering the high educational level of the current generation of young and middle-aged adults and the experiences through which they lived (thermonuclear bomb threats, Vietnam War, Watergate), it is likely that the next two generations of older people will be more liberal than the present one. These future generations may possess greater understanding of the problems of their own age group and those of the wider society, and it can be hoped that they will be more willing and able to do something about those problems.

Figure 8-3 Politically oriented organizations of the elderly are becoming a powerful voice for the rights of the American aged. (*Mental Health*, 1974. Published by the National Mental Health Association, Inc.)

Figure 8-4 Elderly demonstrators in Washington: "Don't agonize—organize." (Photo by Julie Jensen.)

Most politicians realize that the 1980s will be a time to focus on the rights of the aged and that the organized over-65 vote will carry considerable political clout. Political action by organized groups of older people has already been successful in shutting down inadequate nursing homes in certain states, stopping Medicaid cuts in New York, arranging for the placement of traffic lights at busy intersections in Michigan, and obtaining bus fare discounts in dozens of cities.

The hundreds of Golden Age, Senior Citizens, and Live Long and Like It clubs in several American cities are quite active politically. Some of their efforts are directed toward obtaining property- and income-tax reforms, more extensive health-care benefits, better housing, and better transportation for the elderly. Other issues are reforms in social security and private pensions. Considering the great diversity of interests and needs among the elderly, it is not always easy to organize and motivate this minority group for a common cause. Consequently, it is important for organizations concerned with the rights of the elderly to enlist the support of middle-aged and young adults—who will themselves be old before too long and the direct beneficiaries of their own efforts.

STATUS AND ROLES OF ELDERLY MINORITIES

It has been pointed out that the aged in America are similar to minority group members in terms of their status and the roles they are permitted to play. Furthermore, a large percentage of elderly Americans have been discriminated against because they are old and also because they are members of ethnic minorities. The situation of these elderly minorities has been described as one of double jeopardy, or, considering the fact that a substantial proportion are also poor, as one of triple jeopardy.

Because so many elderly members of minority groups in the United States are "invisible," it is difficult to obtain an accurate census. The numbers in Table 8-2, which were obtained by the U.S. Bureau of the Census in 1980, are probably underestimates of the actual numbers. Perhaps a more significant estimate, made by the National Institute on Aging, is that "almost 40 percent of the entire U.S. population in the 1980s will be black or first and second generation Americans belonging to various racial/ethnic subgroups" (National Institute on Aging, 1980, p. 1). Because the percentage of elderly people in all ethnic groups is increasing, the elderly will constitute an even larger proportion of this 40 percent than they now do. It is estimated that the proportion of elderly minorities in the American population will increase from its current ratio of 1 in 10 to 1 in 6 by the year 2035 (Fowles, 1978). As impressive as these numbers may be, lumping all the subgroups comprising the total number of ethnic elderly into a single category is misleading. Thus even within the four groups listed in Table 8-2, there are wide diversities in languages, customs, and expectations.

Common Characteristics of Elderly Ethnic Groups

Whatever the exact count of elderly minorities in the United States, and however extensive their differences, they have certain features in common (Federal Council on the Aging, 1979):

Table 8-2 SIZES OF MINORITY ELDERLY POPULATIONS IN UNITED STATES*

Age Group	Black	Spanish Origin	Asian and Pacific Islander	American Indian, Eskimo, and Aleut	Other Nonwhite
55−59	1,036,601	454,360	130,020	44,792	165,833
60−64	870,734	320,914	97,788	33,881	109,331
65−69	776,597	263,698	79,723	28,256	85,197
70−74	563,377	193,416	58,042	19,886	61,259
75−79	387,231	136,376	39,154	13,742	43,184
80−84	199,760	66,465	21,061	7,052	21,563
85 & over	158,861	48,830	13,854	5,852	16,449

Source: U.S. Bureau of the Census (1981)
*Compare figures with 22,944,033 whites 65 years and older and 42,154,818 whites 55 years and older.

1. The large majority live in metropolitan areas. An exception are American Indians, but for this group there is also a steady urban migration.
2. The average level of formal education is lower than that of their white counterparts.
3. The unemployment rate is higher, and average income is lower than for older white Americans; a smaller percentage own their own homes.
4. Accurate data on the life expectancies of minorities other than blacks are unavailable, but indications are that the average life span is lower than that of whites. Of interest is the "crossover phenomenon," in which blacks who live to be 75 have longer life expectancies than whites.
5. The health status of elderly blacks is poorer than that of elderly whites, but the situation for other minorities is not clear. Indications are that the health of elderly Hispanic-Americans is substantially below average.

Double Jeopardy

The characteristics listed above are both causes and effects of the "double jeopardy" condition of being both elderly and a member of an ethnic minority. In addition to being disadvantaged because of their minority group status, they experience further loss of status because of their age (Dowd & Bengtson, 1978). Thus the problems of low income, poor health, inadequate housing, and loss of status confronting all elderly Americans are particularly acute for elderly minorities.

In the close-knit family structure of many minorities, care and respect for the elderly is often greater in non-white than in white families. Among blacks and Mexican-Americans, for example, multigenerational households in which elderly members make a valued contribution are more common. Coupled with a tradition of respect for the aged, the fact that they are not a severe economic liability creates more positive attitudes toward them. But when westernization or acculturation of young minority group members is combined with poverty and low social status, negative attitudes toward the aged develop in these ethnic groups as well. As a consequence, feelings of being old and negative views of aging are also quite common among minorities (Bengtson, Kasschau, & Ragan, 1977). Like their white counterparts, elderly minority group members deplore the lack of respect that younger people frequently demonstrate toward them and the fact that older people are no longer valued as models by the young. The result is that many elderly in minority groups develop feelings of loneliness and alienation, from the wider American culture as well as from their children and grandchildren (Benetiz, 1973).

Social Services for Elderly Minorities

Social service providers are aware of the special problems of minority elderly, but they also realize that efforts to solve them need to be made with an awareness of the cultural traditions and family dynamics of a particular person. Through research and careful observation, those who work with the minority elderly must attempt to learn more about and understand better whatever variations in the aging process exist within minority groups. Attention by service providers should also be given to communicating in the native language of the older person and to the ethnic and cultural differences of the group to which the older person belongs. Finally, one of the unique features of minority life-style has been maintenance of the elderly within the family unit. One alternative to providing services for the elderly is to work within this family unit as well as through subcultural organizations within the ethnic community.

Although elderly blacks as a group appear to be even more aware than elderly whites of the benefits and services to which they are entitled, many elderly minority group members are unaware of such benefits and services, unwilling to use them, or reside in areas where services are not readily available. This implies a program of providing information, transportation, and other measures that will bring the older person in closer contact with those social services to which he or she is entitled. In addition, because so many blacks and other minority group members who pay social security taxes for a lifetime die before they can collect their benefits, it has been recommended that benefits be given earlier to these subgroups of older people.

SUMMARY

The status accorded the elderly and attitudes toward old age and the aged vary with the culture, the social group, and individual difference variables. Agricultural societies have traditionally held the elderly in higher esteem than gathering/hunting societies or more technological nations. The elderly have also been given greater respect in Eastern than in Western cultures.

Modern society harbors many misconceptions and stereotypes pertaining to the aged, including the beliefs that most old people are in poor health, senile, inflexible, unemployable, sexless, inactive, and alone. The cultural stereotypes and negative attitudes toward aging expressed by adults and the media are transmitted to young children, many of whom also express negative feelings toward aging and the aged. Although the elderly themselves often share the general public's negative perceptions of old age, they do not necessarily agree with younger adults about what problems are most serious in old age. In fact, the results of a national Harris poll indicated that a large majority of the older people who were questioned were pleasantly surprised to discover that old age was not as bad as they expected it to be.

The stereotypes of older people portrayed on television are undergoing changes, as are images of the aged communicated by other sources of information and influence. Unfortunately, attitudes toward aging and the peceived status of the aged are not easy to alter. But presentation of more positive images of the elderly in books, films, and the media, as well as exposure to "normal" older people, should help erode existing stereotypes. Other experimental approaches to attitude change, such as the Empathic Model, show promise. Nevertheless, politically active older people have come to the conclusion that they must work to change society, rather than waiting for society to change its attitudes toward and treatment of the elderly.

Old age has been characterized as a period when the number of social roles that a person plays declines. It would appear, however, that the majority of older people prefer to maintain rewarding friendships in addition to religious and other organizational interactions. Positive interactions with other people, especially with those in their same age group, help the aged retain a sense of belongingness, meaningfulness, and value. An advantage of retirement communities is that by being age-segregated they increase the probability of friendships with other elderly people.

Interest and involvement in religion are greater in older than in younger adults, but the difference is probably a generational rather than an age effect. Many older people are also quite active politically; the great majority are registered, and a larger percentage than average vote in elections. Older people tend to be more politically conservative than younger groups, but they can be quite liberal on issues pertaining to the rights and privileges of the elderly. Many local and national organizations of and for the elderly are quite active politically. Of primary interest to those organizations are the issues and problems discussed in Chapters 3, 8, 9, and 10: health care, nutrition, employment, social security, housing, transportation, and crime.

The situation of elderly minorities in the United States has been characterized as one of double jeopardy: they have low status because they are both old and members of ethnic minorities. Although many minority elderly belong to close-knit family groups, the respect and consideration that they have traditionally enjoyed in such families often change with acculturation of other family members into mainstream American society. In any case, social service providers need to be aware of the special needs and problems of elderly minorities and to seek alternative ways of making older minority group members aware of their rights and benefits and able to take advantage of them.

SUGGESTED READINGS

Cottin, L. *Elders in rebellion*. New York: Doubleday/Anchor, 1979.

Davis, R. H. *Television and the aging audience*. Los Angeles: Andrus Gerontol-ogy Center, University of Southern California, 1980.

Dowd, J. J., & Bengtson, V. L. Aging in minority populations: An examination of the double jeopardy hypothesis. *Journal of Gerontology,* 1978, *33,* 427–436.

Hudson, R. B., & Binstock, R. H. Political systems and aging. In R. H. Binstock & E. Shanas (Eds.), *Handbook of aging and the social sciences.* New York: Van Nostrand Reinhold, 1976. pp. 369–400.

Kessler, J. Aging in different ways. *Human Behavior,* 1976, *5*(6), 56–60.

Northcott, H. C. Too young, too old— age in the world of television. *The Gerontologist,* 1975, *15,* 184–186.

Pratt, F. A. *Teaching about aging.* Boulder, Colo.: Science Education Consortium, 1977.

Richman, J. The foolishness and wisdom of age: Attitudes toward the elderly as reflected in jokes. *The Gerontologist,* 1977, *17,* 210–219.

Stanford, E. P. *The elder black.* San Diego, Calif.: Center on Aging, San Diego State University, 1978.

Valle, R., & Mendoza, L. *The elder latino.* San Diego, Calif.: Center on Aging, San Diego State University, 1978.

NOTES

[1]The desire of these children not to grow old is apparently shared by a sizable number of adults. Kastenbaum (1971) estimated that 25 percent all Americans have such a negative attitude toward old age that many would prefer to die before reaching it.

[2]For some reason, a greater percentage of blacks than whites, or any other ethnic group for that matter, participate in voluntary social organizations (Cutler, 1977).

Employment and Retirement

Sooner or later the question of whether to retire or to keep working at one's occupation arises for those who have a choice. Some people look forward to retirement and the opportunity that it offers to pursue secondary interests and goals. Others, especially those who enjoy their work and perceive it as more than simply a way of making a living, prefer to continue working even after they are eligible for retirement. Such people view the job as a central part of themselves, and becoming permanently separated from it has a marked effect on their self-concepts. This is particularly true of those who are higher up on the occupational ladder rather than of laborers, who may view their work as mere drudgery, which they must do in order to survive.

EMPLOYMENT IN LATER LIFE

Whether to retire or continue working is a decision that is not entirely in the hands of most employees. Management, frequently after consultation with labor unions, makes policies concerning retirement. For most occupations the marker retirement age has traditionally been in the 60s, usually 65. There are, however, extensive individual differences in the rate of aging, and many people can and want to keep working well beyond age 65. On the other hand, there are employees who, because of chronic illness, injury, or other problems, are too disabled to work long before their 65th birthday.

Elderly Employment Statistics

With the exception of wartime, the percentage of elderly people in the work forces of industrialized nations has declined steadily throughout the present century. Nearly 70 percent of American men aged 65 and over were employed in 1900, a figure that had dropped to 46 percent by 1950 and to 19 percent by 1980. In 1980 approximately 3 million older people, representing 13 percent of the labor force, were working or actively seeking work (U.S. Dept. of Health and Human Services, 1981). It is possible that the percentage of older people in the work force will be even lower by the year 2000. Among the probable causes of this decline are technological advances, less agricultural work, and more attractive retirement incentives. The increased educational and training requirements for most jobs have also favored younger workers over older ones.

In contrast to the pronounced decline in the percentage of employed elderly men, the proportion of employed elderly women has remained fairly constant during the past 80 years: It rose from 1 in 12 in 1900 to 1 in 10 during the 1950s and fell back to 1 in 12 in the 1970s (U.S. Dept. of Health and Human Services, 1981). That many of the nonworking elderly—both men and women—prefer to be employed was demonstrated by the results of a 1974 Harris poll. Thirty-seven percent of a representative sample of retired Americans questioned in this poll stated that they would still be working if they could.

The Worker and the Job

Some time during middle age, at the height of their careers as well as their economic needs and responsibilities, most people begin to assess their accomplishments in terms of the time they have left. If their goals are found to be unrealistic, an adjustment may be in order (Neugarten, 1967):

> Men perceive a close relationship between life-line and career-line. Middle age is the time to take stock. Any disparity noted between career expectations and career achievements—that is, whether one is "on time" or "late" in reaching career goals—adds to the heightened awareness of age. One 47-year-old lawyer said, "I moved at age forty-five from a large corporation to a law firm. I got out at the last possible moment, because after forty-five it is too difficult to find the job you want. If you haven't made it by then, you had better make it fast, or you are stuck."

To the middle-ager, faced with Erikson's crisis of generativity versus self-absorption, the job is a central part of the self. Sexual, avocational, cultural, and even family interests may be perceived as less important than the job. People are identified by the kind of work they do, and their status, social relationships, identity, and reason for living are all involved with their work. This is especially true of men, who have traditionally been perceived as the family breadwinner. But with the women's movement and

> **Report 9-1** THE PSYCHOLOGICAL SIGNIFICANCE OF WORK*
>
> Mr. Winter single-handedly ran an operation that nobody else in his company fully understood, nor in fact cared to understand. As Mr. Winter reached his 64th birthday, a bright and talented younger man was assigned as an apprentice to learn the complex set of activities so that at the end of the year, he could take over the operation and the old master could benefit from a well-deserved retirement. Mr. Winter objected, claiming that he did not want to retire, but the company had rules.
>
> Not long after retirement a substantial change in Mr. Winter took place. He began to withdraw from people and to lose his zest for life. Within a year after his retirement this once lively and productive businessman was hospitalized, diagnosed as having a senile psychosis. Friends from work and even family soon stopped coming to visit, as they could evoke no response. Mr. Winter was a vegetable.
>
> About two years after the apprentice had stepped up to his new position of responsibility he suddenly died. The company found itself in a serious predicament. The function that was vacated was essential to company operations but was one which no one else in the company could effectively perform. A decision was made to approach Mr. Winter and see if he could pull himself together enough to carry on the job and train somebody to take over. Four of his closest co-workers were sent to the hospital. After hours of trying, one of the men finally broke through. The idea of going back to work brought the first sparkle in Mr. Winter's eyes in two years. Within a few days, this "vegetable" was operating at full steam, interacting with people as he had years before.
>
> *After Margolis & Kroes (1972).

the associated extension of the social identities of women beyond those of housewife and mother, it is also becoming true of more and more women.

Because a person's job is such an important part of his or her life space, the satisfactions derived from work both affect and are affected by one's physical and mental health. For example, it has been found that severe job stress, produced by heavy responsibilities and dissatisfaction with goal achievements, is related to heart attacks (Romo, Siltanen, Theorell, & Rahe, 1974). Job dissatisfaction is also associated with peptic ulcers, which affect blue-collar and white-collar workers alike (Kahn, 1969). The results of other studies have shown that the rate of suicide is greater among the unemployed than the employed (Rosenfeld, 1976b) and that work satisfaction is positively correlated with longevity (Palmore, 1969; Rose, 1964). Most people who live a long time continue to work at something throughout their lives (see Report 9-1).

Characteristics of Older Workers

The results of a study by Saleh and Otis (1964) showed that job satisfaction reaches a peak in the mid-50s and then declines. Regardless of age, however, people who like their work and see it as meaningful tend to want to keep their jobs as long as possible (Offir, 1974). This is especially true of older workers, who are usually more committed to their jobs and experience greater job satisfaction than young adults. Reflective of these conclusions are the facts that older people are less likely to want to change their jobs, have less absenteeism, and express less job dissatisfaction.

Older workers also resent the assumption that they are incapable of doing a good day's work. Despite the fact that they often perform poorly on laboratory-type tasks, under actual job conditions older men usually do as well or better than younger men (Riley & Foner, 1968). The volume of their work may be less than that of younger adults, but its quality is higher, doing things with less wasted motion and making fewer mistakes (Hurlock, 1980). Older workers are also quite capable of learning new job skills, especially when training methods take their capabilities into account.

The allegation that because of personal problems, older people are hard to get along with on the job has also been contradicted by research. Compared with younger workers, older employees are less restless, less preoccupied with personal problems, and do not manifest any special difficulty in adjusting to other workers. Furthermore, older workers are less "accident-prone" and have fewer illnesses and injuries than one might expect (Hurlock, 1980).

The Unemployed Elderly

Although their job performance is not generally inferior to that of younger workers, the rate of unemployment tends to be higher for the elderly. In addition, once out of work, older people tend to remain unemployed up to 70 percent longer than their younger counterparts (Entine, 1976). Even the official unemployment figures for the elderly, although high, are probably underestimates of the true state of affairs. One reason is that after a time, many older people simply give up and stop looking for jobs, thereby no longer being counted among the unemployed.

The referral rate of older workers to jobs by the U.S. Employment Servce is only about half that of younger workers, even though once he or she is referred to a job an older worker is just as likely to be placed as a younger one (Quirk, 1976). The consequence of the lower referral rate of the elderly is that the older would-be worker is often forced into early retirement, a retirement that should be based on individual needs and capacities rather than on chronological age.

The problem of obtaining employment is even worse when the elderly job seeker is black. In fact, it has been said that as far as employment is concerned, being young and black is functionally equivalent to being old and white in our society (Kastenbaum, 1971). This does not mean that unemployment is necessarily psychologically harder on blacks than on whites. Psychological reactions to being unemployed depend, to some degree, on what a person is accustomed to or prepared for. Margaret Mead (Hechinger, 1977) has suggested, for example, that one reason women live longer than men is that older men are cut off abruptly from their jobs, having a full life one day and nothing to do the next. On the other hand, the typical woman does not retire from her housework but continues doing in old age what she has been doing throughout her married life.

Report 9-2 A CONCERN FOR OLDER WORKERS*

STILLWATER, Okla. (AP)—Despite the stereotypes society has created about the old, older workers can contribute a great deal to businesses, believes Joseph J. Klos, professor of economics at Oklahoma State University.

"Older workers are actually less accident-prone, more careful and more patient," he said. "They have a lower absenteeism rate. Their total output may decline some but that's not always true. On the whole, they are steady, loyal and dependable—more so than younger workers.

"Combine this with increased experience and better judgment, and they make extremely fine employees. For this reason, businesses and industry should show them some consideration."

Klos is particularly concerned with older workers' health problems and how businesses unwittingly contribute to them.

"The pressures of business are hard on individuals," he said. "Young people take it reasonably well, but as people grow older, many prefer less demanding work."

The answer is, he suggests, to offer positions where the pressures of work can be eased but the ego of the worker is not deflated.

"Some might not want to be bumped out of a responsible position, but others would prefer to remain on the payroll and do something less demanding. Companies need not cut their pay, and they probably should still get annual increases, but these could be smaller than those received by other employees."

Klos feels that it's important to realize that extra stress can cause additional physical problems in some situations.

"If you let the individual go just because he has a heart condition and cannot take the hard pressure, the company loses the individual's expertise and wisdom," he said. "If he continues to work under the stress, it may cause another heart attack or death—with the same result to the company.

"It would be a lot easier on the company to lessen the worker's responsibilities—and a lot easier on the company health plan—to place the person in a less stressful job, even if the business has to pay the same salary."

Juggling positions and duties is usually the responsibility of personnel managers, Klos points out. "If they think that the older workers should be doing the same amount of high-pressure work as the younger executive, then they don't understand the process of aging," Klos said.

"If companies will take the aging worker into consideration, make small allowances for him—just as they do younger workers with families and individuals with handicaps—they will have much happier and more productive workers."

*From *Los Angeles Times*, Dec. 5, 1978, Pt. IV, p. 9. Used by permission of the Associated Press.

More Jobs for the Elderly

Many of the unemployed elderly, at least half of whom are physically capable of doing a day's work, are wasting society's and their resources by not working. This may seem to be a harsh judgment, but many older people themselves would agree with it. In any case, the results of surveys indicate that the majority of the elderly want to see the system changed to make employment available to those who need or desire to keep working past retirement age (see National Council on the Aging, 1975). This has been proposed by many authorities and is being done in several European countries. Faced with zero population growth and potentially fewer people in the work force, the governments of many industrialized nations perceive older workers as a valuable resource and attempt to delay their retirement by the use of vaious incentives. The effectiveness of these plans in countries such as Sweden, the Soviet Union, and Japan is seen in statistics that point to a large percentage of those eligible for retirement electing to remain on the job.

A particularly valuable resource in the United States are elderly doctors, lawyers, and businesspersons, who possess professional knowledge and skills that have taken years to develop. For example, retired lawyers can offer legal services to the aged, retired teachers can give courses, and retired doctors and nurses can supply home medical care (Butler, 1975). A few business firms have started skill banks of retirees, which permit former employees of a firm to be hired for specific projects and programs on a full- or part-time basis.

An interesting new phenomenon on the employment scene are the "young–old" retirees aged 55 and over who, having retired from a first career but still in relatively good health, begin looking around for more varied life options (Neugarten, 1975). These well-educated, demanding individuals frequently begin second careers and find new avocational, educational, and even political pursuits. It has even been suggested that, with breakthroughs in prolongevity up to 100 years, people will begin to engage in as many as three different careers in a single lifetime. Legislators and/or chief executives might continue to work for several generations. Members of Congress could be elected for as many as forty consecutive terms, and junior executives may have to wait 50 years for their bosses to retire before they are promoted! (Anderson, 1974)

Whatever the future may hold in terms of superlongevity, the governments of most modern nations are faced with the immediate problem of using the abilities of elderly citizens who want to work. A number of federal employment programs benefiting older Americans are described in Table 9-1. Perhaps the best known of these is the Foster Grandparent Program, which was designed primarily to give elderly people an opportunity to provide love and care to institutionalized and handicapped children. Each of the 15 to 20 thousand Foster Grandparents throughout the United States, Puerto Rico, and the Virgin Islands devotes 4 hours every weekday to the care of two children.

Many other federally aided volunteer programs (e.g., RSVP, SCORE, VISTA) make use of the time and talents of elderly volunteers (see Table 9-1). The largest of these is RSVP (Retired Senior Volunteer Program), in which 250,000 participants receive no remuneration other than the cost of traveling to the places where they serve. Useful services to organizations needing the advice of mature executives are provided by SCORE. Among the other governmental agencies for which elderly people can perform volunteer services are the Veterans' Administration and the Peace Corps.

As the population grows even larger, the service-providing sector will need to expand. Programs such as "Project Green Thumb," which was

Table 9.1   MAJOR FEDERAL EMPLOYMENT PROGRAMS BENEFITING THE ELDERLY*

Program	Agency	Description
Age Discrimination in Employment	Office of Fair Labor Standards, Department of Labor	Investigation of charges of discrimination by certain employers against persons between the ages of 40 and 65.
Comprehensive Employment and Training Act (CETA)	Employment and Training Administration, Department of Labor	Offers help to the economically disadvantaged, underemployed, and unemployed of all ages to compete for, secure, and hold challenging, meaningful jobs.
Foster Grandparent Program	ACTION	Federal grants to public and private nonprofit agencies for creating volunteer services opportunities for low-income persons age 60 and over as companions to children and to older individuals. Volunteers receive at least the federal minimum wage.
Senior Community Service Employment Program (SCSEP)	Employment and Training Administration, Department of Labor	Secretary of Labor may contract with public and private nonprofit agencies to develop and administer part-time work in public service activities for low-income, unemployed persons aged 55 or older; to be paid at least federal minimum wage.
Retired Senior Volunteer Program (RSVP)	ACTION	Federal grants to public or private nonprofit agencies to establish or expand volunteer activities for the elderly; providing compensation for out-of-pocket expenses incidental to their services.
Service Corps of Retired Executives (SCORE)	Small Business Administration	Volunteer services organized through field offices of Small Business Administration; retired professional and businessmen assist persons with business-related problems.

Table 9.1 *(continued)*

Program	Agency	Description
Volunteers in Service to America (VISTA)	ACTION	Provides volunteer service opportunities for persons aged 18 or older in urban and rural poverty areas, on Indian reservations, with migrant families, and in federally assisted institutions for the mentally ill and retarded. Most older VISTA volunteers serve part-time.

*Adapted from Select Committee on Aging. *Federal responsibility to the elderly.* Washington, D.C., U.S. Government Printing Office, 1976, pp. 4–5.

sponsored by the National Farmers Union and paid old people for part-time work in beautification, conservation, and improvement projects in rural areas, may be established. New job opportunities will open up for the elderly in education, social services, and health areas. Elderly people could staff day-care centers and kindergartens, work on historical projects and crafts, and even become small-scale food producers by operating abandoned farms.

Projects at Miami–Dade Community College, New York City Community College, and other educational institutions have been concerned with constructing lists of potential employers of the aged. Cooperating employers in these programs recognize that the primary qualification for employment should be ability to perform the job rather than chronological age. Thus an employer may arrange for two older people or an older and a younger person to share a position, one taking it in the morning and the other in the afternoon. Other possibilities for salvaging the abilities and skills of older people who want to work—and perhaps their self-concepts as well—are being explored. These work options should become even more attractive to the elderly unemployed if inflation continues to grow and the problems with funding social security are not solved.

RETIREMENT: EVENT, STATUS, AND PROCESS

The traditional retirement ages of 65 for men and 60 for women were selected by the U.S. government in the 1930s to serve as a base for paying Old Age and Survivors Insurance, commonly known as social security. These ages were established in a political move to curb unemployment of younger and therefore more productive workers by replacing older workers with them. Although the expected role for older people today involves retirement rather than work, certain professions and organizations have no fixed retirement ages. For example, Bankers Life and Casualty Company of Chicago has never had a mandatory retirement age. By way of contrast, employees of police departments and high-risk jobs in other organizations face early retirement. Still other organizations have policies of gradually reducing employee work load during the years just prior to retirement. In any event, age 65 has served for years as a kind of benchmark or point of passage between middle and old age.

Statistics on Retirement

Owing to the relatively high growth rate of the older population, the number and proportion of retirees in the general U.S. population has increased in recent years. Over 4,000 older Americans retired daily in the late 1970s, bringing the total number of retirees to over 23 million. The total is expected to rise to 33 million, while the average retirement age falls from 62 to 55, by the turn of the century. Consequently, the number of retirees is increasing, and the length of the retirement period may soon be such that people will spend up to one-third of their lives as retirees. At the present time, an average 65-year-old man can look forward to 13 more years of life, and an average 65-year-old woman, to 18 more years. But projections indicate that by the year 2000 the average American will be spending 25 or more years in retirement (Entine, 1976). These statistics are similar to those reported by other industrialized nations.

Another way of looking at retirement statistics is in terms of the ratio of retirees to active workers. As this **dependency ratio** increases, the smaller becomes the number of actively employed who must support one retiree. It is estimated that the dependency ratio, which was 1:3.2 in the United States in 1981, will have increased to almost 1:2 by the year 2000. One important reason for the decreasing average retirement age and the increasing dependency ratio is that many people are being forced to retire before they need or want to, while others are voluntarily deciding to retire early.

Voluntary Retirement

There is a definite trend toward early retirement in the United States, especially in larger companies. In general, larger companies have higher rates of early retirement than smaller companies (Pyron & Manion, 1970). Those who decide to retire early are influenced by factors such as the anticipation of a comfortable income, the relatively high rate of technological obsolescence of workers in their 50s and 60s, increasing relocation of major firms, cyclical employment, and stagnation of certain sectors of the economy (Binstock, 1977). Whatever the reason, a sizable majority of early retirees claim to be satisfied with their lives since retirement. In the Cornell longitudinal study of retirement, for example, one-third of the retirees who were questioned 4 to 6 years after leaving the work force reported that retirement had been a more positive experience than they had anticipated. Only 4 to 5 percent of those surveyed reported that retirement was worse than they had expected (Streib & Schneider, 1971).

The decision to retire early or to keep working is also related to demographic and personal variables. In Streib and Schneider's (1971) study of 1,486 men and 483 women, it was found that people with larger incomes, more education, and occupations of higher social status preferred to continue working longer than those lower on the economic, educational, and occupational scales. Working women as a group were more reluctant to retire than men, but single and married women tended to retire earlier than divorced women and widows.

Another important factor affecting the decision to retire early is the state of one's health. Thus Maddox (1968b) found that nearly 50 percent of the retired people whom he studied chose to do so because of poor health. Also related to poor health is the fact that a larger percentage of minority group than white elderly retire before age 65, the majority presumably for health reasons (Andrus Gerontology Center, 1978).

Mandatory Retirement

Whether or not they elect to retire, an overwhelming majority of elderly people (86 percent in one poll) agree that mandatory retirement policies should be abolished (National Council on the Aging, 1975). There are, of course, pros and cons for a fixed retirement age. As was argued during the Great Depression, jobs vacated by retirees are made available to younger workers and hence help combat unemployment. An argument against this point is that many new jobs become available every year, presumably enough to provide employment for younger workers without forcing older employees to retire. Another argument in favor of mandatory retirement is that it enables employers to get rid of incompetent workers by means of the natural attrition process of retirement without having to prove incompetence to perform the job.

When questioned, supervisors most often indicate that they prefer a variable retirement age that takes individual differences into account. For various reasons, however, supervisors are frequently reluctant to tell employees that they are incompetent, particularly when competence is not easily judged. But when the retirement age is fixed, personnel can be weeded out without engaging in the highly subjective task of evaluating work performance.

On the side against involuntary retirement is the fact that competent elderly workers can be kept on the job and continue to pay in rather than withdrawing money from social security and other retirement plans. Such workers contribute their skills and productivity and also more and more people are maintaining that simple justice and humanity demand that we recognize the value of older lives and the right of older people to continue performing those activities that contribute to their sense of well-being. It is also pointed out that life expectancy has risen since the 1930s, that forced retirement pushes experienced and talented workers aside, and that people have a right to determine their own futures.

Concluding that the idea of a fixed retirement age of 65 is not based on

"And in appreciation of years of dedicated loyal
service, we present this gold watch with
which you can time your descent."

Fig 9.1 Forced retirement can result in physical and mental decline. (Lou Erickson, the *Atlanta Journal*, June 24, 1977. Used by permission.

any scientific findings and is against the public interest, a federal statute signed into law on January 1, 1979, raised the mandatory retirement age from 65 to 70 for most employees in the private sector as well as in the state and local governments. This same law completely eliminated the upper age limit for most civilian employees of the federal government. Even before the law was passed, many private companies had done away with mandatory retirement for employees as long as they could do their jobs and pass annual physical examinations. In addition, union contracts with other companies had already called for increasing the retirement age from 65 to 67 years. Such contractual agreements, recognizing that a variable retirement age was needed to take individual differences in health and ability into account, allow for additional years of optional employment, depending on a joint decision between worker and management.

Planning for Retirement

Many older employees look forward to retirement with optimism and eagerness for release from work and routine. Others, however, are concerned about money or anxious about how they will use their time. The anxiety felt by these people about retiring tends to increase as they reach retirement age, but once they have retired and become adjusted to a new way of life, their level of anxiety decreases (Reichard, Livson, & Peterson, 1962). At least some of this anxiety and "postretirement shock" could be eased by planning and preparing for retirement; this is the goal of preretirement planning programs. As stated in the proposed Federal Employees Preretirement 'Assistance Act of 1975 (Mondale, 1975, p.S.19393):

> A person's retirement years are perhaps the most challenging and potentially devastating period of his or her life. It can be satisfying and rewarding, a culmination of a successful life. Or it can be a cruel, gradual, or sudden breakdown in the person's life style. "Retirement shock" is a common phenomenon. A combination of confusion and anxiety accompanying retirement is added to declining health and reduced income to produce not only general unhappiness but often physical symptoms as well.
>
> Planning for retirement can help workers make the transition from years of active employment to their leisure-time years. Our society is work oriented and youth oriented: retirement can produce a real identity crisis, and often a loss of interest in living. Yet, with adequate advance preparation, retirement from a job does not need to mean retirement from life. By learning to avoid the pitfalls of retirement, and how to get the most from the new opportunities being opened up, preretirement planning can facilitate the vital and necessary continuation of personal growth.

According to Porter (1977), at least ten questions should be asked by anyone considering retirement:

1. When will I retire?
2. Will I lead a life of leisure or continue to work?
3. How much am I worth today?
4. Where will I retire?
5. What can I save by retiring?
6. How much money do I need in retirement?
7. When can I start drawing social security and my other pension benefits?
8. What precisely is my benefit deal under my corporation's pension plan?
9. Will I have enough health insurance?
10. What kind of investments can help me obtain additional retirement income?

It will be noted that more than half of these questions are concerned with money matters, which is a realistic emphasis during a time of rising inflation when many workers are wondering whether they can afford to retire. In addition to financial security, preretirement planning should also be concerned with health maintenance and activities after retirement.

In a nationwide survey conducted a few years ago (National Council on the Aging, 1975), a sample of older Americans was asked what they had done to prepare for retirement. Although many of the respondents reported having made some preparations, the plans of the group as a whole were considered inadequate in terms of savings, preparing a will, arranging for part- or full-time employment, and enrolling in retirement counseling programs. Furthermore, only a small proportion (19 percent) had taken a preretirement planning course or expected to do so. This was characteristic of the state of affairs in the early 1970s, but since then several events have transpired that have led to increased participation in preretirement planning workshops.

The Employee Retirement Income Security Act (ERISA) of 1974, which required that employees be kept more fully informed of their pension benefits, was the stimulus for the development of preretirement planning programs in many companies. A further impetus was provided by the 1979 federal law increasing the retirement age from 65 to 70. Persisting inflation, and the resulting concern of employees about whether they can afford to retire, has also encouraged the development of preretirement planning programs and increased the number of participants.

Depending on the objectives of the program designers, a preretirement planning program may involve literature handouts, lectures on rights and benefits, and in-depth seminars and workshops held during or after work hours. Preretirement planning workshops cover such topics as providing for adequate retirement income, how to develop a realistic budget for the retirement years, social relationships, avocational and new vocational pursuits, as well as physical and mental health needs. Other topics of discussion are legal rights and procedures, sexual behavior, adjusting to changing morals and values, and even such mundane matters as planning and cooking meals. The use of leisure time for hobbies, entertainment, and further education is a sometimes neglected subject for discussion in these workshops. This subject would seem to be especially important for those older people whose work-value systems have until now permitted little indulgence in leisure activities.

A number of larger business and industrial firms have developed their own preretirement planning programs, one of the most ambitious being that of Philadelphia's Sun Company. Other companies have adopted the programs of the American Management Association or the American Association of Retired Persons (AARP). The topics in the AARP Retirement Planning Seminar series are: Challenge of Retirement, Health and Safety, Housing and Location, Legal Affairs, Attitude and Role Adjustments, Meaningful Use of Time, Sources and Amounts of Income, and Financial Planning. Each of the 2-hour sessions devoted to each topic includes a series of organizing questions, brief readings, and filmstrips to use as discussion aids.[1] As the list of topics suggests, these programs emphasize the practical aspects of retirement rather than more subtle psychosocial matters. Among the latter are stresses within the family and the loss of a sense of being important to others (Ullmann, 1976). These are circumstances the preretiree may be unable to anticipate, pointing to the need for postretirement as well as preretirement counseling (Sheldon,

McEwan, & Ryser, 1975). Furthermore, the fact that retirement affects the retiree as well as the entire family is one reason why the spouses of preretirees are also encouraged to participate in preretirement planning and counseling sessions.

Psychological Reactions to Retirement

A 65-year-old man whose job gives him a sense of importance and meaning may view retirement as an insulting indication that society views him as old and useless. The activity orientation and work ethic of Western culture do little to prepare such a person for the trauma of leaving his job and forced idleness for a long time. When people are almost religiously devoted to their work, the experience of suddenly being unemployed and presumably unproductive can be very damaging to one's sense of self-esteem. Retirement in these cases is often accompanied by feelings of diminished usefulness, significance, and independence, and perhaps a sense that life is over. A rather dismal picture is presented by Perlman (1968, p. 152):

> After his first weeks or even months of freedom from work, relished as his just deserts, the old man without a regular job begins to feel lost, somehow, missing the affiliation and regularization of his daily life that was present in his work role. He may find these in part in some forms of leisure activity or in various kinds of volunteer good works. He may attach himself to other old men for shared opinions and fragmental chit-chat and for the comfortableness of being in the company of his peers, the "retired." But with a few exceptions, the sense of being-to-a-purpose has gone out of his life, and it is hard to know whether his unconscious need for withdrawal and for husbanding his energies makes his investment in relationships and activity superficial or whether some increasing emotional withdrawal and lack of social purposefulness and value results from his loss of role. The old woman holds on to her householding duties long after her role as mother and spouse has ended. But when she has tidied up the house and washed her cup and saucer and talked to her grandchild on the telephone—what, then, is she to be or do? And when she is no longer able—sight dim, hearing dulled, legs a-totter—to manage for herself and is taken into her child's home or put to live in a "home for senior citizens," when all tasks are dispatched by the swifter, stronger, more efficient others, what is she?

The loss of meaning and significance in one's life, which has been referred to as the "retirement syndrome," can accelerate the processes of physical and mental deterioration with age. Among the physical symptoms of the retirement syndrome are gastrointestinal difficulties, nervousness, and instability—all of which are reactions to stress. Other indicators of postretirement stress are the increases in alcoholism, divorce, and suicide that have been noted.

Although the retirement syndrome is not uncommon, it is far from universal. Rather than causing negative reactions, research has shown that, for the most part, satisfaction with life, self-acceptance, and overall adjustment do not decrease after retiring (Neugarten, 1971). Most old people look at retirement as providing an opportunity to satisfy previously neglected needs, rather than as being "put on the shelf." When immediate postretirement anxiety and depression occur, they are usually mild and shortlived. And when severe, acute depression occurs, it is usually attributable to physical disabilities or illness rather than to retirement (Lowenthal, 1964; Spence, 1966).

Physical health is obviously a factor in one's attitude toward and

---

Report 9-3 DOCTORS CHALLENGED ON THEIR BELIEF THAT
RETIREMENT POSES HEALTH RISKS*
HARRY NELSON, *Times Medical Writer*

Doctors who routinely advise patients not to retire because they believe retirement raises the risk of illness and death should reevaluate their belief, a leading authority on aging contends.

"The medical community should recognize that there are no scientific data to substantiate the idea drawn from isolated impressions, that retirement is associated with illnesses, deterioration and premature death," says Dr. Valery A. Portnoi, chief of the division of geriatrics at George Washington University Medical School.

Portnoi says in an article in the current issue of the Journal of the American Medical Assn. that sociologists have long suspected that retirement has no negative effects on personal adjustment.

1972 Warning

But many physicians, he said, believe the frequency of death and disease increases after retirement and that the act of retiring is the cause.

He noted that the Committee on Aging of the American Medical Assn. stated in 1972 that retirement may lead to a feeling of uselessness and worthlessness and marital conflict as a result of retirees spending more time with their families.

Portnoi says that while some people do experience these problems, a survey of the medical literature on life satisfaction, health and retirement reveals little evidence to support a negative association with retirement for the great majority of people.

Pre-Retirement Health

Poor health before retirement, rather than retirement itself, is more likely to be the factor predicting a higher death rate soon after retirement, he said.

In a telephone interview Portnoi said he surveyed the medical literature after being told by a number of retired persons that they had been "frightened by doctors" in talks about retirement.

He said some physicians are highly anxious about their own retirement and that this biases them on the subject.

Physicians should be in a position to provide appropriate counseling to patients, Portnoi said in the journal article, but "when they add their own negative attitudes to those of the patients, the needed adjustment is less likely to occur."

*From *Los Angeles Times*, May 1, 1981, Pt. I, p. 3. Copyright 1981, Los Angeles Times. Reprinted by permission.

Table 9-2 THINGS RETIRED PEOPLE 65 AND OVER MISSED ABOUT THEIR JOBS*

	Percent Missing
The money it brings in	74
The people at work	73
The work itself	62
The feeling of being useful	59
Things happening around you	57
The respect of others	50
Having a fixed schedule every day	43

*After National Council on Aging, 1975, p. 218.

enjoyment of retirement. Therefore the results of studies that have found retirees to be more poorly adjusted than nonretirees may have been caused by inadequately controlling for the fact that less healthy workers retire earlier than healthy ones. Also, because mental attitude affects physical health, it is not surprising that the health of individuals who react negatively to retirement often deteriorates. On the other hand, physical health can improve after retirement, especially for individuals whose work involved a great deal of physical or mental stress (see Butler & Lewis, 1977).

Health is undoubtedly a very important factor in one's reactions to retirement, but economic status, social interactions, and other variables are also significant. Thus the results of a poll conducted for the National Council on the Aging (1975) in 1974 showed that what the greatest percentage of retired people missed about their jobs was the money it brought in. Almost as many, however, missed the people at work, and approximately 60 percent missed the work itself and the feeling of being useful (see Table 9-2).

Types and Phases of Adjustment to Retirement

As with any change in a person's life, reactions to retirement depend to a great extent on the effectiveness of his or her adjustment mechanisms or coping behaviors. These mechanisms, not unique to old age, are behavioral patterns reflective of deep-seated personality characteristics that have persisted throughout the person's life. In a now classic investigation of the relationships between personality characteristics and adjustment to retirement, Reichard, Livson, and Petersen (1968) identified three types of personalities associated with good adjustment and two with poor adjustment. The largest category in the "well-adjusted" group consisted of "mature men," who accepted retirement easily without regrets about the past; these men were able to find new tasks and to cultivate new relationships to occupy their time. A second category of well-adjusted retirees, the "rocking chair men," welcomed retirement as a time to sit back, relax, and passively enjoy their old age. The final category of well-adjusted retirees, labeled "armored men," developed an active, highly organized life-style to defend themselves against the anxiety of growing old. The two categories

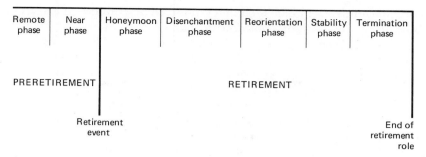

| Remote phase | Near phase | Honeymoon phase | Disenchantment phase | Reorientation phase | Stability phase | Termination phase |

| PRERETIREMENT | | RETIREMENT |

Retirement event

End of retirement role

Figure 9-2 Phases of retirement. (From *The Social Forces in Later Life, an Introduction to Social Gerontology,* Second Edition, by Robert C. Atchley. © 1977 by Wadsworth Publishing Company, Inc. Reprinted by permission of Wadsworth Publishing Company, Belmont, California 94002.)

of poorly adjusted retirees were labeled "angry men" and "self-haters." The former, unable to face the prospect of growing old, bitterly blamed others for their failure to achieve their life goals. In contrast to the "angry men," the "self-haters" blamed themselves for their misfortunes; they reacted with depression rather than with anger.

Adjustment to retirement can also be characterized as a series of progressive stages such as those described by Atchley (1976) (see Fig. 9-2). During the two preretirement phases the individual changes his or her perception of retirement as a **remote event** to viewing it as a **near event** and developing realistic or unrealistic fantasies about it. Realistic fantasies serve to ease the transition to retirement, but unrealistic fantasies lead to false expectations and more severe disenchantment. Retirement itself is divided into five phases. The first of these is the **honeymoon phase,** in which a euphoric attitude of being able to do all the things one never had time to do before prevails. This phase usually gives way to the retirement routine, but for some people a **disenchantment phase** characterized by a letdown, a feeling of emptiness, and even depression ensues. People who are disenchanted with retirement often go through a **reorientation phase** in which they "take stock," "pull themselves together," and develop a more realistic set of life alternatives. When they have developed stable criteria for making choices, whether it be at the end of the honeymoon phase or the reorientation phase, they enter a **stability phase.** For some people, retirement becomes irrelevant to their lives and they go back to work. This **termination phase** can also be entered as a result of illness, disability, or loss of financial support, in which the retirement role is replaced by the sick role or dependent role.

Roles in Retirement

Viewed from a sociological perspective, retirement is a time when people exit from certain roles and seek other roles to replace those that have been terminated (Blau, 1973). Society's attitude toward the older person's social status as one of "role obsolescence" may also cause that person to withdraw into a feeling of outlived usefulness. This feeling appears to be especially pronounced in our century of rapidly changing life-styles and the consequent isolation of generations. The segregation of old people from the rest of society is unfortunate, but those who have at least one or two close friends (confidants) are much better able to deal with the use of time and changing roles.

Because there are few formal roles for retirees in our society, they have to more or less work out their own social roles. This may be less troublesome for the older woman, especially the housewife, than for her retired husband who now finds himself spending almost all his time in his wife's domain. The role of "mother-without-children" whose retired husband is always around represents a change that can create new marital tensions. Nevertheless, role changes in retirement are usually not as great nor adjustment as difficult for a woman. An exception is when the woman becomes a widow and is unable to establish supportive social interactions.

On the whole, retirees adjust rather well to their changed occupational, familial, and other social roles. Some find the sick role or eccentric role easier to tolerate than the role of failure, and so they become hypochondriacs or neurotics (Busse & Pfeiffer, 1969). But for most, and especially those who engaged in some preretirement planning of postretirement roles, activities, and interests, retirement itself is a challenge and an opportunity.

Retirement may signal a decrease in interpersonal interactions and activities, but this is not necessarily bad. The **theory of disengagement** (Cumming, Dean, Newell, & McCaffrey, 1960; Cumming & Henry, 1961) characterizes old age as a time of declining involvement of the individual with society and society with the individual. According to this theory, aging brings about a change in self-perception such that the individual is less interested in being actively involved in things but is content to reflect on his or her past life and accomplishments. To the disengaged person, adjustment comes through gradual withdrawal from responsibility and participation rather than from continued activity.

Disengagement does occur, beginning as early as the 40s, but in many instances it is forced on older people as a consequence of society's failure to provide for them to continue being productive (Havighurst, Neugarten, & Tobin, 1973). Contrasting with the position that disengagement is voluntary is the **activity theory** that continued productivity and social interaction are essential to satisfaction and a sense of well-being (Maddox, 1968a, 1970). An extreme form of this concept sees the individual as "dying with his boots on," but the usual form of the theory incorporates the facts of reduced activity and partial retirement due to decreased energy. Depending on interests, temperament, health, and environmental circumstances, some retirees find satisfaction in a greater degree of activity than others. It is noteworthy that 79 percent of the retirees in Maddox's (1970) sample showed a high activity life-style pattern, which was accompanied by high satisfaction. On the other hand, only 14 percent showed the disengagement pattern and high satisfaction. Regardless of how active an individual retiree elects to remain, society should obviously make adequate provisions for those who want to stay involved.

RETIREMENT PENSIONS

In most agrarian societies the aged have traditionally been kept within the shelter of their own families, contributing whatever they could and being respected for their age and experience. Furthermore, the giving of alms and the construction of institutions for the elderly have been fostered by religious organizations for over a thousand years. However, it was not until the late nineteenth and early twentieth centuries that comprehensive pension programs for the elderly were mandated by law in Western nations. The first large-scale national pension program for retired workers was established in 1889 by Otto von Bismarck, Chancellor of Germany.[2] Similar programs were inaugurated during the same era or shortly thereafter in the Scandinavian countries and Great Britain.

Among the Western nations, the United States was rather late in enacting comprehensive federal pension legislation for the elderly. Proposals in this direction were made by the Social Democratic and Progressive political parties during the 1900 and 1912 presidential campaigns, respectively, but no legislation resulted from the proposals. A dozen individual states and Alaska enacted "old age pension laws" during the period 1915–1935, but it was not until the mid-1930s that President Roosevelt was able to get a national pension program through both houses of Congress. At that time, the high unemployment rate of the Great Depression provided the stimulus and rationale for legislating support of old and disabled workers.

Social Security

The major federal pension programs benefiting the elderly, their dependents, and survivors are listed in Table 9-3. The most extensive and costly of these programs are the Old Age and Survivors Insurance Program ("social security") and the Supplemental Security Income Program (SSI), both administered by the Social Security Administration. The social security program, which was passed into law in 1935, provides for federally administered old-age, survivors', and disability insurance payments. Retired workers are eligible for 80 percent of full monthly old-age benefits at age 62 and for full benefits at 65. The amount of a family's benefits is higher if the wife is 62 or older and/or there is a disabled child under 18 or a child aged 18 to 21 in school. Among those receiving social security payments in 1981, persons under 65 could earn up to $4,080 and persons 65 to 71, up to $5,500 a year and still obtain these benefits without penalty. For persons 72 and over, there is no ceiling on the amount that may be earned ("Social Security Increase," 1980).

The magnitude of the social security program is indicated by the fact

Table 9-3 MAJOR FEDERAL PENSION PROGRAMS BENEFITING THE ELDERLY*

Program	Agency	Description
Civil Service Retirement	U.S. Civil Service Commission	Principal retirement system for federal civilian employees; financed by employee contributions matched by employing agency plus congressional appropriations. Provides monthly retirement benefits based on past earnings and length of service to eligible retirees and their survivors.
Old-Age, Survivors Insurance Program	Social Security Administration, HEW	Financed through the payroll tax on employees, employers, and self-employed persons. Social security pays monthly cash benefits to retired workers (their dependents or survivors). Entitlement and level of benefits is based in part on covered earnings. Eligibility at 65 or may opt for permanently reduced benefits at 62.

that in 1980 the system paid out $123.6 billion in old age, survivors, and disability benefits. Over 35 million individuals, approximately one of every six Americans, received a check each month. Persons 65 and older received two-thirds of the checks, with the remainder going to the following groups: retirees between the ages of 62 and 64; children of retired, disabled, or deceased workers; disabled workers themselves; widows with children under 18 and other survivors and dependents. In addition, supplemental security income (SSI) payments were made to the 10 percent of the aged, blind, or disabled whose financial needs could not be completely met by social security.

Since its inception the social security system has been supported by employee paycheck deductions matched with employer contributions, but it has received no funds from general federal revenues. In 1937, when social security taxes were first levied, the rate paid by an employee was 1 percent of the first $3,000 of income. This tax remained unchanged until 1950, when it began to rise. As a consequence of continued inflation and a resulting increase in the cost of administering the program, it became necessary to tie social security payments to the consumer price index. The fact that this index increased by 14.3 percent in 1980 helps explain why by 1981 the tax rate had risen to 6.65 percent and the maximum income

Table 9-3 *(Continued)*

Program	Agency	Description
Railroad Retirement Program	Railroad Retirement Board	Financed through a payroll tax on employees and employers. Monthly benefits are paid to retired workers (their wives and survivors) after 10 years' employment. Coverage for individuals with less than 10 years' service is transferred to the Social Security system.
Supplemental Security Income Program	Social Security Administration, HEW	Aged, blind, and disabled persons, with no other income or with limited resources, are guaranteed monthly income. States may, and in some cases, must, supplement federal payments.
Veterans Pension Program	Veterans Administration	Provides monthly cash benefits to veterans aged 65 or older with at least 90 days military service, including 1 day wartime service, and who meet income limitation requirements. Benefits are also paid to designated survivor. Benefits vary according to veteran's annual income.

*Adapted from Select Committee on Aging. *Federal responsibility to the elderly.* Washington, D.C., U.S. Government Printing Office, 1976, pp. 12−13.

subject to the tax (the "wage base") had climbed to $29,700. Both the tax rate and wage base are expected to increase gradually during the 1980s, and by 1990 the tax rate is scheduled to be 7.65 percent on every dollar earned up to $66,900 ("Social Security Increase," 1980).

Although the social security system was designed to be self-supporting, the ratio of wage earners to recipients had decreased from a comfortable margin of 35 to 1 in 1945 to approximately 3 to 1 in 1980. As a consequence, the system is now paying out more than it takes in, a pattern that may ultimately bankrupt it. Even with the increases in the tax rate and wage base, there is no assurance that the system's reserve fund will not be depleted in a few years. So what can be done?

One suggested solution to the problem of financing the social security system is to accept the fact that it can no longer be self-supporting and requires contributions from federal income tax revenues. In this regard, the Medicare portion of social security funding could be shifted to general tax revenues, while leaving the pension plan aspects of the system to be funded as they are currently. Other possibilities are to raise the retirement age[3] and/or reduce the benefits paid.

Whatever the source and level of financial support of the social security system may become, as the cost of living and the number of elderly people increase still further, future generations of young and middle-aged adults will probably find themselves contributing more and more to the economic welfare of their elders. Consequently, the following conclusion drawn by the American Council on Life Insurance from a 1978 survey of the social and financial attitudes of young Americans is reassuring: "Young people seem to be willing to shoulder the burden of providing adequate benefits to the elderly even if the burden increases" (Porter, 1980b).

Despite the difficulties of sustaining the present level of support, many public officials and social scientists have maintained that old-age assistance programs in the United States are inadequate (Eisdorfer, 1975). They point to the more comprehensive programs of Sweden, England, and the Communist countries. Several of the Communist countries also provide incentives to workers who are willing to postpone retirement, the effectiveness of which is demonstrated by the fact that 10 percent of Russia's workers are working pensioners. In contrast, the American and British systems penalize those who work while receiving social security payments by decreasing their benefits by a sizable portion of their income.

Other Pension Plans

The first federal pensions in the United States were the military pensions granted in 1792 to the veterans of the American Revolution. The present-day counterpart of those pensions is the Veterans Pension Program. Other federal pension programs are the Civil Service Retirement and the Railroad Retirement Program (see Table 9-3). In addition to government pensions, many business, industrial, and professional organizations have their own retirement plans. These pension programs, which cover less than 20 percent of retirees, are experiencing many of the same problems as the social security system. The costs of all retirement programs have soared during recent years, and the ratio of the number of workers who contribute to the plans to the number of retirees has decreased by over 50 percent in the past decade.

Certain individuals, referred to somewhat disparagingly as "double-dippers," draw two or more retirement pensions at the same time. For example, many military personnel and government employees are young enough after serving the requisite number of years for retirement to begin a new career and take a second and even a third job. By working long enough at each successive job to qualify for a pension from the particular organization, they may eventually be eligible for pensions from several sources. Added to the social security payments to which they are entitled at age 65, the total sum that these individuals receive every month during later life can make their retirement years a time of relative affluence and leisure.

SUMMARY

The percentage of elderly men in the U.S. labor force has declined steadily during this century, whereas the percentage of employed elderly women has remained fairly constant. The retirement rate among elderly men has been increased by those who have been enticed by improvements in retirement benefits and also by those who have been forced to retire before they are ready to do so. A sizable proportion of the latter group consists of men, who, like their younger counterparts, view their jobs as essential to a positive self-concept and want to continue working as long as possible.

Lack of satisfying work can affect both mental and physical health. This is particularly true of older workers, who are even more committed to their jobs than younger people. Research findings demonstrate that the former group typically performs as well as the latter on the job. Despite this fact, both the rate and length of unemployment are greater among older than among younger men, especially in the case of minority groups. In response to lower population growth and the increasing cost of retirement pensions, many countries have raised the retirement age, provided special incentives, and made other moves to increase the number of elderly in the active work force.

The traditional retirement ages of 60 for women and 65 for men were established by social security legislation in 1935 and have no real medical or psychological foundation. Federal legislation in 1979 raised the mandatory retirement age to 70 for most private as well as state and local government employees; there is no retirement age limit for civilian employees of the federal government.

Retirement is a rite of passage between middle and late life that may be anticipated with pleasure or foreboding. It is not necessarily a dreaded event; many people look forward to retiring and pursuing other goals. Even among those who do not relish the prospect of retiring, a large number discover that it is not as bad as they expected. In any event, when, where, how, and with what to retire are decisions that, insofar as possible, should be made by retirees themselves. Preretirement planning can help the individual face and prepare for retirement. Clearly, not all the stresses of retirement can be anticipated, but this fact can also be pointed out in preretirement counseling sessions.

Reactions to retirement vary with the personality and socioeconomic status of the retiree and whether he or she continues to have meaningful social roles to play after retirement. Reichard, Livson, and Peterson described five types of personalities in terms of their adjustments to retirement, whereas Atchley depicted adjustment to retirement in terms of five phases. Blau emphasized the tendency of modern society to view the social status of retirees as one of role obsolescence. The lack of meaningful roles to play is less true of the older women, who continue to take care of the home, than of unemployed older men. The theory of disengagement views old age as a time of reduced involvement with society, whereas the activity theory emphasizes the importance of continuing productivity and social interaction after retirement.

The social security pension system is the most general basis of financial support for elderly Americans. The system is, however, in financial trouble, necessitating changes in the methods of funding and benefit payments in the very near future. Approximately 20 percent of retirees also receive private pensions, but because of increases in the cost and the dependency ratio, many of these plans are, like the social security system, ineffectively financed.

SUGGESTED READINGS

Atchley, R. C. *The sociology of retirement.* New York: Wiley, 1976.

Baugher, D. Is the older worker inherently incompetent? *Aging and Work,* 1978 (Fall), 243–250.

Fisher, D. H. *Growing old in America.* New York: Oxford University Press, 1978.

Jaslow, P. Employment, retirement, and morale among older women, *Journal of Gerontology,* 1976, *31,* 212–218.

Kalt, N. C., & Kohn, M. H. Pre-retirement counseling: Characteristics of programs and preferences of retirees. *The Gerontologist,* 1975, *15,* 179–181.

Kart, C. S., & Manard, B. (Eds.). *Aging in America: Readings in social gerontology.* Part IV. Work, retirement and leisure. Port Washington, N.Y.: Alfred Publishing, 1976.

Plonk, M. A., & Pulley, M. A. Financial management practices of retired couples. *The Gerontologist,* 1977, *17,* 256–261.

Sheppard, H. L. Work and retirement. In R. H. Binstock & E. Shanas (Eds.), *Handbook of aging and the social sciences.* New York: Van Nostrand Reinhold, 1976. pp. 286–309.

NOTES

[1]Available from the American Association of Retired Persons, 1909 K Street, N.W., Washington, D.C. 20006.

[2]Rather than being based on humanitarian concern for the welfare of older Germans, Bismarck's reason for instituting such a program was to disarm the Socialist opposition to his government. Because few Germans in the late nineteenth century lived to be 65, the cost to the state of granting pensions to those who did was not great.

[3]The current retirement age in Sweden, which has the most comprehensive old-age assistance program in the Western world, is 67.

Living Conditions and Activities

According to authorities, the most serious problems of elderly Americans are those concerned with income, health, housing, nutrition, and transportation. Insufficient income is a source of difficulty for the majority of older Americans, inadequate housing for a slightly lower percentage, and poor health for over 75 percent. These problems are obviously not independent of one another. For example, health is affected by nutrition, housing, and transportation, and all four are influenced by income. In fact, insufficient income is a contributing factor in almost all the problems encountered by the elderly. Other sources of difficulty in later life include loss of social roles, use of leisure time, safety, and a host of other matters, ranging from the filling out of income tax forms to coping with theft and assaults against person and property.

INCOME OF THE ELDERLY

The median income of elderly Americans is significantly lower than that of younger adults, but variations among incomes are quite large. In 1979, for example, the average yearly income of older Americans ranged from $20,000 or more for 1.8 million couples with the husband over age 65 to less than $3,000 for 1.6 million unrelated individuals. In general, the income of elderly women was less than that of elderly men, blacks received less than whites, and unrelated individuals had lower incomes than married couples (U.S. Dept. of Health & Human Services, 1981).

Social security is the main source of income for two-thirds of the unrelated old people and half the married couples in the United States. Other sources of income include private pensions, earnings, assets, and a small amount (1 percent) from sons, daughters, or other relatives. Many older people have also accumulated substantial material assets over a lifetime of working and saving. On the average, however, the income of a retired man is only about half that of a working man and that of an elderly woman is half that of a retired man. It has been argued that the resulting 50 percent reduction in purchasing power after retirement is not as serious as it may seem, because less income is needed for job-related and social activities. Nevertheless, on the average 32 percent of an elderly person's income is spent on housing, 25 percent on food, 15 percent on transportation, and 10 percent on medical care. This leaves only about 18 percent for clothing, personal care, gifts, and whatever social or recreational activities he or she wants to engage in (U.S. Dept. of Health and Human Services, 1981).

The Aged Poor

There is a great deal of truth in the saying that being sick but rich is better than being healthy but poor. Denials of the poets notwithstanding, money is related to happiness in old age. Income determines to some extent what people do with their time—whether they sit idly at home and brood or get out, interact with other people, and take an interest in something other than themselves.

With respect to the statistics of poverty, approximately 3.6 million (15.1 percent) elderly Americans were below the official poverty level in 1979 (Table 10-1); another 2.3 million were below the "near-poverty" level. About two-thirds of the elderly poor in that year lived alone or with nonrelatives, and a larger percentage lived in nonmetropolitan than in metropolitan areas. Owing to federal assistance programs, the number of older Americans below the poverty level decreased from one in three in 1967 to approximately one in seven in 1979. Furthermore, most of the income of poor families came from social security, supplemental security, and public assistance (U.S. Dept. of Health & Human Services, 1981).

As was noted above, race is related to economic status. Only 13 percent of elderly whites were below the official poverty level in 1979, whereas 27 percent of elderly Hispanics and 35 percent of elderly blacks were in the same category. Low income was also characteristic of American Indians and other minority groups (U.S. Dept. of Health & Human Services, 1981).

Although the total number of elderly people who are destitute has declined appreciably during the last decade, a disproportionate number remain poor. Those elderly couples whose annual incomes are less than $5,000, the majority of whom live in large cities, wage a daily battle against the rising costs of food, clothing, housing, and medical care. This group includes many people who have not been accustomed to poverty but whose savings have long since been depleted and who are now attempting to live

Table 10-1   PERCENTAGES OF ELDERLY AMERICANS BELOW POVERTY LEVEL IN 1979*

	Percent Below Poverty Level
Ethnic Group	
White	13
Black	35
Hispanic	27
Living Situation	
In families	8
Alone or with nonrelatives	29
Location of Residence	
Metropolitan	20
Nonmetropolitan	12
Total	15

*Data from U.S. Dept. of Health & Human Services, 1981.

on social security payments. Unlike the traditional order of importance—food, clothing, shelter—the elderly poor spend the greatest amount of their income for rent and utilities, with clothing second and food in last place. The difficulties that the aged poor may encounter in attempting to live on fixed incomes was dramatically illustrated by a newspaper story of an elderly New York couple who froze to death after the heat in their apartment was turned off because they were unable to pay the fuel bill.

The Affluent Aged

At the other end of the economic scale from the aged poor are the affluent elderly who retire to a life of relative leisure. Currently, about 700,000 men and women 65 years or older, representing 3 to 4 percent of the elderly population of the United States, live in retirement villages or adult communities. These communities provide lifetime facilities for people who are able to invest a sizable initial payment plus a maintenance charge in an apartment or house and who have a sizable annual income. Among the best known of the "gerontopolises," which have blossomed throughout the nation but especially in the Southwest and Florida, are Sun City near Phoenix; Rossmoor Leisure Worlds of California, New Jersey, and Maryland; Park West in Miami; and The Sequoias in San Francisco. Two of the major developers were Del E. Webb, who founded Sun City with the slogan "happiness equals activity plus friendliness," and Ross W. Cortese, the entrepreneur of Leisure Worlds and Rossmoor (Walnut Creek, California). These retirement communities vary in luxuriousness and the restrictions that are imposed on residents and visitors. For example, no one under 50 can buy property in Sun City, and Park West bars dogs and has a time limit of 3 weeks for visits by children (Fig. 10-1).

The cost of a condominium apartment in a large metropolitan area or suburb or a house in a retirement village is usually beyond the financial

Figure 10-1. Shuffleboard game with visiting granddaughter at Miami's Park West Community. (© 1978 Paul Barton.)

resources of most retirees. This is especially true of the expensive facilities of Leisure World, a cluster of Spanish-style dwellings in Laguna Hill, California for retirees aged 52 and up. Despite the cost, Leisure World has had no scarcity of applicants. It features several heated swimming pools, tennis courts, a 27-hole golf course, bowling greens, restaurants, libraries, classrooms, a medical clinic, closed-circuit television, and free bus rides to Los Angeles. Life at Leisure World, which is protected by 6-foot high walls and security guards who patrol around the clock, consists of a diversity of activities in physically safe surroundings. About the only activity that it does not offer is employment, but some of its residents hold full- or part-time jobs.

There are, of course, disadvantages to retirement communities, even in the plush atmosphere of Leisure World. One retiree declared that Leisure World is a "pain in the neck" if you don't play golf or pool. Living exclusively with one's own age and socioeconomic group can also be boring and, one might argue, unrealistic. Some of the most successful and talented people in our society, which badly needs their problem-solving "knowhow," may become segregated from real life and stultified in a community dominated by play and relaxation.

LIVING ENVIRONMENTS

The living environment of a person includes the house, apartment, or room in which he or she lives, as well as encompassing the neighborhood or community in which the dwelling unit is located. Carp (1976) described the

Table 10-2 LIVING SITUATIONS OF ELDERLY AMERICANS IN 1980*

Living Situation	% Men	% Women
Family householder	75	10
Spouse of family householder	3	36
Other family member	5	11
Living alone	15	41
Living with nonrelatives	2	2

*Data from U.S. Dept. of Health & Human Services, 1981.

major features of living environments to be considered by the elderly as: (1) age and ownership of dwelling units, (2) physical condition and availability of funds for maintenance and repair, (3) location with regard to services needed by older people, (4) proximity to commercial and recreational activities, (5) proximity to relatives and age peers, (6) accessibility and usability of transportation, and (7) congeniality or threat in the surrounding environment, whether related to physical hazards or personal hazards.

Older people have a variety of living environments. The large majority reside in rural areas, small towns, and the poorer sections of cities, and only about 5 percent live in nursing homes or other institutions. Most elderly people, and especially elderly men, live in family settings. The remainder, primarily older women, live alone or with a nonrelative (Table 10-2).

Location of Residence

Few older people can afford the accommodations of a posh retirement community. Rather, the residences of people who are 60 years and older tend to be clustered in special buildings of large cities, in certain neighborhoods within suburbs, and even in specific regions of the nation. Although large numbers of older people live in the large cities of the northeastern and midwestern United States, during the past 20 years there has been a steady migration of retirees to Sunbelt states such as Florida, Arizona, and California. Report 10-1 summarizes the results of a survey of the economic, climatic, and recreational characteristics of the various states in terms of their appropriateness for retirement. According to the survey findings, the ten states in which retirement living is easiest and cheapest are: Utah, Louisiana, South Carolina, Nevada, Texas, New Mexico, Alabama, Arizona, Florida, and Georgia. On the other hand, because of high taxes, expensive utilities, and high unemployment, the worst retirement areas are the New England states, New York, and New Jersey.

The Sunbelt has its attractions, but most retirees remain in the same homes after retirement; only about 4 percent, usually the more affluent, move out of state. Leaving one's lifetime friends, relatives, and familiar surroundings to move out of state (or even across town) can be a stressful experience, which is not for everyone. For this reason, and economic

Report 10-1   SOUTH, WEST FOUND BEST FOR RETIREMENT*

NEW YORK (UPI) — A survey of the best states in the United States to retire to, based on economy as well as climate and recreational facilities, concluded that 10 states in the South and West best fill retirees' needs.

The study by Chase Econometrics Associates, Inc., released in Money magazine, said the 10 states where the living is easiest and comparatively cheap are: Utah, Louisiana, South Carolina, Nevada, Texas, New Mexico, Alabama, Arizona, Florida and Georgia.

All ranked high as areas where it is not only pleasant to live but which offer opportunities for part-time work, low living costs, low taxes, low fuel costs, availability of housing and proximity to medical services and shopping.

The survey also listed the worst retirement areas—New England, New York and New Jersey—because of high taxes, expensive utilities and unemployment. It said Massachusetts is the poorest bet in the nation for retired people.

Following is a state-by-state ranking:

—**Utah:** Moderate living costs and low utility rates. Exclusion of up to $6,000 a year pension income for people over 65 in computing state income tax. Recommended: around Salt Lake City and St. George.

—**Louisiana:** A cost-of-living 10% below the national average. A $400 tax exemption for people over 65. Incredibly low property taxes. Recommended: St. Tammany Parish.

—**South Carolina:** A special tax exemption of $800 and $12,000 deduction from property value assessments for 65 and over. Free hunting and fishing licenses. Recommended: coastal islands and Summerville.

—**Nevada:** No income or inheritance taxes, but high hospital costs. Recommended: Boulder City.

—**Texas:** A $15,000 exemption on the assessed value of houses for people over 65. Recommended: Austin and the Brownsville-McAllen area.

—**New Mexico:** A cost of living 10% below the national average, low taxes, low fuel costs. Recommended: Albuquerque and Roswell.

—**Alabama:** Low food costs. Recommended: Fairhope.

—**Arizona:** About the best medical care you can get anywhere. A personal income tax exemption of $1,000 for people over 65. Recommended: Tucson, Phoenix, Green Valley, Prescott.

—**Florida:** Many medical services geared to older people. A $5,000 deduction on property tax assessments for the over 65ers who are five-year residents. Recommended: away from the costly coastal areas.

—**Georgia:** Cost of living about 9% lower than the national average. Good medical services. Recommended: the Golden Isles area and Savannah.

*From *Los Angeles Times*, Sept. 19, 1979, Pt. 1-B, p. 8. Reprinted by permission of United Press International.

reasons as well, in spite of deteriorating neighborhood conditions, poor health, and frequent loneliness, retirees tend to "stay put."

Whether or not they take it, the opportunity to retire to another geographical location is usually reserved for those who are financially solvent. Thousands of older occupants of single rooms of old hotels located in the shabbiest sections of large cities are at the lower end of the economic scale. When they are not in these rooms, many urban elderly wander the streets or congregate in large outdoor parks, at bus terminals, and in other sheltered public places. Because of accelerating rents, a large portion (approximately 25 percent) of the small incomes of these inner-city residents goes for shelter. Consequently, malnutrition and other health problems are common. Because of somewhat lower rents and a different life-style, health problems and malnutrition are less characteristic of elderly residents of publicly supported housing projects. Such housing projects have the advantages of improved living conditions and, particularly in age-segregated facilities, greater social interaction with one's age group.

Although sizable numbers of old people live in low-cost public housing units and other rental accommodations, 72 percent own their own homes. A large percentage of these individuals, valuing their independence, prefer to live alone rather than with family members. Because they live in their own households and require more services, the expense of maintaining older people is greater than that for other age groups. However, only when they reach a point at which they can no longer fend for themselves do these older "loners" usually express a willingness to live with a family member. An alternative arrangement that may be acceptable to a widowed older person is to live with another elderly individual of the same sex.

Elderly Homeowners

Their incomes are usually low, but a lifetime of work and house payments has resulted in 60 percent of the elderly being mortgage-free homeowners and another 12 percent having homes with mortgages. Whites are more likely than blacks and other minorities to own their own homes, and elderly married are more likely than singles to be homeowners (U.S. Dept. of Health & Human Services, 1979). Elderly homeowners spend 80 to 90 percent of their lives in their homes (Hansen, 1975), many of which are fairly humble dwellings built 40 or more years ago. Consequently, they are frequently deteriorating or substandard as well as unsafe and/or unhealthful. Most are in need of repairs, which the owners do not have the physical ability to make themselves and cannot afford to have done.

The spiraling costs of home repairs, property taxes, and utilities in recent years have all made it difficult for persons on fixed incomes to maintain independent households. It is true that nearly all states give a property-tax break to senior citizens,[1] but housing and associated costs are still more than older people with average retirement incomes can handle. Faced with the rising costs of home ownership, some older people opt for mobile-home living or rental housing in a public project or retirement community. This is not the usual pattern, however, and most single or married elderly people choose not to move but continue to reside in quarters that may actually be too roomy for them. Only a serious physical problem, loss of a spouse, or some other severely stressful circumstance can induce them to move voluntarily.

Better Housing for the Elderly

Government statistics indicate that 30 percent of the housing units for the elderly are substandard, unsafe, and in disrepair; many lack private bathrooms, hot water, and other conveniences that Americans have come to expect (U.S. Senate Special Committee on Aging, 1977). These facts, combined with increases in the number of older people and the rising cost of housing, have created a high priority for housing among the many federal programs concerned with older Americans.

The major federal housing programs that benefit the elderly are described in Table 10-3. These programs are particularly concerned with subsidizing the construction and repair of housing for older people who are now living on low or moderate incomes. Another service, a directory of

Table 10-3 MAJOR FEDERAL HOUSING PROGRAMS BENEFITING THE ELDERLY*

Program	Executive Agency	Description
Housing for the Elderly	Housing Production and Mortgage Credit of HUD	Federal loans for construction or rehabilitation of multifamily rental housing for elderly (aged 62 and over). Tenants may qualify for rent supplements under the Section B program.
Low and Moderate Income Housing	Housing Production and Mortgage Credit of HUD	Provides housing assistance payments for low-income persons and families who cannot afford "decent and sanitary housing in the private sector." Rent supplements cover the difference between the community's fair market rent down to 15 to 25 percent of the tenants' adjusted income.
Mortgage Insurance on Rental Housing for the Elderly	Housing Production and Mortgage Credit of HUD	Federal government insures against loss on mortgages for the construction and rehabilitation of multifamily rental housing for the elderly (aged 62 or over) or disabled whose income is higher than the low or moderate income level.
Rural Rental Housing Loans	Farmers Home Administration of Dept. of Agriculture	Federal government makes direct and guaranteed loans to construct, improve, or repair rental or cooperative housing in rural areas for low-income persons including senior citizens aged 62 or over.

Table 10-3 *(Continued)*

Program	Executive Agency	Description
Community Development	Community Planning and Development of HUD	Formula grants to urban communities, based on poverty population and other economic and population factors, for variety of community development activities, including construction of senior citizens' centers.
Rental and Co-operative Housing for Lower and Moderate Income Families	Housing Production and Mortgage Credit of HUD	The federal government subsidizes down to 1 percent of the interest on mortgages for private developers of multifamily housing for low and moderate income families, persons aged 62 and over, and handicapped individuals.
Low Rent Public Housing	Housing Production and Mortgage Credit of HUD	Local housing authorities receive federal loans to aid in the purchase, rehabilitation, leasing, or construction of multifamily housing for low-income families, individuals aged 62 and over, and handicapped individuals. Housing designed for the elderly may have congregate dining rooms and other special features. Rents may not be more than 25 percent of the family's income.

*Adapted from Select Committee on Aging. *Federal responsibility to the elderly.* Washington, D.C.: U.S. Government Printing Office, 1976, pp. 8–9.

housing constructed especially for older people, is provided by the National Council on the Aging. Information on low- to moderate-income housing, tax relief, and grants for rent payments can also be obtained from local housing authorities, tax collection agencies, and Senior Citizens Centers in the community.

Social designers and space managers have usually failed to give enough attention to the physical and psychological needs of future residents in planning living environments for the elderly. Such engineers and architects have not been sufficiently aware of the profound effect that the intimate environment can have on the health and morale of older people. For example, apartments that are designed by architects who are insensitive to the activities and life-styles of the elderly make it impossible for older people to retain their valued furnishings or to create a setting consistent with their

Table 10-4 RECOMMENDED ADJUSTMENTS IN HOUSING FOR THE ELDERLY*

Entrances

For persons with limited mobility, single-story or ground floor residences are best. At least one incline should have a ramp, properly mounted handrails being placed on either side of the ramp. An open space adjacent to the door should be provided. Entrances should be well-lighted.

General Structural Features

Doors should be designed for disabled persons lacking in strength, grasping power, coordination, or visual acuity. They should be large enough to accommodate wheel chairs; sliding rather than swinging internal doors are best. Eliminate raised thresholds if possible; if not, paint them with a contrasting color. Cover floors with nonslip but easy-to-maneuver surfaces. Make walls smooth.

Kitchen

Storage facilities should allow for easy retrievability of items. Open storage shelves, revolving and pull-out shelves, pegboards, and magnetic catches are recommended. Kitchen counters should be low and have recesses. Dishwasher, washer, dryer, oven, and other large appliances should be front-opening. Sinks and plumbing in kitchen and bathrooms should be built for use by someone in a wheelchair.

Bathrooms

Should be larger than customary in new homes to allow for wheelchair or walker. Bathroom doors should open outward. Install grab-bars near tub, shower, sink, and toilet. Have extra wide tubs, mount shower heads on flexible hoses, and install seat in tub or shower. Bathroom floors should be nonslip, with the shower floor flush with the outside floor and sloping slightly toward the drain. A wall-hung toilet that is higher than usual is an advantage in transferring from a wheelchair. Other fixtures should be low enough to permit easy use by those with limited mobility. Easily moved, nonscald handles and other controls rather than knobs or faucets, and wooden handles rather than cold, slippery metal railings are recommended. Help buttons, warm air dryers, counters on either side of the lavatory, and sinks positioned for ease of access are also good features.

Bedrooms

Should be large enough to permit an elderly person to move around with ease. Mattresses should be level with wheelchair seat height. Closets should have sliding or swing-out doors and at least one rod. Light switches, telephone, and alarm units must be near the head of the bed. Windows should be constructed low enough so someone in a wheelchair or lying in bed can see outside.

Lighting

Light switches must be approximately 90 cm. (3 ft.) from the floor, and wall outlets 45 to 60 cm. (18 to 24 in.) high. Lights must be placed near bed, bath, and medicine cabinet.

Other Considerations

Large elevators should be provided in multiple family dwellings. Easy accessibility to public transportation, parking spaces adjacent to units if single-story, and patios or balconies for entertaining friends are suggested. Emergency buzzers or bells in several locations and an alarm system connected directly to police headquarters would be helpful and reassuring in some units. Climate, air quality, and noise control are also recommended.

*Data from Agan, Casto, Day, & Schwab (1977) and Ryan (1978).

life-styles (Howell, 1980). More attention obviously needs to be given to the kinds of communities and housing that are adequate now and will be appropriate for older people in the foreseeable future. This requires the combined efforts of architects, home economists, builders, and developers in designing living spaces that are suitable during later life.

Regarding the design of the community or neighborhood itself, consideration should be given to factors such as nearness to medical and shopping facilities, availability and convenience of public transportation, air temperatures and pollution, degree of privacy and noise, safety and freedom from crime, and recreational facilities. In selecting a living environment, elderly people themselves will want to consider these factors and also closeness to relatives and friends of similar age. Finally, many of the structural features listed in Table 10-4 are important to elderly residents.

In 1977 there were only about 3 million housing units in the United States designed specifically for the aged, including everything from apartments to intermediate and advanced medical care facilities ("Housing for the Aging," 1977). These facilities may be classified according to the age groups for which they were intended as: (1) fully independent, including apartments for "go-go" people in the 65 to 75 year age range; (2) partially dependent, comprising something in between apartments and nursing homes for "slow-go" people in the 75 to 85 year age range; (3) totally dependent, including nursing homes for the "no-go" people over age 85.

Promises made during the 1976 presidential campaign included better housing for the elderly, but relatively little was done to keep those promises. A primary reason for this failure was undoubtedly rising construction costs and shortage of money, but many of the adjustments needed to make housing more suited to the needs of the elderly are neither difficult nor terribly expensive to make (see Table 10-4). Furthermore, lack of government funding should not interfere with thinking about and proposing solutions to the housing problems of the aged. There are many questions that should be discussed more fully before taking action. For example, should there be more planned towns, one-level apartments, and single-person family dwellings, or are other alternatives more plausible?

Even when considerable thought has gone into the planning of a retirement home, geriatric clinic, or other living environments for the aged, mistakes are made. Thus designers may emphasize the provision of more space for social interaction, only to have the increased space result in decreased interaction. Perhaps the most serious error in designing a living environment for elderly people is to assume that because of their age, all older people have the same requirements. Nothing could be further from the truth. Individual differences in needs and preferences are, if anything, greater among older than younger adults. A special age-segregated environment, for example, may help some old people maintain social interactions and a sense of dignity in the face of advancing years, whereas for others it produces only feelings of detachment and loneliness. It is noteworthy that despite the seeming social advantages of age-segregated environments, two-thirds of the elderly people questioned in one survey preferred to live among people of various ages (Lawton, 1975).

Transportation

The ability to extend one's environment and participate in the wider community depends greatly on communication and transportation facilities. Transportation is often a problem for the elderly, in rural areas that have little public transportation as well as in many suburban and urban communities. Whenever food stores, doctors' offices, banks, and other shops and facilities are not near their residences, problems of transportation can arise for older people. Those who are impaired by disease or disability have special difficulty in getting from place to place, particularly when they do not drive and public transportation is scarce and costly. Even when public buses and trains are available, the high steps, sudden stops and starts, and rapidly closing doors are often nerve rattling and unsafe for older people. They are also inconvenient and potentially dangerous modes of travel for the older person who has to wait on a cold street corner in a high-crime area. Because of their greater expense, one would expect taxi service to be a more efficient means of traveling than riding buses. But waiting for a taxicab can also be a problem for older people when cab drivers, viewing the elderly as passengers who take more time and tip less, simply pass them by.

Having to depend on other people to take them from place to place restricts the life space and life-style of many elderly individuals. This is especially true in the case of the poor, who, because of lack of money for transportation or the nonexistence of public transportation in their areas, become isolated and lonely. Transportation is less of a problem in places where transit companies offer reduced fares to senior citizens and in those states that provide free statewide public transportation to the elderly. "Medicabs" for persons confined to wheelchairs and "dial-a-ride" programs in which elderly passengers can reserve reduced-fare tax rides are other examples of special transportation services for the elderly at the community level (Kimmel, 1980). Illustrative of elderly fare reductions at the national level is Amtrak's policy of offering a 25 percent ticket discount to senior citizens and handicapped people.

The U.S. Department of Transportation administers several federal programs under which grants are made to public and nonprofit groups to support mass transit and reduced-fare programs for the elderly and handicapped. In addition, grants are awarded under the Federal Highway Act for projects aimed at developing and improving the use of public mass transportation in rural areas—where many aged Americans live. These federal programs, and those at the state and local levels, have not taken care of the transportation needs and problems of elderly Americans, but they have made important contributions.

ACTIVITIES OF THE AGED

The problem of how to use one's time in old age is probably not so serious for the 4.4 million individuals who continue to work full- or part-time after age 65. Whether they work for pay or volunteer, these individuals are usually not at a loss for something to do. In addition, workers who see their occupations as dull or taxing and those who have become accustomed to long vacations (e.g., teachers) are less likely to experience problems in occupying themselves after retirement. Many other retirees, however, have to learn by themselves or be taught how to cope with their newly found leisure time. Retired urban office workers who have failed to plan for postretirement activities and whose circumstances do not permit part-time work may find themselves with nothing but time on their hands. In contrast, retired farmers or mechanics can continue to till or tinker within the limits of their strength and ability.

People who are facing retirement often worry about how they will use their time, and, to be sure, the complaint of "too much time on my hands" is often heard from the recently retired. Those who fail to develop hobbies or other interests can easily become worried and anxious when faced with a succession of empty days. For this reason, preretirement counselors stress that it is just as important for the retiree to develop a program of activities as it is to make financial plans.

Planning for the use of leisure time should certainly not be confined to later life. As people put in fewer and fewer hours each day on the job and retire earlier, the question of how the increased leisure time can be used to help them grow and fulfill their potentialities becomes crucial for all age groups. Just as people are taught to have the traditional, culturally prescribed "right" attitude toward work, so too they must learn a newer "right" attitude toward leisure (Neulinger & Raps, 1972).

Using Leisure Time

The ways in which older people fill their time are greatly influenced by the leisure activities in which they engaged during middle age. The activities and avocations developed in early and middle adulthood provide a greater number of role options and hence increase the likelihood of successful adjustment in later life. These activities need not be limited to the traditional retirement pastimes of fishing, gardening, shuffleboard, pool, and golf. Only 15 percent of noninstitutionalized retirees are seriously restricted in their activities, and many take up tennis, jogging, and other vigorous activities. It is true that only a few exceptional individuals are able to approach the feat of 98-year-old Dimitri Iordanidis, who, by training religiously and giving up sex at age 85, was able to run a 42-mile marathon in 7 hours and 40 minutes![2] For most elderly individuals, daily walks rather than marathon running constitute the best kind of physical exercise.

Sun City's slogan that "happiness equals activity plus friendliness" is subscribed to by a number of organizations for the elderly. There is merit in the slogan, because people who continue to interact with others and pursue outside activities seem to adjust better to old age than those who become isolated and idle after retirement. Unfortunately, retirees are not always able to do what they desire. Many cannot afford to pursue the crafts and hobbies or the intellectual and artistic pursuits that interest them. Arbitrary age limits may also inhibit the minority who try to become proficient in a new craft or vocation. A case in point is that of a retired furniture salesman who finally had the time to become what he had always wanted to be—a carpenter. Offering to work free as an apprentice to learn the trade, he was told that unions would object or that insurance would not cover the risk. Because he was too old to join a trade school carpentry class, he was directed to a hobby shop where he was forced to settle for wood-burning rather than the furniture-making that he had always wanted to learn (Curtin, 1972).

Surveys of leisure activities in later life have found that the types or range of activities participated in by older people are more restricted and narrow than those in which young and middle-aged adults engage (Robinson, 1969; Gordon, Gaitz & Scott, 1976). Dancing, drinking, attending movies, participating in sports or physical exercise, using guns, performing outdoor activities, traveling, reading, and doing cultural productions are all reportedly less frequent in older than younger adults. On the other hand, the frequencies of television viewing, discussion, spectator sports, cultural consumption, entertaining participating in organizations, and home embellishment are about the same in older people as in other adult age groups. The fact that activities are more sedentary and restricted to the home in later life is indicated by the greater incidence of solitary pursuits and cooking (by men) (Gordon, Gaitz, & Scott, 1976).

Care must be taken in interpreting the findings of the preceding survey, because the effects of age are confounded with cohort (generational) differences. In addition, the averaged results do not indicate the wide range of differences in the leisure-time activities of various elderly individuals. Thus the survey results suggest that interest in reading declines in old age, but any public librarian knows that many older people read a great deal. Acknowledgment of this fact is shown by the publication of magazines aimed especially at older Americans (e.g., *Active Aging, 50-Plus, Modern Maturity, Prime Time*). In addition, various newspapers throughout the nation (e.g., *Louisville Courier-Journal* and *Miami Herald*) have columns or entire pages devoted exclusively to matters of interest to senior citizens.

The facilities of libraries are used extensively by the aged for recreational purposes and for obtaining information on health, financial, and vocational matters. Special book lists, books with large print, and places where older people can meet for discussions are also made available by librarians. At the national level, the Library of Congress offers free library services (e.g., Braille, cassette, and disc books and magazines) to persons with visual or physical handicaps. The Older Reader Services program of the Department of Education also makes grants available to public libraries for the purchase of special materials and the development of other programs and services for the aged.

Many organizations that sponsor activities for the elderly (e.g., Senior Citizens Centers and Golden Age clubs) provide discount tickets for entertainment programs, travel, and other forms of recreation and services. The National Park Service offers Golden Age passports to permanent U.S. residents 62 years of age and older. These passes enable the holder to pay a reduced fee for use of the facilities of any national park, monument, or recreation area.

As noted earlier, older people also use their leisure time by engaging in volunteer work and club and lodge activities and by visiting friends and relatives. The Older American Volunteer Programs sponsored by the federal ACTION agency, for example, enable the elderly to perform volunteer services for day-care centers, hospitals, schools, and other public service agencies. Additional activities of the aged include going to church and other meeting places, shopping, listening to the radio, and watching television. Among the most popular television shows are "Lawrence Welk," "60 Minutes," "All in the Family," "Over Easy," and the nightly news. Closed-circuit radio and television programs designed especially for the elderly, whether in households or institutions, are also broadcast in many cities.

Although leisure-time activities tend to become more solitary in old age, the role that certain activities play in socialization should not be overlooked. Daniel Rubinstein, a social researcher who wondered what attraction racetracks, bus depots, bingo parlors, and jai alai frontons could have in common for elderly people, spent years studying the life- and love-styles of men and women over 60 who congregate in such places. Rubinstein concluded that rather than simply providing gambling or amusement, the places represent social organizations for older people (McCormack, 1979).

An obvious conclusion that can be drawn from personal observation as well as from research findings is that the leisure activities of the older generation differ in many respects from those of younger people. However, the differences are undoubtedly due as much to upbringing and cultural contrasts between generations as to chronological age. Because the prior experiences of tomorrow's elderly will have been different from those of today's, we should expect their behavior to be different, too. Consequently, rather than playing checkers or shuffleboard and doing gardening, the next generation of older people may spend more of their leisure time swimming, playing musical instruments, visiting museums, and in other ways continuing to engage in the interests of today's young and middle-aged adults.

The Aged Consumer

Although inflation has eroded the value of the U.S. dollar during the past quarter of a century, the steady expansion of social security and pension programs has made the purchasing power of America's elderly citizens greater than ever before. Increasing numbers of older Americans are becoming freer spenders, no longer feeling so concerned with the traditional practice of saving everything for their heirs.

Older people are not nearly as homogeneous in their purchasing behavior as teenagers, but the disproportionate growth of the elderly population and the likelihood that the trend will continue in the foreseeable future has been affecting the plans of manufacturers of consumer products and the advertisers of those products. Manufacturers and advertisers continue to view this "maturity market" with some caution, but they have begun to tailor their products and messages to the changing age structure of the population ("Rich New Market . . . ," 1979).

It is now recognized that vitamins, laxatives, and other health and beauty aids are not the only items purchased by the elderly. Sales of clothing, books, games, art supplies, and vacation trips also thrive in the over-65 group. Adult toys and games like backgammon and mah-jongg, as well as electronic games of all kinds, are becoming popular at Senior Citizens centers and in the homes of older people. Considering the high price of gasoline, smaller automobiles, motor homes, and campers are also doing better than might be expected in the elderly market.

The large number of readers of magazines such as *Prime Time* and *Modern Maturity,* which are aimed specifically at older Americans, has attracted ads by travel firms, restaurants, clothing stores, banks, and many other business organizations. Awareness of the over-65 market is also indicated by discounts to senior citizens offered by tour companies, motion picture theatres, hotels, airline and bus companies, and even Fred Astaire Dance Studios and McDonald's. Cosmetic and clothing companies are designing products especially for the over-50 set, which are being demonstrated by older models. To entice the older homemaker, General Electric offers Braille-style (feeler) knobs on many of its ranges and home laundry appliances at no extra charge. Free bus rides are also being offered as an allurement for seniors to shop at discount grocery stores, and banks offer free travelers checks to elderly customers. The fact that these methods are effective points to a new generation of older people—one not so willing to sit back, let the world go by, and remain "brand-loyal."

SUMMARY

The low income of the majority of older people has an effect on many of the other problems that they experience—problems with housing, health, nutrition, transportation, and the use of leisure time. The income of retired elderly people is, on the average, about half that of the actively employed. The average income of elderly men is higher than that of elderly women, and the average for older whites is higher than that for blacks and other minority elderly.

Social security is the major income source for most older people, but private pensions, assets, earnings, and gifts contribute to the income of some. In spite of the low average, the income range of older Americans is actually quite large. The percentage of older Americans below the official poverty level has declined substantially during the past decade, and the number of those who are destitute is quite small. Of those who continue to live in poverty, a disproportionate number are members of minority groups. Unlike the traditional order of food, clothing, and shelter, the elderly poor must spend the greatest amount of their income for rent and utilities, with clothing in second place and food third.

Older people live in a variety of shelters—houses, mobile homes, apartments, rooms, and the like. These residences are also in various locations, although they tend to be clustered in certain suburban neighborhoods, in special buildings of large cities, and in rural areas. There has been a growing migration of retirees to the Sunbelt states, but the majority remain in their home communities. Certain states, depending on their cost of living index, climate, and recreational facilities, are considered better than others as places to retire.

Over 70 percent of the elderly own their own homes, but most of these homes are quite old and in need of repairs. The deteriorating or substandard condition of much of the housing for the elderly makes it unsafe and unhealthful. Consequently, improved housing has a high priority among the many federal programs benefiting older Americans.

Great concern about the living environments of older people has been expressed by the general public and professionals. The living environment of a person includes the neighborhood or community of residence as well as the dwelling unit itself. The expertise of architects, engineers, home economists, and social psychologists is being applied to the design of safe and comfortable living environments for the elderly. Many of the recommended changes in current housing are not particularly expensive, but entire communities designed for older people run into millions of dollars.

Less serious than income and housing, but also a problem for elderly people is the lack of adequate transportation. Federal, state, and local programs have made buses, trains, and taxicabs less expensive, more convenient, and safer modes of transportation for elderly passengers, but difficulties still exist.

Individuals who have not engaged in any preretirement planning of how they will use their leisure time often find themselves restless and dissatisfied after retirement. On the other hand, those who have developed hobbies during early or middle adulthood and are accustomed to long vacations are less likely to be at a loss for something to do. In addition to the traditional activities of fishing, gardening, and the like, many take up jogging, tennis, and other vigorous activities. They also enjoy arts and crafts, reading, and travel, none of which is necessarily very costly.

Research has shown that the leisure-time activities of older people tend to be more solitary and restricted than those of younger people. Although a certain amount of disengagement is to be expected in old age, the slogan that "happiness equals activity plus friendliness" is as good a prescription as any for effective adjustment in later life. Thus appropriate amounts of physical and mental exercise, combined with pleasant and mutually rewarding social interaction with one's peers, appear to contribute to a long and interesting life.

The growth of the elderly population, the amount of money that many older people have, and their increasing willingness to spend it have stimulated manufacturers and advertisers to pay closer attention to the needs and desires of this age group. Some of the effort that in the past has gone into capturing the teenage "Pepsi-generation" market is now being expended on the "Geritol generation." Special products, services, and messages are all being provided for or directed toward older consumers; among these are discounts, free rides, product adaptations, and special sales for elderly shoppers.

SUGGESTED READINGS

Beverley, E. V. How to choose the right milieu for your later years. *Geriatrics*, 1975, *30*(4), 150–154, 157–160.

Carp, F. M. Housing and living environments of older people. In R. H. Binstock & E. Shanas (Eds.), *Handbook of aging and the social sciences*. New York: Van Nostrand, 1976, pp. 244–271.

Davis, R. H. *Television and the aging audience*. Los Angeles: University of Southern California Press, 1980.

Gordon, C., Gaitz, C. M., & Scott, J. Leisure and lives: Personal expressivity across the life span. In R. H. Binstock & E. Shanas (Eds.), *Handbook of aging and the social sciences*. New York: Van Nostrand. 1976. pp. 310–341.

Lawton, M. P. *Environment and aging*. Belmont, Calif.: Brooks/Cole, 1980.

Parker, S. *The sociology of leisure*. New York: International Publications Service (G. Gallen), 1976.

Peppers, L. G. Patterns of leisure and adjustment to retirement. *The Gerontologist*, 1976, *16*, 441–446.

Schultz, J. H. *The economics of aging* (2d ed.). Belmont, Calif.: Wadsworth, 1980.

Stirner, F. W. The transportation needs of the elderly in a large urban environment. *The Gerontologist*, 1978, *18*(2), 207–211.

Struyk, R. J., & Solda, B. J. *Improving the elderly's housing*. Cambridge, Mass.: Ballinger, 1979.

NOTES

[1]California goes even further than most states, allowing older people with incomes of less than $20,000 to defer their property taxes indefinitely. In this voluntary program the state takes a lien on the house and charges an annual interest of 7 percent on the unpaid taxes.

[2]From the *Albuquerque Journal*, August 27, 1977, p. B-12.

Crime, Justice, and the Elderly

The problem of increasing crime in the United States, as publicized continuously in the media, is a topic of great concern to law enforcement officials, politicians, and especially the victimized public. Daily newspapers and television news programs are full of reports of robberies, rapes, murders, and kidnappings at all levels of society. To document the crime problem, each year the FBI issues its *Uniform Crime Reports,* consisting primarily of detailed lists of statistics on arrests for the many categories of criminal offenses committed during the preceding calendar year. Consequently, it is not surprising when a public opinion poll finds that a sizable percentage of respondents sampled from the general population consider crime to be the nation's number one problem.

THE ELDERLY CRIMINAL

Although crime against the elderly has received more public and professional attention than crime by the elderly, approximately 1 percent of those arrested each year in the United States are people who have reached their 65th birthday. As indicated in Figure 11-1, however, considering the fact that 11 percent of the American population is 65 years and older, 1 percent of all those arrested is a disproportionately small number. Compared to the 22.5 percent of those arrested in 1979 who were 18 and under, the incidence of criminal activity by elderly people is quite unimpressive. In fact, close inspection of Figure 11-1 reveals that the elderly have the lowest crime rate of any age group. The overall trend is an increase in the relative frequency of arrests until young adulthood, and then a gradual decline through middle and late adulthood.[1]

One percent is clearly a small portion of the total number of people who are arrested every year, but in 1969 it translated into 86,624 arrests and in 1979 to 94,264 arrests. For what crimes were these older people arrested and why did they commit them? The "why" question is difficult, but some insight into an answer to the "what" question can be obtained by examining Table 11-1. The largest numbers of arrests of older people, both in 1969 and 1979, were for drunkenness, disorderly conduct, driving under the influence, larceny-theft, and gambling. Over 90 percent of the elderly people arrested in both these years were men, the ratio of women to men committing crimes being even less in old age than it is in young and middle adulthood.

Although difficult to interpret, the changes in the number of arrests of older people for specific crimes from 1969 to 1979 are interesting. Table 11-1 shows, for example, that there was a disproportionate increase in the number of elderly people arrested for driving under the influence, larceny-theft, fraud, aggravated assault, and drug-abuse violations. On the other hand, there were pronounced decreases in arrests for drunkenness, gambling, and vagrancy. Interpretation of these differences should take into account the changing material conditions and social roles of the elderly and the population as a whole and also differences in arrest procedures and the reporting of crime statistics. For example, it has been alleged that law enforcement officers are more likely to overlook less serious crimes such as drunkenness and disturbing the peace when they are committed by

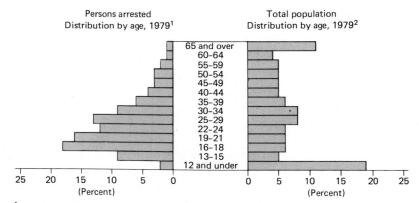

Persons arrested
Distribution by age, 1979[1]

Total population
Distribution by age, 1979[2]

[1]Persons arrested is based on reports received representing 204,622,000 population.
[2]The total population is 220,099,000 for the U.S., based on Bureau of Census Provisional estimates, July 1, 1979

Figure 11-1 Percentage distributions of persons arrested and total U.S. population in 1979. (From U.S. Dept. of Justice, *FBI Uniform Crime Reports*. Washington, D.C.: U.S. Government Printing Office, 1980.)

Table 11-1   TOTAL ARRESTS OF PERSONS 65 AND OLDER IN 1969 AND 1979*

Offense Charged	1969	1979
Drunkenness	56,099	28,400
Disorderly conduct	7,795	6,421
Driving under the influence	6,178	19,130
Gambling	4,406	2,418
Larceny-theft	3,634	12,223
Vagrancy	2,615	365
Liquor law violations	1,566	1,914
Aggravated assaults	1,129	2,389
Weapons; carrying, possessing, etc.	847	1,374
Sex offenses (except forcible rape and prostitution)	712	908
Fraud	311	1,207
Murder and nonnegligent manslaughter	259	304
Burglary	223	460
Drug-abuse violations	198	574
Prostitution and commercialized vice	188	336
Offenses against family and children	182	190
Vandalism	120	547
Motor vehicle theft	56	147
Forgery and counterfeiting	37	110
Forcible rape	37	130
Total	86,624	94,264

*From U.S. Dept. of Justice, *FBI Uniform Crime Reports*. Washington, D.C.: U.S. Government Printing Office, 1970, 1980.

older persons than when the perpetrator is a younger person. Only in the case of more serious crimes (e.g., larceny, assault, narcotics law violations) are the elderly likely to be treated in the same way as younger offenders. When the strictness of law enforcement varies with time and the age of the offender, the result is an apparent but not necessarily real difference in criminal activities.

Many authorities maintain that criminal behavior in older people is associated with mental deterioration and personality disorders (Shichor & Kobrin, 1978). This would seem to be a likelier explanation in the case of crimes against person, in which a brain-damaged or psychotic individual is more apt to lose control and commit an impulsive act of violence. Vagrancy, drunkenness, and certain other crimes may also be indicative of a loss of control due to senility. Nevertheless, there are perfectly sane elderly people who, for various reasons, commit misdemeanors and felonies. In addition to economic needs, criminal activities may serve social needs. Thus Barrett (1972) referred to certain crimes committed by the elderly—for example, drunkenness, disorderly conduct, gambling—as "companionship delinquencies," because he considered these crimes as stemming primarily from a search for companionship.

A crime that has reportedly increased among the elderly during the past decade is larceny-theft, and shoplifting, in particular (see Table 11-1). One elderly woman, for example, devised an effective technique for shoplifting in department stores. Pretending to be senile, she would "accidentally and awkwardly" knock piles of items off the shelves and slip them under her clothes during the ensuing confusion. We may smile at the ingenuity of this woman, but shoplifting by an older person is frequently a desperate act with heart-rending consequences. Consider the case of the 91-year-old, white-haired widow who, having been caught shoplifting in a supermarket, was forced to spend 24 hours in jail. On being released, she stated that she had not slept all night and that the experience of being locked up was terrible. Then she sighed deeply and added: "I wish God would close my eyes. I'm so tired of living." The feelings of shame and guilt experienced by this woman are not uncommon among elderly people who have committed petty theft, and they can persist over many years in a person who has had a strong moral upbringing (see Report 11-1).

Report 11-1   WAS IT ALL FOR NAUGHT?
46 YEARS LATER, OLDSTER TRIES TO PAY $1.50 BILL*
DORIS A. BYRON   *Times Staff Writer*

SANTA ANA—Somewhere among the 20,000 inhabitants of the Missouri boot-heel town of Poplar Bluff, there is at least one very honest old soul.

How else can one explain the one-page unsigned letter containing $10 that arrived recently in the Orange County recorder's office bearing a Poplar Bluff, Mo., postmark and an April 1 date?

The letter was addressed to the recorder's office at the "Court House Annex"—an extension of the old county courthouse that was vacated by the recorder and his staff nearly 10 years ago.

"In what used to be Santa Ana Gardens, at corner of Edinger and Sullivan St., was a filling station owned by a Mr. Forbes—I think," the handwritten letter read.

"Anyway I or we left there owing $1.50 for gas which was forgotten. I do not know how to settle this unless someone there will look up records and forward half of $10 enclosed to heirs and keep the other half for yourself.

"Thanks."

There was no signature, but there was a postcript.

"PS," the letter closed, "this was in 1934."

Assistant Recorder Ella M. Smith said the letter apparently came from someone whose conscience was troubled by the depression-era debt that was never paid.

Though the missive was dated on April Fool's Day, the $10 was real, and only someone who knew his or her way around Santa Ana could have known about Santa Ana Gardens, Edinger Avenue and Sullivan Street and the old courthouse annex.

But if the sender is the honest soul he or she appears to be, there's at least one not-so-honest soul walking the corridors of Orange County government.

Smith said the recorder didn't know what to do with the $10 bill when it arrived—there's no provision for accepting unpaid gasoline bills in the county law—so he tucked it back into its envelope and left it on his desk.

And when he arrived at work Thursday morning and opened the envelope, one person's good deed had been undone by another's bad one: The $10 bill was gone.

*From *Los Angeles Times*, April 22, 1980, Pt. I, p. 20. Copyright, 1980, Los Angeles Times. Reprinted by permission.

VICTIMIZATION AND EXPLOITATION OF THE ELDERLY

"Widow, 87—Mugged—Home Set Afire"
"Elderly Woman Clubbed, Robbed by Intruder"
"Elderly Frequently Abused by Children"
"How Con Artists Rob Elderly"

These are just a sample of headlines of newspaper stories detailing incidents in which elderly people have been victimized and exploited. Typically, such stories give a few details without adequately describing the anxiety and pain of defenseless elderly people who are the repeated victims of crimes against themselves and their property, or who have been exploited by con artists.

Incidence and Types of Crime

Older people are not usually victimized by crime, especially violent crime, more than the rest of the population. According to unpublished data from the National Crime Survey, the elderly are victimized less often than younger adults by rape, robbery, assault, and larceny (see Table 11-2). Only about 1 percent of known rape victims are women over 50 years of age, and a very small percentage of these are over 65 (U.S. Dept. of Justice, 1979). Likewise, as indicated in Figure 11-2, only about 2 percent of the total number of murder victims are 65 years of age or older. However, despite the fact that rape, murder, and other violent crimes are the ones occurring least often, they are the very crimes that older people fear the most. This is especially true of elderly women and blacks, who, to a

Table 11-2 VICTIMIZATION FROM SELECTED CRIMES AGAINST PERSONS, FOR THE POPULATION 12 YEARS AND OVER AND 65 YEARS AND OVER, BY RACE: 1977 (RATE PER 1000 POPULATION)*

Crime	Persons 12 Years Old and Over			Persons 65 Years Old and Over		
	Total	White	Black	Total	White	Black
Crimes of violence	33.9	33.0	41.9	7.5	7.0	13.4
Rape and attempted rape	0.9	0.9	1.0	0.1	0.1	-
Robbery and attempted robbery	6.2	5.4	13.0	3.4	3.0	7.9
With injury	2.2	1.9	5.2	1.9	1.8	3.4
Without injury	4.0	3.5	7.9	1.4	1.1	4.4
Assault	26.8	26.8	27.9	4.0	3.9	5.6
Aggravated	10.0	9.6	13.9	1.2	1.0	2.7
Simple	16.8	17.2	14.0	2.8	2.8	2.8
Personal larceny	97.3	98.2	90.0	23.6	23.1	26.9

*Source: U.S. Department of Justice, Law Enforcement Assistance Administration, National Criminal Justice Information and Statistical Service, unpublished data from the National Crime Survey.

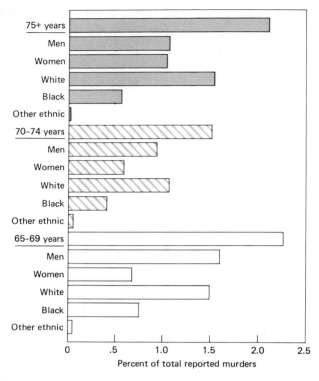

Figure 11-2 Percent total murder victims 65 years and over by sex and race. (Adapted from U.S. Dept. of Justice, *FBI Uniform Crime Reports*. Washington, D.C.: U.S. Government Printing Office, 1980.)

significantly greater degree than elderly men and whites, confess to being afraid of crime. The fears of these people are, of course, not totally unrealistic. Inner-city residents, for example, express greater fear than those who live in the suburbs, a fact correlated with the reported incidence of crime in the two locales. The magnitude of the relationship is not entirely clear, because, through fear of retaliation or whatever reasons, the great majority of crimes probably go unreported.

More common than crimes of violence are property crimes, which are much likelier to occur when the property is unoccupied. In the case of the elderly, however, personal larceny with contact, in which a purse, wallet, or cash is taken directly from the victim's person, has the highest rate (Goldsmith & Tomas, 1974).

Why Designate Elderly Victims for Special Attention?

Elderly people may be more afraid of crime than victimization statistics seem to warrant, but there are reasons for their fears and for singling out the elderly for special consideration. One reason is that the effect of any economic loss on the elderly because of their lower average income is greater than it would be for a younger adult. Associated with diminished income is residence in high-crime, inner-city neighborhoods rather than more affluent suburbs. Low-income elderly of all ethnic groups who live in neighborhoods that may once have been safe but now have a high-crime rate are often trapped because of their reluctance to move to new, unfamiliar surroundings. By remaining in these neighborhoods, a large percentage of older people become victims because of their physical proximity to their most frequent victimizers—school dropouts and other unemployed teenagers and young adults. The proximity, and hence the probability of being victimized, is greater for those old people who live in age-integrated rather than age-segregated housing.

Although the results of studies indicate that the elderly are no more likely than juveniles to be victimized by younger people, it has been found that fear of teenagers keeps many older people at home (Goldsmith & Tomas, 1974) (see Report 11-2). Like most people who live in high-crime areas, they tend to be suspicious and distrustful of strangers and usually do not try to make friends with their neighbors (Conklin, 1976).

Unfortunately, strangers are not the only ones who victimize and abuse the elderly. It has been estimated, for example, that each year more than

---

Report 11-2 FEAR OF TEEN-AGERS KEEPS ELDERLY HOME, STUDY SHOWS*

UNIVERSITY PARK, PA (UPI)—Elderly persons living in cities are so afraid of teen-agers many of them remain indoors after 3 P.M., a new study reports.

The study of Geoffrey C. Godbey, Pennsylvania State University professor of recreation and parks, also found that fear of crime keeps many of the elderly away from senior citizen centers, parks and other places where they would normally go.

Godbey found that 66% of about 2,000 people in his study said fear of crime affected the use of such facilities.

"Everyone knows that many older people are afraid to leave home after dark, but we were surprised to find that 3 P.M. is a cutoff hour, too." Godbey said, "About one-fifth of the elderly in our study wanted to be home by the time school let out."

The fear of teen-agers is so great, the study found, that 88% of those surveyed said that many times they cross the street or change directions to avoid them.

Funding for the study came from the Andrus Foundation of the American Association of Retired Persons. It was conducted in several cities, including Pittsburgh, Philadelphia, Boston, Baltimore, and Newark, N.J.

Nine percent of the elderly in the study had been crime victims within the 12 months before the survey. Most had been robbed or had their homes burglarized.

"There is a tendency to think old people are unreasonable in their fear, that they curtail activities when there is no need to do so," Godbey said. "But we found a high correlation between fear and victimization."

A total of 33 robberies, 22 assaults, and 5 other crimes had been committed against the elderly en route to senior citizen centers in a 12-month period, the researcher was told.

*From *Los Angeles Times*, Mar. 2, 1980, Pt. VIII, p. 7. Reprinted by permission of United Press International.

2.5 million elderly Americans are physically, psychologically, sexually, or financially abused by their children or other caretakers (McCormack, 1980). Examples of this "battered elderly syndrome," in which a parent or other older relative is physically abused, are plentiful:

> A woman, 70, is placed in a tub of cold water by her daughter and left there for several hours.
> A woman, 19, confesses to torturing her father for 7 days by chaining him to a toilet and hitting him with a hammer when he is asleep.
> A son, 22, fights with his parents over money late at night. He hits his mother with a frying pan and clubs his father. (McCormack, 1980, p. 2).

Congressional hearings on elder abuse have revealed many such incidents—600,000 cases per year on the average, including both physical and psychological (threats, "beating with words") mistreatment. The reasons for such abuse are varied (e.g., financial gain, revenge, hatred of the aged and old age), but it is generally agreed that the problem is growing. As a result, proposals for establishing a National Center on Adult Abuse have not fallen on deaf ears.

Another reason why older people are more afraid and deserve special consideration is their poorer physical strength and health. Older people are less able to defend themselves and otherwise escape from threatening situations and also are more easily hurt and have greater difficulty recuperating once they are injured. An elderly victim of a purse-snatching can sustain a broken arm or fall that causes permanent injury. Thus sensory-motor problems and various chronic disorders make the elderly more vulnerable to attack, and it takes longer for their torn flesh to heal and their broken bones to knit.

Awareness of the more fragile physical condition of the elderly causes potential criminals to view them as easy targets. Perhaps the fact that they are less able to defend themselves, and therefore not as likely as younger adults to be confronted with weapons, explains why older people are less apt to be injured during a criminal act. The chances of injury and even death are increased when a person attempts to resist a crime. But even when they are not physically injured, a larger proportion of older than younger victims are emotionally debilitated by a criminal act against them. The emotional stress provoked by an attack is usually greater in the elderly, and they frequently take longer to recuperate psychologically.

Greater physical vulnerability, coupled with the tendency to live alone, increases the vulnerability of the elderly to crime and the likelihood of being victimized repeatedly—often by the same thieves or attackers. This likelihood is especially high for the large number of elderly people who, not having access to a private automobile, must rely on public transportation. Being alone, defenseless, and having a small lifetime accumulation of keepsakes and cash makes them tempting prey to potential thieves.

Knowing the dates of receipt of monthly pension and benefit checks, and consequently when older people are more likely to have cash, young hoodlums may lie in wait for the vulnerable elderly at these times. Quite often the victimizer does not even wait for the check to be cashed. Thousands of social security and relief checks are stolen each year in purse-snatchings, muggings, and burglaries of homes and mailboxes.

Because of their inability to resist, aged widows and others who live alone are the favorite targets of teenage and young-adult hoodlums. Unable to sleep at night through fear of being robbed or mugged, elderly people in large cities may be forced to sleep during the day. Some are so afraid that in spite of the need to get out and enjoy exercise and social interaction, they literally become prisoners in their own homes. One 82-year-old woman who overcame her fear of going outside was robbed of her groceries and money as she reentered her apartment, and then raped. Adding insult to injury, she contracted a venereal disease from the incident (Loether, 1975). Occasionally, an elderly victim of continued muggings and thefts is murdered or simply gives up out of weariness and despair and decides to die by his or her own hand. Others, perhaps manifesting more spunk, refuse to give in to their attackers or let them destroy their self-esteem and sense of purpose in life (see Report 11-3, p. 234).

Exploitation of the Aged

Assaults on the elderly who are walking or traveling by bus to the supermarket or bank, or robbery in their homes, are not the only ways in which they are fleeced. Con men, door-to-door salesmen, and medical quacks also exploit them by falsely promising renewed health, physical attractiveness, a comfortable estate in the South or Southwest, or a way to get rich quick by making a small monetary investment. Loneliness, pain, and fear, combined with the desire to improve their economic, physical, and social status, make many aged the gullible victims of smooth, fast-talking promoters or newspaper ad "come-ons."

According to a former director of the California Department of Public Health, quackery kills more people than all violent crimes combined (Geis, 1976). Defrauding of elderly people is also a lucrative business in California, where they are the victims of 90 percent of the swindles. The amount of money that old people lose from con games in Los Angeles alone in a given year is greater than the total netted in bank robberies in that city ("Step-up in Fight . . . ," 1977). And on the national level, the annual "take" from swindling operations is estimated to be several billions of dollars.

Ranking high on the list of swindles are hearing aid and insurance ripoffs, health quackery, and work-at-home rackets (Lipman, 1979). A common type of fraud is the retirement land deal in which an elderly person, sight unseen, purchases a distant property that sounds attractive. All too often the property is a swamp in Florida or a lizard patch in

Report 11-3 VICTIM, 85, HAS SURPRISE FOR MUGGERS*

OAKLAND (UPI)—Mary Fuller, 85, the most mugged senior citizen in Oakland, now has lost her hearing aid to two young toughs, but she remains undaunted and vows to strike back.

"The hell with them—I'm still going out," said the plucky grandmother, who packs a can of tear gas spray up her sleeve.

On Monday night, two young men followed her as she walked to a store near her apartment. "Oh, oh, here we go again," she thought.

They accosted her and "told me I had no use for that hearing aid, and I told them they had even less use for it," she recalled.

But they forced her to take it off and hand it over, she said. "Then they told me I had no use for that ring, either."

She was referring to her gold wedding band. She said it had been given to her by her husband, "the most wonderful man who ever lived." He died 51 years ago.

The attempt to take the ring was the last straw. "I just whipped it (the tear gas spray) out and gave the boy a whiff," she said. "I told the police that a person had the right to protect herself."

The muggers? They ran off—with the $300 hearing aid but without the ring.

Police said Mary has been mugged so many times on the street that she doesn't carry a purse anymore. Her grocery bags have been yanked from her arms outside stores, her 5-foot, 90-pound body stripped by thugs of objects valuable only to her. And her small apartment has been invaded by robbers.

Mary said one young man who snatched her groceries told her, "We need this food more than you."

If this really was the case, she said, "then I really don't mind. Nobody should go hungry."

Mary said that from now on she is going to be more careful, "but I'm not afraid of them. What's left for them to take, my life? I'm 85 years old. I hate to be afraid."

"If necessary, I'll walk in the middle of the street. A person has to get out once in a while—some fresh air, sunshine."

And to show her spunk she has pinned this sign on her apartment door:

"You bastard thieves.

"I know who you are. If you take one more article from this place, I'm going to police, and you're going to jail."

*From *San Diego Evening Tribune*, Nov. 21, 1980. Reprinted by permission of United Press International.

Arizona, miles from the nearest roads and facilities. And sometimes it turns out that the "seller" of a piece of property does not even own it:

> Typical is the story of one old man who lost $3,400 in a housing swindle. The $3,400 was a 10 percent down-payment on a house that was soon to be built. It turned out that the developer—who netted $100,000 in the operation—had no intention of ever building. How could he? He didn't even own the land he was selling.
>
> "I couldn't believe it," the victim said sadly. "He was such a nice, pleasant fellow—well-dressed, with a fancy office and a Lincoln Continental. Why, I talked to him just four days before he disappeared, and he was as cheerful as could be." (Lipman, 1979, p. 23)

Certain types of swindles are so common that they have been christened with special names. Two of these bunco schemes are the "pigeon drop" and the "bank examiner swindle"[2]:

The pigeon drop.   The victim is approached by one of the swindlers and engaged in a conversation on any sympathetic subject. Let's say the victim is an older man. When the swindler has gained his confidence, she mentions a large sum of money found by a second swindler who, at the moment, "happens" to pass by. The victim is led to believe that whoever lost the money probably came by it unlawfully. The swindlers discuss with the victim what to do with the money. One of the swindlers says that she works in the vicinity, and decides to contact her "employer" for advice. She returns in a few minutes and states that her boss has counted the money and verified the amount, and that he agrees that as the money undoubtedly was stolen or belonged to a gambler (or some such variation on a theme), they should keep and divide the money three ways. *But* that each should show evidence of financial responsibility and good faith before collecting a share. The victim is then induced to draw his "good faith" money from his bank. After he has done this, either alone or in the company of one of the swindlers, the money is taken by the swindler to her "employer." Upon the swindler's return, the victim is given the name and address of the employer and told he is waiting with his share of the money. The victim leaves and, of course, cannot find the employer or sometimes even the address. When he returns to where he left the swindlers they, of course, are gone.

The bank examiner swindle.   A phony bank or savings and loan "investigator" calls you or comes to your home. He is very serious, and may have brought along deposit slips from your bank and other official-looking papers. He tells you that the bank is checking up on a dishonest employee, and explains how you can help. He says he wants to make a test to see what the suspected employee does when a customer draws money out of his account. He suggests that you go to your bank, draw out a specified amount of money, then let him use it for the test. Either he or a "bonded messenger" or some other official will pick up the money at some nearby point. You withdraw the money. Advised of the need for "absolute secrecy" and that the money must be cash "in order to check serial numbers," you ignore the bank teller's concern that you are drawing out such a large sum of cash. You give the money to the "examiner," who hands you a receipt, thanks you for your "cooperation," and may tell you how he plans to use it to trap the suspected employee. Once he's gone, you'll never see him again, or your money. The bank, of course, has never heard of him.

PREVENTING AND COPING WITH CRIME

A generally accepted principle of crime prevention is that potential victims should be informed of the dangers, how to take precautions against them, and how to respond when danger becomes imminent. In recent years, workshops, seminars, and training programs in crime prevention and self-defense for people of all ages have blossomed throughout the United States and especially in large cities. Although training in self-defense is probably not very effective with older people, they can be educated to take precautions both inside and outside their places of residence.

Crime Prevention Tips for Elderly Residents

Whether an elderly person lives in an apartment or house, the following precautions can help prevent crimes against person and property in the place of residence (California Dept. of Justice, 1979; Gross, 1979):

1. Have deadbolt locks rather than chain locks installed on outside doors, and always lock doors and windows when leaving.
2. Change door locks if keys are lost, which clearly identify the location of the residence or automobile ownership, or if your place of residence was previously occupied.
3. Separate house keys from car keys when leaving an automobile in a public garage or at a service station.
4. Be wary of unsolicited telephone calls and "wrong numbers." Do not give information to strangers over the telephone; hang up and report nuisance callers.
5. Do not keep large amounts of money and valuables in predictable or accessible places; use a bank safety deposit box. Have social security and/or pension checks deposited directly to your bank account.
6. Leave a light and maybe a radio on when away for short periods of time. Discontinue mail, dairy, newspaper, and other deliveries when away for long periods of time. If you have a lawn, have it tended while you are away.
7. Notify the police immediately when you see suspicious-looking persons loitering about your place of residence, going from door to door and trying doors, sitting in parked cars or repeatedly cruising by. The description of the person(s); color, make, and license number of car; time and location should be noted and reported.
8. Set up a neighborhood security watch or mutual protection system. Neighbors can watch out for each other, go shopping together, and the like.
9. Consider keeping a pet—even a small dog—if the rules permit animals.
10. Ring your doorbell just before entering your place of residence to give burglars ample time to escape. This will prevent a confrontation. Never rush into dark rooms without reasonable caution. Before closing and securing the door, take a quick look around to determine if there is an intruder hiding somewhere inside. Should this be the case, leave the door open for a hasty retreat.

In addition to the preceding precautions, apartment residents would do well to follow these recommendations:

1. Do not ride in the elevator with a person who looks suspicious.
2. List your name in the entrance and the telephone directory as "M. Smith" rather than as "Mary Smith."

3. Never use the laundromat in your apartment complex by yourself; team up with a neighbor.

Precautions When Walking or Traveling

The New York City Police Department and the New York Department of Aging (1978) have recommended a number of precautions that elderly people are advised to exercise when walking or traveling. First, *be alert:* Do not be afraid, but look around occasionally to see who is standing near you or walking toward you. Second, *be determined:* If you are on an unfamiliar or lonely street, quicken your pace and act as if you are going to meet someone who is waiting for you. Third, *walk carefully:* Walk where it is well lighted, staying away from darkened building entrances, doorways, alleyways, and high shrubbery. Fourth, *walk or travel together:* Travel and shop with companions whenever possible during the daytime and especially at night, remembering that there is greater safety in numbers. Fifth, *plan ahead:* Know where you are walking, know the general day and evening conditions of the streets you use, and know which stores are open late at night. If an emergency situation arises, walk to these stores rather than down your own quieter residential street.

When going out, an elderly person should carry as little money as possible and even that in an inconspicuous place. It is best not to carry a purse, but if one is needed for shopping purposes it should not be left unattended at any time. And when returning home, the elderly shopper or traveler should not spend time at the door searching through a purse or pocket for the key; it should be in hand on arrival at the door.

Rules for Self-Protection against Fraud

The increasing susceptibility of the general public, and the elderly in particular, to fraud has prompted responsible public agencies to expand their efforts to inform potential victims on how to protect themselves. One of the first rules for self-protection against fraud is never to expect to get something for nothing. "Unbelievable bargains" are usually just that— unbelievable, especially when the seller or promotor is a stranger. When doing business, it is always advisable to know the person(s) with whom one is dealing and to refuse to discuss personal finances with strangers. An example of a potential pitfall of failing to investigate before giving cash to a stranger is the "bank examiner swindle" described previously. The rule is: Investigate before investing. Never sign anything hastily, and don't give money to strangers.

One type of exploitation of the elderly that may be blatant embezzlement or may simply tread the fine line between the legal and illegal is tax fraud. An example of the former is the situation in which a bogus "IRS collector" telephones a newly bereaved widow or widower to arrange for an audit or payment of back taxes owed by the deceased. The would-be extortionist in this case can be stopped dead in his tracks by a widow(er) who is smart enough to examine his identification carefully and call the local office of the Internal Revenue Service for verification. Potential victims of this racket should also know that before making personal contact with a taxpayer the Internal Revenue Service sends a written notice of intent to audit and that the IRS does business from 9 to 5 weekdays and not at odd hours.

The complexity of federal and state income tax laws also leads many elderly taxpayers to consult a tax preparer for assistance in preparing their returns. Whenever this is done, it is advisable to ask in advance how much the tax preparer's fee will be and whether it includes both federal and state forms. Forms containing blank spaces that could be filled in later should never be signed, and copies of all prepared documents should be obtained by the taxpayer. Finally, because many preparers rent office space between January and April, it is wise to obtain a year-round address for a tax preparer (California Dept. of Justice, 1979).

Crime Prevention Programs

Top priority is being given in many American cities to the prevention of crime against the elderly and assisting its victims. Representative of these efforts are specially trained police units that perform surveillance and escort services for the elderly at times when the latter are most vulnerable—at night, while shopping, going to the bank, and the like. The officers in these special teams are also charged with the mission of dealing with older victims. Their duties consist of providing information on crime prevention, referral sources, and emergency services to older people. The officers may also counsel and advise the elderly and help them prepare for court appearances (Goldsmith & Goldsmith, 1976). Among the activities of the Bronx Senior Citizens Robbery Unit, for example, are to inform the elderly about recent trends in crime, how to detect criminal behavior, and how to serve as witnesses in criminal cases. However, these officers are trained in the prevention of crimes against the elderly as well as in helping older victims cope with the shock and loss resulting from a crime and in being of assistance in apprehending and prosecuting the criminal(s).

Other programs that have been instituted in many cities include "Neighborhood Watch," which teaches people how to spot ongoing crimes and to protect themselves against burglaries and other felonies. Special monitoring equipment in high-crime areas, special buses and drivers (especially on "checkday"), "ride along" escorts and security aids to walk the streets in high-crime areas, and the encouragement of direct depositing of checks are other features of crime-prevention programs in certain cities. Furthermore, not all the programs cost the taxpayers money. New York City's service of 1,000 teenage escorts for the elderly, for example, is completely voluntary. The use of teenagers for this purpose is particularly helpful, because it serves to persuade the elderly that those teenagers who victimize them are not representative of teenagers in general. Another volunteer program is that of RSVP, which has made progress in organizing the elderly themselves to fight crime in cities such as Baltimore, Las Vegas, and Oklahoma City.

Anticrime programs having the purpose of providing help for the elderly have also been established at the state level, for example, in California, Connecticut, Florida, Michigan, New York, and Pennsylvania (Weaver, 1980). Much of the support for state and national efforts at combating crime against the aged comes from the federal government. The Administration on Aging, for example, has sponsored projects designed to reduce the effects of crime on elderly victims and potential victims in several cities throughout the nation (U.S. Dept. of Health, Education & Welfare, 1977b). Information and assistance is also provided by each state's Criminal Justice Planning Agency, which receives funds from the Law Enforcement Assistance Administration. Activities pertaining to security against residential theft are funded by the Department of Housing and Urban Development, the Federal Housing Administration, and the Farmers Home Administration.

Elderly Victims

Victim compensation laws, according to which restitution to the victim of a crime is made by the offender or the state, are in existence in many states. Under these laws, victims of burglary and assault are entitled to a variety of compensations, for example, money and medical care. Such compensation is needed especially by those who are so often the victims—the elderly poor.

Other legal measures that have been advocated to cope with crime against the elderly are stronger laws against misrepresentation and fraud and more effective enforcement of those laws. Of course, stronger laws and stricter law enforcement alone will not protect the elderly from medical quackery and other forms of exploitation. Improvements in legitimate medical care and public education campaigns directed against fraud are also essential. Special orientation services for elderly victims/witnesses and mandatory penalties for crimes involving body injury of the elderly and handicapped have also been proposed (Nat. Ret. Teach. Assn.–Amer. Assn. Ret. Per., 1978).

Reporting, Testifying, and Assisting by the Elderly

Although the elderly are no less likely than others to report crimes (Dussich & Eickman, 1976), they are often reluctant—through embarrassment or fear of retaliation—to report a crime or serve as a witness in a criminal trial. Because it is impossible to apprehend and sentence criminals unless people are willing to report crimes and serve as witnesses, older people who have been victimized are urged to report the crime to the police. A report should also be made to the Better Business Bureau when an individual suspects that he or she has been swindled or otherwise exploited in some way by a businessperson or organization.

Programs for training the elderly in the identification and reporting of suspicious activities and crimes are offered by a number of police departments. When a criminal is caught and brought to trial, efforts are also made to convince the elderly victim that his or her testimony will help curtail further illegal activities on the part of the culprit. Unfortunately, elderly people do not always make good witnesses in court trials. Because of transportation problems and physical difficulties in walking, they may fail to arrive at court on time. Poorer memory for details and overreaction to the stress of cross-examination may also cause them to become more easily confused and flustered under a defense attorney's unremitting probing.

Despite the shortcomings of many elderly people in reporting and testifying, certain police departments have made effective use of elderly volunteers in crime prevention. Many of these older aides already possess skills in human relations and other aspects of police work, and some can be easily trained to provide services that release officers for more demanding tasks. Most older volunteers are viewed as conscientious, dependable, and ethical in their performance of the community relations tasks or other activities assigned to them by law enforcement officials (U.S. Dept. of Justice, 1979).

LEGAL SERVICES AND ELDER ADVOCACY

Crime is a serious matter, but the elderly also need assistance with a host of other legal matters. These problems include social security, old age assistance, pension rights, Medicare, special housing, probate matters, workmen's compensation, and other concerns pertaining to disability. The need for legal counsel and advocacy is greater with poor elderly people, many of whom do not know their rights and are unable to find their way through the bureaucratic maze of red tape involved in social security, SSI, Medicaid, and Medicare (Weaver, 1980).

Efforts to develop legal services for the aged in all states and territories of the United States have been fairly extensive. Under Title III of the Older Americans Act of 1965, each state and more than 550 city and county governmental agencies on aging are designated to serve as advocates for older persons, coordinate activities on their behalf, and provide information to them about services and opportunities (U.S. Dept. of Health, Education & Welfare, 1977b). Legal service centers for the aged have also been established in a number of American universities (e.g., Syracuse University's Legal Center on Aging) to help older people cope with the bureaucracies in both the governmental and private sectors. In addition, a National Senior Citizens Law Center has been established to act as a legal services clearinghouse.

Attorneys as Elder Advocates

The various area agencies on aging are required by law to cooperate with local bar associations in arranging legal services for the elderly. The American Bar Association has responded by encouraging lawyers to launch outreach programs. Workers in outreach programs in states such as Florida, Georgia, New Hampshire, and Ohio identify elderly people who have legal problems requiring the assistance of an attorney. Attorneys then offer low-cost legal services to these persons. Alternatively, lawyers may go to senior homes or other centers on certain days to consult with elderly people in need of legal assistance. The initial consultation for clients 60 years and older is usually free, and subsequent services are paid for at a reduced rate.[3]

Basically, the lawyers in these programs, and all lawyers with elderly clients, provide three types of services to older people: (1) information and referral, (2) routine litigation, and (3) law reform activity (Nathanson, 1977). In the first type of service, lawyers provide older people with information and educational material concerning their rights and benefits under the Social Security and Older Americans acts. In routine litigation, lawyers contest on behalf of older clients or defend them against evictions, involuntary commitments, and the like; they also prepare suits for clients to establish their eligibility for benefits or to protect them against repossessions and unfair contracts (Nathanson, 1977).

Routine litigation may also be referred to as **case advocacy,** in that the attorney functions in the interest of an older client so that the kind of treatment to which the client is legally entitled can be obtained. The concept of **elder advocacy,** however, is broader than case advocacy. The term **advocate,** which has traditionally referred to a person who pleads another's case before a tribunal or judicial court, has been broadened in this context to mean concern for and action on behalf of a particular group of people—namely, the elderly. Elder advocacy includes the third type of service provided by lawyers—law reform activity, or **monitoring.** Attorneys concerned with the monitoring function keep watch to make certain that laws and programs pertaining to the elderly are carried out as intended by the legislators who drafted them. In cases where a law is being incorrectly applied, a **class action suit** on behalf of an entire group of elderly people may be necessary. Such a procedure, for example, might be used to improve conditions in nursing homes or in the treatment of elderly customers by utility companies.

Two other types of advocacy that are important in ensuring the legal rights of the elderly are legislative advocacy and administrative advocacy. Efforts to make certain that the Older Americans Act, the Social Security Act, and other laws pertaining to the elderly are appropriate to their needs is known as **legislative advocacy.** Legislative advocates for the elderly apply pressure, usually by lobbying, on state and federal lawmakers to draft and vote for legislation that better meets the needs of older people. Finally, the notion of **administrative advocacy** is a recognition of the fact that the administrators of governmental agencies are often in a position to take action in support of older Americans (Suran & Rizzo, 1979).

Commitment

The "routine litigation" issue of commitment versus release has been hotly debated in recent years and has led to laws requiring that more attention be given to the rights of the elderly and other mental patients. Because these laws state that a patient must be either treated or released, mental hospitals and other institutions can no longer serve as "dumping grounds" for older people who are unwanted by their families. In every case, however, an attempt must be made to balance the rights of the patient against the welfare of the larger society. Although some people argue that the practice of involuntary commitment should be abolished entirely, others maintain that society has a right to protect itself against potentially dangerous mental patients, both young and old. With sufficient legal safeguards of a patient's civil rights and periodic reviews of his or her therapeutic progress, most experts now agree that families need not feel guilty about having an older relative admitted to an institution with good treatment facilities.

Competency and Testamentary Capacity

The question of **competency** to handle one's life and property arises when a relative makes a legal declaration that because of physical or mental infirmity resulting from old age, the person is unable to take care of his or her property and other affairs, and it is formally requested that the court appoint someone to handle these matters. Obviously, legal action of this sort should be considered only after other possibilities have been examined carefully. Being forced to become entirely dependent on someone else may be the last straw for an elderly person who is barely managing to hold on. For this reason, Butler (1975) has suggested that a legal concept of "partial competency" is needed. Such a concept would preserve the civil rights of a person and yet protect the person against exploitation and victimization when his or her judgment becomes poor.

Testamentary capacity is, in a sense, a kind of partial competence, in that it refers specifically to competency to make a will. An individual possessing testamentary capacity, which is also legally determined, knows the nature and extent of his or her property, that he or she is making a will, and who his or her natural beneficiaries are (Freedman, Kaplan, & Sadock, 1972).

SUMMARY

The problem of crime in the United States is a topic of great concern to Americans, but only a small percentage of criminals are elderly people. Because a fraction of the crimes committed lead to arrests, the number of arrests is not a precise indicator of criminal activity. For whatever reasons, only about 1 percent of those arrested in the United States each year are 65 years old or over. The crimes for which elderly people, and particularly elderly men, are most frequently arrested are drunkenness and disorderly conduct. However, there has been a substantial increase in the number of arrests of older Americans for larceny-theft during the past decade.

The elderly are apparently not victimized any more often than other age groups, but the economic, physical, and psychological effects of crime tend to be more serious in the case of older victims. A variety of crimes are committed against the elderly—theft, mugging, and fraud in particular, but more serious crimes of violence such as murder and rape occur less often. Many of the victimizers of older people, and especially older poor people living in high-crime areas of large cities, are teenagers. In any event, the elderly are swindled and abused by people of all ages—including their own age group and their own relatives.

Gullible, lonely, and perhaps somewhat greedy older people are easy targets for exploiters and con artists. Among the most common types of fraud are those involving health cures and real estate. Confidence games such as the pigeon drop and the bank examiner swindle are also widely practiced.

The key to crime control is crime prevention, and there are many precautions that elderly residents, walkers, and travelers can take to prevent crime against themselves and their property. Education in crime prevention also involves learning the rules for self-protection against fraud and exploitation. Law enforcement agencies in many large cities have special programs designed to inform the elderly about crime and how to protect themselves against it. Victim compensation laws, under which restitution is made to crime victims by the state or offender exist in many states.

Elderly people are no less likely than others to report crimes, but because of fear of embarrassment or retaliation, they are often reluctant to testify in court. A number of elderly people, however, cooperate fully with law enforcement officials in reporting and testifying with regard to crimes committed against themselves and also by acting as volunteer workers in criminal justice activities.

Older people require legal assistance for a variety of reasons, but many do not know their civil rights and the appropriate legal procedures and are too poor to afford the services of an attorney. As a result of the Older Americans Act, all states and territories now have agencies that provide information and coordinate legal activities on the part of the elderly.

Through local outreach programs, older people in need of legal help are identified and attorneys are able to provide consultation and other legal services to them on a discount basis. Attorneys also serve as elder advocates in several ways: by providing information and referrals, routine litigation services (case advocacy), and law reform activity (monitoring and class action suits). Two other types of elder advocacy are legislative advocacy— applying pressure on legislators to draft and vote for certain measures, and administrative advocacy—action on behalf of a group (the elderly) by agency administrators.

The questions of commitment, competency, and testamentary capacity are serious matters to older mental patients. Commitment refers to legal admission (voluntary or involuntary) to an institution for purposes of treatment for a mental disorder. Diagnosis of a mental disorder and commitment do not automatically imply incompetency; this must be determined at a separate legal hearing. The purpose of a competency hearing is to determine whether an individual is able to handle his life and property. The question of testamentary capacity is more narrow than that of competency. The determination of testamentary capacity involves a legal hearing to decide whether an individual knows what property he or she has, who his or her beneficiaries are, and that he or she is making a will.

SUGGESTED READINGS

Can, L. D. Aging and the law. In R. H. Binstock & E. Shanas (Eds.). *Handbook of aging and the social sciences*. New York: Van Nostrand Reinhold, 1976. pp. 342–368.

Clemente, F., & Kleinman, M. B. Fear of crime among the aged. *The Gerontologist*, 1976, *16*, 207–210.

Cook, F. L., Skogan, W. G., Cook, T. D., & Antunes, G. E. Criminal victimization of the elderly. *The Gerontologist*, 1978, *18*, 338–349.

Goldsmith, J., & Goldsmith, S. S. (Eds.). *Crime and the elderly—challenge and response*. Lexington, Mass.: Heath, 1976.

Goldstein, A. P., Hoyer, W. J., & Monti, P. J. (Eds.). *Police and the elderly*. New York: Pergamon Press, 1979.

Jaycox, V. H. The elderly's fear of crime: Rational or irrational? *Victimology: An International Journal*, 1978, *3*(3-4), 329–334.

Malinchak, A. A. *Crime and gerontology: The venerable (vulnerable) Americans*. Englewood Cliffs, N.J.: Prentice-Hall, 1978.

Rifai, M. A. (Ed.). *Justice and older Americans*. Lexington, Mass.: Heath, 1977.

Weiss, J. A. *Law and the elderly*. New York: Practicing Law Institute, 1977.

NOTES

[1]A possible exception to this age decline in crime is suicide, which, especially in white males, increases with age (see Chapter 5). Many authorities, however, criticize

the classification of suicide as a crime. In the seriously ill it may well be viewed as self-euthanasia rather than criminal activity.

[2]From *Your Retirement Anticrime Guide,* pp. 26–27. Copyright 1973, 1978 by American Association of Retired Persons and National Retired Teachers Association.

[3]Further information on these programs may be obtained from: Commission on Legal Problems of the Elderly, American Bar Association, 1800 M Street, N.W., Washington, D.C. 20036.

Death
and
Bereavement

The realization that humans are mortal and the fear of death begin very early in life, but it is often difficult to conceive of and accept the inevitability of one's own demise. People in modern societies, which keep the dying and deceased from public view, usually go through life without thinking much about death. Consequently, they are surprised when someone whom they know—particularly someone in their own age group—dies.

As one grows older, the physical changes accompanying aging, coupled with the aging and dying of family members and friends, force a person to face the event in life that is looked forward to the least. Erikson (1968) maintained that the realization that time is short and death imminent precipitates the integrity versus despair crisis of the terminal period of life. Attempting to cope with death, however, is not something that waits for the final developmental period. Conquest of the fear of death usually begins in young adulthood or middle age, and by the time one reaches old age the process of dying is feared more than death itself.

RESEARCH AND VIEWPOINTS ON DEATH

Until recent years, death and dying were rather taboo topics for research and study. The research of Kübler-Ross (1975), Kastenbaum (Kastenbaum & Aisenberg, 1978), Shneidman (1980) and other researchers has now changed the situation, and thanatology—the study of death—has become more acceptable. There are currently research investigations and writings on various aspects of dying and death—biological, psychological, philosophical, religious, and legal.

Biology of Dying

The death of a human being does not occur in a single instant. Certain body structures, such as the thymus gland, deteriorate before a person is fully mature. In fact, body cells are constantly dying and being replaced by new cells even before an individual is born. The building up and breaking down of body cells and structures, known as anabolism and catabolism, respectively, are complementary metabolic processes. As a person ages, the rate of breaking down begins to exceed the rate of building up, a point reached earlier in some body structures than others.

The traditional definition of death as the cessation of heartbeat has been a topic of controversy and debate in medical and legal circles. The usually accepted medical definition of death is cessation of all electrical activity of the brain for a certain period of time. When a patient is "dying," the cells of the higher brain centers, which are very susceptible to oxygen deficiency, die first—within 5 to 10 minutes after their oxygen supply is cut off. Next, cells in the lower brain centers die, including those in the medulla oblongata, which regulates respiration, heartbeat, and other vital reflexes. Thus "brain death," indicated by a flat or no-response pattern on the electroencephalogram (EEG), leads to death in other body organs.

Cessation of heartbeat is a natural consequence of brain death, but the brain is not always dead when the heart stops. The heart can stop, and its pumping action be restored before the vital centers of the brain are affected. Restoration of the heartbeat by use of electric shock ("counter-shock") is a common procedure in hospitals today. Unfortunately, if the heart has stopped for too long, or for other reasons the blood supply to the brain is interrupted, the higher brain cells will be deprived of oxygen and their functioning affected. In this case, the sensory-motor and mental skills of the person may undergo some deterioration.

The cells of certain glands and muscles die only after the medulla has ceased functioning, but skin and bone cells can live for several hours longer. The growth of fingernails even after interment, for example, has often been noted. Intestinal tissue also continues to function for some time after a person is pronounced clinically dead, and such tissue has been kept "alive" for years when placed in a special physiological solution (Selkurt, 1975).

Even when an individual is medically dead, there are cases in which a resurrection, of the soul and of the entire body of the deceased, is planned. Occasionally, one reads a newspaper story about a deceased person whose body was deep-frozen in liquid nitrogen at the time of death and is being kept in a special aluminum capsule. It is an article of faith of the Cryonics Society that a body preserved in this manner can be thawed and restored to life at some time in the future when a cure for the disease of which the person died is found. Whether those few bodies that are being preserved in this way can be restored to life is debatable, but most authorities are doubtful.

Helplessness and Choice

A wealth of data, both anecdotal and experimental, support the notion that a feeling of helplessness or simply "giving up" and refusing to resist any longer can lead to death under certain circumstances. This "giving up" syndrome has been observed in animals, primitive tribesmen, and highly civilized people (see Seligman, 1975). Instances of death attributed to "giving up" have often been observed in prisoners of war, convicts, and other institutionalized persons. An occurrence in a psychiatric hospital was reported by Lefcourt (1973, p. 242):

> This writer witnessed one such case of death due to a loss of will within a psychiatric hospital. A female patient who had remained in a mute state for nearly 10 years was shifted to a different floor of her building along with her floor mates, while her unit was being redecorated. The third floor of this psychiatric unit where the patient in question had been living was known among the patients as the chronic, hopeless floor. In contrast, the first floor was most commonly occupied by patients who held privileges, including the freedom to come and go on the hospital grounds and to the surrounding streets. In short, the first floor was an exit ward from which patients could anticipate discharge fairly rapidly. All patients who were temporarily moved from the third floor were given medical examinations prior to the move, and the patient in question was judged to be in excellent medical health though still mute and withdrawn. Shortly after moving to the first floor, this chronic psychiatric patient surprised the ward staff by becoming socially responsive such that within a two-week period she ceased being mute and was actually becoming gregarious. As fate would have it, the redecoration of the third-floor unit was soon completed and all previous residents were returned to it. Within a week after she had been returned to the "hopeless" unit, this patient, who like the legendary Snow White had been aroused from a living torpor, collapsed and died. The subsequent autopsy revealed no patholgy of note, and it was whimsically suggested at the time that the patient had died of despair.

A similar type of reaction was produced in wild rats in a series of experiments by Richter (1957). It was found that rats, placed in a vat of warm water, would swim for approximately 60 hours before drowning. But if they were restrained by a human hand until they stopped struggling and then placed in the water, they swam for only a few minutes before sinking to the bottom. Death due to drowning occurred even sooner when the animals were both restrained and their sensitive whiskers cut prior to placing them in the water. The rats that stopped swimming long before they were exhausted apparently "gave up" because they had learned during the restraint period that escape was impossible.

One physiological explanation of the deaths of Richter's rats and similar occurrences in humans is that they were caused by excessive activity of the parasympathetic nervous system, resulting in extreme relaxation, slowing down of heart action, and consequently decreased blood pressure. Parasympathetic death is different from the sympathetic deaths of most mammals. In the latter the heartbeat speeds up rather than slowing down, and the blood pressure increases just before dying. At any rate, the data on death caused by feelings of helplessness underscore the recommendation that nursing home patients and people in related circumstances should be given as much control as possible over decisions affecting their own lives. They should be encouraged to plan their own meals and activities, select their own clothes, and in other ways become involved in choices related to the management of their lives.

Evidence underscoring the importance of individual choice was obtained in Ferrare's (1962) study of nursing home applicants. On the basis of interviews, 55 female applicants (average age, 82 years) to a nursing home were classified into one of two categories: those who perceived that they had no choice but to go to the home, and those who perceived that they had other alternatives. No medical differences between the two groups were observed on admission. Of the 17 women in the "no-choice" group, 8 were dead after four weeks and 16 after ten weeks following admission to the home. However, only one of the 38 women in the "choice" group died during the initial period.

Existentialism and Euthanasia

The importance of making decisions or having a choice as to what one's life will mean has also been stressed by existential philosopher Jean-Paul Sartre (1957). Sartre, Martin Heidegger, and other writers have also maintained that the awareness of our mortality creates a condition of anxiety and concern over whether we are living meaningful lives. As a result, it is said that the true meaning of one's life comes from the awareness that it will end. By accepting one's own finiteness, life becomes more meaningful and valuable. This is because, by facing the inevitability of a personal ending, the individual is spurred into action to live a life that will have some significance. Fearing not death so much as an absurd, valueless life, existential philosophers see death as losing much of its terror for the person whose life has been filled with meaning. Thus the very fact of death energizes the drive toward a meaningful existence, the attainment of which overcomes the fear of death and nothingness.

The existentialist philosophy, emphasizing freedom of action, maintains that even in death one has a choice. This choice has been expressed succinctly by Albert Camus in "The Myth of Sisyphus": "Is one to die voluntarily or to hope in spite of everything?" Or, as asked by an old man named Charlie who had been rescued after sticking his head in a gas oven: "But a man has a right to die, don't he? He don't have to sit and wait, sit and wait for death." (Curtin, 1972, p. 167)

The decision to end one's life is not limited to the existentialists and the Charlies. It may be a very rational choice in a helpless, hopeless person who feels that he or she has no meaningful reason to continue living. The fact that the decision for death is more likely under certain conditions is seen in the relatively high suicide rate for patients suffering from malignant neoplasma or other terminal illnesses (Farberow, Shneidman, & Leonard, 1963; Abram, Moore, & Westervelt, 1971).

To My Family, My Physician, My Lawyer and All Others Whom It May Concern

Death is as much a reality as birth, growth, maturity and old age—it is the one certainty of life. If the time comes when I can no longer take part in decisions for my own future, let this statement stand as an expression of my wishes and directions, while I am still of sound mind.

If at such a time the situation should arise in which there is no reasonable expectation of my recovery from extreme physical or mental disability, I direct that I be allowed to die and not be kept alive by medications, artificial means or "heroic measures". I do, however, ask that medication be mercifully administered to me to alleviate suffering even though this may shorten my remaining life.

This statement is made after careful consideration and is in accordance with my strong convictions and beliefs. I want the wishes and directions here expressed carried out to the extent permitted by law. Insofar as they are not legally enforceable, I hope that those to whom this Will is addressed will regard themselves as morally bound by these provisions.

Signed_____

Date _____

Witness_____

Witness_____

Copies of this request have been given to _____

_____

_____

_____

Figure 12-1 A "Living Will." Prepared by Concern for Dying, it expresses the signer's wish to avoid the use of "heroic measures" to preserve his/her life in the event of irreversible disease or injury. (Reprinted with permission from Concern for Dying, 250 West 57 Street, New York, N.Y. 10107.)

The "mercy killing" of animals and humans too ill or injured to recover is known as **euthanasia** (from the Greek, meaning good death). Most of the legal debate over the concept of euthanasia is concerned with passive euthanasia, that is, letting a patient die naturally rather than exercising extreme, artificial means (transplants, life-sustaining drugs, heart-lung machines, respirators, etc.) to sustain life, perhaps in a state of constant suffering or unconsciousness. Some people, concerned with the physical and financial cost to themselves and their loved ones of a long terminal illness, are beginning to assert their "right to die" in the form of a "living will" (Fig. 12-1). Although such a document is not legally binding, it does represent an attempt to permit the dying individual some choice, even during the last days or months of life.

Although physicians subscribe to the Hippocratic oath, with its emphasis on preserving life at any cost, medical authorities are usually opposed to employing artificial, life-sustaining procedures with patients having extensive, irreversible brain damage. In the case of a conscious, rational, terminal patient who ostensibly wishes to die, agreement is not so general. To begin with, the great majority of terminally ill patients do not want to die (Hall & Cameron, 1976). And even those who express death wishes frequently change their minds (see Report 12-1).

Religion and Death

Unlike Oriental philosophies in which life an death are viewed as complementary experiences, most people in Western societies think of death as being outside of life and foreign to the self. The emphasis of Western culture on individualism, action, and self-determination makes death—something beyond our control, to be feared and denied—an insult and outrage to the living. Thus the mythology and literature of Western culture have tended to depict death, the "Grim Reaper," as man's greatest enemy. The threat of death and what may follow have also been used with effectiveness by rulers and religions to make people obey.

Faced with the inevitable, many people draw strength from music, literature, and the visual arts. Strong philosophical or religious convictions can also be a comfort to people on their deathbeds. This was attested to in a statement by thanatologist Ernest Becker as he lay dying of terminal cancer (Keen, 1974, p. 78): "What makes death easier is . . . to know that . . . beyond what is happening to us is the fact of the tremendous creative energies of the cosmos that are using us for some purposes we don't know."

Several researchers have observed that people who believe in some form of God and have truly integrated religion into their lives are able to face death with greater composure than nonbelievers (Kübler-Ross, 1974; Ross, Braga, & Braga, 1975). On the other hand, Erikson (1976) felt that acceptance of death is not contingent on conventional religious beliefs. To Erikson, an identification with the human race is the best defense against death. Also noteworthy is the finding that the greatest fears of death are experienced by people who are undecided about religion or have inconsis-

Report 12-1 'DEATH WITH DIGNITY': SHOULD PATIENTS DECIDE?*

BOSTON (AP) — Doctors should be reluctant to accept the requests of sick persons for "death with dignity," because their desire to die may change, be based on needless fears or be a quest for attention, two physicians say.

In recent years, doctors have paid increasing attention to patients' wishes for quiet death as the development of respirators and other advances allowed them to keep people alive long after they lost consciousness.

A team of physicians who treat people with bad burns recently recommended that patients be allowed to make life-and-death decisions, because "who is more likely to be totally and lovingly concerned with the patients' best interests than the patient himself?"

Now, two Cleveland doctors say this view "may be somewhat naive and, in certain clinical situations, potentially dangerous."

In today's New England Journal of Medicine, the doctors said that before pulling the plug, doctors should make sure the patient who seeks death really means what he says.

"Physicians who are uncomfortable or inexperienced in dealing with the complex psycho-social issues facing critically ill patients may ignore an important aspect of their professional responsibility by taking a patient's statement at face value without further exploration or clarification," they wrote.

The doctors, David L. Jackson and Stuart Younger, described six cases they encountered in the intensive care unit at University Hospitals of Cleveland.

In one case, an 80-year-old man with lung disease at first said he did not want to be kept alive by a respirator. However, later, he changed his mind several times. The case, they said, shows that "one must be cautious not to act precipitously on the side of the patient's ambivalence with which one agrees, while piously claiming to be following the principle of patient autonomy."

In another case, a 52-year-old man with multiple sclerosis said he did not want doctors to try to save him if he developed serious complications. However, he later admitted he was upset with his family for not paying attention to him.

An 18-year old woman with chronic asthma resisted treatment with a respirator. But after she was questioned by doctors, she said she was afraid of the hospital equipment. Her fears were calmed and she was discharged eight days later.

A 56-year old woman with cancer urged doctors to do all they could to help her because she wanted to live long enough to see the birth of her first grandchild. When her condition worsened and she lost consciousness, her family asked that treatment be stopped. But the doctors refused, and the woman recovered enough to go home and see the child.

The doctors said they hoped their experience would help other physicians cope with situations in which "superficial and automatic acquiescence to the concepts of patient autonomy and death with dignity threaten sound clinical judgment."

*From *News-Chronicle*, Thousand Oaks, Calif., Aug. 29, 1979, p. 32. Used by permission of The Associated Press.

tent beliefs. The fewest death fears are reported by both the strongly religious and confirmed atheists (Kalish, 1976).

The notions of immortality, the afterlife, heaven, and hell form a part of many religions. The results of older surveys (see Cavan, Burgess, Havighurst, & Goldhamer, 1949) indicate that a sizable majority of 65-year-olds believe in an afterlife—a percentage that increases during later life. Although those who believe usually do not arrive at their conclusions from personal experience, in the past few years physicians have interviewed a number of patients who were revived after having been judged clinically dead. The experiences described by these patients who reportedly visited the "other side" are generally pleasant, but in some cases terrifying (Moody, 1975; Rawlings, 1978). Siegel (1980) points out, however, that these afterlife visions are similar to drug-induced hallucinations. They can be interpreted as evidence that people survive death, but a more parsimonious explanation is to view them as dissociative hallucinatory phenomena produced by abnormal brain activity.

Report 12-2   IS THERE LIFE AFTER DEATH*

Life After Life author Raymond Moody believes that there is life after death. He came to his belief while interviewing "hundreds" of persons who had been clinically dead. They told Dr. Moody that before they were revived they "left their physical bodies" and "crossed to the other side." They did not remember re-entering their physical bodies prior to returning to consciousness.

While not everyone relates the same details upon resuscitation, Dr. Moody said that most remember that they:

- Were sucked out of their physical bodies through the head;
- Were aware of a loud, unpleasant noise (descriptions have included buzzing, clicking, sound of trap drums, roaring, vibration) which was "sensed" rather than heard;
- Were drawn rapidly through a darkness (tunnel, funnel, cave, well, valley, pipe, dark cylinder) toward an intense, brilliant light at the end of the darkness;
- Recognized the presence of dead relatives who were there to help them in their transition to the other side;
- Felt only love in the presence of the "being of light" to which they were drawn, a brilliance which could be described as "love" as well as light;
- Were asked—not in spoken words but in "terms of a very living presence"—"What have you done with your life that you want to show me?" and "Are you ready to die?" and "'Are you satisfied with your life?'"
- Saw a panoramic review of their lives—in color, three dimension, third person and simultaneously—and heard their own words repeated from the time of an action, felt their own thoughts and sensed what effect their words and deeds had on others present at the time of the action;
- Were given total acceptance by the "being of light" even though some of their past actions embarrassed them;
- Did not want to return to their physical bodies but were sent back to complete unfinished tasks on earth, to care for dependent loved ones or, in some cases, to tell others what it is like on "the other side";
- Were told that learning is an eternal process, to never stop gaining knowledge; and
- Can never adequately describe their experiences because the English language has no words capable of so doing.

The revived persons usually say they are glad to be back with an opportunity to live out their natural lives, that they now know love and how to give it, are not afraid of death any longer, and have a more positive attitude toward life, Dr. Moody said.

*From *Greensboro Daily News*, August 1, 1977, p. A12. Used with permission.

TREATMENT OF THE DYING

Unlike preindustrial societies, in which personal contacts with the dead and dying were fairly commonplace, modern society keeps the terminally ill and deceased away from public view. Over two-thirds of the dying in the United States is done outside the home, usually in health care institutions ("Acceptance," 1975). Yet most dying people would rather spend their last days at home, in familiar surroundings and among those whom they know and love. Dying at home, however, may impose a heavy burden on the family. Therefore the dying person often ends his or her life in a hospital or nursing home, feeling abandoned and humiliated (Weisman, 1972).

Attitudes toward Death

Negative attitudes toward death can easily generalize to old people, acting as a factor in the lack of respect shown for them. The aged may be perceived as a homogeneous group of decayed organisms merely sitting around waiting to die and not as individuals. To demonstrate the point, Curtin (1972) enlisted the services of a Mrs. Duffy to pose as a prospective

Figure 12-2 Mark Jury and his dying grandfather. Despite the fact that the old miner refused to eat during his last days, the Jurys abided by his wish to die in his own way at home rather than moving him to a hospital where he would be fed intravenously and die in a strange place with tubes stuck in him. (From *Gramp*, by Mark Jury and Dan Jury. Copyright © 1975, 1976 by Mark and Dan Jury. Reprinted by permission of Viking Penguin Inc.)

resident of a retirement community. When describing the features of the community to Mrs. Duffy, the salesman boasted: "Here you are free from worry. We have a security patrol 24 hours a day, just looking after your welfare so you can sleep in peace." Not one to be bested, the skeptical Mrs. Duffy replied: "That's exactly what the man said when I bought a plot in the cemetery for me and my husband." (Curtin, 1972, p. 116).

As with attitudes toward the elderly, attitudes toward death are not all negative. They vary with sex, emotional adjustment, educational level, financial security, experiences with the deaths of others, family relationships, and religious orientation. Men are more likely than women to view death as an evil antagonist who must be fought. Women, in contrast, tend to view death in a more accepting, benevolent way— as a compassionate mother rather than as an opponent (Back, 1971).

Attitude toward death is positively related to both educational level and emotional adjustment: A more accepting attitude is characteristic of those with higher educational levels and those with better emotional adjustment. Educational level, however, is also positively related to emotional adjustment, and all three variables—educational level, emotional adjustment, and attitude toward death—are associated with financial security.

Most elderly people believe in an afterlife, but as they approach the end of life few people emphasize the religious side of death—heaven, hell, the last judgment, and so on. Furthermore, it is the quality of the affiliation that is related to a person's attitude toward dying (Carey, 1976), rather than merely the affiliation with some religious organization. Experiences with the deaths of others and strong interpersonal ties to family and friends, which help provide the strength to face the inevitable and a sense of the continuity of life, are also associated with more accepting attitudes toward death.

A Conspiracy of Silence

Although they may accept death in the abstract, the reactions of most people to the actual facts of dying and death are sufficiently negative to make them inadequate in dealing with the concerns of terminally ill patients. Even medical personnel, who are trained primarily to save lives and hence to consider death as an enemy, are often uncomfortable with the topic and do not like being present when their patients die. But many dying patients, as well as their family and friends, could benefit from discussing their feelings with doctors and nurses.

An important and anxiety-provoking question that the attending physician must face is whether to tell a patient he or she is dying. According to Butler (1975), less that 20 percent of attending physicians voluntarily tell their patients they are going to die. Physicians feel, sometimes justifiably, that patients will be unable to handle the prospect of their own demise and that the knowledge will cause their physical condition to worsen. On the side of telling the patients is the fact that most older people view death as inevitable, have made some preparation for it, and are willing to discuss it with others. Too often physicians, as a result of training that emphasizes only the physical and technical side of medical treatment and the saving of lives, overlook the human needs of patients to ask questions and to receive emotional support and understanding from the medical staff.

In general, the reactions of a typical hospital staff toward terminally ill patients are technically efficient but impersonal (Buckingham et al., 1976). Trapped in a "conspiracy of silence" on the part of medical personnel, family, and friends, the dying patient is left to face death alone or with impersonal nursing care—a frightened, machinelike object attached to life-giving equipment, rather than a valuable human being. This conspiracy of silence was described nearly a century ago by Tolstoy (1886) in "The Death of Ivan Ilych" (pp. 137–138):

> What tormented Ivan Ilych most was the deception, the lie, which for some reason they all accepted, that he was not dying but was simply ill, and that he only need keep quiet and undergo a treatment and then something very good would result. He, however, knew that do what they would nothing would come of it, only still more agonizing suffering and death. This deception tortured him—their not wishing to admit what they all knew and what he knew, but wanting to lie to him concerning his terrible condition, and wishing and forcing him to participate in that lie. Those lies—lies enacted over him on the eve of his death and destined to degrade this awful, solemn act to the level of their visitings, their curtains, their sturgeon for dinner—were a terrible agony for Ivan Ilych. And strangely enough, many times when they were going through their antics over him he had been within a hair-breadth of calling out to them: "Stop lying! You know and I know that I am dying. Then at least stop lying about it!" But he had never had the spirit to do it. The awful, terrible act of his dying was, he could see, reduced by those about him to the level of a casual, unpleasant, and almost indecorous incident (as if someone entered a drawing-room diffusing an unpleasant odor) and this was done by that very decorum which he had served all his life long. He saw that no one felt for him, because no one even wished to grasp his position. Only Gerasim recognized it and pitied him. And so Ivan Ilych felt at ease only with him.

Psychological Treatment of the Dying

Elisabeth Kübler-Ross (1969) found that most dying patients want to talk about their fears and feelings and to be given the opportunity to make some decisions pertaining to their lives and deaths. They may need to spend this time working through unresolved conflicts with others, expressing meaningful farewells, and generally putting their lives in order. Weisman (1972) advocated giving dying patients some autonomy, as in deciding how much medication they want. Most important, however, is that the dying person have a relationship of mutual trust with a compassionate individual to help him or her face fears of the unknown.

There is a growing emphasis in medical schools on teaching doctors to assist dying patients and their families in accepting death as a natural event rather than the frightening consequence of a medical mistake. The aim of these efforts is to help patients and their families view death less fearfully and thus make the passage from life a more diginified experience for all. One procedure designed to train medical personnel for such a service is the **psychological autopsy** (Weisman & Kastenbaum, 1968). This is a post-mortem analysis of the psychosocial aspects of a patient's death, with the goal of helping hospital personnel to become more aware of the importance of psychological factors in dying.[1]

Hospice Care

A growing movement in terminal care that provides pain- and symptom-free treatment while meeting the patient's emotional needs is hospice care. Hospice care was initiated by Dr. Cecily Saunders at St. Christopher's Hospice in London as a method of fostering a positive attitude toward death in terminally ill cancer patients (Saunders, 1980). It was introduced in the United States at St. Luke's Hospital in New York and New Haven Hospice in Connecticut and has since spread to other British and American cities and throughout the world. By 1981 more than 50 hospice units had been started in Great Britain and more than 100 such projects in America.

In hospice care, the dying are surrounded with people who act as if death were not the end; these people treat the dying as valuable individuals whose significance is in no way diminished. There are four major features of hospice care: control of the patient's pain and discomfort; personal, caring contact between patients and staff; discussions of death and dying between patients and medical staff; death with meaning and dignity and not alone. To alleviate pain, patients are sometimes given a mixture of morphine, cocaine, ethyl alcohol, and a sweetener. This "Brompton's mixture" is said to provide maximum relief of pain with minimum sedative effect.

The efforts of the entire staff in a hospice center are directed toward helping patients feel accepted and significant and to use wisely the time remaining. Patients are urged to communicate with counselors, family, and others, showing their feelings and exploring the meaning of death. Through such procedures terminal patients are helped to die with dignity and grace, and to believe that their lives have meaning even if they are about to die.

THE PROCESS OF DYING

Although thoughts of death are not uncommon in the elderly, death is viewed with less fear in older than in young and middle-aged adults. As noted earlier, the elderly fear the process of dying more than death itself (Kalish & Reynolds, 1976). In any event, awareness of death can become quite strong after a serious accident, a prolonged illness, or the death of someone close. Whether the resulting preoccupation with death induces motivational paralysis on the one hand or a beneficial or destructive change in the individual's life on the other varies from person to person.

Life Review

A phenomenon of particular interest triggered by the awareness of death is the life review. The term **life review** can refer to either a prolonged reminiscence or preoccupation with the past, or a split-second review of one's life during an actual experience of dying or near death. To Butler (1968, 1971), the life review is a universal process, occurring at any time of life and providing the opportunity to relieve old pleasures and sufferings and to work out persisting conflicts. The fact that this process is going on may be signaled by frequent "mirror gazing" and an enhanced interest in discussing the past.

Ideally, a life review culminates in a sense of continuity with the past, an integrated life, and resulting wisdom and inner peace. To quote Curtin (1972, pp. 76–77): "There seems to be a particular point in the lives of old people when they've reached the top of the mountain, when they seem . . . to see everything with dreadful clarity. All ambition gone, all sense of having a coherent future lost, they have no veils to shield a vision of themselves, their past, the world. Some old people cannot bear this 'amazing grace' because it seems to signal their closeness to death." Reminiscing about the past can also result in feelings of guilt, anger, and depression, and even suicidal impulses. In any event, Cameron (1972), who was unable to confirm the supposition that old people think more about the past than the future, concluded that the life review process is not so common in old age as it is presumed to be.

Individual Differences in Dying

Throughout this book it has been emphasized that individual responses to stress situations and crises vary widely and that personality makes its imprint on almost all behavior. This is very true of dying; reactions and attitudes toward dying are quite different in different individuals. For example, Weisman and Kastenbaum (1968) observed two broad response patterns in their dying patients. Some seemed unaware of impending death or accepted it, gradually withdrawing into inactivity; others remained actively involved in hospital life right up until the day they died.

Reactions to impending death usually reveal something about the personality of the dying person and the kind of life he or she has lived. One person may view death as a punishment for hostile impulses, whereas in another it arouses early fears of separation; in a third it represents a reunion with departed loved ones. Some older people possess a strong religious faith in the significance of human existence and in an afterlife, and this faith helps them approach death with composure. Others, perhaps those who have lost too much—including the will to keep trying and enduring, embrace death as a solution to their personal problems. Kastenbaum (1971) found, for example, that 25 percent of the terminally ill patients whom he interviewed wanted to die before their time.

For still other people, rather than being a solution, death represents a highly stressful event that is approached with fear and conflict. Afraid of dying, but also afraid of becoming unable to cope with prolonged illness and pain, these people continually vacillate between the desire to live and the desire to be released from pain and suffering. Added to the fear of being unable to cope and of being a burden on others is the concern about what will happen to surviving relatives and friends who depend on the patient.

Stages of Dying

As a result of interviews with over 200 dying patients, Elisabeth Kübler-Ross (1969) postulated five psychological stages through which people pass as they become aware of their impending death. She maintained that most people, whether they die slowly or quickly, pass through these successive stages in their attempts to deal with death. Throughout the five stages, the patient continues to hope for recovery or a cure. Kübler-Ross believes that this feeling of hope should be supported by telling patients that everything humanly possible will be done to help them.

During the first stage, **denial,** the patient refuses to accept the doctor's diagnosis and consults other medical and nonmedical people. It is always important for a seriously ill patient to ask for a second opinion on medical matters, but in an attempt to defend himself against the realization that he is dying, the patient may spend a great deal of money on faith healers and medical quacks. According to psychoanalysts, most people at the uncon-

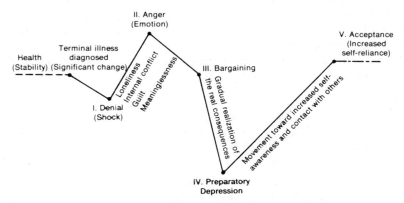

Figure 12-3 Psychological stages in the dying process. (Courtesy of Dr. Elisabeth Kübler-Ross; 1975, p. 161.)

scious level do not really believe they are going to die, and by refusing to accept the fact of death they protect themselves against anxiety resulting from the realization that their time is short.

As the patient's health continues to deteriorate, it becomes increasingly difficult to deny the imminence of death. Thus denial gradually fades into a partial acceptance of the inevitable. During this second stage, which Kübler-Ross refers to as **anger,** the patient feels angry and even enraged at the unfairness of having to die before his or her work has been completed and while other people continue to live. It is important for the family and hospital staff to be alert to this stage, because they may be the apparent targets of the patient's anger. The anger, however, is actually directed not so much toward them but toward the unfairness of death.

Patience and understanding on the part of the hospital staff and family are very important during the second stage. In any event, the anger slowly abates, to be replaced by desperate efforts on the part of the patient to buy time by **bargaining**—with fate, God, the doctors, or anyone who offers the possibility of hope. The patient promises to take his medicine and go to church regularly, prays for forgiveness, and even engages in rituals or magical acts to ward off the demon Death. The bargaining state is not obvious in all patients, but when it occurs it appears to represent a healthier, more controlled approach than denial and anger.

During the fourth stage, **depression,** the patient now fully accepts his impending death, but becomes depressed by all that he has suffered and all that he will be giving up by dying. Depression, at least to some degree, is a necessary part of the acceptance of death and the final peace that comes with acceptance. Consequently, the patient should be allowed to feel depressed for a while, and not be continually pestered by denying, "sweet lemon" Pollyannas. He should be permitted to share his grief with people who are important to him, and, after he has been sad for a time, then reassured and cheered up.

The last psychological stage of dying, **acceptance,** is characterized by "quiet expectation." The patient, who is now very weak and tired, accepts the inevitability of death and desires only freedom from pain. This is a time to be alone with one or two loved ones, erasing old hurts and saying last goodbyes. The calm acceptance of death has been expressed poetically by William Cullen Bryant ("Thanatopsis"), and Robert Louis Stevenson ("Requiem").

> Under the wide and starry sky
> Dig my grave and let me lie.
> Glad did I live and gladly die,
> And I laid me down with a will.
>
> This be the verse that you grave for me:
> Here he lies where he longed to be,
> Home is the sailor, home from the sea,
> And the hunter home from the hill.
>
> Robert Louis Stevenson

Just before he died, the noted journalist Stewart Alsop wrote: "A dying man needs to die as a sleepy man needs to sleep, and there comes a time when it is wrong, as well as useless, to resist" (Alsop, 1973, p. 299).

Kübler-Ross has made important contributions to attitudes toward dying and an understanding of the dying process, but her theory of stages has not gone unchallenged. Kastenbaum and Costa (1977) noted, for example, that the notion of a fixed sequence of stages in dying has not been verified by research. Shneidman (1973) went somewhat further by concluding from his observations that there is no inevitable progression of stages in the dying process, but rather a continual alternation between denial and acceptance. Perhaps an even more serious criticism of Kübler-Ross's theory is the way in which it is sometimes applied in working with the dying. Thus, medical personnel, subscribing to the theory of a fixed sequence of stages in dying, have been known to chide terminally ill patients for not going through the stages in the proper order and not completing the required emotional tasks on time.

BEREAVEMENT AND MOURNING

Death during old age is usually considered a normal occurrence rather than a tragedy. The elderly are seen as having had their chance to attain happiness and make whatever contributions they wish, and so death in later life is only fair. Dying is considered more of a tragedy when it occurs in a young person, who has not been given a sufficient opportunity to experience life and achieve his or her goals. It would seem, then, that death in old age, especially if the deceased's dying trajectory has been long, would not be the cause of so much grief and mourning in the survivors. Even when expected, however, the death of an elderly loved one can be a very stressful experience for the family and friends of the deceased.

The Funeral

Historically, the purpose of the funeral rite was to honor the deceased, supply him or her with things thought to be needed in the other world, and to gain favor with the gods. The term "funeral" comes from the Sanskrit word for "smoke," presumably stemming from the early practice in northern India of burning the dead. Another ancient custom was **suttee,** in which the widow threw herself on the funeral pyre of her deceased husband—to be burned alive. This practice was fairly common in India until being outlawed by the British in the nineteenth century.

Another ancient custom was for newly bereaved Egyptian widows to run through the streets, beating their breasts and tearing their hair. With respect to treatment of the corpse of the deceased, both cremation and earth burial were practiced by the ancient Greeks and Romans. Anointing and decorating the dead in preparation for the afterlife were also practiced in ancient times, as they are today. Many of our own funeral customs—wearing black, walking in procession, raising a mound over the grave—were introduced into Britain by the Romans and subsequently transported by the British to North America (Hambly, 1974).

Mandelbaum (1959) described several functions of the funeral in our culture, including public acknowledgment of the death of a person and disposal of the body. The funeral also serves as an institutionalized way of reaffirming family ties and, secondarily, the stability of society. Furthermore, by extending the period of mourning over several days, the funeral and other ritualized features of bereavement help the survivors to readjust and reorient themselves to the world of the living. This therapeutic function of the social and religious rites associated with death has been recognized by most societies.

The Stress of Bereavement

Mourning for the deceased and grief at his or her departure do not automatically cease when the funeral is over. The death of a loved one, and a spouse in particular, is often an extremely stressful experience from which the bereaved has difficulty recovering. Preoccupied with loss and grief, the bereaved may ignore other people and let things go, having little or no energy left to cope with the external world.

There are various household and business duties that the bereaved must now perform alone without the help and guidance of the deceased. Medical bills and funeral expenses need to be taken care of, a difficult chore even when life insurance and/or savings cover the costs and a severe burden when they do not. Payment of income, inheritance, and gift taxes, and the implementation of conditions stated in the will are other duties of survivors.

Survivors are usually eligible for some kind of death benefit or burial payment from social security, typically a lump sum for burial expenses and a burial plot. They may also be entitled to veterans' benefits in cases where the deceased had a service-connected disability and to funds from a labor union or fraternal organization. Whatever the benefits, when there has been a terminal illness a good portion of the total usually goes for hospital bills. The cost of a casket, a hearse, a cemetery plot or use of a crematory, use of a funeral home, flowers, obituary notices, clergyman's honorarium, and music for the funeral service must also be taken into account in the overall bill. Considering the rising costs of funerals, it is no wonder that memorial services are becoming more popular.[2]

Perhaps because of their greater dependence on the deceased, the stress of bereavement tends to be greater for women than for men. Men also seem to accept death more readily than women and find it harder to express grief (Glick, Weiss & Parks, 1974). Whether the survivor is a man or a woman, the death of a loved one deprives the survivor of various kinds of satisfaction. The deceased served as a satisfier of the physical needs of the bereaved as well as a source of emotional gratification. As a consequence, over the years the bereaved's sense of identity and the meaning of his or her life may have become intertwined with the personality of the deceased. Somehow he or she must now learn to cope with the loss and the resulting stress.

The period of greatest stress for the bereaved is usually immediately after the death of the deceased. This is the time when the reactions of the bereaved are most intense. Among the behavioral reactions observed during the first month of mourning are periodic crying, difficulty sleeping, loss of appetite, and problems in concentrating or remembering (Fig. 12-4). A study of 109 widowed persons found that the emotional disturbances and insomnia associated with bereavement can also lead to dependence on tranquilizers, sleeping pills, and/or alcohol (Clayton, Halikes & Maurice, 1971).

The emotional reactions of a surviving spouse, who in 75 percent of the cases is the wife, may be so intense that severe physical illness, a serious accident, or even death—occasionally from suicide—occurs. It was found in

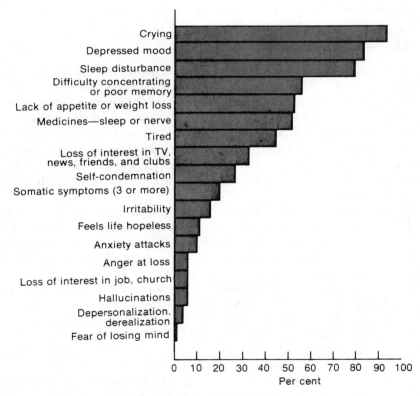

Figure 12-4 Percentages of recently widowed persons expressing various symptoms. (Reprinted from Kimmel, 1980, p. 525. Adapted from Clayton, Halikes, and Maurice, 1971, Table 1.) Courtesy of Physicians Postgraduate Press, Inc.)

a study of 4,500 British widowers aged 55 and over, for example, that 213 died during the first 6 months of their bereavement (Parkes, Benjamin & Fitzgerald, 1969). The rate of death, most instances of which apparently resulted from heart problems, was 40 percent higher than expected in this age group. Concluding from a series of related investigations that grief and consequent feelings of helplessness make people more vulnerable to pathogens, Seligman (1975) suggested that individuals who have recently lost a spouse would do well to be very careful about their health. He recommended monthly medical checkups during the first year after the loss.

Although anxiety and depression are the most common reactions to bereavement, anger, guilt, and even psychotic symptoms (hallucinations, feelings of depersonalization, etc.) have been observed. Depression is a normal response to any severe loss, but it is augmented by feelings of guilt in cases where interpersonal hostilities and conflicts with the deceased have not been resolved. Anger may be expressed—toward nurses, physicians, friends, and family members whom the bereaved believes to have been negligent in their treatment of the deceased. For various reasons, survivors may also experience anger toward the deceased or relief at his or her death—both of which can lead to feelings of guilt.

Stages of Mourning

It has been observed that many bereaved people appear to go through several stages of mourning. Similar to Kübler-Ross's (1969) psychological stages in dying, Bowlby (1960) found evidence for five stages in mourning: (1) concentration on the deceased; (2) anger toward the deceased or others; (3) appeals to others for help; (4) despair, withdrawal, and disorganization; (5) reorganization and direction of love toward a new object. There has been relatively little research on Bowlby's stages, but, as with Kübler-Ross's stages in dying, it is recognized that not all mourners go through them in the order listed.

Kavanaugh (1974) described seven stages in the process of grieving or mourning for a loved one: shock, disorganization, volatile emotions, guilt, loss and loneliness, relief, and reestablishment. Kavanaugh also recognized that a particular mourner may not go through all these stages and not necessarily in the order listed.

Somewhat more parsimonious than Bowlby's (1960) and Kavanaugh's (1974) descriptions is Gorer's (1965) three-stage conception of mourning. The first stage, **initial shock,** lasts only a few days and is characterized by a loss of self-control, reduced energy, and lack of motivation. The mourner is bewildered, disoriented, and loses perspective. As the initial shock wears off, the second stage, **intense grief,** takes over. This stage is characterized by periodic crying and a confused inability to comprehend what has actually happened. The second stage can last for several months, but it gradually gives way to a **gradual reawakening of interest.** During this third and last stage the mourner accepts the reality of the loved one's death and all that it means.

Readjustment and Renewal

For a variety of reasons, survivors often find it difficult to let go of the dead. In contrast to Mark Antony's famous dictum[3], they tend to purify and idealize the deceased in their memory. The result can be a persistence of grief beyond a reasonable period of time. Nevertheless, the old cliché that time heals all things is to a large extent true. Some people never get over the death of a loved one completely, but in most instances the emotional effects of death do not persist more than two years. In one study, for example, 48 percent of the widows who were interviewed one year after their husbands had died reported that they had gotten over their husbands' deaths. Only 20 percent said that they had not yet recovered and did not expect to do so (Lopata, 1973).

The problem of adjusting to the death of a person to whom one has been very close is especially painful when the death was unexpected and if there was insufficient time for the survivors, as well as the deceased, to prepare for it. But when the family members and friends are given ample warning that the person is dying, there is an opportunity to talk through problems with the dying person and each other.

In any event, the ability to go on living and developing new social relationships depends on the kind of gratification that was gained from the relationship with the deceased. It is difficult to begin anew when there are persisting interpersonal problems and negative emotions. But when the relationship has been built on mutual trust and fulfillment and there are no serious unresolved conflicts, the bereaved can more easily begin the process of readjustment and self-renewal.

SUMMARY

The medical definition of death as being the cessation of the heartbeat and brain activity has been a topic of considerable debate. Not all parts of the body die simultaneously; certain tissues can live for hours and even days after the heart and brain have ceased to function. Furthermore, by using countershock it is possible to "resurrect" a person whose heart has stopped beating.

As witnessed by the "giving up" syndrome in lower animals and humans, psychological factors play an important role in dying. Parasympathetic death, resulting from relaxation of the body, apparently stems from feelings of helplessness.

Music, literature, and the visual arts, as well as philosophical and religious beliefs, can be a comfort in the face of death. Existential philosophers have stressed the fact that the true meaning of one's life comes from the awareness that it will end. Western culture, with its emphasis on individualism and self-determination, has tended to view death as man's worst enemy and as outside of life. On the other hand, oriental philosophies view life and death as complementary experiences.

Perceiving themselves as trained to save lives, even physicians are sometimes uncomfortable in the presence of death and the dying. Whether or not a patient should be informed of impending death and encouraged to talk about it is not always an easy question to answer. Kübler-Ross, however, has found that most dying patients want to discuss their fears and feelings and to be permitted to make decisions concerning their lives. There is certainly no routine psychological prescription for assisting the dying person, but hospital personnel should be made aware of the importance of psychological factors in dying. Hospice care, which attempts to provide pain- and symptom-free treatment while meeting the emotional needs of terminally ill patients, is especially noteworthy for its efforts in helping them die with dignity.

Butler perceives the life review as a universal therapeutic process in the aged and dying, but Cameron maintains that it is not so common as it is presumed to be. Whether or not a life review takes place depends, as do other reactions and attitudes toward life and death, on the individual. Attitude toward death varies with emotional adjustment, experiences with the deaths of others, family relationships, education, economic security, and religion.

Kübler-Ross noted five successive psychological stages in the reactions of the dying person: denial, partial acceptance (anger), bargaining, depression, and acceptance. These five stages have been the subject of controversy, and they need not follow one another in the order listed. In any event, reactions to dying vary greatly with the personality and circumstances of the patient.

The rituals of the modern funeral stem from several historical practices and serve a number of therapeutic functions. The death of a relative or close friend is a stressful experience that can have wide-ranging psychological and physical consequences for survivors. The reactions of the bereaved include anxiety, depression, guilt, anger, and even psychotic behavior. Bowlby listed five stages, Kavanaugh seven stages, and Gorer three stages (initial shock, intense grief, gradual reawakening of interest) in the psychological response pattern known as mourning.

In addition to psychological reactions, the loss of a loved one can result in pronounced physical changes and even death in the bereaved. The quality and intensity of the psychological and physical changes of mourning, and whether or not the bereaved is able to readjust, depend on the kind of gratification gained from the relationship with the deceased and the resolution of any interpersonal problems or negative emotions in regard to the latter.

SUGGESTED READINGS

Conroy, R. C. Widows and widowhood. *New York State Journal of Medicine,* 1977, 77, 357–360.

Feifel, H. (Ed.). *New meanings of death.* New York: McGraw-Hill, 1977.

Jury, M., & Jury, D. *Gramp.* New York:

Grossman Publishers, 1976.

Kastenbaum, R., & Aisenberg, R. *The psychology of death*. New York: Springer, 1978.

Pattison, M. *The experience of dying*. Englewood Cliffs, N.J.: Prentice-Hall, 1977.

Portwood, D. A. A right to suicide? *Psychology Today*, 1978, *11*(8), 66–76.

Russell, O. R. *Freedom to die: Moral and legal aspects of euthanasia* (Rev. ed.).

New York: Human Sciences, 1977.

Schultz, R. *The psychology of death, dying, and bereavement*. Reading, Mass.: Addison-Wesley, 1978.

Shneidman, E. S. *Death: Current perspectives* (2d ed.). Palo Alto, Calif.: Mayfield, 1980.

Siegel, R. K. The psychology of life after death. *American Psychologist*, 1980, *35*, 911–931.

NOTES

[1]A discussion of counseling the dying and their families is presented in Chapter 6.

[2]It is now generally recognized that embalming and "seal-type" caskets do not retard decay, and so at least these expenses can be avoided.

[3]"The evil that men do lives after them.

The good is often interred with their bones."

Old age has yet his honour and his toil;
Death closes all: but something ere the end,
Some work of noble note, may yet be done,
Not unbecoming men that strove with Gods."

—Tennyson, *Ulysses*

Agencies and Organizations for the Aging

ACTION. Retired Senior Volunteer
   Program (RSVP), Foster
   Grandparents and Senior
   Companions
806 Connecticut Ave., N.W.
Washington, DC 20525

Administration on Aging
Office of Human Development Services
U.S. Dept. of Health and Human
   Services
330 Independence Ave., S.W.
Washington, DC 20201

American Aging Association
c/o Denham Harman, M.D.
University of Nebraska College of
   Medicine
Omaha, NE 68105

American Association of Homes for the
   Aging
1050 17th Street, N.W.
Washington, DC 20036

American College of Nursing Home
   Administrators
4650 East-West Hwy.
Bethesda, MD 20014

American Geriatrics Society
Ten Columbus Circle
New York, NY 10019

American Health Care Association
1200 15th Street, N.W.
Washington, DC 20005

Asociacion Nacional Pro Personas
   Mayores
1730 W. Olympic Blvd., Suite 401
Los Angeles, CA 90015

Concerned Seniors for Better
   Government
1346 Connecticut Ave., N.W.
Washington, DC 20036

The Gerontological Society
1835 K Street, N.W.
Washington, D. C. 20006

Gray Panthers
3700 Chestnut Street
Philadelphia, PA 19104

International Association of
   Gerontology
Section of Biological Ultrastructure

The Weizmann Institute of Science
P.O.B. 26
Rehovot, Israel

International Center for Social
   Gerontology
425 13th St., N.W.
Washington, DC 20004

International Federation on Aging
1909 K St., N.W.
Washington, DC 20049

International Senior Citizens
   Association
11753 Wilshire Boulevard
Los Angeles, CA 90025

National Alliance of Senior Citizens
777 14th St., N.W.
Washington, DC 20005

National Association of Area Agencies
   on Aging
1828 L St., N.W.
Washington, DC 20036

National Association of Mature People
918 16th St., N.W.
Washington, DC 20006

National Association of Retired Federal
   Employees
1533 New Hampshire Ave., N.W.
Washington, DC 20036

National Association of State Units on
   Aging
1828 L St., N.W.
Washington, DC 20036

National Center on Black Aged
1424 K Street, N.W., Suite 500
Washington, DC 20005

National Citizens Coalition for Nursing
   Home Reform
1424 16th St., N.W.
Washington, DC 20036

National Committee on Careers for
   Older Americans
1414 22nd St., N.W.
Washington, DC 20037

National Council of Senior Citizens
1511 K Street, N.W.
Washington, DC 20005

National Council on the Aging
1828 L Street, N.W.
Washington, DC 20036

National Geriatrics Society
212 W. Wisconsin Ave., Third Floor
Milwaukee, WI 53203

National Indian Council on Aging
P.O. Box 2088
Albuquerque, NM 87103

National Institute on Aging
National Institutes of Health
U.S. Dept. of Health and Human
   Services
9000 Rockville Pike
Bethesda, MD 20205

National Pacific/Asian Resource Center
   on Aging
927 15th St., N.W., Room 812
Washington, DC 20005

National Retired Teachers
   Association—American Association
   of Retired Persons
1909 K St., N.W.
Washington, DC 20049

Office of Long Term Care
Public Health Service
U.S. Dept. of Health and Human
   Services
5600 Fishers Lane
Rockville, MD 20852

Service Corps of Retired Executives
   (SCORE) and Active Corps of
   Executives (ACE)
Small Business Administration
1441 L St., N.W.
Washington, DC 20416

Social Security Administration
U.S. Dept. of Health and Human
   Services
6401 Security Blvd.
Baltimore, MD 21235

Urban Elderly Coalition
1828 L St., N.W.
Washington, DC 20036

Glossary

Ability The extent to which a person is capable of performing a certain task, such capability being the joint product of hereditary endowment and experience.

Acceptance According to Kübler-Ross, the final stage in a person's reactions to impending death. This phase is characterized by "quiet expectation" and acceptance of the inevitability of death. The dying person wants to be alone with one or two loved ones and desires only freedom from pain.

Accommodation The automatic change in the shape of the lens of the eye so that an image can be brought into sharper focus on the retina.

Activity theory The theory that active, productive people are happiest at any age.

Acute brain syndrome Reversible, but frequently severe, brain disorder resulting from disease, injury, malnutrion, alcoholism, and so on.

Adjustment The ability to get along in society and satisfy most of one's needs.

Administrative advocacy Activities by administrators of governmental agencies on behalf of a person or group.

Affective psychoses Functional psychoses characterized by extremes of emotion (elation or depression).

Ageism Social stereotyping of and/or discrimination against older people.

Age norm The average or expected characteristics or behaviors of a person of a particular chronological age.

Aging The continuous process (biological, psychological, and social), beginning with conception and ending with death, by which organisms mature and decline.

Alienation A state of indifference to or withdrawal from the world of other people.

Alzheimer's disease A type of presenile dementia characterized by progressive mental deterioration.

Anger According to Kübler-Ross, the second stage in a person's reactions to impending death. During this stage the person partially accepts the knowledge that he/she is going to die but becomes angry at the unfairness of having to die while others go on living.

Angor anima A fear of impending death, often accompanying a heart attack.

Angry type According to Reichard, a maladjusted personality pattern, persisting into old age. The person is bitter and blames other people for his/her failures.

Anxiety neurosis A type of psychoneurotic disorder in which persistent anxiety is the major symptom.

Apoplexy See *Cerebrovascular accident.*

Aptitude The ability to profit from further training and experience in an occupation or skill.

Arcus senilis A cloudy ring that forms around the cornea of the eye in old age.

Armored-defended personality According to Reichard, a personality pattern, persisting into old age, in which the person defends against anxiety by keeping busy.

Arteriosclerosis Abnormal hardening and thickening of the walls of the arteries in old age.

Arthritis Degeneration and/or inflammation of the joints.

Atherosclerosis A type of arteriosclerosis resulting from an accumulation of fat deposits on artery walls.

Attitude A tendency to react positively or negatively to some person, object, situation, or event.

Audiometer A frequency generator for measuring a person's sensitivity to various frequencies in the audible range of human hearing; used to determine degree of deafness.

Autoimmunity theory Theory that the immunological defenses of a person decrease with age, causing the body to "turn on itself," and consequently increasing the likelihood of autoimmune diseases such as arthritis.

Autointoxication A state of being poisoned by toxic substances produced within the body.

Bargaining According to Kübler-Ross, the third stage in a person's reactions to impending death. This stage is characterized by the person's attempts to buy time by bargaining with the doctors, God, or with anyone or anything that the person believes can protect him from death.

Behavior modification A group of counseling or psychotherapeutic techniques based on principles of conditioning and other kinds of learning.

Behavior therapy Psychological methods of treatment employing the principles of learning theory. Specific techniques include reinforcement, desensitization, counterconditioning, and extinction.

Bereavement   The loss of a loved one by death.

Biological age   Anatomical or physiological age of a person, as determined by changes in organismic structure and function; takes into account such features as posture, skin texture, hair color and thickness, strength, speed, and sensory acuity.

Case advocacy   Routine litigation in which lawyers contest on behalf of clients.

Centenarian   A person who is at least 100 years old.

Cerebral arteriosclerosis   Chronic hardening and thickening of the arteries of the brain in old age.

Cerebrovascular accident (CVA)   A sudden rupture (hemorrhage) or blockage (thrombosis) of a large cerebral blood vessel, leading to impairment of brain functioning (stroke, apoplexy).

Cherry angiomas   Small red spots on the skin in the trunk area of the body.

Chronic brain syndrome   Mental disorder caused by long-standing injury to the brain; gradual, insidious changes in personality occur.

Class action suit   Litigation on behalf of an entire group of people.

Climacterium   Changes in the ovaries, and associated processes, including menopause, in middle-aged women.

Cockayne's syndrome   A childhood form of progeria (premature aging).

Cohort   A group of people of the same age, class membership, or culture (e.g., all people born in 1900).

Cohort differences   Differences between individuals born in different time periods and hence belonging to different generations.

Collagen   Fibrous protein material found in the connective tissue, bones, and skin of vertebrates; becomes gelatinous on heating.

Competency   Legal determination that a person's judgment is sound and that he or she is able to manage his or her own property, enter into contracts, and so on.

Concurrent validity   See *Validity*.

Conduction deafness   Deafness resulting from failure of the mechanical vibrations corresponding to sound waves to be transmitted adequately through the three small bones in the middle ear into the cochlea of the inner ear.

Confabulation   Filling in memory gaps with plausible guesses or untruths.

Construct validity   See *Validity*.

Content validity   See *Validity*.

Contingency management   Control of institutionalized persons by differentially reinforcing them for socially approved and socially disapproved behavior; makes pleasures or privileges of certain kinds contingent upon keeping neat and clean, eating properly, interacting with other patients, or other socially acceptable behaviors.

Coronary A heart attack, resulting from obstruction of a coronary artery and usually destroying heart muscle.

Corpus luteum Ductless gland developed within the ovary following ovulation.

Correlation The degree of relationship between two variables, signified by an index ranging from -1.00 to $+1.00$ (correlation coefficient).

Counseling A general term for giving advice and guidance to individuals who need assistance with vocational, academic, or personal problems.

Creatine A white crystalline substance found in the muscles of vertebrates.

Cross-linkage Inadvertent coupling of large intracellular and extracellular molecules, causing connective tissue to stiffen.

Cross-sectional investigation Comparisons of the physical and psychological characteristics of different age groups of people.

Crystallized intelligence Intelligence that is specific to certain fields, such as school learning, and is applied in tasks where habits have become fixed.

CVA See *Cerebrovascular accident.*

Death rattle A rattling or gurgling sound produced by air passing through mucus in the lungs and air passages of a dying person.

Defense mechanisms In psychodynamic theory, psychological techniques that defend the ego against anxiety, guilt, and loss of self-esteem resulting from awareness of certain impulses or realities.

Delusion A false belief, characteristic of paranoid disorders. Delusions of grandeur, persecution, and reference are common in these psychotic conditions.

Denial According to Kübler-Ross, the first stage in a person's reactions to impending death. During this stage the person refuses to accept the fact of death and seeks assurance from other medical and nonmedical people.

Dependency ratio The ratio of the number of dependent (retired) persons to the number of active wage earners in a population.

Dependent variable The variable in an experiment that changes as a function of changes in the independent variable. Variations in magnitude of the dependent variable, plotted on the Y axis of a graph, can be viewed as the experimental effect.

Depression According to Kübler-Ross, the fourth stage in a person's reactions to impending death. The patient fully accepts the fact of death but becomes depressed by all that has been suffered and all that will have to be given up.

Desensitization The extinction of anxiety evoked by a stimulus or situation, resulting from repeated exposure of the individual to that situation under "safe" conditions.

Disenchantment phase The second of Atchley's five phases of retirement, characterized by a let-down, a feeling of emptiness, and even depression.

Disengagement theory   Cumming's theory that aging brings a change in self-perception, and adjustment occurs through withdrawal from responsibility and participation.

Ego   Loosely speaking, the "I" or "self" of personality. In psychoanalytic theory, the executive, reality-oriented aspect of personality, which acts as a mediator between the id and superego.

Elder advocacy   Concern for and legal action on behalf of the elderly.

Electroshock therapy (EST)   A form of treatment for severe depression and certain other mental disorders; a high-voltage current is passed briefly through the head, producing unconsciousness and convulsions.

Embolism   Obstruction of a blood vessel by an air bubble or other abnormal particle (thrombosis).

Empathic Model   Use of special devices (earplugs, special glasses, etc.) to simulate the sensory-motor disturbances of old age. It assists younger people to experience the world from the perspective of an elderly person, and hence to help the young understand the old.

Euthanasia   Either active or passive contribution to the death of a human being or animal suffering from a terminal illness or injury.

Excitement phase   The first phase in the sexual response cycle. In the male, the penis becomes erect, the scrotal sac is flattened and elevated, and the testes are partially elevated; vaginal lubrication and enlargement and vasocongestion of the clitoris occur in the female. Muscle tension, blood pressure, and heart rate increase in both sexes.

Family counseling   Simultaneous counseling of two or more people who are members of the same family.

Fertility rate   Average number of children per woman of child-bearing age in a population.

Fixation   Any stereotyped form of behavior resulting from frustration and resistance to change.

Fraternal twins   Twins resulting from coincident pregnancies in the same person. Originating from two separately fertilized eggs, fraternal twins are genetically no more alike than nontwin siblings.

Free radicals   Highly reactive molecules or parts of molecules, which may connect and damage other molecules; thought to play a role in the process of aging.

Full scale IQ   See *Wechsler Adult Intelligence Scale.*

Functional psychosis   A psychotic disorder having no clearly defined structural (organic) basis.

Geriatrics   Branch of medicine dealing with the prevention and treatment of health problems of the elderly.

Geronto   An old person (Greek *gerōn* = old man).

Gerontocracy Government by the aged; a social organization in which a group or council of old people govern.

Gerontology A branch of knowledge (science) concerned with the characteristics and problems of the aged.

Gerontophobia Unreasonable fear and/or hatred of old people.

Gingivitis Inflammation of the gums.

Glomerulus (i) · A compact cluster of capillaries, especially in the kidneys.

Gradual reawakening of interest The last stage of Gorer's three-stage conception of mourning, during which the mourner finally accepts the reality of the loved one's death and all that it means.

Gray Panthers A politically active group concerned with legislation and programs for the aged.

Hallucination Perception of an object or situation in the absence of an external stimulus.

Hemorrhage Heavy discharge of blood from a blood vessel; uncontrollable bleeding. (See also *Cerebrovascular accident.*)

Honeymoon phase The first of Atchley's five phases of retirement during which a euphoric attitude of being able to do things that one has never had time to do prevails.

Huntington's chorea A progessive disorder of the central nervous system, presumably hereditary, characterized by jerking movements and mental deterioration.

Hutchinson-Gilford syndrome See *Progeria.*

Hyperoxygenation Breathing of 100% oxygen under high atmospheric pressure, a process that in certain investigations has improved learning and retention of information in the elderly.

Id In the psychoanalytic tripartite conception of personality, the reservoir of instinctive impulses and strivings. The id, or "animal nature" of man, is concerned only with immediate gratification of the pleasures and destructive impulses.

Identical twins Twins produced by a single fertilized egg. Because they are genetically identical, they are often used in studies of the effects of heredity on structure and behavior. Also called monozygotic twins.

Imipramine A tricyclic drug used in the treatment of depression (Tofranil).

Incompetency Legal decision that a person is suffering from a mental disorder causing a defect of judgment so that the person is unable to manage his/her own property, enter into contracts, and so on.

Independent variable The variable whose effects are being assessed in an experiment. On a graph depicting the results of an experiment, changes in the independent variable (the "cause") are plotted on the horizontal axis.

Infant mortality   Death before the age of one year.

Initial shock   The first stage of Gorer's three-stage conception of mourning. It lasts only a few days, and is characterized by a loss of self-control, reduced energy, lack of motivation, bewilderment, disorientation, and a loss of perspective by the mourner.

Insanity   An imprecise legal term for severe mental disorders involving lack of responsibility for one's actions. According to the M'Naghten Rule, an insane person is one who cannot distinguish right from wrong. However, other precedents such as the Durham decision are used in some states to determine insanity.

Intelligence   Many definitions of this term have been offered, such as "the ability to judge well, understand well, and reason well" (Binet) and "the capacity for abstract thinking" (Terman). Most intelligence tests measure the ability to succeed in academic-type tasks.

Intense grief   The second stage of Gorer's three-stage conception of mourning. It often lasts for several months and is characterized by periodic crying and confusion about what has happened.

Interiority   A turning inward of the personality, or movement from active to passive mastery, observed in many people during old age.

Involuntary commitment   Legal process by which a person is committed to a mental hospital against his/her will.

Involutional period   Decline in body energy during middle age or early old age, signaled by the menopause in women.

Involutional psychosis (melancholia)   A disorder characterized by deep depression or paranoia, presumably precipitated by the "change of life" in middle-aged women and somewhat older men.

Korsakoff's syndrome   Chronic brain disorder associated with alcoholism.

Legislative advocacy   Applying pressure, usually by lobbying, on lawmakers to draft and vote for specific legislation.

Life cycle group therapy   Life review therapy extended to a group of 8–10 members of different chronological ages.

Life expectancy   The average life span of people born in a certain year; probable length of life of an individual.

Life review   Reminiscence or a split-second review of one's life just prior to impending death.

Life review therapy   Form of psychotherapy in which patients reminisce about their personal experiences.

Lipofuscin ("age pigment")   A pigmented granule containing lipis, carbohydrates, and protein. The number of these granules in various body cells increases with aging.

Longevity   Length of life; long duration of life.

Longitudinal investigation   Studying the development of the same individual(s) at different ages over a period of months or years.

Long-term memory (LTM, or secondary memory)   Memory which lasts at least 10−20 minutes, involving more permanent storage mechanisms of the brain.

Major stroke   Heart failure resulting from blockage of a large cerebral blood vessel. (See also *Cerebrovascular accident.*)

Manic-depressive psychosis   An affective disorder characterized by severe mood swings and excitability.

Manic disorder   Excessive agitation and excitability, which may or may not alternate with depression. (See also *Manic-depressive psychosis.*)

Mature type   According to Reichard, a personality pattern that persists into old age, in which the person is relatively free of neurotic conflicts and can accept him- or herself and grow old with few past regrets.

Maximum breathing rate   Amount of air moved through the lungs in 15 secs. while breathing as rapidly as possible.

Menopause   Cessation of menstruation, usually occurring sometime between ages 45 and 50.

Mercy killing   See *Euthanasia.*

Monitoring   Law reform activity in which steps are taken to make certain that laws and programs are carried out as intended by the legislators who drafted them.

Monozygotic twins   See *Identical twins.*

Near event   The second phase of preretirement, during which individuals orient themselves toward a specific retirement date (Atchley).

Nerve deafness   A form of deafness caused by damage to the inner ear or auditory nerve; usually involves a loss of sensitivity to sounds of high frequency. Also called presbycusis.

Octogenarian   A person who is 80 to 90 years old.

Organic brain damage   Damage to brain tissue caused by disease or injury; may result in mental disorder.

Organic psychosis   Severe mental disorder caused by organic brain damage resulting from alcoholism, encephalitis, cerebral arteriosclerosis, and other diseases, drugs, and injuries.

Orgasmic phase   The third phase in the sexual response cycle. Breathing rate, blood pressure, and heart rate reach a maximum, resulting in a release of muscular tension and vasoconstriction built up during the first two phases. The orgasmic phase ends with ejaculation by the male and contractions of the orgasmic platform in the female.

Osteoporosis   A gradual, long-term loss in the mass of bones in old age, especially in elderly women; the bones become less dense, more porous, and fracture more easily.

Paranoid disorder   A general term for a broad class of mental illnesses of varying severity characterized by suspiciousness, projection, excessive feelings of self-importance, and frequently complex delusions of grandeur, persecution, and ideas of reference.

Parkinsonism   A progressive brain disorder resulting from damage to the basal ganglia and occurring most often in later life. The symptoms are muscular tremors; spastic, rigid movements; propulsive gait; and a masklike, expression-less face. Also called Parkinson's disease.

Performance IQ   See *Wechsler Adult Intelligence Scale*.

Personality   The sum total of all those qualities, traits, and behaviors that characterize a person's individuality and by which, together with his physical attributes, the person is recognized as a unique human being.

Phenomenal field   That part of a person's physical environment that is perceived by and has meaning for the person.

Pick's disease   A type of presenile, degenerative brain disorder.

Placebo effect   Change in behavior resulting from the administration of a chemically inert substance to people who believe they are receiving an active drug.

Plaque   Accumulation of fatty tissue and calcified material in the cerebral blood vessels of old people, resulting in clogged arteries and interference with blood circulation.

Plateau phase   The second stage of the sexual response cycle; muscle tension, blood pressure, and heart rate changes become intensified, terminating in the production of an orgasmic platform in the female and rapid breathing in both sexes.

Predictive validity   See *Validity*.

Presbycusis   See *Nerve deafness*.

Presbyopia   Literally, "old-sightedness," a condition of farsightedness resulting from a loss of elasticity of the lens of the eye due to aging.

Progeria   A very rare disorder that mimics premature aging. A progeric child typically begins to look old as early as age 4. Also called Hutchinson-Gilford syndrome.

Psychodrama   A method of psychotherapy, devised by J. L. Moreno, in which the problems and experiences of a person are acted out in a stage setting by the person himself (herself) and other "actors."

Psychological age   The age of a person as determined by his or her feelings, attitudes, and life perspective.

Psychological autopsy   Postmortem analysis of the psychosocial aspects of a person's death.

Psychosis Severe mental disorder characterized by faulty perception of reality, deficits of language and memory, disturbances in the emotional sphere, and other bizarre symptoms. Psychoses are classifed as organic or functional, depending on whether they are associated with a known organic change.

Psychotherapy Psychological methods of treating mental disorders, involving communications between patient(s) and therapist and other special techniques.

Reciprocal inhibition A behavioral therapy technique involving presentation of the conditioned stimuli for an anxiety response while the individual is making responses incompatible with anxiety.

Refractory period A period of time, after orgasm, during which sexual arousal cannot recur.

Regression Return or reinstatement of an early stage of development; a common response to frustration (e.g., thumbsucking in an older child or adult).

Reliability The extent to which a psychological test or other measuring instrument is consistent. A reliable test is relatively free from errors of measurement and can therefore be depended on.

Remote event The first phase of the preretirement period, during which the individual views retirement as a vague, positive thing that will occur someday (Atchley).

Reorientation phase The third of Atchley's five phases of retirement, during which retirees take stock, pull themselves together, and develop more realistic life alternatives.

Resolution phase The final phase of the sexual response cycle; there is a gradual return to the physiological state that prevailed prior to the excitement phase.

Retirement Withdrawal from one's occupation or from active work.

Rigidity Inflexibility or unwillingness to change one's way of thinking or behaving; allegedly a characteristic of older people.

Rocking chair type According to Reichard, a personality pattern persisting into old age, in which the person views old age in terms of freedom from responsibility and as an opportunity to indulge passive needs.

Role A social behavior pattern that an individual is expected to display under certain conditions or in certain situations.

Role exit theory Blau's sociological theory of old age as a time for abandoning certain roles and assuming others.

Schizophrenia A broad category of psychotic disorders characterized by distortions of reality and disturbances of thought, behavior, and emotional expression.

Scribotherapy Form of psychotherapy in which group members write out their feelings about certain topics and then, after group discussion and individual interviews, develop them into a news format.

Self   That part of an individual's phenomenal field (or "awareness") that he (she) perceives as his (her) own personality.

Self-actualization   Fulfillment of one's potentialities; attaining a state of congruence or harmony between one's real and ideal selves.

Self-concept   Fairly consistent cluster of feelings, ideas, and attitudes toward oneself.

Self-hating type   According to Reichard, a maladjusted personality pattern persisting into old age, in which the person is depressed and blames him- or herself for his or her disappointments and misfortunes.

Senescence   The state of being old or the process of growing old.

Senile dementia   An organic brain disorder occurring in older people. The symptoms are childishness, self-centeredness, and difficulty in reacting to new experiences.

Senile keratoses   Brown spots dotting sun-exposed areas of the skin.

Senile purpura   Purplish skin spots caused by cutaneous bleeding.

Senility   An imprecise term used to refer to deterioration in the brain and behavior observed in some elderly individuals; disability caused by illness or injury as a person ages.

Senium praecox   Premature senility. (See also *Progeria* and *Werner's Syndrome*.)

Septuagenarian   A person who is 70 to 80 years old.

Serial anticipation (method of)   System for investigation of learning, in which the learner attempts to anticipate successive items in a list.

Short-term memory (STM)   Process of retaining items of information from one second to several minutes at most.

Small stroke   Blockage of a small blood vessel in the brain.

Social age   Age of a person as determined by the social roles and activities in which he or she is expected to participate or which are considered appropriate for an individual at a particular age or stage of maturity.

Social gerontology   Subfield of gerontology dealing with social factors in aging, elderly group behavior, and the causes and effects of growth in the elderly segment of the population.

Stability phase   The fourth of Atchley's five phases of retirement. It may succeed either the honeymoon phase or the reorientation phase.

Stimulus persistence theory   Theory that aging causes recovery from the short-term effects of stimulation to be slowed down.

Superannuation   Retirement and pensioning because of age or infirmity.

Superego   In psychoanalytic theory, that aspect of personality representing the internalization of parental prohibitions and sanctions—the moral aspect of personality, or conscience.

Suttee   Old Hindu custom in which a devoted wife is voluntarily cremated on the funeral pyre of her husband.

Synovial fluid   Lubricating fluid in the joints, a loss of which characterizes osteoarthritis.

Terminal drop   Decline in intellectual functions (IQ, memory, cognitive organization), sensorimotor abilities (e.g., reaction time), and personality (assertiveness, etc.), during the last few months of life; observed in many elderly people.

Termination phase   The last of Atchley's five phases of retirement, in which the retirement role is replaced by the sick or dependent role.

Testamentary capacity   The legally determined competency of a person to make a will.

Thanaphobia   An unreasonable fear or dread of dying and death.

Thanatology   A branch of knowledge concerned with the study of dying and death.

Three-component method (model).   Schaie's model (including cross-sectional, longitudinal, and time-lag comparisons) for determining the differential effects of age, cohort, and time of measurement on developmental characteristics.

Thrombosis   See *Embolism.*

Time-lag design   Schaie's procedure for examining several cohorts, each in a different time period; part of the three-component model.

Tofranil   See *Imipramine.*

Tranquilizer   Psychotherapeutic drug such as Valium or Mellaril having anti-anxiety or antipsychotic effects.

Transactional analysis   Method of psychotherapy, devised by Eric Berne, that consists of analyzing the interactions, or transactions, among a person's three ego states (adult, parent, child).

Validity   The extent to which a test measures what it was designed to measure. Validity can be assessed in several ways: by analysis of a test's content (*content validity*), by relating scores on the test to a criterion of interest (*predictive* and *concurrent validity*), by a thorough study of the extent to which a test is a measure of a certain psychological construct (*construct validity*).

Verbal IQ   See *Wechsler Adult Intelligence Scale.*

Voluntary commitment   Unforced submission of oneself to a mental hospital for examination and treatment. (See also *Involuntary commitment.*)

Wechsler Adult Intelligence Scale (WAIS)   An individual intelligence test designed for adults aged 16 years and over. It consists of 11 subtests grouped into Verbal and Performance scales, and yields three intelligence quotients: Verbal IQ, Performance IQ, and Full Scale IQ.

Werner's Syndrome   A condition of arrested growth occurring between the ages of 15 and 20; thought to be a later-developing progeria.

References

Abram, H. S., Moore, G. L., & Westervelt, F. B., Jr. Suicidal behavior in chronic dialysis patients. *American Journal of Psychiatry*, 1971, *127*, 119–121.

Acceptance of the idea of mortality. *Intellect*, 1975, *103*(2362), 215–216.

Adamowicz, J. K. Visual short-term memory and aging. *Journal of Gerontology*, 1976, *31*, 39–46.

Adams, B. N. Interaction theory and the social network. *Sociometry*, 1967, *30*, 64–78.

Agan, T., Casto, M. D., Day, S. S., & Schwab, L. O. Adjusting the environment for the elderly and the handicapped. *Journal of Home Economics*, 1977, *69*(3), 18–20.

Aging: Primitives handle it better. *Science Digest*, 1976, *79*(3), 17–18.

Aiken, L. R. Problems in testing the elderly. *Educational Gerontology*, 1980, *5*, 119–124.

Alpaugh, P., & Haney, M. *Counseling the older adult: A training manual*. Los Angeles: University of Southern California Press, 1978.

Alsop, S. *Stay of execution*. Philadelphia: Lippincott, 1973.

American Psychiatric Association. *Diagnostic and statistical manual of mental disorders*. Washington, D.C.: Author, 1968.

Anderson, B. G. *The aging game*. New York: McGraw-Hill, 1979.

Anderson, K. Science probes ways to prolong life. *Science Digest*, 1974, *76*(3), 36–41.

Andrus Gerontology Center. *Project MASP retirement fact sheet*. Los Angeles: Andrus Gerontology Center, University of Southern California, Sept. 1978.

Arehart-Treichel, J. How you age. *Science News*, 1972, *102*, 412–413.

——— Human reproduction and aging. *Science News*, 1976, *110*, 297.

Arenberg, D. Cognition and aging: Verbal learning, memory, and problem solving. In C. Eisdorfer & M. P. Lawton (Eds.), *The psychology of adult development and aging*. Washington, D.C.: American Psychological Association, 1973.

Atchley, R. C. *The social forces in later life: An introduction to social gerontology* (2d ed.). Belmont, Calif.: Wadsworth, 1977.

Axelrod, S., Thompson, L. W., & Cohen, L. D. Effect of senescence on the temporal resolution of somesthetic stimuli presented to one hand or both. *Journal of Gerontology*, 1968, *23*, 191–195.

Back, K. W. Metaphors as a test of personal philosophy of aging. *Sociological Focus*, 1971, *5*, 1–8.

Bahr, M. H. Aging and religious disaffiliation. *Social Forces*, 1970, *49*, 59–71.

Baller, W. R., Charles, D. C., & Miller, E. L. Mid-life attainment of the mentally retarded: A longitudinal study. *Genetic Psychology Monographs*, 1967, *75*, 235–329.

Baltes, P. B. Longitudinal and cross-sectional sequences in the study of age and generation effect. *Human Development*, 1968, *11*, 145–171.

Baltes, P. B., & Schaie, K. W. On life-span developmental research paradigms: Retrospects and prospects. In P. B. Baltes & K. W. Schaie (Eds.), *Life-span developmental psychology: Personality and socialization*. New York: Academic Press, 1973.

—— Aging and IQ: The myth of the twilight years. *Psychology Today*, 1974, *7*(10), 35–40.

—— On the plasticity of intelligence in adulthood and old age: Where Horn and Donaldson fail. *American Psychologist*, 1976, *31*, 720–725.

Barns, E. D., Sack, A., & Shore, H. Modalities and methods for use with the aged. *The Gerontologist*, 1973, *13*, 513–527.

Barrett, J. H. *Gerontological psychology*, Springfield, Ill.: Charles C Thomas, 1972.

Bayley, N., & Oden, M. H. The maintenance of intellectual ability in gifted adults. *Journal of Gerontology*, 1955, *10*, 91–107.

Bell, A., & Zubek, J. The effect of age on the intellectual performance of mental defectives. *Journal of Gerontology*, 1960, *15*, 285–295.

Bellak, L., & Bellak, S. S. *Senior Apperception Technique*. Larchmont, N.Y.: C.P.S., 1974.

Benet, S. *Abkhasians: The long-living people of the Caucasus*. New York: Holt, Rinehart and Winston, 1974.

—— *How to live to be 100: The life-style of the people of the Caucasus*. New York: Dial Press, 1976.

Benetiz, R. Ethnicity, social policy, and aging. In R. Davis & M. Nieswander (Eds.), *Aging: Prospects and issues*. Los Angeles: Andrus Gerontology Center, University of Southern California, 1973.

Bengtson, V. L., Kasschau, P. L., & Ragan, P. K. The impact of social structure on aging individuals. In J. E. Birren & K. W. Schaie (Eds.), *Handbook of the psychology of aging*. New York: Van Nostrand Reinhold, 1977.

Bennett, R. Attitudes of the young toward the old: A review of research. *Personnel & Guidance Journal*, 1976, *55*, 136–139.

Ben-Yishay, Y., Diller, L., Mandelberg, I., Gordon, W., & Gerstman, L. Similarities and differences in block design performance between older normal and brain-injured persons. *Journal of Abnormal Psychology*, 1971, *78*, 17–25.

Berne, E. *Games people play*. New York: Grove Press, 1964.

—— *Principles of group treatment*. New York: Oxford University Press, 1966.

Biehler, R. F. *Child development: An introduction* (2d. ed.). Boston: Houghton Mifflin, 1981.

Binstock, R. H. Aging and the future of American politics. In R. A. Kalish (Ed.), *The later years: Social applications of gerontology*. Monterey, Calif.: Brooks/Cole, 1977.

Birren, J. E. Increments and decrements in the intellectual status of the aged. *Psychiatric Research Reports*, 1968, *23*, 207–214.

Birren, J. E., Butler, R. N., Greenhouse, S. W., Sokoloff, L., & Yarrow, M. R. (Eds.). *Human aging: A biological and behavioral study*. Pub. No. (HSM) 71-9051. Washington, D.C.: U.S. Government Printing Office, 1963.

Bischof, L. J. *Adult psychology*. New York: Harper & Row, 1969.

Blau, Z. S. *Old age in a changing society*. New York: New Viewpoints, 1973.

Blazer, D., & Palmore, E. Religion and aging in a longitudinal panel. *The Gerontologist*, 1976, *16*, 82–85.

Bloom, K. L. Age and the self-concept. *American Journal of Psychiatry*, 1961, *118*, 534–538.

Blue, G. F. The aging as portrayed in realist fiction for children. *The Gerontologist*, 1978, *18*, 187–192.

Blum, J. E., Fosshage, J. L., & Jarvik, L. F. Intellectual changes and sex differences in octogenarians: A twenty-year longitudinal study of aging. *Developmental Psychology*, 1972, *7*, 178–187.

Botwinick, J. *Cognitive process in maturity and old age*. New York: Springer, 1967.

—— *Aging and behavior*. (2d. ed.). New York: Springer, 1978.

Botwinick, J., & Thompson, L. Age differences in reaction: An artifact? *The Gerontologist*, 1968, *8*, 25–28.

Bower, G. H. A descriptive theory of human memory. In D. P. Kimble (Ed.), *Learning, remembering and forgetting* (Vol. 2). New York: New York Academy of Science, 1966.

Bowlby, J. Grief and mourning in infancy and early childhood. *Psychoanalytic Study of the Child*, 1960, *15*, 9–52.

Brink, I. L. Psychotherapy after forty. *MH*, 1976, *60*(2), 23–24.

Brown, J. H. U. Physiological parameters of human potential. In H. A. Otto (Ed.), *Explorations in human potentialities*. Springfield, Ill.: Charles C Thomas, 1966.

Brown, N. K., & Thompson, D. J. Nontreatment of fever in extended-care facilities. *New England Journal of Medicine*, 1979, *300*, 1246–1250.

Brown, S. Taking senior citizens off the shelf. *Education Digest*, 1977, *40*(9), 45–47.

Buckingham, R. W., III, Lack, S. A., Mount, B. M., MacLean, L. D., & Collins, J. T. Living with the dying: Use of the technique of participant observation. *Canadian Medical Association Journal*, 1976, *115*, 1211–1215.

Busse, E. W., & Blazer, D. G. *Handbook of geriatric psychiatry.* New York: Van Nostrand Reinhold, 1980.

Busse, E. W., & Pfeiffer, E. Functional psychiatric disorders in old age. In E. W. Busse & E. Pfeiffer (Eds.), *Behavior adaptation in late life.* Boston: Little, Brown, 1969.

Butler, R. N. The life review: An interpretation of reminiscence in the aged. In B. L. Neugarten (Ed.), *Middle age and aging.* Chicago: University of Chicago Press, 1968.

—— Age: The life review. *Psychology Today*, 1971, *5*(7), 49–55ff.

—— Successful aging. *MH*, 1974, *58*(3) 7–12.

—— *Why survive? Being old in America.* New York: Harper & Row, 1975.

Butler, R. H., & Lewis, M. I. *Sex after sixty: A guide for men and women in their later years.* New York: Harper & Row, 1976.

—— *Aging and mental health* (2d ed.). St. Louis: Mosby, 1977.

Buttenwieser, P. *The relation of age to skill of expert chess players.* Unpublished Ph.D. dissertation. Palo Alto, Calif.: Stanford University, 1935.

California Department of Justice, Office of the Attorney General. *Senior Crime Preventers' Bulletin*, 1979, *7*(1), 2–3.

Cameron, P. The generation gap: Time orientation. *The Gerontologist*, 1972, *12*, 117–119.

Campbell, D. P. A cross-sectional and longitudinal study of scholastic abilities over twenty-five years. *Journal of Counseling Psychology*, 1965, *12*, 55–61.

Can oxygen fight senility? *Business Week*, March 25, 1972 (No. 2221), 94.

Carey, R. G. Counseling the terminally ill. *Personnel & Guidance Journal*, 1976, *55*, 124–126.

Carkhuff, R. R. *Helping and human relations*, (Vols. 1 & 2). New York: Holt, Rinehart and Winston, 1969.

Carp, F. M. Housing and living environments of older people. In R. H. Binstock & E. Shanas (Eds.), *Handbook of aging and the social sciences.* New York: Van Nostrand Reinhold, 1976.

Cavan, R. S., Burgess, E. W., Havighurst, R. J., & Goldhamer, H. *Personality in old age.* Chicago: Science Research Associates, 1949, 58.

Charles, D. C., & James, S. T. Stability of average intelligence. *Journal of Genetic Psychology*, 1964, *105*, 105–111.

Clayton, P. J., Halikes, H. A., & Maurice, W. L. The bereavement of the widowed. *Diseases of the Nervous System*, 1971, *32*, 597–604.

Coleman, J. C. *Abnormal psychology and modern life* (5th ed.). Glenview, Ill.: Scott, Foresman, 1976. Ch. 13.

Comfort, A. *The prospects of longevity.* Paper read at the Gerontological Society, San Juan, Puerto Rico, December 1972.

—— *A good age.* New York: Crown Publishers, 1976.

Conklin, J. E. Robbery, the elderly, and fear: An urban problem in search of a solution. In G. Goldsmith & S. S. Goldsmith (Eds.), *Crime and the elderly—challenge and response.* Lexington, Mass.: Heath, 1976.

Cooper, A. F., Curry, A. R., Kay, D. W. K., Garside, R. F., & Roth, M. Hearing loss in paranoid and affective psychosis of the elderly. *The Lancet*, 1974, *2*(7885), 851–854.

Cottin, L. *Elders in rebellion.* New York: Doubleday/Anchor, 1979.

Cowdry, E. V. (Ed.). *Problems of aging: Biological and medical aspects.* Baltimore: Williams & Wilkins, 1939.

Craik, F. I. M. Age differences in human memory. In J. E. Birren & K. W. Schaie (Eds.), *Handbook of the psychology of aging.* New York: Van Nostrand Reinhold, 1977.

Cumming, E., Dean, L. R., Newell, D. S., & McCaffrey, I. Disengagement—A tentative theory of aging. *Sociometry*, 1960, *22*, 23–35.

Cumming, E., & Henry, W. E. *Growing old: The process of disengagement*, New York: Basic Books, 1961.

Curtin, S. R. *Nobody ever died of old age.* Boston: Little, Brown, 1972.

Cutler, S. J. Age differences in voluntary association membership. *Social Forces*, 1976, *55*, 43–58.

—— Aging and voluntary association participation. *Journal of Gerontology*, 1977, *32*, 470–479.

Davis, R. H. *Television and the aging audience.* Los Angeles: Andrus Gerontology Center, University of Southern California, 1980.

De Beauvoir, S. *The coming of age* (Trans. P. O'Brien). New York: Putnam's, 1972.

Denckla, W. D. Role of the pituitary and thyroid glands on the decline of minimal O_2 consumption with age. *Journal of Clinical Investigation*, 1974, *53*, 572–581.

Dennis, W. Creative productivity between the ages of twenty and eighty years. *Journal of Gerontology*, 1966, *21*, 1–8.

De Vries, H. The physiology of exercise and aging. In D. Woodruff & J. Birren (Eds.), *Aging: Scientific perspectives and social issues*. New York: Van Nostrand, 1975.

Dibner, A. S. The psychology of normal aging. In M. G. Spencer & C. J. Dorr (Eds.), *Understanding aging: A multidisciplinary approach*. New York: Appleton-Century-Crofts, 1975.

Docs find geriatric difficulties. *Stockton* (Calif.) *Record*, March 19, 1978, p. 19.

Doppelt, J. E., & Wallace, W. L. Standardization of the Wechsler Adult Intelligence Scale for older persons. *Journal of Abnormal & Social Psychology*, 1955, *51*, 312–330.

Dowd, J. J., & Bengtson, V. L. Aging in minority populations: An examination of the double jeopardy hypothesis. *Journal of Gerontology*, 1978, *33*, 427–434.

Dussich, J. P. J., & Eickman, C. J. The elderly victim: Vulnerability to the criminal act. In J. Goldsmith & S. Goldsmith (Eds.), *Crime and the elderly—challenge and response*. Lexington, Mass.: Heath, 1976.

Duvall, E. M. *Marriage and family development* (5th ed.). Philadelphia: Lippincott, 1977.

Eisdorfer, C. The WAIS performance of the aged: A retest evaluation. *Journal of Gerontology*, 1963, *18*, 169–172.

Eisdorfer, C., Nowlin, J., & Wilkie, F. Improvement in learning in the aged by modification of autonomic nervous system activity. *Science*, 1970, *170*, 1327–1329.

Elderly demanding equal TV time. *Los Angeles Times*, Aug. 10, 1977, Pt. VI, p. 1.

Ellis, A. *Reason and emotion in psychotherapy*. New York: Lyle Stuart, 1962.

Entine, A. D. Mid-life counseling: Prognosis and potential. *Personnel & Guidance Journal*, 1976, *55*, 112–114.

Erikson, E. H. *Childhood and society* (2d ed.). New York: Norton, 1963.

—— *Identity, youth, and crisis*. New York: Norton, 1968.

—— Reflection on Dr. Borg's life cycle. *Daedalus*, 1976, *105*(2), 1–28.

Farberow, N. L., Shneidman, E. S., & Leonard, C. Suicide among general medical and surgical hospital patients with malignant neoplasms. Veterans Administration, Dept. of Medicine and Surgery, *Medical Bulletin* MB-9, Feb. 25, 1963, pp. 1–11.

Federal Council on the Aging, U.S. Dept. of Health & Human Services. *Policy issues concerning elderly minorities*. DHHS Pub. No. (OHDS) 80-20670. Washington, D.C.: U.S. Government Printing Office, 1979.

Ferrare, N. A. *Institutionalization and attitude change in an aged population: A field study and dissidence theory*. Unpublished doctoral dissertation, Western Reserve University, 1962.

Fletcher, C. R. How not to interview an elderly clinic patient: A case illustration and the interviewer's explanation. *The Gerontologist*, 1972, *12*, 398–402.

Fowles, D. G. *Some prospects for the future elderly population. Statistical reports on older Americans*. DHEW Pub. No. (OHDS) 78-20288. Washington, D.C.: U.S. Government Printing Office, January 1978.

Freedman, A. M., Kaplan, H. I., & Sadock, B. J. *Modern synopsis of psychiatry*. Baltimore: Williams & Wilkins, 1972.

Gal, P. Mental disorders of advanced years. *Geriatrics*, 1959, *14*, 224–228.

Gallup, G. To be happy is to be young, married, with a college background. *The Gallup Poll Release*, Sunday, Dec. 25, 1977.

Galton, L. Senility: Attacking the problem. *Parade*, Aug. 13, 1978, p. 20.

—— Best friend, best therapy? *Parade*, June 3, 1979, p. 20.

Geis, G. Defrauding the elderly. In J. Goldsmith & S. S. Goldsmith (Eds.), *Crime and the elderly—challenge and response*. Lexington, Mass.: Heath, 1976.

Gergen, K. J., & Back, K. W. Cognitive construction in aging and attitudes toward international issues. In I. H. Simpson & J. C. McKinsey (Eds.), *Social aspects of aging*. Durham, N.C.: Duke University Press, 1966.

Glasser, W. *Reality therapy: A new approach to psychiatry*. New York: Harper & Row, 1965.

Glick, I. O., Weiss, R. S., & Parkes, C. W. *The first year of bereavement*. New York: Wiley, 1974.

Goldhamer, J., & Marshall, A. W. *Psychosis and civilization*. Glencoe, Ill.: Free Press, 1953.

Goldsmith, J., & Goldsmith, S. S. (Eds.). *Crime and the elderly—challenge and response*. Lexington, Mass.: Heath, 1976.

Goldsmith, J., & Tomas, N. E. Crimes against the elderly—a continuing national crisis. *Aging*, 1974 (236-237), 10–13.

Gordon, C., Gaitz, C. M., & Scott, J. Leisure and lives: Personal expressivity across the life span. In R. Binstock & E. Shanas (Eds.), *Handbook of aging and the social sciences*. New York: Van Nostrand Reinhold, 1976.

Gorer, G. *Death, grief and mourning in contemporary Britain*. London: Cresset, 1965.

Gots, D. E. The long life diet. *Family Circle*, 1977, *90*(9), 14, 20, 166, 168, 170.

Gove, W. Sex, marital status, and mortality. *American Journal of Sociology*, 1973, *79*(1), 45–67.

Gray Panther power. An interview with Maggie Kuhn. *The Center Magazine*, 1975, *8*(2), 21–25.

Gross, P. J. Crime prevention and the elderly. In A. P. Goldstein, W. J. Hoyer & P. J. Monti (Eds.), *Police and the elderly*. New York: Pergamon Press, 1979.

Grossberg, J. M. Behavior therapy: A review. *Psychological Bulletin*, 1964, *62*, 73–85.

Gubrium, F. F. Being single in old age. *International Journal on Aging and Human Development*, 1975, *6*(1), 29–41.

Gutmann, D. An exploration of ego configurations in middle and later life. In B. L. Neugarten (Ed.), *Personality in middle and late life: Empirical studies*. New York: Atherton Press, 1964.

—— Aging among the Highland Maya: A comparative study. *Journal of Personality & Social Psychology*, 1967, *7*, 28–35.

—— The cross-cultural perspective: Notes toward a comparative psychology of aging. In J. E. Birren & K. W. Schaie (Eds.), *Handbook of the psychology of aging*. New York: Van Nostrand Reinhold, 1977.

Hall, E., & Cameron, P. Our failing reverence for life. *Psychology Today*, 1976, *9* (11), 104–108, 113.

Hall, G. S. *Senescence: The second half of life*. New York: Appleton-Century-Crofts, 1922.

Hambly, W. D. Funeral customs. *The world book encyclopedia* (Vol. 9). Chicago: Field Educational Enterprises, 1974.

Hansen, G. O. Meeting housing challenges: Involvement—the elderly. In *Housing issues. Proceedings of the Fifth Annual Meeting, American Association of Housing Educators*. Lincoln, Neb.: University of Nebraska Press, 1975.

Hansen, J. C., Stevic, R. R., & Warner, R. W. *Counseling theory and process* (2d ed.). Boston: Allyn & Bacon, 1977.

Harman, D. The biological clock: The mitochondria? *Journal of the American Geriatric Society*, 1972, *20*, 145–147.

Harman, D., Heidrick, M. L., & Eddy, D. E. *Free radical theory of aging: Effect of antioxidants on humoral and cell-mediated response as a function of age*. Paper read at the 6th Annual Meeting of the American Aging Assn., Washington, D.C., September 1976.

Havighurst, R. J., Neugarten, B. L., & Tobin, S. S. *Disengagement and patterns of aging*. Paper presented at the meeting of the International Association of Gerontology, Copenhagen, August 1973.

Hayflick, L. Aging under glass. *Experimental Gerontology*, 1970, *5*, 291–303.

Hechinger, G. Margaret Mead: Growing old in America. *Family Circle*, 1977, *90*(8), 27–32.

Hendricks, J., & Hendricks, C. D. *Aging in mass society*. Cambridge, Mass.: Winthrop, 1977.

Herr, J. J., & Weakland, J. H. *Counseling elders and their families*. New York: Springer, 1979.

Hickey, T., & Kalish, R. A. Young people's perceptions of adults. *Journal of Gerontology*, 1968, *23*, 215–219.

Hochschild, A. R. *The unexpected community*. Englewood Cliffs, N.J.: Prentice-Hall, 1973.

Hodgkins, J. Influence of age on the speed of reaction and movement in females. *Journal of Gerontology*, 1962, *17* (4), 385–389.

Holmes, T. H., & Rahe, R. H. The social readjustment scale. *Journal of Psychosomatic Research*, 1967, *11*, 213–218.

Horn, J. L., & Donaldson, G. On the myth of intellectual decline in adulthood. *American Psychologist*, 1976, *31*, 701–719.

Housing the aging. *Architectural Record*, 1977, *16*(May), 123–138.

Howell, S. C. *Designing elderly housing: Patterns of use*. Cambridge, Mass.: MIT Press, 1980.

Hurlock, E. B. *Developmental psychology: A life-span approach* (5th ed.). New York: McGraw-Hill, 1980.

Inglis, J., Ankus, M. N., & Sykes, D. H. Age-related differences in learning and short-term memory from childhood to the senium. *Human Development*, 1968, *11*, 42–52.

Ingram, C. State panel to examine "sexual minority" issues. *Los Angeles Times*, Oct. 19, 1980, Pt. I, p. 1.

Jacobs, E., Winter, P. M., Alvis, H. J., & Small, S. M. Hyperbaric oxygen: Temporary aid for senile minds. *Journal of the American Medical Association*, 1969, *209*, 1435–1438.

Jacobs, R. H., & Vinick, B. H. *Reengagement in later life: Re-employment and remarriage*. Stamford, Conn.: Greylock Publishers, 1979.

Jacoby, S. Waiting for the end: On nursing homes. *New York Times Magazine*, March 31, 1974, pp. 13ff.

Jenkins, C. D., Rosenman, R. H., & Friedman, M. Development of an objective psychological test for the determination of the coronary-prone behavior pattern in employed men. *Journal of Chronic Diseases*, 1967, *20*, 371–379.

Jones, H. E., & Conrad, H. S. The growth and decline of intelligence. *Genetic Psychology Monographs*, 1933, *13*, 223–298.

Jowsey, J., & Holley, K. E. Influence of diphosphonates on progress of experimentally induced osteoporosis. *Journal of Laboratory Clinical Medicine*, 1973, *82*, 567–575.

Kahana, B., & Kahana, E. Grandparenthood from the perspective of the developing grandchild. *Developmental Psychology*, 1970, *3*, 98–105. (a)

——— Changes in mental status of elderly patients in age-integrated and age-segregated hospital milieus. *Journal of Abnormal Psychology*, 1970, *75*, 177–181. (b)

Kahn, R. L. Stress: From 9 to 5. *Psychology Today*, 1969, *3*(4), 34–38.

Kalish, R. A. Death and dying in a social context. In R. Binstock & E. Shanas (Eds.), *Handbook of aging and the social sciences*. New York: Van Nostrand Reinhold, 1976.

Kalish, R. A., & Reynolds, D. K. *Death and ethnicity: A psychocultural study*. Los Angeles: University of Southern California Press, 1976.

Kallmann, F. J., & Jarvik, L. F. Individual differences in constitution and genetic background. In J. E. Birren (Ed.), *Handbook of aging and the individual*. Chicago: University of Chicago Press, 1959.

Kallmann, F. J., & Sander, G. Two studies on senescence. In R. G. Kuhlen & G. G. Thompson (Eds.), *Psychological studies of human development*. New York: Appleton-Century-Crofts, 1963.

Kaplan, H. B., & Pokorny, A. D. Self-derogation and psychosocial adjustment. *Journal of Nervous and Mental Disease*, 1969, *149*, 421–434.

Kastenbaum, R. (Ed.). The reluctant therapist. *Geriatrics*, 1963, *18*, 296–301.

——— On the meaning of time in later life. *Journal of Genetic Psychology*, 1966, *109*, 9–25.

——— Age: Getting there on time. *Psychology Today*, 1971, *5*(7), 52–54, 82–84.

Kastenbaum, R., & Aisenberg, R. *The psychology of death*. New York: Springer, 1978.

Kastenbaum, R., & Candy, S. The 4% fallacy: A methodological and empirical critique of extended care facility population statistics. *International Journal of Aging and Human Development*, 1973, *4*, 15–21.

Kastenbaum, R., & Costa, P. A. Psychological perspectives on death. In M. R. Rosenzweig & L. W. Porter (Eds.), *Annual review of psychology*, (Vol. 28). Palo Alto, Calif.: Stanford University Press, 1977, pp. 225–249.

Kastenbaum, R., & Durkee, N. Young people view old age. In R. Kastenbaum (Ed.), *New thoughts on old age*. New York: Springer, 1964, pp. 237–250.

Kavanaugh, R. E. *Facing death*. Baltimore: Penguin Books, 1974.

Keen, S. The heroics of everyday life: A theorist of death confronts his own end. *Psychology Today*, 1974, *7*(11), 71–75ff.

Kimmel, D. C. *Adulthood and aging* (2d ed.). New York: Wiley, 1980.

Kinsey, A. C., Pomeroy, W. B., & Martin, C. C. *Sexual behavior in the human male*. Philadelphia: Saunders, 1948.

Kirchner, W. K. Age differences in short-term retention of rapidly changing information. *Journal of Experimental Psychology*, 1958, *55*, 352–358.

Kisker, G. W. *The disorganized personality* (2d ed.). New York: McGraw-Hill, 1972.

———*The disorganized personality* (3d ed.). New York: McGraw-Hill, 1980.

Kivett, V. R. The aged in North Carolina: Physical, social, and environmental characteristics and sources of assistance. *Technical Bulletin No. 237*. Raleigh, N.C.: Agricultural Experiment Station, 1976.

Kleinmuntz, B. *Essentials of abnormal psychology*. New York: Harper & Row, 1974.

Knopf, O. *Successful aging*. New York: Viking, 1975.

Kobrin, F., & Hendershot, G. Do family ties reduce mortality? Evidence from the United States, 1966–68. *Journal of Marriage and the Family*, 1977, *39*, 737–745.

Kogan, N. Attitudes toward old people. *Journal of Abnormal Psychology*, 1961, *62*, 44–54.

Kogan, N., & Shelton, F. Beliefs about old people: A comparative study of older and younger samples. *Journal of Genetic Psychology*, 1962, *100*, 93–111.

Kubey, R. W. Television and aging: Past, present, and future. *The Gerontologist*, 1980, *20*, 16–35.

Kübler-Ross, E. *On death and dying*. New York: Macmillan, 1969.

——— *Questions and answers on death and dying*. New York: Macmillan, 1974.

——— (Ed.). *Death: The final stage of growth*. Englewood Cliffs, N.J.: Prentice-Hall, 1975.

Kuhlen, R. G. Changing personality adjustment during the adult years. In J. E. Anderson

(Ed.), *Psychological aspects of aging.* Washington, D.C.: American Psychological Association, 1956.

Landis, J. T. What is the happiest period of life? *School and Society,* 1942, *55,* 643−645.

Langer, E. J., & Rodin, J. The effects of choice and enhanced personal responsibility for the aged: A field experiment in an institutional setting. *Journal of Personality & Social Psychology,* 1976, *34,* 191−198.

Lawton, M. P. *Social and medical services in housing for the elderly.* Philadelphia: Philadelphia Geriatric Center, 1975.

Leaf, A. Getting old. *Scientific American,* 1973, *229,* 45−52.

Learning for the aged. *Time,* 1972, *100*(3), 48.

Lefcourt, H. M. The function of illusions of control and freedom. *American Psychologist,* 1973, *28,* 417−425.

Lehman, H. C. *Age and achievement.* Princeton, N.J.: Princeton University Press, 1953.

────── The creative production rates of present versus past generations of scientists. *Journal of Gerontology,* 1962, *17,* 409−417.

────── The psychologist's most creative years. *American Psychologist,* 1966, *21,* 363−369.

Lieberman, M. A. Psychological correlates of impending death: Some preliminary observations. *Journal of Gerontology,* 1965, *20,* 181−190.

────── Grouchiness: A survival asset. *University of Chicago Alumni Magazine,* April 1973, pp. 11−14.

Lieberman, M. A., & Coplan, A. S. Distance from death as variable in the study of aging. *Developmental Psychology,* 1969, *2,* 71−84.

Lipman, V. How con artists rob elderly. *Parade,* July 8, 1979, pp. 22−23.

Lobsenz, N. M. Sex and the senior citizen. *New York Times Magazine,* Jan. 20, 1974, pp. 8−9.

Loether, H. J. *Problems of aging* (2d ed.). Belmont, Calif.: Dickenson Publishing, 1975.

Lombana, J. H. Counseling the elderly: Remediation plus prevention. *Personnel & Guidance Journal,* 1976, *55,* 143−144.

Longworth, R. C. Soviets' geriatric sensations: They're old, but not that old. *San Francisco Chronicle,* April 9, 1978, p. 3.

Lopata, H. Z. Widows as a minority group. *The Gerontologist,* 1971, *11*(1), Pt. 2.

────── *Widowhood in an American city.* Cambridge, Mass.: Schenkman, 1973.

Lowenthal, M. F. Social isolation and mental illness in old age. *American Sociological Review,* 1964, *29*(1), 54−70.

Lowy, L. Social welfare and the aging. In M. G. Spencer & C. J. Dorr (Eds.), *Understanding aging: A multidisciplinary approach.* New York: Appleton-Century-Crofts, 1975, 134−178.

Maddox, G. L. Persistence of life style among the elderly: A longitudinal study of patterns of social activity in relation to life satisfaction. In B. L. Neugarten (Ed.), *Middle age and aging.* Chicago: University of Chicago Press, 1968. (a)

────── Retirement as a social event in the United States. In B. L. Neugarten (Ed.), *Middle age and aging.* Chicago: University of Chicago Press, 1968. (b)

────── Persistence of life style among the elderly. In E. Palmore (Ed.), *Normal aging.* Durham, N.C.: Duke University Press, 1970.

Mandelbaum, D. G. Social uses of funeral rites. In H. Feifel (Ed.), *The meaning of death.* New York: McGraw-Hill, 1959.

Manion, U. V. Preretirement counseling: The need of a new approach. *Personnel & Guidance Journal,* 1976, *55,* 119−121.

Margolis, B., & Kroes, W. Work and the health of man. Paper commissioned by the Special Task Force, *Work in America.* Cambridge, Mass.: MIT Press, 1972.

Marshall, J. R. Changes in aged white male suicide: 1948−1972. *Journal of Gerontology,* 1978, *33,* 763−768.

Masters, W. H., & Johnson, V. E. *Human sexual response.* Boston: Little, Brown, 1966.

────── *Human sexual inadequacy.* Boston: Little, Brown, 1970.

McCormack, P. Race tracks, bus depots: Social centers for elderly. *Los Angeles Times ,* Aug. 15, 1979. Pt. 1-B, p. 2.

────── Elderly victims of abuse may be getting needed help soon. *Los Angeles Times,* Nov. 9, 1980, Pt. I, pp. 2, 24.

McFarland, R. A., Tune, G. S., & Welford, A. T. On the driving of automobiles by older people. *Journal of Gerontology,* 1964, *19* (4), 190−197.

McKain, W. C. *Retirement marriage.* Storrs, Conn.: Storrs Agricultural Experiment Station, University of Connecticut, 1969.

Medley, M. Satisfaction with life among persons sixty-five years and older: A causal model. *Journal of Gerontology*, 1976, *31*, 448–455.

Meltzer, H., & Ludwig, D. Age differences in positive mental health of workers. *Journal of Genetic Psychology*, 1971, *119*, 163–173.

Moberg, D. O. Religiosity in old age. In B. L. Neugarten (Ed.), *Middle age and aging: A reader in social psychology*. Chicago: University of Chicago Press, 1968.

Moberg, D. O. *Spiritual well-being*. (White House Conference on Aging background papers). Washington, D.C.: U.S. Government Printing Office, 1971.

Mondale, W. S.2632 Federal Employees Preretirement Assistance Act of 1975. *Congressional Record*, 121(164), pp. S.19393-4. Nov. 6, 1975.

Moody, R. A., Jr. *Life after life*. Atlanta: Mockingbird Books, 1975.

Morgan, C. M. The attitudes and adjustments of recipients of old age assistance in upstate and metropolitan New York. *Archives of Psychology*, 1937, *30*(214).

Mortimer, E. A., Monson, R. R., & MacMahon, B. Reduced coronary heart disease mortality in men residing at high altitude. *New England Journal of Medicine*, 1977, *296*, 581–585.

Myers, G. C., & Pitts, A. M. *The demographic effects of mortality reduction on the aged population of the U.S.: Some baseline projections*. Paper presented at the meeting of the Gerontological Society, San Juan, Puerto Rico, December 1972.

Nathanson, P. S. The necessity for legal services. In R. A. Kalish (Ed.), *The later years: Social applications of gerontology*. Monterey, Calif.: Brooks/Cole, 1977.

National Center for Health Statistics. *Vital statistics of the United States, 1973*. (Vol. 2), Part A: Mortality. Rockville, Md.: U.S. Dept. of Health, Education, and Welfare, 1974.

National Council on the Aging. *The myth and reality of aging in America*. Washington, D.C.: Author, 1975.

National Institute on Aging. *Age page. Accidents and safety*. Bethesda, Md.: Author, July 1980.

———— *Age page. Minorities and how they grow*. Bethesda, Md.: Author, August 1980.

National Retired Teachers Association, American Association of Retired Persons. *1978 Federal and State Legislative Program*. Washington, D.C.: Author, 1978.

Neugarten, B. L. The awareness of middle age. In R. Owen (Ed.), *Middle age*. London: British Broadcasting, 1967.

———— Adult personality: Toward a psychology of the life cycle. In E. Vinacke (Ed.), *Readings in general psychology*. New York: American Book, 1968.

———— Grow old along with me! The best is yet to be. *Psychology Today*, 1971, *5*(7), 45–48ff.

———— Personality changes in late life: A developmental perspective. In C. Eisdorfer & M. P. Lawton (Eds.), *The psychology of adult development and aging*. Washington, D.C.: American Psychological Association, 1973.

———— The rise of the young–old. *New York Times*, Jan. 18, 1975, p. 29.

———— The psychology of aging: An overview. *Master lectures in developmental psychology*. Washington, D.C.: American Psychological Association, 1976. (Cassette tape)

———— Personality and aging. In J. E. Birren & K. W. Schaie (Eds.), *Handbook of the psychology of aging*. New York: Van Nostrand Reinhold, 1977.

Neugarten, B. L., Havighurst, R. J., & Tobin, S. S. Personality and patterns of aging. In B. L. Neugarten (Ed.), *Middle age and aging*. Chicago: University of Chicago Press, 1968.

Neugarten, B. L., & Weinstein, K. K. The changing American grandparent. In B. L. Neugarten (Ed.), *Middle age and aging*. Chicago: University of Chicago Press, 1968.

Neulinger, J., & Raps, C. S. Leisure attitudes of an intellectual elite. *Journal of Leisure Research*, 1972, *4*(3), 196–207.

New image for the old stereotype. *Los Angeles Times*, Aug. 11, 1977, Pt. VI, p. 1.

Newman, G., & Nichols, C. R. Sexual activities and attitudes in older persons. *Journal of the American Medical Association*, 1960, *173*, 33–35.

New York City Police Department-New York City Department of Aging. *Crime prevention for senior citizens*. New York: Police Dept. City of New York, Crime Prevention Section, 1978.

Nisbet, J. D. Intelligence and age: Retesting after twenty-four years' interval. *British Journal of Educational Psychology*, 1957, *27*, 190–198.

Nowak, C. *Concern with youthfulness and attractiveness in adult women*. Unpublished master's thesis, Wayne State University, 1974.

O'Brien, J., & Streib, G. *Evaluative research on social programs for the elderly*. AOA DHEW Pub. No. (OHD) 77-20120. Washington, D.C.: U.S. Government Printing Office, 1977.

Odell, C. Counseling for a third of a lifetime. *Personnel & Guidance Journal*, 1976, *55*, 145–147.

Offir, C. Old people's revolt—"At 65, work becomes a four-letter word." *Psychology Today*, 1974, *7*(10), 40.

Overall, J. E., & Gorham, D. Organicity versus old age in objective and projective test performance. *Journal of Consulting & Clinical Psychology*, 1972, *39*, 98–105.

Owens, W. A., Jr. Age and mental abilities: A longitudinal study. *Genetic Psychology Monographs*, 1953, *48*, 3–54.

———— Age and mental abilities: A second adult follow-up. *Journal of Educational Psychology*, 1966, *57*, 311–325.

Packer, L., & Smith, J. R. Extension of the lifespan of cultured normal human diploid cells by vitamin E. *Proceedings of the National Academy of Sciences*, 1974, *71*, 4763–4767.

———— Extension of the lifespan of cultured normal human diploid cells by vitamin E: A reevaluation. *Proceedings of the National Academy of Sciences*, 1977, *74*, 1640–1641.

Palmore, E. Physical, mental and social factors in predicting longevity. *The Gerontologist*, 1969, *9*, 103–108.

———— (Ed.). *Normal aging*. Durham, N.C.: Duke University Press, 1970.

———— (Ed.). *Normal aging II*. Durham, N.C.: Duke University Press, 1974.

———— The Facts on Aging quiz: A review of findings. *The Gerontologist* , 1980, *20*, 669–672.

Palmore, E., & Cleveland, W. Aging, terminal decline, and terminal drop. *Journal of Gerontology*, 1976, *31*(1), 76–86.

Parkes, M. C., Benjamin, B., & Fitzgerald, R. G. Broken heart: A statistical study of increased mortality among widowers. *British Medical Journal*, 1969, *1*, 740–743.

Pastalan, L. A. The stimulation of age-related sensory losses. A new approach to the study of environmental barriers. *The New Outlook for the Blind*, October 1974, pp. 356–362.

People in Hawaii live longer. *San Francisco Chronicle*, Dec. 14, 1977, p. 3.

Perlman, H. H. *Persona: Social role and personality*. Chicago: University of Chicago Press, 1968.

Perry, P. W. The night of ageism. *MH*, 1974, *58*(3), 13–20.

Peterson, J. A. Marriage and sex and the older man and woman. *Modern Maturity*, December 1970–January 1971.

Peterson, L. R., & Peterson, M. J. Short-term retention of individual verbal items. *Journal of Experimental Psychology*, 1959, *58*, 193–198.

Pfeiffer, E. Psychopathology and social pathology. In J. E. Birren & K. W. Schaie (Eds.), *Handbook of the psychology of aging*. New York: Van Nostrand Reinhold, 1977.

Pfeiffer, E., Verwoerdt, A., & Davis, G. C. Sexual behavior in middle life. *American Journal of Psychiatry*, 1972, *128*, 1264.

Pfeiffer, E., Verwoerdt, A., & Wang, H. S. Sexual behavior in aged men and women. *Archives of General Psychiatry*, 1968, *19*, 755–758.

———— The natural history of sexual behavior in a biologically advantaged group of aged individuals. *Journal of Gerontology*, 1969, *24*, 193–198.

Phillips, B. S. *The aged in a central Illinois community*. Urbana: University of Illinois Press, 1962.

Pines, M. Age-ism . . . slashing our own tires. *APA Monitor*, 1976, *7*(12), 7.

Population Reference Bureau. *1981 world population data sheet*. (Prepared by Carl Haub, Demographer.) Washington, D.C.: Population Reference Bureau, Inc., April, 1981.

Porter, S. Retirees' cost of living jumps. *Greensboro* (N.C.) *Daily News*, August 17, 1977, p. A8.

———— The graying of America. *San Francisco Chronicle*, July 28, 1980a, p. 58.

———— Elderly face gaps in Medicare coverage. *Stockton* (Calif.) *Record*, July 31, 1980b, p. 52.

Puner, M. *To the good long life: What we know about growing old*. New York: Universe Books, 1974.

Pyron, H. C., & Manion, U. V. The company, the individual, and the decision to retire. *Industrial Gerontology*, 1970, *4*, 1–11.

Quirk, D. A. Life span opportunities for the older adult. *Personnel & Guidance Journal*, 1976, *55*, 140–142.

Rawlings, M. *Beyond death's door*. Nashville, Tenn.: Thomas Nelson, 1978.

Reichard, S., Livson, F., & Petersen, P. G. *Aging and personality*. New York: Wiley, 1962.

———— Adjustment to retirement. In B. L. Neugarten (Ed.), *Middle age and aging*. Chicago: University of Chicago Press, 1968.

Reimanis, G., & Green, R. F. Imminence of death and intellectual decrement in the aging. *Developmental Psychology*, 1971, *5*, 270–272.

Reports show decline in cardiovascular disease death rates. *Los Angeles Times*, August 12, 1979, Sec. A, p. 13.

Rich new market among nation's elderly. *U.S. News & World Report*, 1979, *81*(Nov. 12), 80–81.

Richter, C. P. On the phenomenon of sudden death in animals and man. *Psychosomatic Medicine*, 1957, *19*, 191–198.

Riley, M. W., & Foner, A. (Eds.). *Aging and society.* New York: Russell Sage, 1968.

Robinson, J. P. Social changes as measured by time budgets. *Journal of Leisure Research*, 1969, *1*, 75–77.

Rodin, J. & Langer, E. Long-term effects of a control-relevant intervention with institutionalized aged. *Journal of Personality & Social Psychology*, 1977, *35*, 897–902.

Roffwarg, H. P., Muzio, J. N., & Dement, W. C. Ontogenetic development of the human sleep-dream cycle. *Science*, 1966, *152*, 604–619.

Rollins, B. C., & Feldman, H. Marital satisfaction over the life cycle. *Journal of Marriage and the Family*, 1970, *32*(1), 20–28.

Romo, M., Siltanen, P., Theorell, T., & Rahe, R. H. World behavior, time urgency, and life-dissatisfactions in subjects with myocardial infarction: A cross-cultural study. *Journal of Psychosomatic Research*, 1974, *18*(1), 1–8.

Rose, A. M. The subculture of aging: A framework in social gerontology. In A. M. Rose & W. A. Peterson (Eds.), *Older people and their social world.* Philadelphia: Davis, 1965, pp. 3–16.

Rose, C. L. Social factors in longevity. *The Gerontologist*, 1964, *4*, 27–37.

Rosenfeld, A. *Prolongevity.* New York: Knopf, 1976. (a)

———— The Willy Loman complex. *Saturday Review*, 1976, *3*(22), 24–26. (b)

Ross, K., Braga, J., & Braga, L. D. Omego. In E. Kübler-Ross (Ed.), *Death: The final stage of growth.* Englewood Cliffs, N.J.: Prentice-Hall, 1975.

Ross, M. D. Effects of aging on the otoconia. In S. S. Han & D. H. Coons (Eds.) *Special senses in aging.* Proc. Symposium on Biology of Special Senses in Aging, University of Michigan, Oct. 10–11, 1977. Ann Arbor: Institute of Gerontology, University of Michigan, 1977.

Ryan, R. Seniors want some surprising things. *Los Angeles Times*, Jan. 22, 1978, Sect. VIII, p. 1.

Saleh, S. D., & Otis, J. L. Age and level of job satisfaction. *Personnel Psychology*, 1964, *17*, 425–430.

Sarton, M. More light. *New York Times*, Jan. 30, 1978, p. A21.

Sartre, J. P. *Existentialism and human emotions.* New York: Philosophical Library, 1957.

Saul, S. *Aging: An album of people growing old.* New York: Wiley, 1974.

Saunders, C. St. Christopher's Hospice. In E. S. Shneidman (Ed.), *Death: Current perspectives* (2d ed.). Palo Alto, Calif.: Mayfield, 1980.

Savitz, H. A. Mental health and aging. *MH*, 1974, 58(3), 21–22.

Schaie, K.W. Age changes and age differences. *The Gerontologist*, 1967, *7*, 128–132.

Schaie, K. W., & Labouvie-Vief, G. Generational versus ontogenetic components of change in cognitive behavior: A fourteen-year cross-sequential study. *Developmental Psychology*, 1974, *10*, 305–320.

Schaie, K. W., & Parham, I. A. *Manual for the Test of Behavioral Rigidity* (2d ed.). Palo Alto, Calif.: Consulting Psychologists Press, 1975.

———— Cohort-sequential analysis of adult intellectual development. *Developmental Psychology*, 1977, *13*, 649–653.

Schaie, K. W., & Strother, C. R. A cross-sequential study of age changes in cognitive behavior. *Psychological Bulletin*, 1968, *70*, 671–680.

Schonberg, W. B., & Potter, H. C. Friendship fluctuations in senescence. *Journal of Genetic Psychology*, 1976, *129*, 333–334.

Schonfield, D. Memory changes with age. *Nature*, 1965, *208*, 918.

Schultz, J. H. *The economics of aging.* Belmont, Calif.: Wadsworth, 1976.

Schwartz, A. N., & Peterson, J. A. *Introduction to gerontology.* New York: Holt, Rinehart and Winston, 1979.

Scientists hope to lift elderly spirits. *Los Angeles Times*, March 13, 1980. Pt. I, pp. 3, 26.

Scott-Maxwell, F. *The measure of my days.* New York: Knopf, 1968.

Seligman, M. E. P. *Helplessness: On depression, development, and death.* San Francisco: Freeman, 1975, Chapter 8.

Selkurt, E. E. Death. *The world book encyclopedia* (Vol. 5). Chicago: Field Enterprises Educational Corp., 1975.

Selye, H. *The stress of life* (Rev. ed.). New York: McGraw-Hill, 1976.

Senior citizens showing up for drug counseling. *Stockton* (Calif.) *Record*, June 22, 1978, p. 31.

Serock, K., Seefeldt, C., Jantz, R. K., & Galper, A. As children see old folks. *Today's Education*, 1977, *66*(2), 70–73.

Shanas, E., Townsend, P., Wedderburn, D., Friis, H., Milhoj, P., & Stehouwer, J. (Eds.). *Old people in three industrial societies*. New York: Atherton, 1968.

Sheldon, A., McEwan, P. J. M., & Ryser, C. P. *Retirement patterns and predictions*. National Institute of Mental Health, DHEW, Publ. No. (ADM)74-79, 1975.

Shichor, D., & Kobrin, S. Criminal behavior among the elderly. *The Gerontologist*, 1978, *18*, 213–218.

Shneidman, E. *Deaths of man*. New York: Quadrangle, 1973.

—— *Voices of death*. New York: Harper & Row, 1980.

Shock, N. W. Aging and psychological adjustment. *Review of Educational Research*, 1952, *22*, 439–458. (a)

—— Aging of homeostatic mechanisms. In A. I. Lansing (Ed.), *Cowdry's problems of aging* (3d ed.). Baltimore: Williams & Wilkins, 1952. (b)

—— The physiology of aging. *Scientific American*, 1962, *206*(1), 100–111.

—— Biological theories of aging. In J. E. Birren & K. W. Schaie (Eds.), *Handbook of the psychology of aging*. New York: Van Nostrand Reinhold, 1977.

Siegel, R. K. The psychology of life after death. *American Psychologist*, 1980, *35*, 911–931.

Signorielli, N., & Gerbner, G. *The image of the elderly in primetime network television drama* (Report No. 12). Institute for Applied Communication Studies, Annenberg School of Communications, Univ. of Pennsylvania, 1977.

Silverman, P. The -widow-to-widow program: An experiment in preventive information. *Mental Hygiene*, 1969, *53*, 333–337.

Simmons, L. Your chances of living to be 100. *Los Angeles Times*, Nov. 20, 1977, Pt. V, p. 1, 14–15.

Sinaki, M., Opitz, J. L., & Wahner, H. W. Bone mineral content: Relationship to muscle strength in normal subjects. *Archives of Physical Medicine and Rehabilitation*, 1974, *55*, 508–512.

Smith, B. B. Aging: What we'll be we'll be. *Los Angeles Times*, July 22, 1979, Pt. VII, p. 4.

Smith, M. E. Delayed recall of previously memorized material after forty years. *Journal of Genetic Psychology*, 1963, *102*, 3–4.

Social security increase—here it comes. *News Chronicle* (Thousand Oaks, Calif.). Dec. 29, 1980, p. 20.

Soviets say work spurs longevity. *Greensboro* (N.C.) *Daily News*, August 22, 1977, p. A11.

Spence, D. L. Patterns of retirement in San Francisco. In F. M. Carp (Ed.), *The retirement process*. U.S. Dept. of Health, Education and Welfare, PHS Publ. No. 1778. Washington, D.C.: U.S. Government Printing Office, 1966.

Spence, D. L., Feigenbaum, E. M., Fitzgerald, F., & Roth, J. Medical student attitudes toward the geriatric patient. *Journal of American Geriatrics Society*, 1968, *16*, 976–983.

Steinbaum, B. *Attitudes toward the aged in nursing students before and after a course in gerontology*. Unpublished doctoral dissertation, Columbia University, 1973.

Stephens, J. *Loners, losers, and lovers: Elderly tenants in a slum hotel*. Seattle: University of Washington Press, 1976.

Step-up in fight on crimes against elderly. *U.S. News & World Report*, 1977, *82*(23), 62.

Streib, G. F., & Schneider, C. J. *Retirement in American society*. Ithaca, N.Y.: Cornell University Press, 1971.

Streib, G. F., & Thompson, W. E. The older person in a family context. In E. Shanas & G. Streib (Eds.), *Social structure and family: Intergenerational relations*. Englewood Cliffs, N.J.: Prentice-Hall, 1965.

Study finds underweight people have shorter life spans too. *Los Angeles Times*, May 5, 1980, Pt. I, p. 17.

Suran, G. B., & Rizzo, J. V. *Special children: An integrative approach*. Glenview, Ill.: Scott Foresman, 1979.

Sussman, M. B. The family life of old people. In R. H. Binstock & E. Shanas (Eds.), *Handbook of aging and the social sciences*. New York: Van Nostrand Reinhold, 1976.

—— *Incentives and family environments for the elderly*. Final Report AOA Grant No. 90-A-316. Washington, D.C.: Administration on Aging, Feb. 12, 1977.

Symonds, M. New CJE counselor. *Criminal Justice and the Elderly*, 1978(Fall), 4–5.

Taves, M. J., & Hansen, G. O. 1700 elderly citizens. In A. M. Rose (Ed.), *Aging in Minnesota*. Minneapolis: University of Minnesota Press, 1963.

Terry, R., & Wisniewski, H. Sans teeth, sans eyes, sans taste, sans everything. *Behavior Today*, 1974, *5*, 84.

The graying of America. *Newsweek*, 1977, *89*(9), 50–52; 55–58; 63–65.

Tolstoy, L. The death of Ivan Ilych. In L. Tolstoy, *Death of Ivan Ilych and other stories*. New York: New American Library, 1960. (Originally published in 1886.)

Troll, L. C. The family of later life: A decade review. *Journal of Marriage and the Family*, 1971, *33*, 263–290.

Tuckman, J., & Lorge, I. Attitudes toward old people. *Journal of Social Psychology*, 1953, *37*, 249–260.

Tuddenham, R. D., Blumenkrantz, J., & Wilkin, W. R. Age changes in AGCT: A longitudinal study of average adults. *Journal of Counseling & Clinical Psychology*, 1968, *32*, 659–663.

Ullmann, C. A. Preretirement planning: Does it prevent postretirement shock? *Personnel & Guidance Journal*, 1976, *55*, 115–118.

U.S. Bureau of the Census. Projections of the population of the United States: 1977 to 2050. *Current Population Reports*, Series P-25, No. 704. Washington, D.C.: U.S. Government Printing Office, 1977.

———— *Estimates of the population of the United States by age, sex, and race: 1970–1978* (P-25, No. 800). Washington, D.C.: Superintendent of Documents, U.S. Government Printing Office, 1978.

———— 1980 Census of population. *Supplementary Reports*, PC80-S1-1. Washington, D.C.: U.S. Government Printing Office, 1981.

U.S. death rate falls. *San Francisco Chronicle*, Dec. 12, 1978, p. 21

U.S. Department of Health, Education, and Welfare. *Fact sheet*. DHEW Pub. No. (OHDS) 77-20222. Washington, D.C.: U.S. Government Printing Office, 1977. (a)

———— *Fact sheet*. DHEW Pub. No. (OHDS) 77-20223. Washington, D.C.: U.S. Government Printing Office, 1977. (b)

U.S. Department of Health & Human Services. *Facts about older Americans, 1979*. HHS Pub. No. (80-20006). Washington, D.C.: U.S. Government Printing Office, 1979.

———— *Facts about older Americans, 1980–81*. HHS Pub No. (81-20006). Washington, D.C.: U.S. Government Printing Office, 1981.

U.S. Department of Justice, Law Enforcement Assistance Administration. *A mutual concern: Older Americans and the criminal justice system*. Rockville, Md.: NCJRS Document Distribution, 1979.

U.S. Senate Special Committee on Aging. *Developments in aging: 1976*. Washington, D.C.: U.S. Government Printing Office, 1977.

Vaillant, G. E. Natural history of male psychologic health: Effects of mental health on physical health. *New England Journal of Medicine*, 1979, *301*, 1249–1254.

Verwoerdt, A. Biological characteristics of the elderly. In R. R. Boyd & C. G. Oakes (Eds.), *Foundations of practical gerontology*. Columbia, S.C.: University of South Carolina Press, 1969. (a)

———— Psychiatric aspects of aging. In R. R. Boyd & C. G. Oakes (Eds.), *Foundations of practical gerontology*. Columbia, S.C.: University of South Carolina Press, 1969. (b)

Vinick, B. *Remarriage in old age*. Paper presented at the annual meeting of the American Sociological Association, Chicago, September 1977.

Volpe, A., & Kastenbaum, R. Beer and TLC. *American Journal of Nursing*, 1967, *67*, 100–103.

Wallace, D. J. The biology of aging. *Journal of the American Geriatrics Society*, 1977, *25*(3), 104–111.

Warped view of the old folks. *Newsweek*, 1979, *94*(Nov. 12), p. 124.

Weaver, P. Ways that the elderly can afford legal services. Syndicated by King Features, 1980.

Wechsler, D. *The measurement and appraisal of adult intelligence* (4th ed.). Baltimore: Williams & Wilkins, 1958.

Weisman, A. D. *On dying and denying: A psychiatric study of terminality*. New York: Behavioral Publications, 1972.

Weisman, A. D., & Kastenbaum, R. The psychological autopsy: A study of the terminal phase of life. *Community Mental Health Journal*, Monograph No. 4. New York: Behavioral Publications, 1968.

Welford, A. T. *Aging and human skill*. New York: Oxford University Press, 1958.

Wesman, A. G. Intelligent testing. *American Psychologist*, 1968, *23*, 267–274.

Wilkie, F., & Eisdorfer, C. Intelligence and blood pressure in the aged. *Science*, 1971, *172*, 959–962.

Williamson, J. B., Evans, L., & Munley, A. *Aging and society*. New York: Holt, Rinehart and Winston, 1980.

Winokur, G. The types of affective disorders. *Journal of Nervous & Mental Diseases*, 1973, *156*, 82–96.

Wolk, R. L., & Wolk, R. B. *The Gerontological Apperception Test.* New York: Behavioral Publications, 1971.

Wolpe, J., & Lazarus, M. *Behavior therapy techniques.* New York: Pergamon Press, 1966.

Woodruff, D. S. *Can you live to be 100?* New York: Chatham Square, 1977.

Woodruff, D. S., & Birren, J. E. Age changes and cohort differences in personality. *Developmental Psychology*, 1972, *6*, 252–259.

Yerkes, R. M. Psychological examining in the U.S. Army. *Memoirs: National Academy of Science*, 1921, *15*, 1–890.

Young, M. L. Age and sex differences in problem solving. *Journal of Gerontology*, 1971, *26*, 330–336.

Index of Authors and Names

Abram, H. S., 250, 284
Adamowicz, J. K., 87, 284
Adams, B. N., 172, 284
Agan, T., 216, 284
Aiken, L. R., 79, 284
Aisenberg, R., 246, 267, 289
Alpaugh, P. K., 96, 129, 138, 139, 284
Alsop, S., 261, 284
Alvis, H. J., 90, 288
Anderson, B. G., 171, 284
Anderson, K., 48, 188, 284
Ankus, M. N., 86, 288
Arehart-Treichel, J., 40, 142, 284
Arenberg, D., 84, 96, 284
Arnold, M., 165
Atchley, R. C., 26, 162, 199, 206, 284
Averill, J. H., 16
Axelrod, S., 37, 284

Back, K. W., 84, 91, 255, 284, 287
Bacon, F., 18
Bahr, M. H., 174, 284
Baller, W. R., 81, 284
Baltes, P. B., 23, 81, 84, 284, 285
Barns, E. D., 134, 139, 285
Barrett, J. H., 17, 38, 106, 227, 285
Barrows, C. H., 72
Barry, J. R., 139
Baugher, D., 206
Bayley, N., 80, 285
Becker, E., 251
Bell, A., 81, 285
Bell, B., 51
Bellak, L., 102, 285
Bellak, S. S., 102, 285
Benet, S., 15, 26, 285
Benetiz, R., 179, 285

Bengtson, V. L., 173, 179, 181, 285, 287
Benjamin, B., 264, 292
Bennett, R., 171, 285
Ben-Yishay, Y., 83, 285
Berg, R. C., 140
Bergman, M., 50
Berne, E., 127, 285
Beverley, E. V., 224
Biehler, R. F., 100, 285
Bierman, E. L., 4, 73
Binstock, R. H., 182, 191, 206, 224, 285, 286, 287, 294
Birren, J. E., 26, 42, 50, 51, 73, 83, 96, 102, 121, 285, 288, 289, 291, 292, 294, 296
Bischof, L. J., 96, 206, 285
Bismarck, O., 201
Blackburne, 75
Blazer, D. G., 111, 174, 285, 286
Blau, Z. S., 172, 285
Bloom, K. L., 104, 285
Blue, G. F., 171, 285
Blum, J. E., 82, 285
Blumenkrantz, J., 81, 295
Booth, C., 19
Botwinick, J., 39, 41, 42, 81, 90, 96, 106, 285
Bower, G. H., 86, 285
Bowlby, J., 264, 285
Boyd, R. R., 295
Braga, J., 251, 293
Braga, L. D., 251, 293
Brink, T. L., 125, 285
Britton, J. A., 121
Britton, J. H., 121
Brody, S. J., 72
Brown, J. H. U., 18, 285
Brown, N. K., 66, 285
Brown, S., 92, 285

Index of Terms and Organizations

Numbers in *italics* refer to pages in the Glossary.

Ability (mental), 74−85, *272*
Abkhasian(s), 11−12, 14−15
Abnormal, 109
Acceptance, stage of, 260, *272*
Accidents, 55−56
Accommodation, 36, *272*
Activities of the aged, 218−222
Activity theory, 200, *272*
Acute brain syndrome, 58, *272*
Adjustment, 97−101, *272*
   to retirement, 198−199
Administration on Aging, 23, 239, 270
Administrative advocacy, 242, *272*
Advocate, 241
Affective psychosis, 116−118, *272*
Affluent aged, 209−210
Age Discrimination in Employment, 189
Ageism, 165, *272*
Age norm, 2, *272*
Aging, *272*
Aging clock, 47, 48
Alcoholism, 115
Alienation, *272*
Alzheimer's disease, 60−61, *272*
American Aging Association, 270
American Association of Homes for the
   Aging, 270
American Association of Retired Persons,
   175, 195, 206, 271
American Bar Association, 241, 245
American College of Nursing Home
   Administrators, 270

American Geriatrics Society, 18, 270
American Health Care Association, 270
American Management Association, 195
Anger, stage of, 260, *273*
Angor animi, 57, *273*
Angry type, 199, *273*
Antisocial personalities, 115
Anxiety neurosis, 113, *273*
Apathetic, 108
Apoplexy, *273*
Aptitude, *273*
Arcus senilis, 30, *273*
Armored type, 197, 198
Armored defended personality, 108, *273*
Army Alpha, 80
Arousal, learning and, 88−89
Arteriosclerosis, 58−59, *273*
   cerebral, 59
Arthritis, 53, *273*
Asociacion Nacional Pro Personas Mayores,
   270
Atherosclerosis, *273*
Attitude(s), *273*
   toward death, 254−255
   toward old age, 63−65, 163−171
   toward sex, 145−146
Audiometer, *273*
Autoimmunity theory, 47, *273*
Autopsy, psychological, 257

Bank examiner swindle, 235
Bargaining, stage of, 260, *273*

Elderhostel, 92–93, 96
Electroencephalogram (EEG), 247
Electroshock therapy (EST), 119, *276*
Embolism, *276*
Empathic Model, 44, 136, 171, *276*
Employee Retirement Income Security Act,
  195
Employment, 183–190
Empty nest syndrome, 157
Environmental (milieu) therapy, 135
Ethnic differences (in longevity), 10
Euthanasia, 251, *276*
Excitement phase, 144, *276*
Exercise, importance of, 62
  longevity and, 14
Existentialism, 249
Exploitation of the aged, 233–235

Family counseling, 133–134, *276*
Family relationships, 156–160
Farmers Home Administration, 214
Federal Bureau of Investigation, 226–227
Federal Employees Preretirement Assistance
  Act, 194
Federal Highway Act, 218
Fertility rate, 5, *276*
Fixation, 127, *276*
Flexibility, 106–107
Fluid intelligence, 85
Focused type, 108
Folie á deux, 115
Folie á trois, 115, 116
Food Stamp Program, 62–63
Foster Grandparent Program, 188, 189
Fraternal twins, *276*
Fraud, 233–235
Free association, 127
Free radicals, 47, 49, *276*
Friendships, 172–173
Full Scale IQ, 77, *276*
Functional psychosis, 115, *276*
Funeral, 261–262

Gastrointestinal system, 33–34
General intelligence, 76–83
Genitourinary system, 34
Geography, longevity and, 12–14
Geriatrics, 18, *276*
Geronto, *276*
Gerontocracy, *276*
Gerontological Apperception Test, 102
Gerontological Society, 19, 270
Gerontology, 18–20, *277*
Gerontophobia, *277*
Gerontopolis, 209
Gerovital, 49
Gingivitis, *277*
Giving-up syndrome, 248
Glaucoma, 36
Glomerulus, *277*
Golden Age Club, 125, 155, 177, 221

Golden Age Passport, 221
Gradual reawakening of interest, 264, *277*
Grandparent(s), 159–160
Gray Panthers, 146, 175, 270, *277*
Grief, 137
Group counseling and psychotherapy,
  132–134

Hallucination, 115, *277*
Health care, 61–71
Health care insurance, 68–71
Hearing, 38–40
Hebephrenic schizophrenia, 117
Helplessness, 248, 249
Hemorrhage, 58, *277*
Heredity, longevity and, 15, 17
Hill-Burton Program, 69
Holding on, 108
Homosexuality, 147
Homeostatic imbalance theory, 47
Homeowners, elderly, 213
Honeymoon phase (of retirement), 199, *277*
Hormonal theories (of aging), 47
Hospice, 257
Housing, 210–217
Housing Production and Mortgage Credit of
  HUD, 214–215
Hunza, 11–12
Huntington's chorea, 60, *277*
Hyperoxygenation, 90, *277*
Hypertension, 56
Hypothermia, 41, 48

Id, 126, *277*
Identical twins, *277*
Identity, 101
Illusions, perceptual, 36–37
Imipramine, 119, *277*
Immunological theory, 47
Income, of the elderly, 207–210
Incompetency, 242, *277*
Independent variable, *277*
Infant mortality, 5, *277*
Initial shock, 264, *278*
Insanity, *278*
Integrated personality, 108
Integrity vs. despair, 99–101
Intelligence, 76–82, *278*
  decline in, 81–82
Intense grief, 264, *278*
Interference, learning and, 88–89,
  91
Interiority, 105–106, *278*
Internal Revenue Service, 237–238
International Association of Gerontology, 19,
  270
International Center for Social Gerontology,
  271
International Federation on Aging, 271
International Senior Citizens Association,
  175, 271

Involuntary admission (commitment), 118–119, 122, *278*
Involutional period, *278*
Involutional psychosis (melancholia), 117–118, *278*

Jakob-Creutzfeldt disease, 60

Korsakoff's syndrome, 58, *278*

Later longevous period, 17
Law Enforcement Assistance Administration, 239
Law reform activity, 241
Learning, drugs and, 89–90
Legal Center on Aging, 240
Legislative advocacy, 242, *278*
Leisure time, use of, 219–221
Leisure World, 62, 210
Lentigo senilis, 29
Life cycle group therapy, 133, *278*
Life expectancy, 3, 54, *278*
Life review, 133, 258, *278*
Life review therapy, 133, *278*
Limited time perspective, 84, 91
Lipofuscin, *278*
Live Long and Like It Club, 177
Living environment(s), 210–218
Living Will, 250
Loneliness, 105–106
Longevity, 2, *278*
  diet and, 14–15
  ethnic group differences in, 10
  exercise and, 14
  geography and, 12–14
  heredity and, 15, 17
  marital status and, 9–10
  nationality and, 10–12
  sex differences in, 7–9
  state and climate and, 12–14
Longitudinal investigation (study), 21, 80–81, 84, *279*
Long-term memory, 85, *279*

Major stroke, *279*
Manic-depressive psychosis, 116, 117, 118, *279*
Manic disorder, *279*
Marital relationship, 151–153
Marriage, 149–153
  longevity and, 9–10
  problems, 152–153
Masturbation (in old age), 147
Mature type, 107, 198, *279*
Maximum breathing rate, *279*
Meals on Wheels, 62
Means test, 70
Medicab, 219
Medicaid, 68–81
Medicare, 68–71
Memory, 85–90

Menopause, *279*
Mental abilities, 74–6
Mental disorder(s), 109–120
  classification of, 109
  statistics on, 110
  treatment of, 118–120
Mercy killing, 251, *279*
Milieu therapy, 135
Minority aged, 178–180
  characteristics of, 178–179
  roles of, 178
  social services for, 179–180
  status of, 178
Mitochondria, 48
Monitoring, 241, *279*
Monozygotic twins, *279*
Motor abilities, 41–43
Mourning, stages of, 264–265
Müller-Lyer illusion, 36–37
Multigenerational household, 157, 158
Musculoskeletal system, 33

National Alliance of Senior Citizens, 175, 271
National Association of Area Agencies on Aging, 271
National Association of Mature People, 271
National Association of Retired Federal Employees, 271
National Association of State Units on Aging, 271
National Center on Black Aged, 175, 271
National Citizens Coalition for Nursing Home Reform, 271
National Committee on Careers for Older Americans, 271
National Council of Senior Citizens, 175, 271
National Council on the Aging, 168, 174, 271
National Geriatrics Society, 271
National Indian Council on Aging, 271
National Institute of Child Health and Human Development, 23
National Institute of Mental Health, 23, 118
National Institute on Aging, 23–25, 271
National Pacific/Asian Resource Center on Aging, 271
National Retired Teachers Association-American Association of Retired Persons, 271
National Senior Citizens Law Center, 241
Near event (retirement as), 199, *279*
Necker cube illusion, 36–37
Neighborhood Watch, 238
Nerve deafness, *279*
Nervous system, 34–35
Neurosis, 113
Nine-step counseling model, 129–130
Nursing homes, 65–68
Nutrition, 14–15, 62–63
Nutrition Program for Older Americans, 62